The Yacht Navigator's Handbook

For *Mar Del Norte* (K318)
and her co-owner

The Yacht Navigator's
Handbook

Norman Dahl

HEARST BOOKS

House editor Helen Douglas-Cooper
Designed by Viv Harper
Layout by Heather Sherratt

Text filmset in Hong Kong
by Asco Trade Typesetting Limited.

Printed and bound in Spain by Graficomo, S.A., Cordoba.

Acknowledgments

The author and publishers would like to thank the following for permission to use copyright material:
Page 108 US Department of Commerce.
Pages 120, 149 and 151 reproduced by courtesey of the Defense Mapping Agency Hydrographic/Topographic Center, Washington DC.
Pages 131, 133, 138–9, 141, 158 and 162. reproduced by permission of the Controller, HM Stationery Office.
Page 178 reproduced by permission of Thomas Reed Publications Ltd.

The author and publishers would like to thank the following for supplying photographs for the book: Brookes & Gatehouse Ltd pages 36, 48–9, 110 top; Firdell Multiflectors Ltd page 117; Lokata Ltd page 110 centre and bottom; Sestrel/Henry Browne & Son Ltd pages 25 top, centre and bottom, 27, 45, 163.

Line diagrams drawn by Harry Clow.

CONTENTS

As its name suggests, this book contains all the techniques that most yachtsmen are likely to need to conduct their vessels safely from one place to another, wherever on the surface of the earth those places might be. It is intended for use as a self-teaching book at home, as a classroom textbook or as a ready reference to be kept by the chart table at sea. For those seeking some form of yachtsman's qualification, the book is sufficiently comprehensive and detailed to meet the navigational syllabus of most of the various schemes now in operation in different countries.

This book differs from the normal run of yacht navigation manuals in two significant ways:

1) Wherever possible the contents are organized in what publishers call 'spreads'. This means that the words and the pictures for a particular subject are all to be found on two facing pages, so everything can be seen at a single book opening. Where a topic is too large to fit onto two pages, it has been broken up into logical sub-units, each on its own spread. The purpose of this arrangement is to make it as easy as possible for the user, who may be bucking about in a seaway, to find and use the information he wants.

2) One of the dominant themes throughout the book is the understanding and handling of errors. When I was first taught navigation (in the Royal Navy), errors were thought of as being rather disgraceful, the sole result of poor technique by the navigator. Whilst I always accepted (and still accept today) that I was not the most brilliant navigator in the world, I was disappointed to find, that, however hard I tried, errors never seemed to go away. Navigating a submerged submarine, and later yachts of many kinds in many situations eventually made me realise that errors are an integral part of navigation, and need to be studied in their own right. Professional navigators (especially those who fly) have studied errors in detail, but few books intended for the amateur consider them to any extent.

This book is intended to be a practical tool for the working navigator, and so theory has been kept to a minimum; where theory must be described, it is kept on its own 'spreads', away from the practical applications which follow. This has not been done to suggest in any way that theory is unimportant. Quite the reverse is the case; it very often happens that only by understanding the theory of a subject is it possible to understand and make use of the actual circumstances of the moment. However, many people find theory hard to swallow, and merely want to know what to do to get an answer. To help them, a step-by-step description is given so that they can just follow the instructions, 'plugging in' their own numbers to work out what they want.

The book is divided into a number of sections, each more or less independent of the others though some degree of overlap is inevitable.

The navigator's tools describes the various tools, instruments, charts and books that the navigator needs to do his job. Advice is given on the errors to which the various instruments are liable, and how they may (to some extent) be corrected.

The reckoning deals with the problem of dead reckoning, keeping track of the yacht's position by taking account of its own movement through the water and such external factors as tidal stream and current. Dead reckoning is of the greatest importance, as the foundation upon which the various position-finding techniques can be based, and with which they can be compared.

Position is all about the various ways that exist for finding a yacht's position on the surface of the earth. The basic unit is the *position line*, which when combined with other position lines leads to a *fix*.

The environment collects together information on some of the external factors of importance to the yacht – specifically weather, land- and sea-marks, tides, tidal streams and currents.

Radio aids to navigation now range from a simple hand-held medium frequency direction finder to the full-blooded microprocessor controlled satellite navigator.

Astronomical navigation Many yachtsmen think that astronomical navigation – finding your position from the sun, moon, planets or stars – is too difficult. In fact it is not difficult at all, once the basic principles have been mastered. An astronomical position line can often be worked out just as quickly and easily as many other kinds of position line. No navigator can call himself really capable until he can master these straightforward techniques.

Passage making is all about turning the bare bones of information into a practical course of action, so the yacht can sail, conduct herself sensibly and eventually arrive at her destination.

Knowledgeable navigators may notice some errors of fact in this book, which have been included deliberately to make things simpler; in no case do the errors make any significant difference to the yacht navigator. For example, the sea mile and the nautical mile are terms used interchangeably, though they are not in fact the same thing. In plane sailing, mid-latitude is used instead of mean latitude. To repeat, these simplifying assumptions will not cause any appreciable errors in yacht navigation.

Finally, this book has been written to be as international as possible, to reflect the fact that the sea is still a place where nationality matters less than personal qualities. If navigators from many lands find this book useful as they roam the seas and oceans of the world, I shall be well satisfied.

NORMAN DAHL

For the newcomer, navigation can be a trial and a disappointment. Fresh from the winter navigation classes, where dead reckoning, estimated positions and fixes march in ordered progression across the chart, he finds that things are not so simple at sea. His observations never seem to match up with his estimated position; landfalls never appear when and where expected; and conspicuous objects on shore might be printed on a different chart for all the help they are to him. And whilst it is easy to stop a car and ask the way of a passing stranger, it is more difficult (and more embarrassing) to do the same at sea. There are few navigators who can truthfully claim never to have experienced the sickening feeling of being lost.

The reason for the discrepancy between the real world and the classroom is that in the real world, errors appear which can obscure or distort the truth that the navigator is seeking. A major purpose of this book is to show that errors in navigation are normal and natural, and that the most skilful navigator with the most advanced equipment will cheerfully accept that his position is in some doubt – even though the magnitude of his doubt may be only a few metres. It is relatively easy (with practice) to make observations and measurements at sea, and to plot them on the chart. A major skill in navigation lies in the ability to interpret the results in terms of the likely errors; in other words, the navigator must measure doubt as well.

The first step in this process is to analyse the types of error that can occur in an observation, whether caused by the instrument or by the observer. Four types of error are recognized:

Systematic errors

Systematic errors are errors which change very slowly (if at all) with time, so that they can be measured and corrected. They can arise from inaccurate manufacture or from improper adjustment of the instrument. The two most common types are:

Zero error, in which all readings (including the zero reading) are in error by the same amount; for example, an echo sounder may read one metre low on all readings.

Scale error, in which the error of a reading depends on the magnitude of the reading; if the scanning speed of an echo sounder is wrongly set, it may have an error of one metre at ten metres, two metres at twenty metres and so on.

Systematic errors are best corrected by adjusting the instrument, if the design allows; otherwise a correction table or graph can be drawn up, or the appropriate correction factors can be found and then applied arithmetically to each reading.

Semi-systematic errors

There is no firm division between systematic and semi-systematic errors. The difference between them is time; a systematic error varies very slowly or not at all, while a semi-systematic error varies more quickly – over a period of hours or days. One example of a semi-systematic error is the personal error that an observer may have when using a particular instrument; this can vary with time and circumstances. Another example is magnetic variation, caused by the fact that the earth's magnetic pole does not co-incide with the true pole, and is moving (see page 28). Thus the magnetic variation varies both with time and with the position of the vessel on the earth's surface.

Semi-systematic errors can be corrected in the same way as systematic errors, but the actual magnitude of the error must be checked at suitably frequent intervals.

Random errors

Random errors are errors which vary rapidly in a way that can neither be foreseen nor corrected. These errors can arise in many different ways, but the most common are:

Rounding error, where a reading falls between graduations on the scale of an instrument and is rounded up or down to the nearest graduation.

Periodic error, when an instrument is swinging from side to side of the correct reading, it is moving quickly past the correct reading and more slowly at the extremities of the swing. The correct value is less likely to be read than an incorrect one.

Backlash, when the reading lags or leads the true value, because of friction, backlash or damping.

Noise, where the sensitivity of the instrument is reduced or the reading is altered by some outside interference.

As has been said, random errors cannot be foreseen or corrected; however, it is generally true that a good quality instrument used by a practised observer will give smaller random errors than a poor instrument in untrained hands.

Gross errors

Gross errors, which are large and unexpected errors, can arise in three ways:

Blunders, where the operator makes a mistake, such as reading the reciprocal of a compass bearing.

Equipment faults, which can give large and sometimes undetected errors.

Breakdowns, where the equipment ceases to operate. In many ways it is preferable to have equipment that does not work at all rather than faulty equipment telling lies.

Gross errors can never be eliminated entirely, but they can be reduced in frequency; blunders can be avoided by careful and systematic working, and by checking whenever possible against information from some other source. Faults and breakdowns can be minimized by careful attention to installation, operation and maintenance procedures.

Because gross errors are unpredictable, the navigator must be constantly on his guard. He should not rely on one source of information exclusively, but should cross-check at every opportunity with information from some other source. And he should look for inconsistencies, by comparing the present with the past to make sure that the pattern which emerges makes sense.

Error distributions

It is possible to visualize the various types of error by means of graphs. These graphs plot the probability of an error (vertically) against the magnitude of the error (horizontally). For systematic errors, the error is fixed – it is certain that the error has a particular value. Therefore the distribution graph is a vertical straight line (Fig. 1a). For gross errors, the error may have any value with equal probability; therefore the graph is a horizontal straight line (Fig. 1b). Random errors follow the form of Figure 1c, which has been derived from experiment and experience; it approximates to the Gaussian or Normal distribution of statistical theory. The curve means that the reading will most probably be close to the truth (the hump on

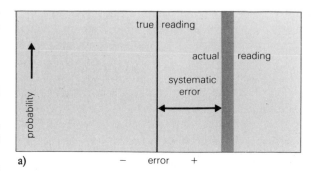

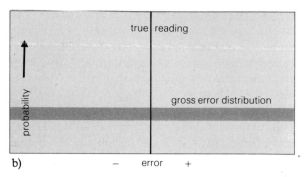

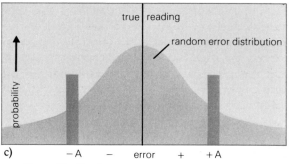

1.1 *Error distributions*.

the graph), whilst it gets less and less likely that a reading will be greatly in error (the skirts of the curve). However, there is always a chance (though it may be very small) of any size of error occuring.

To make use of the idea of random errors, we must put a limit to what we consider to be likely. This we do by choosing a particular error (+ A and − A in Fig. 1c), such that 95 per cent of the area of the curve lies between + A and − A. This is equivalent to saying that it is 95 per cent certain that any error will lie between + A and − A. The odds are 20 to 1 that the error is not greater than A. The value of A is known as the 95 per cent error of the instrument, and this term will be used throughout the book.

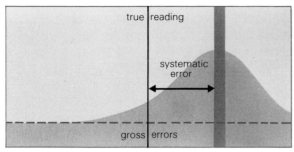

1.2 *Combined error distribution.*

Whilst the 95 per cent error is a useful value for the navigator to use, it is still true that there remains a 5 per cent chance that the error will be greater than A. The possibility must be borne in mind, but theory indicates that the chances of large errors fall very quickly, and the odds are about 1000–1 against an error of 2A.

If we combine the three distributions of Figure 1, we arrive at a picture of the total situation (Fig. 2). The 'hump' of the random component of error has been shifted sideways by the systematic error, and lifted up by the gross error. The strategy that must be followed to reduce errors now becomes obvious. Gross errors must be fought to reduce in particular the chance of large errors; the 'hump' must be re-centred by removing systematic (and semi-systematic) errors; and it must be made as narrow as possible by good quality equipment and careful operation.

Using errors

Having explored the way in which errors are likely to affect the readings that a navigator takes, the next step is to see how these can be used to help the navigator make sensible decisions about his position and future course of action.

The first case to consider is a simple position line (Fig. 3a). If, for example, a bearing of an object is taken with a 95 per cent error of 3°, then the vessel must lie (with 20–1 probability) somewhere in the 'fan' 3° either side of the measured bearing. The actual error distribution gives rise to a ridge of probability.

A fix is generally obtained by the intersection of two (or more) position lines. As each position line is not really a line at all, but rather a band of probability, the true position must lie somewhere in the region where the two bands intersect. In

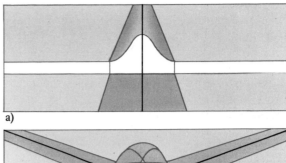

a)

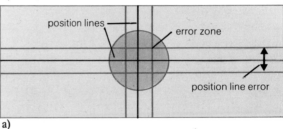

b) **1.3** *Ridges and heaps of probability.*

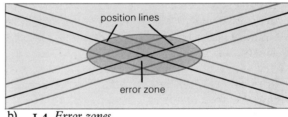

a)

b) **1.4** *Error zones.*

terms of probability, the two ridges of the position lines combine to give a 'heap' of probability for the true position (Fig. 3b).

If the two position lines cross at right angles and have equal 95 per cent errors, then the 'heap' can be represented on the chart by a circle, the radius of which is a little bigger (one and a quarter times) than the position line error (Fig. 4a). If the position lines have unequal 95 per cent errors or cut at an angle other than 90°, the 95 per cent error zone of the fix is an ellipse (Fig. 4b). However, unless the ellipse is very elongated, it is sufficient to assume that the 95 per cent error zone is a circle with radius rather less than the larger position line error; although this is an approximation, it is normally satisfactory and makes for easier working.

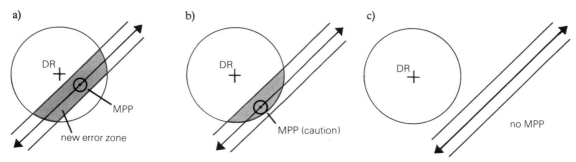

a)   DR   MPP   new error zone

b)   DR   MPP (caution)

c)   DR   no MPP

1.5 *Most probable position.*

The most probable position (MPP)

It is often necessary to estimate a most probable position by combining a position circle with a position line. The most common example is the updating of a dead reckoning position (which may have a large 95 per cent error) by means of a single position line (with its own 95 per cent error). Provided that the two error zones intersect fully, as shown in Figure 5a, then it is possible to select an MPP, with a long, thin error zone parallel with the position line and bounded by the DR error circle. If the error of the position line is less than that of the DR, it is normal to select an MPP at the closest point on the position line to the DR position; if the position line has a larger error than the DR, the navigator may prefer to use the DR position as his MPP.

Figures 5b and 5c show other possible combinations of position circle and position line;

1) The position line and the position circle do not fully intersect. A mistake is probable, either in estimating random errors or some form of gross error.

2) The position line and the position circle do not intersect at all. A gross error is most likely.

In the latter two cases, the navigator should endeavour to discover and put right any mistake that he might have made; if this is not possible, then it may be necessary to increase the error zone of his DR position to include the position line. The situation is an obvious warning that something has gone wrong, and caution will be needed until the situation resolves itself with new information.

Error magnitudes

To put the ideas in this chapter into practice, the navigator needs to arrive at some estimate of the actual magnitudes of the errors he is likely to have to use.

Gross errors By definition, these errors are unforseeable and may have any magnitude. The navigator can only be on his guard. Careful working and good maintenance will reduce their probability, and cross-checking will generally show when they have occurred.

Systematic errors These errors can be found by calibration, and either compensated within the instrument or allowed for in some other way. The sections of this book that deal with various types of equipment include notes on the correction of systematic errors; the actual procedure for an individual instrument is to be found in the maker's handbook.

Random errors These are more difficult to establish, as they are random, and vary with the type and age of the equipment and the circumstances in which they are used. It is only possible to estimate the 95 per cent error of an instrument under the various conditions in which it will be used. This book contains reasonably pessimistic estimates for the various types of instrument in common use in yacht navigation. The newcomer to navigation can use these (cautiously) for an initial estimate, but he should be prepared to revise them in the light of his own experience. Good equipment, good conditions and good operators indicate that the 95 per cent error might be reduced, and *vice versa*.

Putting errors to work

Navigators hate surprises, and any navigator who goes to sea with a clear idea of the errors he is likely to experience in all conditions is much less likely to be surprised. Before going to sea, he will have taken steps to find out what systematic errors there

1.6 *Choosing a position.*

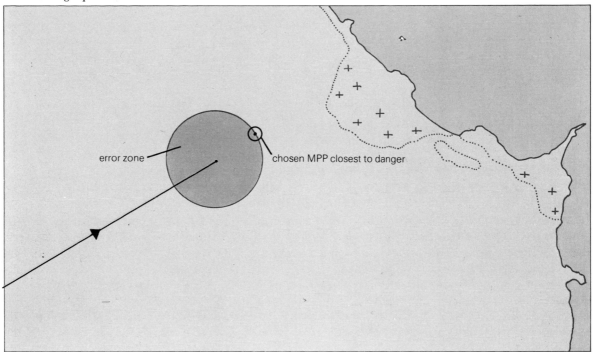

error zone — chosen MPP closest to danger

might be in his equipment, and if necessary he will have compensated for them; whilst at sea, he will take every opportunity to check that these errors have not altered. Cross-checking and tests for consistency will take care of most gross errors, and a pessimistic view of random errors, whilst giving rise to large error circles, means that the unexpected becomes much less likely. Navigation is a suspicious occupation.

When first trying to put these ideas into practice, it is a good idea to plot the error zones and circles on the chart, to help ensure that all errors are allowed for and to give an immediate picture of the scale of errors actually involved. An experienced navigator will probably carry the error information in his head rather than on the chart. The important thing is that the existence of errors and their likely magnitude is never forgotten; nor should the navigator forget the small (5 per cent) probability that he is actually outside his 95 per cent error circle.

Having established an error circle, it is not necessary (nor indeed wise) to choose the most probable position at its centre. In open waters, the centre of the circle will do as well as any other position, but when near dangers it is best to follow that traditional practice of choosing a position within the circle closest to the danger. For example, when making a landfall, it is wise to choose a position on the leading edge of the circle (Fig. 6).

The use of the 95 per cent error should allow the cruising yachtsman to navigate with confidence that he will avoid the unexpected and be in a position to make prudent and seamanlike decisions about his future course of action. A racing navigator will need more than this, because he has the additional task of making his way from point to point in the shortest possible time. He will therefore be interested in the finer structure of the error zone, so that he can calculate the odds in favour of or against any particular tactical decision. He may choose to use a 50 per cent error zone within his 95 per cent zone, accepting the fact that there is an even chance that he is in fact outside this smaller region. The 50 per cent error is approximately half the 95 per cent error. However, the racing navigator must never forget his prime responsibility of keeping the yacht clear of danger, so he should hedge his bets where necessary by reverting to his 95 per cent errors.

THE NAVIGATOR'S TOOLS

2 Position, direction and distance on the earth

The earth

The purpose of navigation is to conduct a vessel from one place to another on the surface of the earth, so any study of navigation properly begins by considering the whole environment in which it takes place. The earth is one of the planets of the solar system, and it moves around the sun in a closed orbit once in each year; at the same time, the earth rotates on its own axis to give the familiar pattern of days and nights as each point on the surface is either exposed to or hidden from the light of the sun. A day, measured with respect to the sun is approximately 24 hours long and a year consists of just over 365 days.

For the purposes of navigation, the earth can be regarded as a sphere, though it is in fact slightly flattened at the poles. A spherical earth is much easier to deal with mathematically and the errors resulting from this assumption are rarely of any significance in the navigation of small craft.

In essence, navigation can be described as a way of answering three basic questions:

Where am I?

Which way should I go?

How far is it to my destination?

With this in mind, we need definitions of the three basic building blocks of navigation – position, direction and distance.

Direction

Directions on the surface of the earth (and indeed of any planet) are defined with respect to its rotation. The direction towards which the earth rotates is defined as *east* and the opposite direction is *west* (Fig. 1) The earth rotates on an imaginary line called its axis; the two points on the surface where the axis cuts it are called the poles. For an observer facing east, the pole on his left hand is the north pole, which lies *north* of him. The pole on his right hand is the south pole, lying *south* of him.

These rules define the four principal, or cardinal, directions at 90° intervals; but the navigator needs to be able to specify a direction much more precisely. The old seamen established a set of 32 points of the compass (see page 26), but the modern practice is to use degrees. Directions are measured clockwise from north (000), using a 360° notation. Thus east becomes 090, south 180 and west 270 (directions are always shown as three figures and the degree symbol is left out).

If the weather is clear, directions can be measured with respect to the heavens, but it is much more convenient to carry some form of directional reference in the craft. As far as yachts are concerned, this is almost invariably a magnetic compass (see pages 26–31). As is explained there, the magnetic compass does not in general point to true north (towards the pole) but towards the magnetic north pole nearby. The magnetic compass in a particular ship may also be affected by iron in the ship or other local influences, deflecting it away from magnetic north. Corrections must therefore be applied to a magnetic compass to obtain true directions.

Great and small circles

If the earth is cut by a plane (as if it were an orange being cut by a knife), a circle is formed on the surface (see Fig. 2). If the plane of cut includes the centre of the earth, the resulting circle on the surface is called a *great circle*; otherwise a *small circle* is formed. The great circle is of considerable importance in navigation: the shortest distance between two points on the earth's surface lies along the great circle which joins them.

Position

Because the earth can be considered as a sphere, a convenient way of defining the position of any point on its surface is by means of angles measured at the centre of the earth (Fig. 3). These angles are measured from two fixed axes:

Latitude is measured north or south of the *equator*, a great circle running east and west exactly midway between the poles. The equator itself is 0° latitude and the two poles are 90°N and 90°S respectively. Any other point has a latitude between these two values. Points with the same latitude lie east and west of each other on a small circle called a *parallel of latitude*.

By international agreement, *longitude* is measured east or west of the half great circle between the poles which passes through Greenwich, near London. This north-south line is called the *meridian of Greenwich*. Each point on the surface

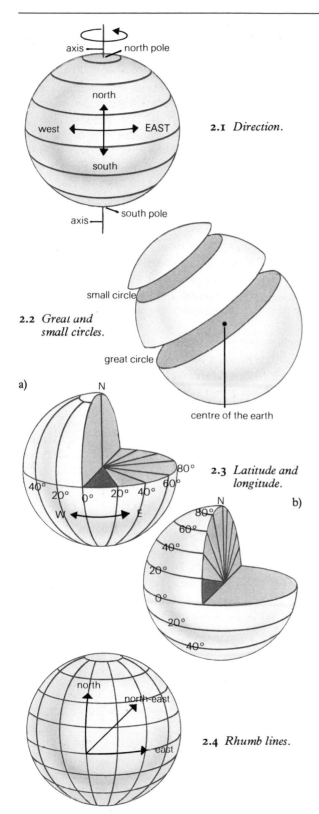

2.1 *Direction.*

2.2 *Great and small circles.*

small circle

great circle

centre of the earth

a)

N

40° 20° 0° 20° 40°

80° 60°

W ← → E

2.3 *Latitude and longitude.*

N

80°

60°

40°

20°

0°

20°

40°

b)

north

north-east

east

2.4 *Rhumb lines.*

of the earth has its own meridian, and longitude is the angle (measured at the equator) between the Greenwich meridian and the meridian of the place. It has a maximum value of 180° east or west.

In defining the position of a point, the latitude is given first, followed by the longitude. In yacht navigation it is often sufficient to define a position to the nearest minute of arc (1 minute = 1/60 degree), but for more precise work, tenths of a minute may be quoted as well. For example:

Greenwich	51°28'.6N	0°00'.0
New York	40°45'N	74°00'W
Sydney	33°53'S	151°10'E

A minute of arc can also be subdivided into 60 seconds of arc.

Distance

There is a fixed relationship between the distance between two points and the angle between them as measured at the centre of the earth. For example, the distance between the equator and one of the poles corresponds to 90° of angle. Because of this, navigators use a unit of distance related to angle. The *sea mile* is the distance on the surface corresponding to one minute of arc at the centre of the earth. As the earth is not truly spherical, the sea mile can vary from 6046 feet (1844 m) at the equator to 6108 feet (1862 m) at the poles. To avoid this variation, the *nautical mile* has been defined as a fixed distance; the British Standard nautical mile is 6080 feet (1853.18 m), and the International nautical mile is 1852 metres. The yacht navigator can ignore these differences and regard the sea mile and the nautical mile as being the same.

The rhumb line

If a vessel travels in a constant direction, it follows a *rhumb line*. If the vessel is travelling due north or south, the rhumb line corresponds with the meridian, and if travelling east or west, the rhumb line corresponds with the parallel of latitude. In all other cases, the rhumb line spirals towards the pole (Fig. 4). As the shortest distance between two points is a great circle and a rhumb line is not (in general) a great circle, it follows that the distance between two points along the rhumb line joining them is greater than the great circle distance. Over short distances, this is unimportant, but for ocean passages it can become significant (see page 180).

3 Chart projections

Having established ways of defining position, direction and distance, the navigator needs to carry with him some form of model of the world so he can establish his present position and decide on the distance and direction of his destination. The most obvious model of the world is a globe, but this is clearly impractical, especially in a yacht! Instead the navigator uses a chart, which is a representation of some part of the earth's surface on a piece of paper. An ideal chart would be an exact model of the area without distortion of any kind; but as the earth is curved and the chart is flat, the ideal is impossible to attain. Chartmakers therefore introduce deliberate distortions by using a *projection* which preserves certain relationships at the expense of others less important for the particular application. The only two projections of any importance to the yacht navigator are *mercator's* projection which reproduces rhumb lines as straight lines, and the *gnomonic* projection which reproduces great circles as straight lines.

Mercator's projection

The course of a vessel (the direction in which it travels) is normally decided with reference to the compass, and is therefore a rhumb line. The mercator projection (first used in 1569) represents rhumb lines as straight lines on the chart, and is therefore the most generally useful projection for nautical charts. By drawing a straight line from his starting point to his destination, the navigator can measure directly the constant course he needs to follow from start to finish.

The mercator projection is derived mathematically, but the principle is shown in Figure 1. A transparent globe with a bright light at the centre is enclosed by a cylinder of paper, touching only at the equator. The details on the surface, including the graticule of latitude and longitude, are projected onto the paper.

The properties of the mercator chart are:
1) Rhumb lines are straight.
2) The direction of a rhumb line is not altered.
3) The equator is a straight line.
4) Meridians appear as equally spaced straight lines.
5) Parallels of latitude appear as straight lines, but their spacing increases as the latitude increases.
6) The poles themselves cannot be shown on the standard mercator chart.
7) The straight line between two points (the rhumb line) is not the shortest distance between the points. This is given by the great circle track, which appears curved towards the nearer pole on a mercator chart.

The gnomonic projection

The second projection of interest to yachtsmen is the gnomonic projection, in which great circles appear as straight lines. The principle of this projection is shown in Figure 2. A flat sheet of paper touches the globe at one point only, called the

3.1 *Mercator's projection.*

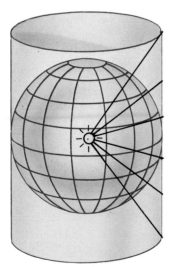

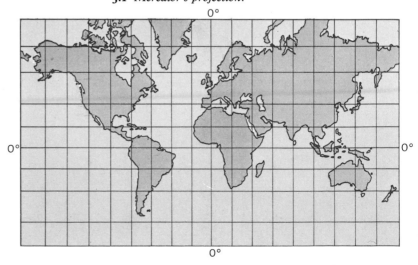

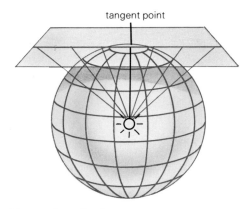

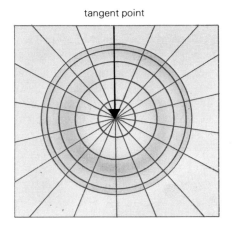

3.2 *Gnomonic projection.*

tangent point. Very often a pole is chosen as the tangent point for an ocean passage planning chart, but this is not essential.

The properties of a gnomonic chart are:
1) Great circles appear as straight lines.
2) Rhumb lines are curved.
3) Parallels of latitude (small circles) are curved.
4) Meridians (great circles) are straight lines which converge towards the poles.
5) Distortion increases with distance from the tangent point.

The gnomonic chart is most often used in ocean passage planning, where the differences between the great circle and the rhumb line tracks become important (see page 180). It is often used for charts of the polar regions (of little interest to yachtsmen) and in a modified form for harbour plans.

Scale and distance on a mercator chart

Because latitude is measured along a great circle (in fact, a meridian), the angle subtended at the centre of the earth by one sea mile is one minute of latitude, and so the scale of latitude and the scale of distance are one and the same. The same is not true of longitude; at the equator, one minute of longitude is indeed equivalent to one sea mile, as the equator is a great circle (Fig. 3). But as the meridians converge, a minute of longitude becomes shorter and shorter on the surface, until at the pole it disappears entirely.

A problem exists with small-scale mercator charts because the parallels of latitude become

more widely spaced as the latitude increases. This distortion is an essential part of the projection as it helps to preserve the shape of the land on the chart, but it means that the latitude scale changes over the chart. The navigator should take care to use the latitude scale adjacent to the position of interest for measuring distance, or considerable errors may arise. This effect is not important on medium or large scale charts (i.e. with a natural scale of 1 : 150,000 or less).

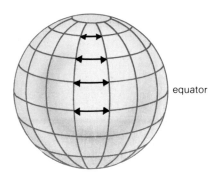

3.3 *Convergence of the meridians.*

4   The chart

A chart is one of the basic tools that a yacht navigator needs to plan and conduct his passage from one place to another. At first sight, it is a complicated and confusing document, but it contains a wealth of information about the part of the world it covers. The difference between a chart and a map is obvious at the first glance; a map deals with the land and there is little or no detail shown of the sea. A chart is exactly the reverse; a navigator is not much interested in the land, except to know where the shoreline runs and to see where prominent objects are for the purpose of fixing his position. On the other hand, he needs to know about buoys and beacons, the nature of the bottom, the depth of water and about underwater hazards that cannot be seen. So a chart is filled with detail over the sea, whilst much of the land area covered by a chart is left blank.

Almost all the charts offered to the mariner are precisely and beautifully produced, but for any particular purpose there are good charts and bad; and as charts are by no means cheap, it is worth considering carefully before buying. A good chart is accurate, comprehensive, easy to use, easy to correct, robust and covers the area of interest at a suitable scale. So, what factors should be considered in choosing a chart? To a large extent, this will depend on the individual navigator and the individual chart under consideration, but there are a number of indicators which can help in making a choice.

Official or commercial?

All maritime countries of any importance maintain a hydrographic service which produces charts for their own mariners and for the rest of the world to use. Most of this information is pooled for the benefit of other countries, so that, for example, a British chart of the River Tagus (Tejo) would be based upon Portuguese government surveys. Apart from these official charts, a number of commercial companies produce charts for a specialized use – for fishermen or for yachtsmen. These commercial charts can vary widely in quality, though those produced by a reputable company are thoroughly trustworthy. They are in general an edited and rearranged form of the official charts of the area, concentrating on aspects of particular interest to the user and omitting detail that is irrelevant. Examples of different kinds of chart are given on pages 61–4. In deciding between official and commercial charts, the key point is that official charts are based on official surveys. *Ipso facto*, the official chart ought to be more accurate, though not perhaps as easy to use.

Scale

Scale is the relation between distance on the chart and distance on the surface of the earth. A large scale chart covers a small area of the earth.

The scale of a chart can vary from 1 : 1,000,000 or more for passage planning to 1 : 10,000 for a harbour plan. For coastal passages, a suitable scale is somewhere between 1 : 50,000 and 1 : 150,000, depending on the complexity of the coastal features. The largest scale chart available should always be used, for two good reasons; the larger scale chart carries more detail, and it is generally the first to be up-dated as the topography alters.

Country of origin

If possible, it is best to use charts prepared and produced by the country concerned, rather than by some other country. Thus a Finnish chart of Helsinki is likely to be more satisfactory than an American or British or French chart, especially as the foreign charts are almost certainly based on the same survey as the original. When using foreign charts, problems of correction and language arise, but the balance is firmly in favour of the local article.

Soundings

For popular and well-travelled areas almost all charts are equally reliable, but for the more remote regions, the pattern of soundings on a chart can often give an idea of its reliability; scattered soundings with gaps in the coverage and incomplete depth contours are both warning signs. Even in well-surveyed areas it is entirely possible for a small, isolated danger to escape detection. In poorly-surveyed areas the risk is all the greater.

Date of survey

The date of survey, which is given on all good charts, can be a useful guide when considered with the type of country involved. Solid, rocky regions change very slowly and an old survey may be quite acceptable; on the other hand, a river estuary with shifting sand- or mudbanks requires a modern survey. The date of a survey may also affect the quality of the soundings; before the 1930s, soundings were all made by hand, using a lead and line. Later surveys have used echo sounders and (nowadays) side-scan sonar, with more systematic results. Modern position-fixing methods have also vastly improved the quality of surveys.

Corrections
It is essential that any chart purchased should be up-to-date with the latest information available to the charting authority or his agent. New editions are brought out from time to time, incorporating any corrections known to date; subsequently, small corrections are published at regular intervals so that chart users can correct them by hand (see pages 20–1).

Appearance
A chart that looks full and 'interesting' is likely to be better than one that is sparse and bare. Charts of remote regions are likely to be bare, and a yachtsman should remember that he may well be testing such a chart for the first time since the original survey. Very considerable caution is required, particularly in the first approach to the coast.

5 Looking after charts

A chart properly cared for is a very accurate and useful guide to the mariner; a chart which is damaged or has been allowed to get out-of-date is a danger. Some yachtsmen choose to buy new copies of charts at frequent intervals, but charts are not cheap and an outfit can represent a substantial investment. It makes good sense to care for your charts for both safety and financial reasons.

The physical care of charts

Charts are printed on strong, stable paper of good quality, but they can still be damaged quite easily if care is not taken. A few common-sense rules can extend the life of a chart considerably.

1) Draw lightly with a good quality soft pencil.
2) Rub out lines with a good quality soft eraser, but not when the chart is wet.
3) Keep the chart as dry as possible. In a yacht in bad weather this may well be impossible, but at least remove a dripping hat and keep the chart sheltered.
4) Protect the edge of the chart nearest you; wet oilskins rubbing on a wet chart can destroy it in seconds.
5) Do not fold a chart into new creases if you can help it. If essential to make it fit the chart table, then fold it carefully. Take the folds out before putting the chart away.
6) Do not keep charts rolled up, as this makes them difficult and annoying to use. Stow them flat, under the mattress of a bunk if nowhere more suitable is available.
7) When you have finished with a chart, rub off all old work (if the chart is dry), so that it is immediately ready for use next time.
8) In general, treat the chart as a valuable document; protect it from falling on the sole, spilt coffee, dropped food and the other detritus of shipboard life.

Chart correction

There is no need for a chart to get out-of-date within its lifetime (before a new edition is published). Corrections are published by all charting authorities at frequent intervals, and are generally available free of charge (except perhaps for postage). If tackled regularly and systematically, cor-recting even a large outfit of charts takes little time, though it can become a daunting task if corrections are allowed to accumulate. Chart agents may offer a correction service, maintaining and correcting a yacht's outfit of charts during the off season.

Chart corrections are published in a number of ways:

Urgent navigational warnings are broadcast by coast radio stations on marine frequencies. These warnings are normally temporary in nature, concerning unlit navigational buoys, new wrecks and the like. Any such warnings received should be noted on the chart in pencil until either cancelled or confirmed in a *Notice to Mariners*.

The majority of chart corrections are published at regular intervals (often weekly) by charting authorities, as *Notices to Mariners*. These Notices contain details of new charts or new editions of charts which have just been published, together with corrections to existing charts and publications. If a notice is described as 'Temporary' or 'Preliminary', the details should be noted on the chart in pencil until cancelled or confirmed.

The process of correcting a chart is reasonably straightforward, though it requires a good knowledge of chart symbols (pages 41–2). Corrections should be made neatly and legibly in waterproof ink using a fine pen (violet is the conventional colour for the ink). An example of a *Notice to Mariners* and the resulting chart correction is given in Figure 1. Neatness should be a matter of pride, and an excellent example to follow is the meticulous work of professional correctors who keep charts up-to-date between the time they are printed and the time they are sold. Having made a correction it is *very important* to make a note of the fact in the appropriate place on the chart so that another user can have confidence that the chart has been corrected. Templates of chart symbols exist (e.g. DMAHTC No. 9998 for US charts). These can help keep your work neat.

Sometimes a correction may be so extensive or complicated that it is difficult to describe in words. In this case, a block is produced; this consists of a reprint of the appropriate section of the chart with all the necessary corrections made. The block should be carefully cut out with scissors and offered up in the right place on the chart to ensure

5.1 *Correcting a chart.*

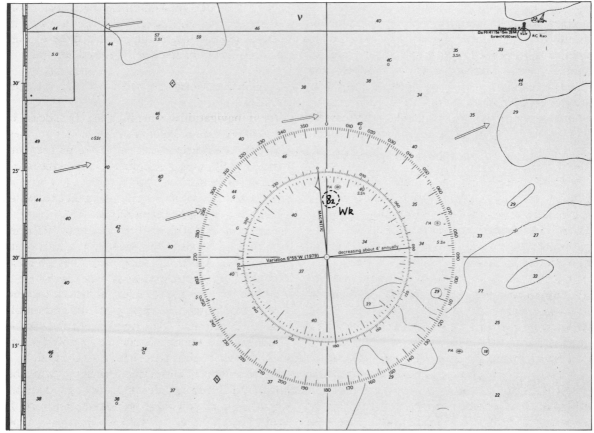

FRANCE, North coast — Bassurelle — Amendment to wreck South-Westward

(1) A depth of 8 metres surrounded by a danger circle ⟨⟩, Wk, is to be inserted in position 50°23′.80N., 0°40′.05E.

(2) The dangerous wreck ⋮+⋮ PA close E. is to be deleted.

Chart [*Last correction*] – **9999** [*1395/81*]
French Notice 11/27/81

that it fits. A few pencil strokes across the block and the chart will help in fixing the block later. When you are satisfied that the block fits as well as possible (paper distortions sometimes prevent a perfect fit), the block can then be pasted into place.

A *Notice to Mariners* may well affect several charts of different scales; when making corrections, put in the same quantity of detail as is already shown on the chart. Large-scale charts contain as much detail as possible. As the scale gets smaller, more and more information is left out to keep the chart from getting cluttered. For ex-

ample, the details of buoys inside a harbour are generally omitted from a chart intended for coastal passage making; on ocean charts, only the major landfall lights are shown, and so on.

Commercial charts are not as easy to correct as those published by a charting authority. Most publishers do their best to ensure the chart is correct when sold, but few have any facilities for publishing corrections. *Notices to Mariners* can of course be used, but there is a difficulty if a correction is published as a block, which will not fit the commercial chart.

6 Books and tables

A vast number of books have been published to give the navigator information he needs. The more important of these are described below. It would be a very unusual yacht that would need all these books at one time, so this list should not be considered as a recommended library; it is rather a guide to what is available for any particular purpose.

The pilot

The most important of the books available to the navigator is the *Pilot*, or *Sailing Directions*. A *Pilot* is a narrative description of coastlines, dangers, harbours and facilities, and is an invaluable supplement to the chart. *Pilots* have a history as old as seafaring itself, as they are descended from the verbal account of a coast that one mariner would give to another, even before charts were dreamed of. The modern *Pilot* is the distillation of many years experience by many seamen and contains a wealth of information that is difficult to find elsewhere.

Pilots are of two kinds; official *Pilots* are published by charting authorities, and yachting *Pilots* are published commercially. Each has its advantages and its disadvantages. Official *Pilots* are thorough and detailed, and cover most parts of the world, but they are written with the larger ship in mind; a safe and pleasant haven may be dismissed with the words 'suitable only for small craft with local knowledge'.

Yachting Pilots are a very mixed bunch; some are excellent and others are awful. With a little experience it is not too difficult to form an opinion about the worth of a particular book; if it has been through several editions at regular intervals, it ought to be more up-to-date and better maintained than one that has been re-published only rarely. Perhaps the best way to choose a yachting *Pilot* is on the recommendation of someone you trust.

The advantage of a yachting *Pilot* over an official one is that it has been written with the yachtsman in mind, and it supplies much valuable information that the bigger *Pilot* leaves out. However, there is a major problem of correction. Official *Pilots* are normally supplied with correc-

tions in the form of a supplement, which is revised every year or so. Very few yachting *Pilots* offer this service. The more reputable publishers will reprint at frequent intervals so that recent information can be included. It should also be remembered that yachting *Pilots* are only published for popular sailing areas, and do not cover places off the beaten track.

List of lights and fog signals

The *Light List* supplements the information on the chart, in that it gives full details of a light or fog signal, rather than the 'shorthand' version printed on the chart. A description of the structure housing the light is also given for daytime recognition. The details of buoys, light floats and lightships over a certain size are also recorded.

List of radio signals

This document (which may be in several volumes) gives information about the use of radio in navigation, including radio and radar beacons, direction-finding services, weather information services, time signals, radio position-fixing systems and details of port radio stations and pilot vessels.

Tide tables

Tide Tables are published for all areas of the world where tide is significant. Predictions are normally made for a number of 'Standard Ports'. In simple cases the height of the tide at a 'Secondary Port' can be established by applying a simple set of corrections to the data for the nearest Standard Port, but in some parts of the world more elaborate techniques are needed (see page 102).

Pilot charts and ocean passage planning aids

The function of these books or charts is to link together the *Pilots* of different parts of the world by giving recommended tracks between ports, distances, details of weather, currents and potential hazards (such as ice) and much other useful information.

Distance tables

Tables are published of the distances (by the most practical route) between the major ports of the world. This book is of little use to yachtsmen.

Nautical Almanac

The *Nautical Almanac* (published annually) is essential for the practice of astronomical navigation. It gives details of the movements of the sun, moon, major planets and brighter stars, together with the times of sunrise, sunset, moonrise and moonset. Calendars and eclipse predictions are included.

Nautical tables

Several volumes of mathematical tables specially prepared for navigators have been published. The more important of the tables normally included are *Traverse Tables* (see page 177), *Distance Tables* and tables for obtaining a position line from observations of heavenly bodies.

Sight reduction tables

Sight Reduction Tables offer another, simpler way of getting a position line from astronomical observations. The tables chosen for use in this book are the *Sight Reduction Tables for Air Navigation* (US Pub 249, British AP3270) in three volumes. The use of these tables is described in detail on page 148 and following.

Combined Almanacs

Some nautical publishers gather together as much of the above information as they consider their customers will need, and publish it all in one (rather fat) volume. These books can save both space near the chart table and money, but it should be remembered that they must of necessity be more limited in their scope than full-size tables.

Tidal stream atlases

For areas where tidal streams are important and complex, atlases are published giving chartlets which show the direction and strength of the tidal streams for each hour of the tide. Though less exact than the tidal stream information given on the chart, these atlases give an excellent overall impression of the way in which the water moves. They are therefore especially useful for passage planning.

Chart catalogues

When planning a passage, a *Chart Catalogue* gives a rapid view of the scale and coverage of available charts.

7 Drawing and plotting instruments

Chartwork consists essentially of plotting and drawing points (representing positions) and lines (representing directions), and measuring distances. To help the navigator do this quickly and accurately, a number of instruments have been evolved for measuring distances and angles, and for drawing parallel lines. As with many aspects of navigation, there is more than one way of killing a cat, and the same job can often be done with a variety of instruments. Which one to use depends more on the training and preference of the user than any inherent advantage. Each navigator will develop his own approach, but he should at least be familiar with other methods, in case he finds himself navigating a boat which does not carry his favourite tools. Plotting instruments should be purchased on the basis of their quality and accuracy; it is a mistake to buy cheap, flimsy and inaccurate instruments.

Pencils
Pencils should be of good quality, with soft leads (grade 2B is perhaps best). Hard leads dig into the chart and are difficult to erase; on the other hand, soft leads wear down quickly and need frequent sharpening. They can also smear and make the chart messy. Fine lead propelling pencils (0.5 mm) are very convenient as they do not need to be sharpened, but their life tends to be rather short in the adverse surroundings of a small boat at sea. Always carry plenty of spare pencils.

Erasers
Carry a good stock of soft, good quality artists erasers for rubbing out old work. Keep them as dry as possible, and avoid using them on wet charts as this tends to rub off the top layer of the paper and the print.

Dividers
Dividers are used for measuring distances. They should be well made, and smooth and firm in operation without being stiff. It should also be possible to take them to pieces for cleaning and lubrication. Most good dividers for marine use are made of brass with stainless steel points. The points should be sharp enough to catch the surface of the chart without digging in and making holes; they will need sharpening from time to time. Dividers are inconvenient if they are too short; arms of about 6 in (15 cm) are very suitable. As Figure 1 shows, there are two kinds of dividers; the conventional straight-armed type, and a bowed version which has the advantage that it can be either opened or closed with one hand. Good quality 'straight' dividers can also be used with one hand, given a little practice.

Parallel rulers
Parallel rulers are used for drawing parallel lines (though protractors can also be used – see below). The most common material for these nowadays is clear perspex, though boxwood and brass are also used. It is obviously essential that the two sides of the ruler are parallel with each other and that the ruler moves with a truly parallel motion. A good test is to use the ruler to compare the opposite borders of a chart; if the instrument can carry a line right across the chart, it is clearly satisfactory. There are two types, as shown in Figure 2. Both have their disadvantages; the rolling type is more difficult to use if the boat is moving violently and is likely to roll all over the place when not in use, unless it is properly stowed. The opening type of parallel ruler has to be 'walked' across the chart and is very likely to twist if it catches in a fold or an obstruction under the chart (such as a hinge). The opening ruler shown in Figure 2 is of Captain Field's Improved Pattern, which incorporates a protractor.

Protractors
Because protractors are used in navigation as much for drawing lines as for measuring angles, square or triangular shapes are more useful than round or semi-circular. It is possible to draw on the reverse side of this instrument for plotting fixes by horizontal angles (see page 82). The triangular protractor is illustrated in Figure 3.

Proprietary plotting instruments
A bewildering variety of more or less complicated plotting instruments are offered to the yachtsman, each claiming to make his life easier. Many of them consist of some form of square protractor with a hinged plotting arm attached. All too often these

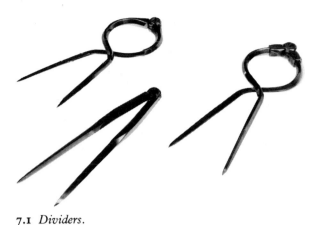

7.1 *Dividers.*

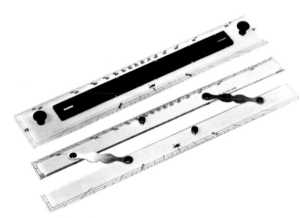

7.2 *Parallel rulers.*

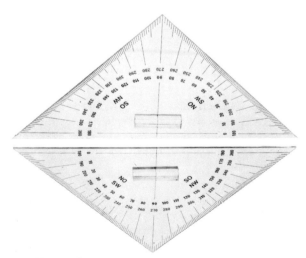

7.3 *Triangular protractors.*

devices are flimsy, clumsy and difficult to stow. It is advisable to try such devices out at sea (by borrowing one) before putting your hand in your pocket.

The station pointer
The station pointer is a protractor with three arms (two of them adjustable). It is used only for horizontal angle fixes (see page 83); on grounds of size, cost and infrequency of use it cannot be recommended for yachts.

Compasses
There are occasions when a pair of compasses is useful for drawing arcs or circles; as with all instruments, a good quality pair should be chosen.

The chart table
The chart table, as the field on which the navigator works, requires some comment, though very few yachtsmen are in a position to have their navigating position designed and built for them. Most yachtsmen have to put up with the arrangements, good or bad, that happen to exist in the boat they buy or are invited to crew in. However, the chart table should be one of the factors in judging a boat. It is difficult to be specific, because a chart table for a fifty-footer would be absurd in a twenty-footer and *vice versa*. The chart table should be as big as practicable with good stowage nearby for books, charts and instruments. It should be protected from the weather, but within easy contact of the helm. It should be strong, with a comfortable seat; some form of restraint should be provided to hold the navigator in place while he works with both hands. And it needs a light which can illuminate the chart at night without troubling off-watch crew members or dazzling the navigator or helmsman.

The techniques for using plotting instruments are described on pages 54–5.

8   The magnetic compass

A compass is a device carried in a vessel to indicate north, so that the heading of the vessel can be known. There are two principal types of compass – the magnetic compass and the gyrocompass. Because of price and a continuous need for electrical power, the gyrocompass is only found on a few large, luxury power yachts. For all practical purposes, the yachtsman's compass is a magnetic compass.

The origins of the magnetic compass are obscure, but it came into general use in European ships in the late Middle Ages. In its earliest form, it consisted of a piece of magnetic iron ore (lodestone) suspended by a thread. The magnetic axis of the stone took up a north-south line. It was later found that this magnetic property could be transferred (by rubbing) to an iron needle. The needle was at first floated in a bowl of water on a piece of cork; later it was suspended from a card, pivoted at the centre. Though vastly improved in materials, construction and accuracy, the modern magnetic compass has altered little in principle.

A typical yacht compass is shown in Figure 1. A number of magnets are suspended below a light

card. The card is free to revolve on a very carefully made pivot. The bowl of the compass is filled with a liquid which helps to damp down oscillations in the card, and which supports much of the weight of the card and needles, thus reducing wear on the pivot. The bowl is fitted with bellows so that the liquid in the bowl may expand and contract in differing temperatures without causing a bubble to form or bursting the bowl.

The compass card

As well as supporting the magnets, the compass card carries graduations to allow the direction of the ship's head to be read. When the compass is installed, a line inside the bowl, called the lubber's line, is lined up with the ship's head. The heading is indicated by the graduation opposite the lubber's line.

Having established the cardinal points of the compass, north south east and west, the early navigators divided the card into half, and half again, and then once more to give the traditional card divided into 32 points, each $11\frac{1}{4}°$. Modern compasses are graduated in degrees clockwise from north; a yacht compass may only have graduations at 5° intervals.

Choosing and installing a compass

Modern yacht compasses are available in many different styles; some have internal gimbals to keep the card level, while some have external gimbals; some are designed for bulkhead mounting, others have to be mounted on a bracket; some carry internal correcting magnets, while others have to be corrected by magnets outside the compass. A steering compass should be selected mainly for its quality; it can be (literally) fatal to make a false economy by buying a cheap, inaccurate and unreliable compass. From different styles of compass, a choice should be made to suit the particular boat and your own preferences; if you are uncertain, the advice of a knowledgeable friend can be invaluable.

The ideal steering compass position is one where the card can be seen easily by the helmsman (on either tack in sailing yachts). It should be remote from any bodies of iron which may cause errors (see page 29), and protected from accidental damage from feet, bodies or equipment. It should

8.1 *A yacht compass.*

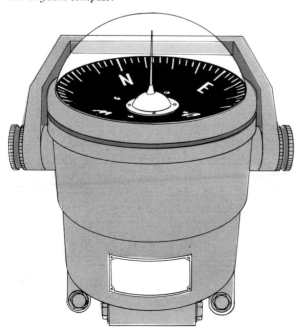

also be out of the way. Fairly obviously, the ideal is generally impossible, but any compass installation should be carried out with a great deal of careful thought, together with expert advice if available.

Hand bearing compasses

The navigator often wishes to take a compass bearing of some object, which means that he wants to measure the direction in which the object lies from him. This can sometimes be done by using the steering compass, but often this is not possible. A hand bearing compass is a small compass which can be held in the hand and taken to any convenient part of the deck to take a bearing. A typical

hand bearing compass is shown in Figure 2. It incorporates a prism or some other optical device to allow the navigator to look at both the object and the compass card at the same time, so he can record the bearing. As with a steering compass, the hand bearing compass must be carefully chosen. It can be a sobering experience to compare hand bearing compasses at the door of a chandler's shop. A variation of 10° or 15° is not uncommon among cheap compasses.

Transmitting compasses

A transmitting compass consists of a master compass unit which can be mounted almost anywhere, with one or more repeater units to indicate the ship's heading wherever desired. Transmitting compasses are inevitably more expensive than normal compasses of the same quality, and they require continuous electrical power; this can be a problem in a sailing craft. The advantages are the ability to mount the master unit in a position remote from magnetic interference (even up the mast), and the ability to position repeaters without having to worry about magnetic influences.

The gyrocompass

Though the gyrocompass is rarely found in a yacht, it may be found in some large power yachts. The principle is related to the child's gyroscope toy. A spinning wheel is made to interact with the rotation of the earth and the force of gravity to cause the axis of the wheel to point to north. The essential difference between a gyrocompass heading and a magnetic compass heading is that a gyrocompass *points to true north*, whereas a magnetic compass points to magnetic north (see pages 28–9). A gyrocompass takes about 90 minutes to settle after it is first switched on; thereafter, the error should not exceed 1–2°. An adjustment has to be made to the gyrocompass as the latitude of the vessel changes. The gyromagnetic compass is a combination of gyrocompass and magnetic compass; it is often used in aircraft, but rarely at sea.

8.2 *A hand bearing compass.*

9 Using the magnetic compass

The entire earth can be considered to be a magnet, probably because the molten iron core of the earth sustains powerful electric currents as a form of generator. Like an ordinary bar magnet, the earth has two magnetic poles, north and south, connected by lines of force along the surface and in nearby space. The magnets of a compass align themselves with these lines of force to give an indication of direction.

The first problem in using a magnetic compass arises from the fact that the magnetic north pole does not coincide with the geographic north pole; therefore, in general, the magnetic compass does not point to true north. The difference between magnetic north and true north is called the *variation* (see below), which varies in an irregular way with time and with position on the surface of the earth. At present, the north magnetic pole is in about 75°N, 95°W – some 1,000 miles from the true pole. It revolves around the true pole about once every 500 years.

Variation

Variation is a semi-systematic error of the magnetic compass (page 9). It varies both with position on the earth's surface and with time; in areas likely to be visited by yachts, it is unlikely to exceed 30° east or west of the true meridian.

The variation at a particular place can be obtained from two sources. A chart showing curves of equal magnetic variation is called an isogonal chart (Fig. 1). Such a chart will also give information about the rate of change of variation with time. The second and more convenient way to discover the variation is to consult a chart of the area. This will contain (probably in or near the compass roses printed at intervals across the chart) a notice in the following form:

['Variation 6°22′W (1979) increasing about 10′ annually.']

Note that the variation will vary across the chart, and in certain areas the change can be quite marked. For example, when approaching Halifax, Nova Scotia from Newfoundland, the variation will change 10° in less than 500 miles. Small scale

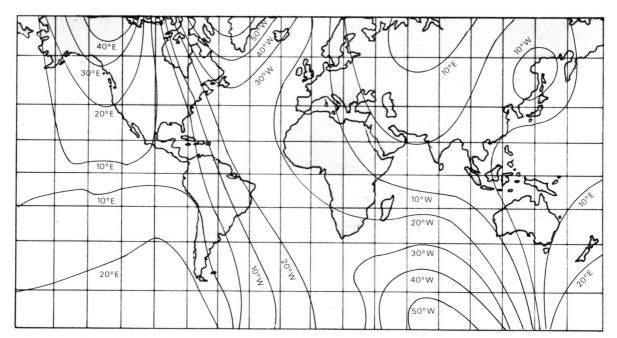

9.1 *Isogonal chart.*

ocean charts often have isogonic lines (lines of equal magnetic variation) printed on them. If the chart has been in circulation for some time without a new edition, the change in variation with time (called the secular change) may also be appreciable.

Variation is expressed as the number of degrees (and minutes) east or west of the true meridian. The navigator often needs to convert a true direction to a magnetic direction and *vice versa*. This is done by applying the variation according to the following rule: (Fig. 2)

Magnetic to true – add easterly variation
True to magnetic – subtract easterly variation
For example:
True direction 155
Variation   6W
Mag direction 161M

True direction 266
Variation   12E
Mag direction 254M

Mag direction 091M
Variation   9W
True direction 082

In certain places, the magnetic variation is disturbed by geological features; details of these local magnetic anomalies are given on charts and in pilot books where they are known. Intense electrical storms can also cause temporary derangement of the magnetic compass.

Deviation

A magnetic compass may also be disturbed by magnetic influences close to it – in a steel vessel, the hull and decks and in wooden or glassfibre boats, the engine or other fittings of ferrous metal (in general, marine grade stainless steels are non-magnetic). These disturbing influences, if they exist, give rise to a systematic error (page 9) called deviation. It varies with the actual heading of the vessel with respect to magnetic north, and can alter with time. Deviation is measured east or west of magnetic north and the process of calibrating a particular compass installation to discover the deviation is called swinging the compass (see page 32). It is most important that a compass is swung periodically (at least once a year), and that

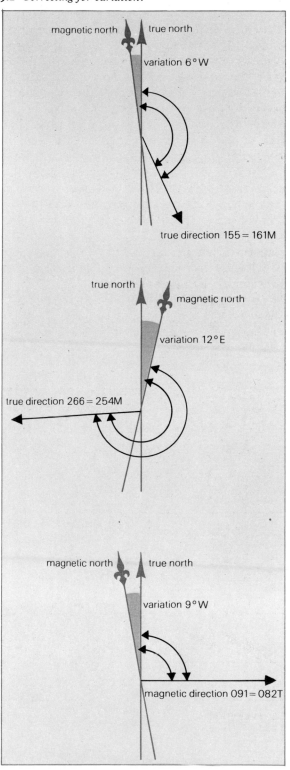

9.2 *Correcting for variation.*

magnetic north   true north
variation 6°W
true direction 155 = 161M

true north   magnetic north
variation 12°E
true direction 266 = 254M

magnetic north   true north
variation 9°W
magnetic direction 091 = 082T

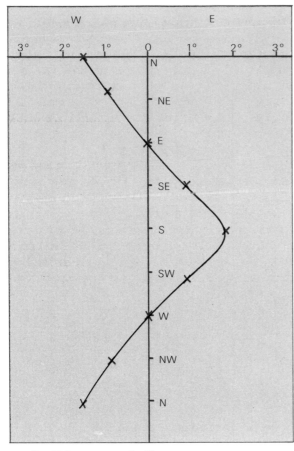

9.3 *Deviation curve and table.*

Ship's Head by Compass		Deviation
N	(000)	1½°W
NE	(045)	1°W
E	(090)	0°
SE	(135)	1°E
S	(180)	1½°E
SW	(225)	1°E
W	(270)	0°
NW	(315)	1°W

frequent checks are made to ensure that no un-suspected change in deviation has occurred. The deviation on any heading is normally shown as a table or as a curve (Fig. 3).

If the deviation on any heading is found to exceed 2–3°, the compass should be adjusted by placing small magnets at suitable locations close to the compass. For the majority of wooden or glass-fibre yachts this is a straightforward operation well within the capacity of the owner, but for more difficult installations (steel or ferro-cement boats, or if the engine is close under the compass) a professional compass adjuster should be engaged. The simple procedure is described on page 33.

Converting between compass, magnetic and true headings

Where both variation and deviation exist, it is necessary to convert between true, magnetic and compass headings. To convert a true heading to a compass heading, first apply the variation (from the chart) to obtain a magnetic heading; then look up the deviation for that heading, and apply it following the same rules as for variation, to obtain the compass heading. To convert the opposite way, from compass to true, this procedure is reversed.

Two examples will show the principle:

True heading	154	
Variation	3E	
Mag heading	151M	
Deviation	2E	(from deviation table)
Compass heading	149C	

Compass heading	357C
Deviation	4E
Mag heading	001M
Variation	11W
True heading	350

Note the use of the suffixes M and C to indicate magnetic and compass headings respectively; true headings are given without a suffix.

If a bearing of an object is taken from the steering compass, the deviation must be applied to the result; this should be the deviation appropriate to the course of the yacht, *not* to the direction of the bearing. Most bearings, however, are taken with a hand bearing compass. If this is held well clear of possible magnetic influences, it can generally be assumed that any deviation will be negligible; in a steel or ferro-cement yacht, hand bearing compasses should be used with caution and held at least three feet (one metre) above deck level.

Heeling error

A large body of iron below the compass can lead to heeling error, which varies in magnitude according to the angle of heel. This can cause an unsteady compass in a rolling vessel, and a sailing yacht may experience different deviations on different tacks for the same heading. Heeling error can only be corrected by a professional adjuster with the proper instruments.

Acceleration errors

Acceleration errors can affect the compass of a high-speed craft making a tight turn, causing the compass either to lag or lead during the turn. The error will disappear as the craft steadies on its new heading.

Summary of errors

Gross errors A good quality compass, overhauled every five years or so, is a thoroughly reliable instrument. Wear in the pivot can cause a sticky card. A bubble in the bowl can cause gross unsteadiness. The most likely cause of gross errors is the careless placing of magnetic objects near the compass; the most common offenders are drink cans and cameras (which have a magnet in the automatic exposure meter).

Systematic errors Apart from variation and deviation, the most common systematic error is misalignment between the lubber line of the compass and the fore-and-aft line of the ship.

Random errors The inherent random errors of a properly adjusted compass are small (1° maximum on 95 per cent of occasions). They are masked by the errors in using the compass in a seaway, discussed on page 52.

10 Swinging and adjusting compasses

Swinging a compass

Swinging a yacht's compass to establish a table or curve of deviation is a relatively quick and easy procedure, which should be done at least once a year. It should not be attempted in a marina, where steel fittings on the pontoons may give unwanted errors. Many different ways of swinging a compass have been described, most of them requiring the use of a pelorus, or dumb compass card, for taking relative bearings of shore objects or a heavenly body. The method described below, whilst marginally less accurate than the best, has the overpowering merit of being both simple and practical*. It can even be done single-handed, if necessary.

The principle is shown in Figure 1. The boat is taken to a convenient location, in smooth water and with land at a reasonable distance off (certainly not less than a mile); then:

1) Head north by compass.

2) Identify *any* object which is right ahead on this heading – a tree, a house, a telegraph pole or anything else that may be readily kept in the mind's eye. If there is no such object right ahead on the heading, then move the boat to a position where there is one.

3) Take a careful bearing of the object with a good quality hand bearing compass.

   The hand bearing compass should be used standing well up and clear of any magnetic influences on the yacht.

   Whilst taking this magnetic bearing, there is no need to keep the boat exactly on the original heading.

4) The difference between the original heading with the object right ahead (north) and the compass bearing of the object is the deviation; if the magnetic bearing is to the left of the heading, deviation is easterly and *vice versa*.

5) Repeat the process on the remaining cardinal points and on the inter-cardinal points (NE, SE, SW, NW). Again, if no object conveniently presents itself on any heading, move to another position where it does.

*This method was suggested by I. McLaren of the City of London Polytechnic's School of Navigation.

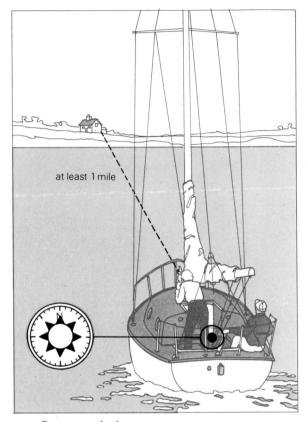

at least 1 mile

10.1 *Compass swinging.*

6) From the results thus obtained, a deviation table or a deviation curve (whichever is preferred) can be drawn up as shown in Figure 2.

If the deviations are large (more than a few degrees), or appear to follow an irregular pattern, the compass needs to be adjusted. An owner can often do this himself as described below, but if he is in any doubt or difficulty, he should engage a professional compass adjuster.

Steering Compass	Hand Bearing Compass	Deviation
N	357	3°E
NE	044	1°E
E	090	0°
SE	137	2°W
S	183	3°W
SW	226	1°W
W	269	1°E
NW	313	2°E

10.2 *Drawing up the deviation table.*

Adjusting the compass

In most cases, the owner of a wooden or glassfibre boat should be able to adjust his own compass, assuming that a swing shows this to be necessary. The owner should be careful if the compass installation is close above the engine (say two feet or 0.6 metres); if so, heeling error may be present, which can only be removed by a qualified compass adjuster. Steel boats and ferro-cement boats (which have large quantities of steel in the reinforcing mesh) are more complicated to adjust, and should be left to the professional.

A theoretical study shows that a deviation curve can be broken down into five components, but the 'do-it-yourself' adjuster assumes that only two of these are of any importance.

Coefficient B is caused by hard iron fore and aft of the compass. It produces a deviation which is zero on north and south headings, and at a maximum (with opposite signs) on east and west (Fig. 3).

Coefficient C is caused by hard iron on either which is zero on east and west headings, and at a maximum (with opposite signs) on north and south (Fig. 4).

To correct for the effects of coefficients B and C, it is necessary to steady the yacht in turn on the four cardinal points (magnetic this time, not by compass). This can be done in a similar way to the swinging of the compass, as follows:

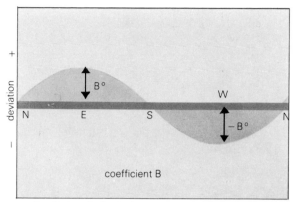

10.3 *Coefficient B deviation.*

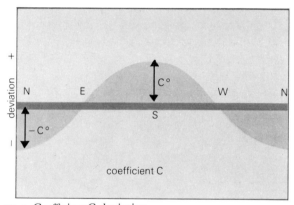

10.4 *Coefficient C deviation.*

1) Using a hand-bearing compass, identify an object on shore which is exactly due north (magnetic) from the yacht; if necessary, move the yacht until you find one.
2) Point the yacht at the object so that it is right ahead.
3) Adjust the compass so that it reads north by means of magnets pointing *athwartships*. Some compasses contain built-in correcting magnets on a special mechanism which can be adjusted by a screwdriver; others have little pockets into which small magnets can be put by 'cut and try' until the deviation disappears. If the compass has no facility at all for correction, it should be rejected as unfit to take to sea.
4) Repeat steps 1, 2 and 3 for a magnetic heading of east, this time adjusting the compass by

means of magnets pointing *fore-and-aft*. This will compensate for coefficient B, in the same way that step 3 compensated for coefficient C.
5) Steady the boat on south (magnetic) and check the deviation; in theory it should be zero but in practice a small deviation may remain. Adjust the athwartships magnets to remove *half* the deviation.
6) Now steady the boat on west (magnetic) and, if necessary, remove half the remaining deviation with the fore-and-aft magnets.
7) Finally swing the ship again to obtain the final deviation table; by now the deviations should be small (no more than 2°).
8) Note that when adjusting a compass, it does not matter which heading is used initially, or which way round the compass the adjustments are made, provided the basic sequence is followed.

Checking a compass

Every opportunity should be taken to check the compass on a variety of headings. Along the coast this can be done by pointing the boat at a known shore object from a known position, and comparing the compass with the magnetic bearing extracted from the chart. A better way is to point the boat along a transit (*range* in US terminology) formed by bringing two charted objects into line (Fig. 5). The opportunities for taking transits are less frequent, but the accuracy is better. Out of sight of land, the compass can be checked by taking bearings of the sun and computing its azimuth (bearing) using the techniques described on page 162. A simpler way is to take the bearing of the sun at sunrise or sunset (when the bottom edge of the sun is about half the sun's diameter above the horizon). Using the boat's latitude and the declination of the sun (from the *Nautical Almanac*), it is possible to work out the azimuth of the sun. A table for this purpose is given in this book (p. 193) and similar tables are published in other books.

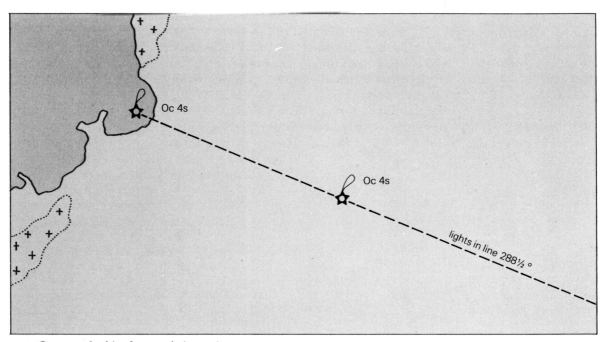

10.5 *Compass checking by transit (range).*

11 Logs and distance measurement

A log is primarily a device for recording the distance travelled through the water by a vessel; most yacht logs now incorporate a speed indicator, which is of more value to the helmsman than to the navigator. The *common log* was invented at the end of the sixteenth century; before then, seamen had estimated the speed of their ship by eye. The common log is shown in Figure 1. It consists of a log-ship of wood, in the form of a quadrant, attached by a bridle to a long line. The log was cast over the stern, and the log line was paid out as the ship sailed away. The line was marked at equal intervals by pieces of knotted cord, and the number of these 'knots' paid out in a fixed time (measured by a sandglass) represented the speed of the ship. At the end of the run, the line was jerked, pulling a pin on one leg of the bridle so that the log-ship lay flat in the water and could be recovered. It is from the common log that the knot, or one nautical mile per hour, is named.

The towed log was invented at the beginning of the nineteenth century and in a developed form is still in use. This consists of a carefully shaped rotor which revolves as it is dragged through the water astern of the ship. The rotation is transmitted along the towing line to a recording device mounted at the stern. Though rather less convenient than other types of log, it is the most accurate.

The majority of modern yacht logs are designed to be fitted to the hull of the yacht. While this is convenient, it leads to the major cause of inaccuracy in such logs. As the hull of the yacht moves through the water, it tends to carry with it a thin layer of water, called the *boundary layer* (Fig. 2). Thus close to the hull (the region in which most hull logs work) the speed of the water past the hull is not the same as the speed of the bulk of the water away from the hull. As the thickness of the boundary layer varies with speed, it is not always possible to correct the log thoroughly for the entire speed range of the boat.

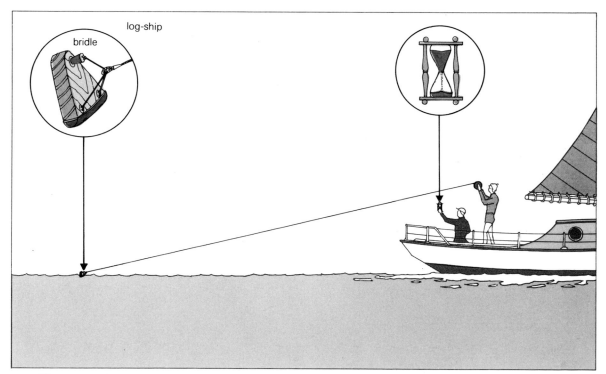

log-ship

bridle

11.1 *The common log.*

Yacht logs are constructed on a variety of physical principles, but it cannot be said that any one type has overwhelming advantages over the others. As with any instrument, accuracy and reliability are related to price and quality.

Impellor logs These consist of a small rotor or paddlewheel projecting into the water through the hull (Fig. 3). The rotation of this device is transmitted to an indicator – sometimes by flexible cable like the speedometer of a car, but more commonly by electronic circuitry. The impellor log tends to be more reliable than other types, but is very prone to fouling by floating weed and marine

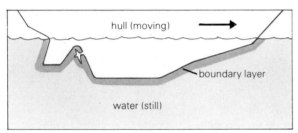

11.2 *Boundary layer*.

growth in spite of the protective measures taken by the manufacturers.

11.3 *Impellor type hull log*.

Electromagnetic logs These work on a principle first discovered by Faraday, that a voltage is induced across the ends of a conductor moving in a magnetic field. In the case of a log, the magnetic field is produced by an electromagnet mounted flush with the skin of the boat and the conductor is the seawater itself (Fig. 4). As the boat moves through the water, a tiny voltage proportional to speed is picked up by two electrodes. This voltage is amplified and applied to the indicating instruments.

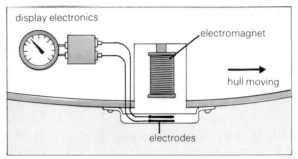

11.4 *Principle of the electromagnetic log*.

Doppler logs These logs use the well-known doppler effect, whereby the pitch of a sound is lower if the source is moving away from the hearer, and higher if the source is moving towards him. In the doppler log, a transducer emits very high frequency sound waves (ultrasound), and a receiver detects the change in pitch caused by the speed of the boat.

Pitot logs The pitot log works in the same way as the air speed indicator in an aircraft. It consists of two tubes (Fig. 5). One tube is bent so that the opening at its end points into the flow of water past it; the other tube has its opening at right angles to the flow. The speed of the boat causes a difference of pressure in the two tubes, which is used to drive a pointer over a scale.

11.5 *The Pitot type log*.

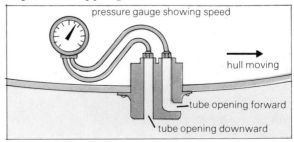

The Dutchman's log This is a way of measuring the speed of a boat when no other means is available. A piece of paper, an empty can or any other scrap object that will float is thrown over the side near the bow, and a stopwatch is used to measure the time it takes this object to pass between two marks a known distance apart on the ship's side. From this, it is easy to calculate the speed of the boat.

For example, if it takes five seconds for the object to move 30 feet, then the speed is given by:

$$\frac{30}{5} \times \frac{3600}{6080} = 3.55 \text{ knots}$$

Or if the object moves ten metres in five seconds,

$$\frac{10}{5} \times \frac{3600}{1852} = 3.9 \text{ knots}$$

Hull logs compared

The impellor type of log is at present the most common; it tends to be more reliable than the other types, though it can be expected that purely electronic logs like the electromagnetic and the doppler type will improve in reliability as development proceeds. In spite of careful design and (in some cases) the fitting of weed deflectors, the impellor log is liable to fouling by floating weed which stops the impellor and makes the log useless until it is cleared. It is also possible for marine growth to slow or stop the rotation. For these reasons, it is essential that an impellor log should be capable of withdrawal into the boat for cleaning. The electromagnetic log is flush with the hull and must be kept clear of marine growth. The doppler log, too, must be kept clean; it can be difficult to find a suitable place for installation, but once that has been done it seems to work satisfactorily. The pitot log has a non-linear scale and only works well at high speed; it is therefore best suited to high-speed motor craft.

Installing a log

A hull log should be installed in a place where it will remain well submerged whatever motion is experienced, and where the flow of water is smooth and undisturbed. For a sailing yacht, a position on the centreline near the forefoot is good. For power yachts, a position well aft but out of the direct slipstream of the propellors is generally best.

Calibration

A good quality towed log will probably not need any calibration, though its accuracy should be checked over a measured distance. All types of hull log *must* be calibrated before they are trusted for navigation. The manufacturer's instructions will explain any adjustments that can be made. The principle is to compare the distance recorded on the log with the distance actually covered. In still water, this can be merely the distance between two known objects, but if a current or tidal stream is running, then two runs should be made, one in each direction.

For example: On the first run over a measured distance of one mile, the log recorded 0.88 miles. On a second run in the opposite direction, it recorded 1.06 miles.

Total distance covered 2 miles
Total distance logged 1.94 miles
Error is 0.06 miles in 2 miles or 3 per cent low.

Summary of errors

Gross errors Any form of impellor log, whether towed or mounted in the hull is liable to fouling by floating weed or debris; it has also been reported that towed log impellors can be swallowed by sharks! Any form of electronic log can suffer serious errors if the batteries driving it are allowed to go flat.

Systematic errors As it works in the boundary layer, any form of hull-mounted log may suffer systematic errors, which may vary with speed. These errors can be corrected by calibration, but only for one speed; it is wise to check for remaining errors at different speeds.

At low speeds, any form of impellor log tends to under-read, due to friction; in rough conditions, the towed log (and probably other types) tends to over-read, as the boat has to travel further over rough seas than it would if the sea were flat.

Random errors The long-term random error of a towed log is probably of the order of 1 per cent on 95 per cent of occasions. A properly calibrated hull log will have an error of 2–5 per cent on 95 per cent of occasions.

12 Depth measurement

One of the primary functions of the navigator is to keep his boat safely afloat in sufficient water, so the measurement of the depth of water is of great importance. The early teachers of navigation used to refer to the three 'Ls' – lead, log and lookout – as the fundamentals of safe navigation. The sounding rod, later replaced by the lead and line, was the first navigational instrument ever devised, and can be seen in use in ancient Egyptian pictures. Depths were traditionally measured in fathoms (1 fathom = 6 feet or 1.8 metres). Most charting authorities now show depths in metres, but many charts marked in fathoms, or fathoms and feet, still remain.

Apart from making sure that there is enough water to float the boat, sounding (the measurement of depth) can also give valuable information to the navigator. The 100 fathom (180 m) line has for centuries been used to warn of the crossing of the continental shelf and the approach of land. On a smaller scale, yachts can use the crossing of chosen depth contours to help fix their position. When doing this, there are two cautions to observe:

1) As is explained on page 100–1, charted depths are referred to as chart datum, a level below which the water rarely falls. Depending on the state of the tide, soundings will generally be deeper than the charted depth (this is a deliberate safety factor). Before it can be compared with a charted depth, a sounding must be *reduced* (see page 104).
2) The value of a sounding for navigation depends very much on the nature of the bottom. If the bottom is irregular, soundings can be difficult to interpret, if not downright misleading.

The lead and line

Every boat should carry a lead and line, even if only for insurance against the failure of an echo sounder. The line should be about ten fathoms (eighteen metres) long, with a seven to eight pound (three and a half kilogram) lead weight on the end. The lead should have a hollow in the bottom for *arming* (see below). After stretching, the line should be accurately marked in feet, fathoms or metres. Any clear system of marking the navigator cares to devise will do, but for interest

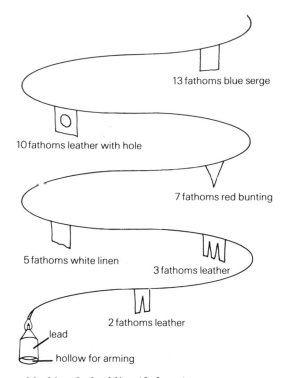

13 fathoms blue serge

10 fathoms leather with hole

7 fathoms red bunting

5 fathoms white linen

3 fathoms leather

2 fathoms leather

lead

hollow for arming

12.1 *Marking the lead line (fathoms).*

the traditional markings are shown in Figure 1. These marks were carefully chosen; they were easy to remember and the different textures of leather, linen and bunting could be felt in the dark. The leadsman would deduct the 'drift', or distance between his hand and the waterline when sounding at night.

Heaving the lead is an operation which requires practice. When reading off the depth, the line must be vertical; so if the boat is moving ahead, as it generally is, the lead must be heaved ahead (Fig. 2). This process leads the beginner very quickly into a tangle. Running a line of soundings also leads to a soaked and aching arm.

Arming the lead

The lead and line offers one advantage over the echo sounder, in that it can bring up a sample of the bottom for examination. This is done by arming the lead, or filling the hollow in the bottom with tallow or stiff grease. A sample of sand, mud, shingle or broken shell from the sea bottom can often be tied in with information on the chart or in the *Pilot*.

12.2 *Using the lead and line*

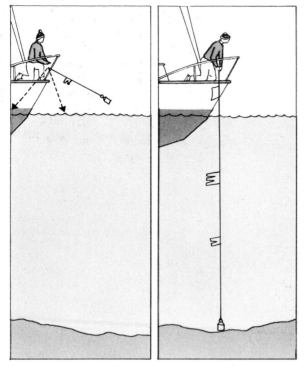

12.3 *Principle of the echo sounder.*

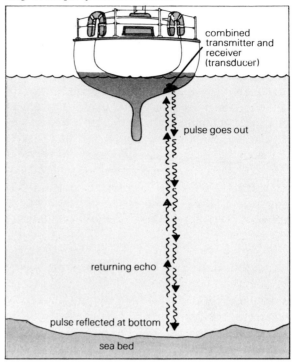

combined transmitter and receiver (transducer)

pulse goes out

returning echo

pulse reflected at bottom

sea bed

The echo sounder

With the advent of modern electronics, the small echo sounder is now both cheap and reliable. For many kinds of sailing they are so convenient as to be almost indispensable. They work by sending out a pulse of sound energy from a transducer mounted in the bottom of the boat. This pulse is reflected off the sea bed, and the echo is detected as it returns to the boat. The time interval between the outgoing pulse and its echo is a measure of the depth of water (Fig. 3).

All echo sounders work on this principle, but there are several different types of display (Fig. 4).

Rotating lamp display A lamp is made to spin around a circular scale in synchronism with the sound pulses. The lamp is made to flash at the zero mark as the pulse is sent out, and it flashes again when the echo is received; the depth can then be read off the scale. This type of display is cheap and simple, but it can be hard to read in bright sunlight.

Meter display This display makes use of a conventional pointer moving over a scale. There is generally provision for a repeater meter to be fitted where the helmsman can see it.

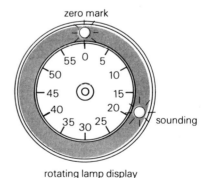

zero mark

sounding

rotating lamp display

12.4 *Types of echo sounder display.*

meter display

12.4 *Types of echo sounder display (cont.).*

digital display

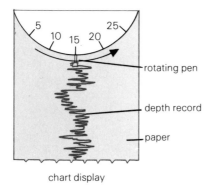

chart display

Digital display The depth is displayed in numerical form on a light-emitting diode or liquid crystal display.

Paper recorder Some echo sounders produce a semi-permanent record of the depths measured on a paper chart. This rather more expensive equipment is of great value for fishermen, and it can help in establishing a profile of the bottom when trying to run a line of soundings.

Video display Echo sounders are now appearing which mimic the paper chart recorder by storing digital information to produce a record of the past few minutes' soundings.

Installation and operation
The installation of an echo sounder is normally quite simple, and the manufacturer's instructions should be followed. In a glassfibre hull, it may be possible to mount the transducer inside the hull with no significant loss of performance. The transducer should be mounted where it has a good 'view' of the seabed and as near the centreline as possible. In a sailing yacht, it may happen that the transducer comes too close to the surface when the yacht is steeply heeled; the solution to this problem is to fit two transducers, one on each side, and to select the 'downhill' transducer with a manual or automatic changeover switch. The more expensive echo sounders can be adjusted to read the depth below the waterline, the depth below the transducer or the depth below the keel. The navigator is free to choose whichever he prefers, but the indicator *must* be clearly marked accordingly.

The principal control in operating an echo sounder is the sensitivity control; this should be adjusted to the minimum level that gives consistent and reliable soundings. Some models are fitted with variable depth alarms, which can be very useful, especially if short-handed.

When using a powerful echo sounder in deep water, it is possible for the echo to be delayed until after the next transmission pulse; the result is a sounding which appears very much shallower than it really is. This can cause considerable alarm until the situation is recognized.

Summary of errors
Gross errors Flat batteries; second-time echoes (see above); using the wrong datum (below waterline, transducer or keel).
Systematic errors The two most likely systematic errors are related. On one hand, the timing speed of the recording device may be wrong; on the other, the velocity of sound through the water may differ from the nominal 1500 metres/sec, which is the agreed average value. The best way of establishing if either of these errors exists is by comparing a depth on the echo sounder with that obtained from a carefully marked lead and line. In general, correction of the scanning speed must be carried out by the maker.
Random errors Most echo sounders are surprisingly accurate, and an error of two to four per cent on 95 per cent of occasions is about right.

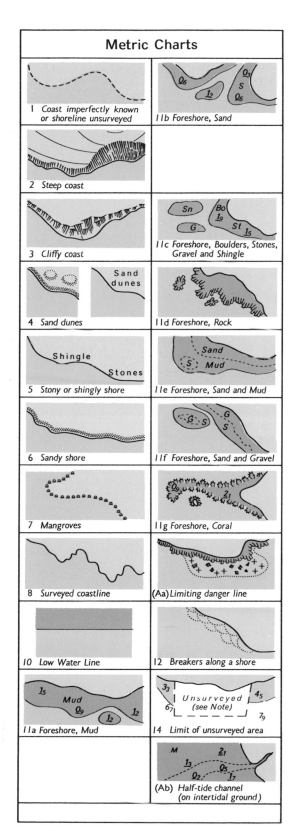

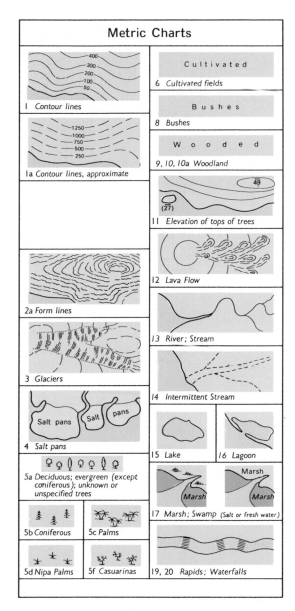

Selection of symbols used on British Admiralty charts: 'The Coastline' (left) and 'Topography: Natural Features' (right).

Reproduced from portions of BA Chart No. 5011 (1979 ed.) with the sanction of the Controller, HM Stationery Office and of the Hydrographer of the Navy.

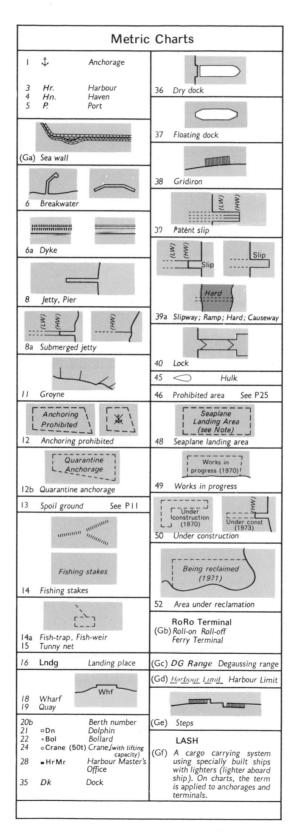

Metric Charts

1	⚓	Anchorage
3	Hr.	Harbour
4	Hn.	Haven
5	P.	Port

(Ga) Sea wall

6 Breakwater

6a Dyke

8 Jetty, Pier

8a Submerged jetty

11 Groyne

12 Anchoring prohibited

12b Quarantine anchorage

13 Spoil ground   See P11

14 Fishing stakes

14a Fish-trap, Fish-weir
15 Tunny net

16 Lndg   Landing place

18 Wharf
19 Quay

20b		Berth number
21	▫ Dn	Dolphin
22	∘ Bol	Bollard
24	∘ Crane (50t)	Crane, (with lifting capacity)
28	■ HrMr	Harbour Master's Office
35	Dk	Dock

36 Dry dock

37 Floating dock

38 Gridiron

39 Patent slip

39a Slipway; Ramp; Hard; Causeway

40 Lock

45 ⬯ Hulk

46 Prohibited area   See P25

48 Seaplane landing area

49 Works in progress

50 Under construction

52 Area under reclamation

RoRo Terminal
(Gb) Roll-on Roll-off Ferry Terminal

(Gc) DG Range Degaussing range

(Gd) Harbour Limit Harbour Limit

(Ge) Steps

LASH
(Gf) A cargo carrying system using specially built ships with lighters (lighter aboard ship). On charts, the term is applied to anchorages and terminals.

Reproduced from portions of BA Chart No. 5011 (1979 ed.) with the sanction of the Controller, HM Stationery Office and of the Hydrographer of the Navy.

Selection of symbols used on British Admiralty charts: 'Ports and Harbours'.

2. LATERAL MARKS

2.1. Definition of "conventional direction of buoyage"

The "conventional direction of buoyage", which must be indicated in appropriate nautical documents, may be either:

2.1.1. The general direction taken by the mariner when approaching a harbour, river, estuary or other waterway from seaward, or

2.1.2. The direction determined by the proper authority in consultation, where appropriate, with neighbouring countries. In principle it should follow a clockwise direction around land masses.

2.2. Buoyage Regions

There are two international Buoyage Regions A and B where lateral marks differ. These buoyage regions are indicated in Section 8.

2.3. Description of Lateral Marks used in Region A

2.3.1. Port hand Marks

Colour :	Red
Shape (Buoys) :	Cylindrical (can), pillar or spar
Topmark (if any) :	Single red cylinder (can)
Light (when fitted) :	
Colour :	Red
Rhythm :	Any, other than that described in section 2.3.3.

2.3.2. Starboard hand Marks

Colour :	Green
Shape (Buoys) :	Conical, pillar or spar
Topmark (if any) :	Single green cone, point upward
Light (when fitted) :	
Colour :	Green
Rhythm :	Any, other than that described in section 2.3.3.

2.3.3. At the point where a channel divides, when proceeding in the "conventional direction of buoyage", a preferred channel may be indicated by a modified Port or Starboard lateral mark as follows:

2.3.3.1. Preferred channel to Starboard :

Colour :	Red with one broad green horizontal band
Shape (Buoys) :	Cylindrical (can), pillar or spar
Topmark (if any) :	Single red cylinder (can)
Light (when fitted) :	
Colour :	Red
Rhythm :	Composite group flashing (2 + 1)

2.3.3.2. Preferred channel to Port :

Colour :	Green with one broad red horizontal band
Shape (Buoys) :	Conical, pillar or spar
Topmark (if any) :	Single green cone, point upward
Light (when fitted) :	
Colour :	Green
Rhythm :	Composite group flashing (2 + 1)

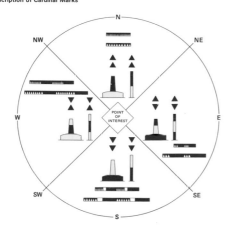

2.4. Description of Lateral Marks used in Region B

2.4.1. Port hand Marks

Colour :	Green
Shape (Buoys) :	Cylindrical (can), pillar or spar
Topmark (if any) :	Single green cylinder (can)
Light (when fitted) :	
Colour :	Green
Rhythm :	Any, other than that described in section 2.4.3.

2.4.2. Starboard hand Marks

Colour :	Red
Shape (Buoys) :	Conical, pillar or spar
Topmark (if any) :	Single red cone, point upward
Light (when fitted) :	
Colour :	Red
Rhythm :	Any, other than that described in section 2.4.3.

2.4.3. At the point where a channel divides, when proceeding in the "conventional direction of buoyage", a preferred channel may be indicated by a modified Port or Starboard lateral mark as follows:

2.4.3.1. Preferred channel to Starboard :

Colour :	Green with one broad red horizontal band
Shape (Buoys) :	Cylindrical (can), pillar or spar
Topmark (if any) :	Single green cylinder (can)
Light (when fitted) :	
Colour :	Green
Rhythm :	Composite group flashing (2 + 1)

2.4.3.2. Preferred channel to Port :

Colour :	Red with one broad green horizontal band
Shape (Buoys) :	Conical, pillar or spar
Topmark (if any) :	Single red cone, point upward
Light (when fitted) :	
Colour :	Red
Rhythm :	Composite group flashing (2 + 1)

2.5. General Rules for Lateral Marks

2.5.1. Shapes
Where lateral marks do not rely upon cylindrical (can) or conical buoy shapes for identification they should, where practicable, carry the appropriate topmark.

2.5.2. Numbering or lettering
If marks at the sides of a channel are numbered or lettered, the numbering or lettering shall follow the "conventional direction of buoyage".

3. CARDINAL MARKS

3.1. Definition of Cardinal quadrants and marks

3.1.1. The four quadrants (North, East, South and West) are bounded by the true bearings NW-NE, NE-SE, SE-SW, SW-NW, taken from the point of interest.

3.1.2. A Cardinal mark is named after the quadrant in which it is placed.

3.1.3. The name of a Cardinal mark indicates that it should be passed to the named side of the mark.

3.2. Use of Cardinal Marks

A Cardinal mark may be used, for example:

3.2.1. To indicate that the deepest water in that area is on the named side of the mark.

3.2.2. To indicate the safe side on which to pass a danger.

3.2.3. To draw attention to a feature in a channel such as a bend, a junction, a bifurcation or the end of a shoal.

3.3. Description of Cardinal Marks

3.3.1. North Cardinal Mark

Topmark[a] :	2 black cones, one above the other, points upward
Colour :	Black above yellow
Shape :	Pillar or spar
Light (when fitted) :	
Colour :	White
Rhythm :	VQ or Q

3.3.2. East Cardinal Mark

Topmark[a] :	2 black cones, one above the other, base to base
Colour :	Black with a single broad horizontal yellow band
Shape :	Pillar or spar
Light (when fitted) :	
Colour :	White
Rhythm :	VQ(3) every 5s or Q(3) every 10s

3.3.3. South Cardinal Mark

Topmark[a] :	2 black cones, one above the other, points downward
Colour :	Yellow above black
Shape :	Pillar or spar
Light (when fitted):	
Colour :	White
Rhythm :	VQ(6) + Long flash every 10s or Q(6) + Long flash every 15s

3.3.4. West Cardinal Mark

Topmark [a] :	2 black cones, one above the other, point to point
Colour :	Yellow with a single broad horizontal black band
Shape :	Pillar or spar
Light (when fitted):	
Colour :	White
Rhythm :	VQ(9) every 10s or Q(9) every 15s

IALA Maritime Buoyage System: Lateral Marks (Regions A and B) and Cardinal Marks.

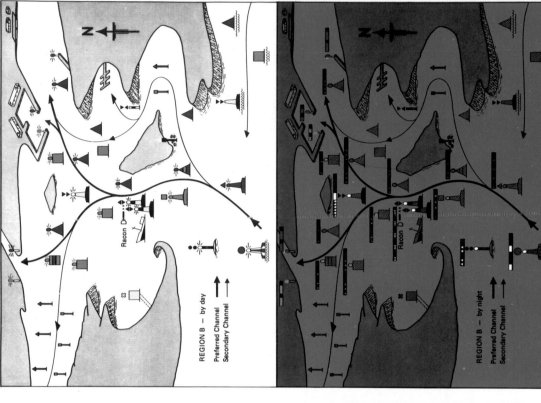

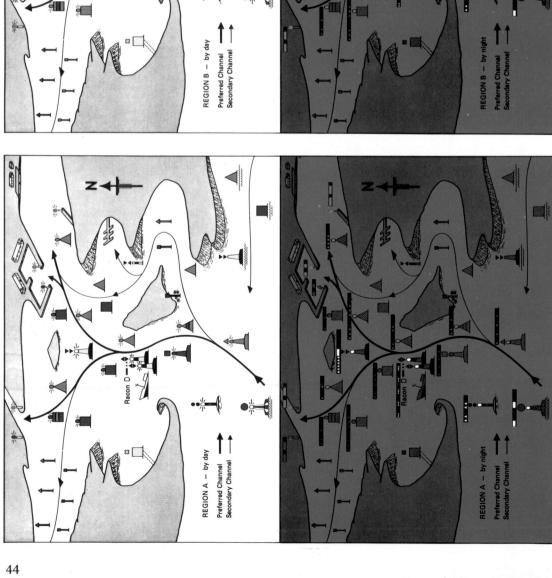

REGION B — by day

Preferred Channel

Secondary Channel

REGION B — by night

Preferred Channel

Secondary Channel

REGION A — by day

Preferred Channel

Secondary Channel

REGION A — by night

Preferred Channel

Secondary Channel

IALA Maritime Buoyage System: Region A and Region B by day and by night.

Reproduced from the IALA Maritime Buoyage System by permission of the Association Internationale de Signalisation Maritime (International Association of Lighthouse Authorities).

13 The sextant

The sextant is an instrument for measuring angles with great accuracy; it is indispensable for astronomical navigation, where it is used to measure the angle between a heavenly body and the horizon, and it can also be of great value for accurate coastal navigation. The sextant was invented in the eighteenth century by Hadley, though an unpublished design for a very similar instrument was later found amongst Sir Isaac Newton's papers. Hadley's instrument was known as a quadrant, though it is better described as an octant (Fig. 1). This means that the scale covers one eighth of a circle (45°). The sextant has a scale covering one sixth of a circle (60°), which means that it is capable of measuring larger angles than the octant; apart from this, there is no practical difference between them. The quintant (one fifth of a circle) was popular at one time.

13.1 *Hadley type quadrant.*

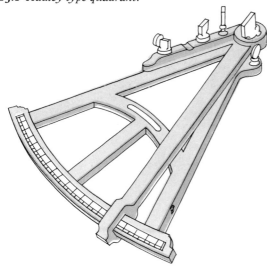

Construction and principle of the sextant
The principle upon which the sextant works is shown in Figure 2. A mirror, called the index glass, is pivoted at the top of the instrument, and the angle to which it has been set is indicated on a scale. A second mirror, called the horizon glass, is only half silvered, so the observer can both look through it to see the object directly in front of him, and at the same time see a second object reflected in the silvered portion of the horizon glass and the

index glass. If the observer adjusts the index glass so that the images of the two objects co-incide, then it can be shown that the angle between the two objects is exactly twice the angle between the two mirrors. The 60° scale of the sextant is therefore capable of measuring angles between objects of up to 120°, and the scale is graduated accordingly.

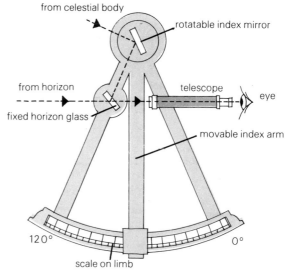

13.2 *The principle of the sextant.*

The construction of a modern sextant is shown in Figure 3. The frame of the instrument carries the scale, marked to 120°. The index glass is

13.3 *A modern sextant.*

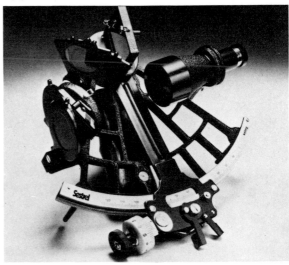

mounted on a pivoted arm, with an indicating mark that moves over the scale; a micrometer device is fitted to allow angles to be read off with great precision (0.1 minutes of arc in the best sextants). The actual observations are made through a telescope mounted on the frame, with the horizon glass in front of it. Both the horizon glass and the index glass are fitted with shades which can be used to reduce the light entering the telescope (for example, when observing the sun). The radius of the scale is usually about six inches (ten centimetres). A light is sometimes provided to illuminate the scale at night.

For accurate work, a good quality, metal-framed sextant with a good telescope is essential, but it costs a lot of money. Plastic sextants are now on the market, and the better ones can be quite satisfactory for use in a yacht; they are rather more difficult to use and adjust (and of course less accurate), but cost only a fraction of the price. A beginner would do well to consider buying a plastic sextant for his first attempts, and the experienced navigator might carry a plastic sextant as a spare in case his good one gets smashed.

Figure 4 shows how to read the scale of the sextant; in general this is easy enough. The degrees are read from the scale along the bottom of

13.4 *The micrometer scale of a sextant.*

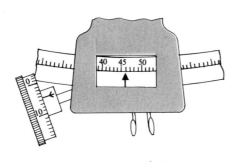

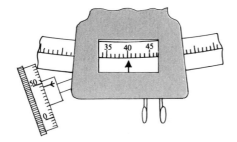

the instrument, and the minutes of arc are read from the micrometer drum. It is easier to estimate fractions of a minute by eye, though a small vernier is provided for accurate interpolation. Care is needed when the reading is close to an exact degree; it is not difficult to get confused about the number of degrees and record, for example, an angle of 49°59′ as 50°59′.

Care of the sextant

Though remarkably robust, a sextant is a precision instrument and should be handled with care; avoid bumps and bangs which can put the sextant out of adjustment. Keep it in its box except when actually using it, and make sure that the box is securely stowed. Fit a lanyard to the handle or the frame so that you can hang it around your neck to prevent it going over the side if you lose your balance in a seaway. It is not a bad idea to keep it buttoned inside a jacket except when actually making observations; this will protect it against knocks and help to keep it dry. If the sextant should be knocked or dropped, it is *essential* to check the calibration (see below) before it is used again.

A sextant should be protected from seawater as much as possible. A little spray is not too bad, provided that the instrument is carefully cleaned and dried before being put away (take care when cleaning the mirrors lest they are put out of adjustment). If conditions are such that the sextant is likely to get soaked, then it should be left in the box until the weather moderates.

Mirrors and telescope lenses should be cleaned with a lens cloth or soft tissue; the scale and micrometer rack can be coated with a thin film of petroleum jelly, and the moving parts can be given a tiny drop of light machine oil occasionally.

The Royal Air Force arranged for their sextant boxes to be marked 'handle like eggs'. It is an excellent principle.

Errors of the sextant

The sextant has a number of systematic errors, which must be corrected as described below. They are:

Perpendicularity error: in which the index glass is not at right angles to the plane of the scale.

Side error: in which the horizon glass is not at right angles to the plane of the scale.

Index error: in which the two mirrors are not parallel when the scale reading is zero.

These errors must be corrected in the following order:

Perpendicularity error This can be checked by setting the arm to about half-way along the scale, and then looking into the index glass from the top of the instrument. By moving the eye, it is possible to find a position in which the edge of the scale and its reflection in the mirror can be seen. If they are not co-incident, then perpendicularity error exists. It is removed by carefully adjusting the adjusting screw on the index glass mounting.

Side error This is corrected in conjunction with the index error (see below). It can be seen by looking at a point (e.g. a star) or a vertical line (a mast, or the horizon if the sextant is held on its side) with the arm set at zero. If the reflected image falls to one side of the direct image, then side error exists (Fig. 5). It is corrected by the outer adjusting screw on the horizon glass mounting.

Index error This is shown by the two images failing to co-incide when the sextant is set to zero. It is corrected by the inner adjusting screw on the horizon glass mounting.

When adjusting side error and index error, the two adjusting screws interact, so the procedure is to remove half the side error, then half the index error, then half the remaining side error and so on. Side error should be removed entirely, but some index error may remain; it should not be allowed to be more than a few minutes of arc.

Index error should be checked every time the sextant is used. Bring the two images of the horizon into coincidence and look at the reading (Fig. 6). Index error may be *on the arc*, in which case it should be subtracted from all readings taken. If it is *off the arc*, it should be added.

Random errors

The random errors inherent in the sextant itself are so small that they are entirely submerged by personal and observational errors, such as the quality of the horizon or the motion of the vessel. These errors are discussed in the sections which describe the actual methods of using the sextant.

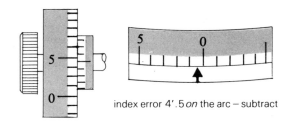

index error 4′.5 *on* the arc – subtract

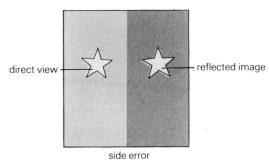

direct view — reflected image

side error

13.5 *Side error.*

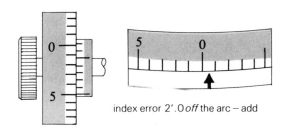

index error 2′.0 *off* the arc – add

13.6 *Index error.*

14 The use of radio in navigation

Though they are entirely a twentieth century development, radio aids to navigation are now of the utmost importance, even to the yacht navigator. They vary in cost and complexity from the very cheap and simple to the present limits of technology, and span a very large section of the electromagnetic spectrum (Table 1). Each radio aid of importance to the yacht navigator is discussed in detail later in this book, but this section summarizes what is available.

A domestic radio receiver capable of working on MF and LF can be used for receiving time signals and weather information near the coast. Some broadcasting organizations transmit special weather forecasts for shipping, but even forecasts intended mainly for shore consumption can give valuable indications of the weather to come at sea.

A communications receiver covers LF, MF and HF bands, and can be used to receive information specially broadcast for the mariner, such as continuous time signals, weather information and navigational warnings. These sets require a properly installed antenna to be effective, but are capable of world-wide reception.

Marine communications equipment (Fig. 1) working on MF, HF or VHF channels, is primarily intended for communications, but is a useful source of weather forecasts and navigational warnings.

Facsimile equipment works with a suitable communications receiver to produce synoptic charts and other weather information, transmitted by national meteorological authorities. Its price makes it very much a luxury item, but it can be found in some larger yachts.

Radiobeacons are perhaps the most useful radio navigational aid for the yachtsman, as they require relatively simple and cheap equipment. A radiobeacon is a transmitter sited at some point of navigational interest, such as a lighthouse or lightship. It transmits on an LF frequency, either continuously or at regular frequent intervals. The ship carries a suitable receiver connected to a directional antenna, with which the operator can

Band		Frequency Range	Wavelength Range	Use at Sea
VLF	Very Low Frequency	3–30kHz	100km–10km	Omega. Submarine Communications
LF	Low Frequency	30–300kHz	10km–1000m	Radio beacons, time signals, Decca, Loran C, Consol
MF	Medium Frequency	300kHz–3MHz	1000–100m	Morse and voice communications, radio beacons, weather broadcasts, domestic radio
HF	High Frequency	3MHz–30MHz	100–10m	Long range communications, weather broadcasts, time signals, facsimile, CB radio
VHF	Very High Frequency	30MHz–300MHz	10–1m	Communications, radio lighthouse, satellite navigation, VOR, domestic radio broadcasts
UHF	Ultra High Frequency	300MHz–3GHz	1m–10cm	Satellite navigation
SHF	Super High Frequency	3GHz–30GHz	10cm–1cm	Radar

1kHz = 1 kilohertz = 1000 cycles per second
1MHz = 1 megahertz = 1,000,000 cycles per second
1GHz = 1 gigahertz = 1,000,000,000 cycles per second

Table 1 *The electromagnetic spectrum.*

take a bearing of the transmitter. This gives him a position line (see page 68) which can be used to help him fix his position. Though useful at any time, radiobeacons are of particular value in poor visibility when visual fixing is not possible.

Consol and the radio lighthouse are methods of giving the navigator a bearing of the transmitter without requiring him to have a directional antenna. Consol operates on LF, and the (experimental) radio lighthouse on VHF. The transmitted signal is made to appear as if it comes from a rotating aerial, so that the navigator can work out his bearing from the transmitter by a simple counting or timing process.

Hyperbolic navigational systems provide navigational information by measuring time delays between signals received from pairs of special transmitters. There are a number of different systems, but they all require special equipment and are uncommon in yachts on the grounds of cost and complexity; as electronic equipment becomes progressively cheaper, this situation may alter.

The major hyperbolic aids are:

Omega operates on VLF and offers global coverage with a network of eight transmitters. Accuracy is of the order of one mile, when properly corrected.

Loran C also works on LF, with a range of some 1,500 nautical miles. The coverage is good in the North Atlantic, near the United States, and in much of the Pacific Ocean. Accuracy depends on a number of factors, but is of the order of a few miles at 1,000 miles from the chain. The earlier Loran A system on MF is now becoming obsolete.

Decca is another LF system, but intended for greater accuracy at shorter ranges. Decca chains are established in many strategic areas of the world, and have a maximum range of about 250 miles. Accuracy is very high, less than 100 yards (100 m) under ideal conditions.

VOR (VHF omni range) is a radio aid primarily used by aircraft. A single transmitter sends out a signal which is received and decoded in the aircraft to operate a pointer giving the magnetic bearing of the transmitter. Where VOR beacons are suitably sited, they can also be of value to yachtsmen.

Radar can be of great value both for navigation and for collision avoidance in poor visibility. A rotating aerial on the ship sends out a pulse of energy in the SHF band (a wavelength of about three centimetres). A big enough object in the path of the beam will reflect back sufficient energy to be detected by the radar receiver. The time taken by the returning echo, allied to the direction in which it was sent, is displayed as a form of electronic map on a PPI (plan position indicator). The maximum range depends mostly on the height of the aerial and the size of the object to be detected. The accuracy of the range displayed is high, of the bearing less so. Some important buoys and lightships are fitted with a *Racon*, a device to enhance and mark the echo so that the object may be positively identified.

Satellite navigation requires a special VHF or UHF receiver and a microcomputer (Fig. 2). It uses a network of earth satellites which transmit information to the receiver; from this data, the computer can calculate a position to within a quarter of a mile with simple equipment or a few metres with the best available. Although a very sophisticated system, the price has recently fallen enough to make it attractive to the better-off yachtsman.

14.1 *Marine radio receiver display unit.*　　**14.2** *Satellite navigator display unit.*

15   Records

Records of various kinds are essential to good navigation, for a number of reasons:

1) It is unwise to rely upon memory in a yacht at sea. A sudden change in circumstances can drive an important piece of information out of your mind, or the significance of some seemingly unimportant fact may be overlooked. If facts are recorded, they will not be forgotten, and can be reviewed later if necessary.
2) No navigator can be on duty for 24 hours a day, so the watch on deck must keep records of the ship's progress while the navigator is resting.
3) Scribbled notes on the chart or on scraps of paper can be rubbed out or thrown away by mistake.
4) As this book stresses throughout, errors are an integral part of the navigation process. Accurate and complete records are the only way of checking and backtracking when things have gone wrong, as they inevitably will from time to time.
5) Apart from its value in navigation, a well-kept log is an invaluable reminder of past enjoyment, and makes evocative reading in times to come.
6) In some cases, the keeping of a log is a legal requirement.

The deck log

The deck log is the most important of the navigational records, as it contains (or should contain) a full record of courses and distances sailed, and notes of any event of navigational importance, such as the raising of a light or the passing of a buoy. The deck log, kept by the watch on deck, is the raw material from which the dead reckoning (see page 56) is determined.

Many of the pre-printed logs offered for sale to yachtsmen carry lines and columns which are not really suitable for the purpose. It is often better to choose a suitably stout notebook and to rule up columns as you wish. A form of log which has proved useful at sea is shown in Figure 1. Most of the columns are obvious and self-explanatory, but the two columns 'course ordered' and 'course steered' may cause surprise. The purpose is to acknowledge the fact that a sailing yacht is controlled by the wind direction; when sailing on the wind, for example, a small change in wind direction may make it impossible for the helmsman to keep on the compass course ordered. If the wind shift was a major one, then clearly the skipper and navigator must be told, but a minor shift only needs a suitable entry in the 'course steered' column. Similar problems may occur when running square to a shifting wind.

The log should be written up frequently; any significant event should be recorded at once; and regular entries of course, distance run, wind, weather and barometer should be made at least once an hour, even when ocean sailing hundreds of miles from land. This is necessary because a close watch must be kept on the barometer; in the tropics, suppression of the diurnal variation of the barometer or a fall of three millibars (0.09 in) may herald the approach of a tropical revolving storm (see page 92).

In coastal waters, it is better to fill in the log at half-hourly intervals and when racing, quarter-hourly intervals may be appropriate. Provided the navigator is firm about keeping the log, crews generally welcome the need to write up the log as a regular incident in their watch. It also helps if the crew are encouraged to use the log to record anything of interest or amusement such as marine life seen, comments on the cooking, or a description of a hilarious misadventure on the foredeck.

Navigator's work book

The navigator should keep his own work book, in which he writes down information from the deck log, and any calculations he may make such as the times and heights of high water, times of sunrise and sunset, details of fixing information and passage notes. The format for this work book is entirely a matter of choice, but some clear and consistent scheme should be adopted and every entry should include the date and time.

Sight book

Many navigators choose to keep the records and calculations for astronomical sights in a special book, though they can equally well be kept in the work book if desired. In either case, a suitable format is given on page 157.

15.1 *Layout for a yacht's log.*

Time	Course Ordered	Course Steered	Log Reading	Wind & Weather	Barometer	Remarks

Barometers and barographs

The importance of keeping a record of barometer readings has already been mentioned in the section on the deck log. In conjunction with other meteorological data, the barometer can give warning of the weather to come; in tropical regions it is often the first sign you get of impending bad weather.

A barograph can be used to keep a continuous record of barometric pressure on a paper chart for a week. A barograph must be suitably designed for use at sea in a small yacht, as the motion of the vessel can otherwise shake the recording pen to such an extent as to obliterate the record. The instrument should always be mounted on a resilient bed with the recording arm lying athwartships. It should be firmly secured in position as befits any delicate instrument.

16   Boat and crew

As the object of navigation is to guide the vessel on her way from place to place, the performance of the boat and the crew is obviously of great importance; if either differ from that expected, then errors in navigation will arise. It is necessary to monitor and 'calibrate' the boat and the crew, in particular each individual helmsman.

Leeway Unless the wind is coming from right ahead or right astern, it exerts a force which tends to push the boat (sail or power) sideways. The extent to which it succeeds depends upon several factors:

1) Obviously, the strength of the sideways component of the wind.
2) The underwater profile of the boat. Deep keel sailing yachts and displacement power craft will resist leeway better than shoal draught cruisers or power boats with little sideways 'grip' of the water.
3) Boats with high freeboards offer more windage than those without.
4) Large or confused seas increase leeway by checking the forward component of the vessel's progress.

Various methods of measuring leeway have been suggested, such as measuring the angle at which the line of a towed log streams astern, or by watching the bearing of floating objects thrown over the stern; however these measurements are not easily taken and are unreliable. An educated guess is perhaps the best approach, and as the navigator gains experience in different conditions, these guesses will improve in accuracy. Because of the wide variation in boats and conditions, it is not possible to give much guidance in a book, but noticeable leeway can be expected if the wind and sea cause the boat to labour (see page 60).

Leeway is normally allowed for as an error in the heading, as shown in Figure 1.

Weather helm and lee helm Sailing yachts are generally trimmed to give some weather helm, so that the boat tends to luff up into the wind. An experienced helmsman will allow for this effect and steer the course that he is given, but the majority of helmsmen will actually make good a course somewhat to weather of the course they have been given. By a happy coincidence, it very

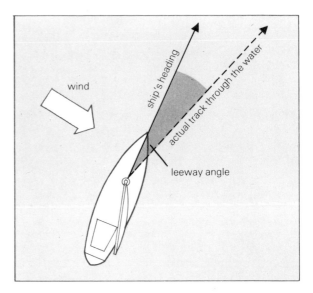

16.1 *Allowing for leeway.*

often happens that the weatherway made in this manner cancels out the leeway described above. Trimming the boat to give lee helm should be avoided, not only because it makes the boat more difficult to handle, but also because additional leeway is generated by inexperienced helmsmen.

Broaching If the wind and sea are such that the boat tends to broach from time to time, the actual course achieved will be somewhat to weather of that ordered; again, the effect is not so marked if the helmsman is experienced.

Dead running In a sailing yacht with the wind right aft, most helmsmen will flinch away from a possible gybe, and so make good a course to weather. The best thing to do in these circumstances is to alter course to put the wind on the quarter. Not only does this give the helmsman peace of mind; it also increases boat speed to a useful extent. Otherwise, rig a strong preventer on the main boom.

Helmsman errors It is not easy to steer a proper course in a yacht when the compass card is swinging about all the time; an inexperienced helmsman will often fail to ensure that the boat swings equally on either side of the desired course, so that an error accumulates while he is steering. Equally, such a helmsman will often report a course which is not in fact his actual mean course. The solution to this problem is to study (unobtrusively) the performance of each helmsman and apply a suitable correction when necessary. It sometimes helps to restrict the choice of courses to even 5° intervals, as indifferent helmsmen find it easier to steer on a prominent mark on the compass card.

It is not uncommon for helmsmen to steer the wrong course, generally because of a blunder in handing over from one helmsman to the next. This often takes the form of transposed digits, so that he steers 335 instead of 353 for example. Some navigators like to write the course to be steered on a slate beside the compass, but this in itself can be a source of error if it is not kept up to date at all times.

Another point to watch, with experienced sailing helmsmen, is that they will generally try to sail the boat to its best speed by altering course to follow changes in the wind. This is a good thing if they are punctilious about recording what they do in the deck log; otherwise it can lead to serious errors in the reckoning.

THE RECKONING

17   Plotting techniques

Plotting navigational information on a chart is a very straightforward process, though the techniques depend upon the actual equipment used; English-speaking navigators tend to prefer a parallel ruler for laying off directions and parallel lines, whilst European navigators often use a pair of triangular set squares for the same purpose. Various types of protractor and proprietary plotting aids are also on the market, each with its adherents. The newcomer is advised to experiment with as many of these devices as he can, to find out which suits him best.

It must always be remembered that a chart is a precise and valuable document and it must always be treated with care; when plotting, a soft-leaded pencil should be used, with as little pressure as will lead to a distinct line.

Some of the more common plotting tasks are illustrated, using different types of plotting aids.

1) Chart graduations at different scales.
2) Plotting and recording position in latitude and longitude.
3) Ways of drawing a line parallel to another.
4) Drawing a line in a given direction; measuring the direction of a line.
5) Position by direction and distance; direction and distance between two points.

17.1 *Chart graduations.*

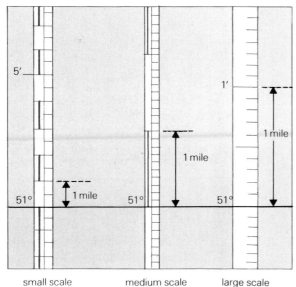

small scale   medium scale   large scale

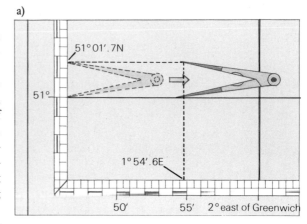

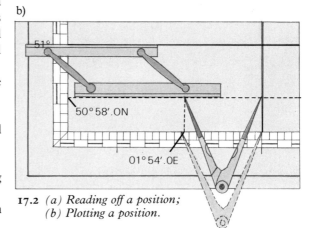

17.2 *(a) Reading off a position;*
(b) Plotting a position.

17.3 *Drawing parallel lines with: (a) parallel ruler;*
(b) protractor.

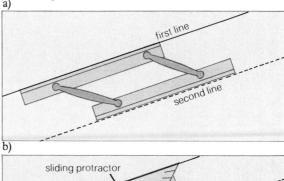

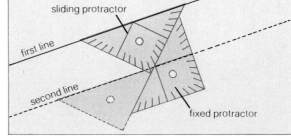

17.4 *Drawing or measuring directions with: (a) parallel ruler; (b) protractor.*

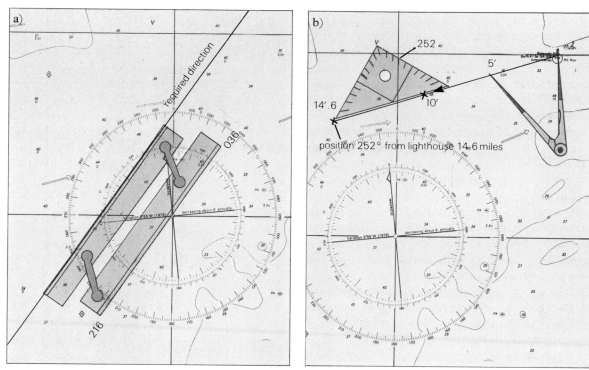

17.5 *(a) Position as a bearing and distance; (b) Course and distance between two points.*

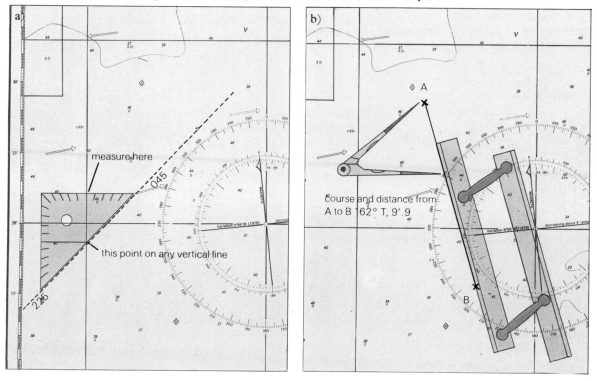

18 Dead reckoning

Dead reckoning is the name given to the process of estimating the position of a vessel by taking account of the direction and distance that the vessel travels, together with other factors such as estimations of current, tidal stream and leeway (see Note, page 67). At one time the dead reckoning position was also known as the *position by account*, which expresses the situation very well; the position is derived by accounting, rather like a book-keeper, for all the factors that have affected the progress of the ship. The term *dead reckoning* is generally thought to be a corruption of ded (= deduced) reckoning.

Dead reckoning is an essential corner-stone of the whole edifice of navigation, because it is the only way in which an estimate can be made of the position without any reference to the world outside the vessel. Whatever the conditions, a DR can always be kept up, using the simple and almost totally reliable instruments of compass, log, chart and pilot book. Obtaining a position by observing outside objects requires objects to observe and instruments and visibility with which to observe them; these may not be available when they are most wanted, but a DR is.

If dead reckoning could be made totally accurate, then there would be no need for any other form of navigation (except perhaps as a check). Inertial navigation is merely a very sophisticated automatic DR system; the inertial navigation equipment in inter-continental ballistic missiles can guide them to within a few tens of metres of a chosen point across a distance of thousands of miles. Manual DR, especially at sea in a small craft, is very substantially less accurate than this, and unless outside objects can be observed at suitable intervals, the errors of the DR will rapidly grow to a point where it becomes difficult to make sensible decisions. Despite this drawback, a navigator should always maintain a dead reckoning plot, for the following reasons:

1) As has been said, a DR is derived from sources within the vessel and is always available.
2) Because it is totally independent of outside observations, it acts as an invaluable check on such observations. Consistency between independent sources of information is a great comfort.
3) For some types of observation (e.g. astronomical position lines), a dead reckoning position is needed as a starting point for the calculations.

The simplest aspect of dead reckoning is illustrated in Figure 1. In this example, account is taken only of the direction and distance travelled by the yacht, as recorded in the log. A starting position is needed to begin the process; when setting off on a passage, this could be typically a pinpoint fix on the fairway buoy or some other mark near the harbour entrance. A fix is marked as a dot with a small circle around it, the time and (generally) the log reading.

In Figure 1, the deck log records that the departure fix was taken at 0800, at which time the log was set to 0.0 (Beware the confusion between log or deck log, a document, and log in the sense of an instrument for recording distance travelled.) The yacht set off on a course of 075 compass. With a variation of 6°W and a deviation of 2°E, this represents a true course of 075 − 6 + 2 = 071 (see page 30). A line can now be drawn on the chart from the departure point in the direction 071 true, to represent the course of the yacht across the sea.

At 0900, the deck log records that the log read 5.6 miles; therefore in the hour since the fix, the yacht has travelled 5.6 nautical miles. This distance can be measured off with dividers against the latitude scale of the chart and pricked off along the course line. A tick across the line represents the DR position at 0900.

At 1000, the log read 11.7, whilst the course has been held constant at 075 compass or 071 true. In the hour since 0900, the yacht has travelled 11.7 − 5.6 = 6.1 miles. This distance can now be pricked off along the course line to give the 1000 DR position.

At 1025, course was altered to 150 compass (variation still 6°W, deviation now 1°W), with the log reading 14.5. The yacht therefore continued past the 1000 DR on the original course of 071 true a distance of 14.5 − 11.7 = 2.8 miles; the DR position for 1025 can now be plotted. From this point a new course line can be drawn in the direction 150 − 6 − 1 = 143 true.

At 1100 the log read 17.5, which represents a distance travelled along the new course line of 3.0 miles since the alteration at 1025; the 1100 DR can now be plotted.

18.1 *Basic DR plotting: log entries and resulting plot.*

Time	Course Ordered	Course Steered	Log Reading	Wind & Weather	Barometer	Remarks
0800			0·0	NW4		Position 235M Bassurelle L.V 4·5mi Set course 260M
0900	260	260	5·6	NW4		
1000	260	255	11·7	WNW5		Headed off by windshift
1025	260	255	14·5			Tacked to 350M
1100	350	350	17·5	WNW 4		
	NB: Variation 6°W throughout,					

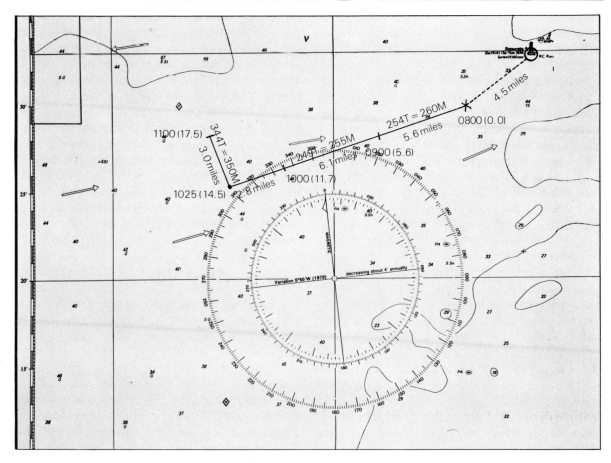

At its simplest, dead reckoning navigation requires no more than this – the meticulous recording of courses, times and log readings, followed by a very simple plotting exercise. There are many areas, notably in the Mediterranean and the Baltic, where the procedure described above is often all that is required; however in general it is necessary to allow also for external influences on the boat, notably those caused by tidal streams or currents. This is described overleaf.

19 Allowing for tides, currents and leeway

Two main factors generally complicate the plotting of a dead reckoning position. They are:
1) Movement of the water in which the boat floats.
2) The effect on the boat of the wind.

Water movement – tidal streams and currents

The simple dead reckoning so far described plots the movement of the boat through the water under the influence of its sails or its engine. But the navigator needs to know his position relative to the land, rather than the water; the positions of harbours, rocks, shoals and navigational marks of all kinds are defined with respect to the land. If the water in which the boat moves is itself moving, then the navigator will not know where he is unless he makes a suitable allowance.

The body of water which supports a boat may move under one of two influences (sometimes, but rarely, found in combination). These are:

1) Currents, caused by the long-term circulation of water around the globe, or by winds blowing in the same direction for a prolonged time.
2) Tidal streams, caused by the gravitational influence of the sun and the moon. Tidal streams are cyclic in nature, continually varying in strength and direction.

In order to make allowances for the effects of tidal streams or currents, the navigator must be able to find out their likely magnitudes and directions. For currents, the best place to find this information is in a suitable pilot book for the region. Methods of discovering the forecasted tidal streams are described on pages 106–9. In both cases, more accurate information for the moment can sometimes be obtained by direct observation – for example by watching the flow of water past some fixed object such as a navigational buoy.

If a boat is moving through water which is itself moving, the resulting motion will be a combination of the two (Fig. 1). In air navigation it is common to combine the two influences (in this case the aircraft's velocity and the wind velocity)

19.1 *Combined effect of boat and water movement.*

19.2 *Boat and water movement treated separately.*

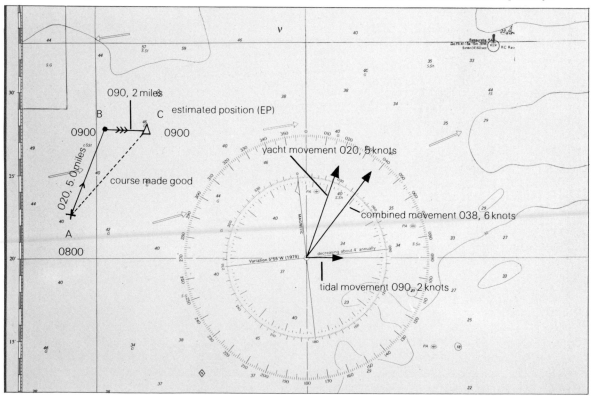

by using an instrument such as a Dalton computer. The normal approach at sea is to consider the two velocities as acting separately, as shown in Figure 2. In this example, it is assumed that the vessel is steering a course of 110 at five knots; after one hour, the yacht will have moved five miles from its starting position at A to position B. However, during this same hour, the water itself will have moved one mile in a direction of 220. If this movement is plotted from B, it leads to the corrected DR position (C); this is the position that the yacht would reach under the combined influences of its own motion and the tidal stream. Of course, in the real world these two influences are acting together so that the ship follows the line AC directly, rather than travelling along two sides of a triangle – from A to B to C. It is a convenient fiction to pretend otherwise.

The effects of both tidal streams and currents can be estimated in this way; the difference is that it will normally be necessary to revise the estimate of tidal stream every hour, whereas a current will set in much the same direction and speed for days

19.3 *Sailing into a fair or foul stream.*

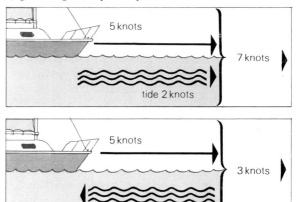

or weeks (in some cases, permanently). Sometimes it is possible to simplify the procedure; if a yacht is steaming directly into a foul stream, the position can be derived merely by subtracting the speed of the water flow from the speed of the boat (Fig. 3). On the other hand, if the boat is travelling exactly with the flow, the speeds can be added.

19.4 *Setting course to allow for the stream.*

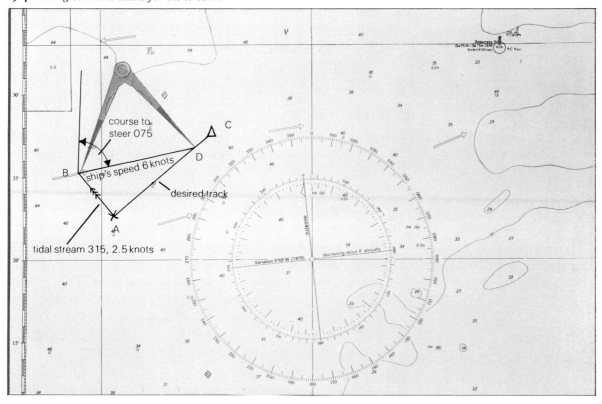

The effect of a current or tidal stream, unless it is directly fair or foul, is to set the vessel to one side or the other of its chosen course. Frequently the navigator will wish his craft to follow a particular line across the sea bed, and wants to know what course to steer so that the resulting movement is correct (Fig. 4). To do this, he must plot the tidal triangle 'in reverse'. He knows the direction in which he wants to go (AC in the diagram), the speed and direction of the stream, and the speed at which his own boat will travel. The first step is to plot the tidal stream or current for a suitable interval (say, an hour) *backwards* from C to B. This is equivalent to saying that a floating object dropped at B will get to C after the given interval of time, solely by virtue of the water movement. The next step is to take a pair of dividers set to a distance corresponding to the boat's speed (for the same time interval as that chosen for the water flow). One point is set on position B, and an arc is struck to cut the line AC (at position D). The course to steer is given by the direction DB; even though he starts from A, he will track along the line AC if he steers in that direction.

Leeway

The wind, acting on the topsides of a yacht, can also affect its progress. A wind directly ahead or astern will simply slow down or speed up the boat – an allowance very easily made. If, however, the wind is blowing from the side, then the vessel will be blown downwind of her proper course (Fig. 5).

It is difficult to say how much allowance should be made for leeway, as circumstances can vary so much. Clearly, the stronger the wind, the more it is on the beam and the surface area of the topsides and superstructure will all tend to increase leeway; so will the underwater shape of the vessel, as it controls the 'grip' of the boat on the water. Sea state is also a factor, because a boat that is continually stopped by an awkward sea will make more leeway than one that is sailing smoothly. Very strong winds also cause a surface drift (the beginnings of a current) which can be significant, and a

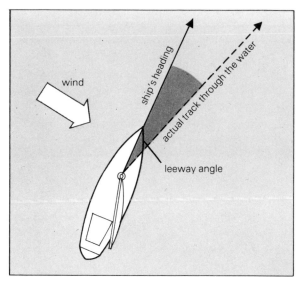

19.5 *Allowing for leeway.*

boat that slides down the face of a breaking wave will also be pushed to leeward. The following suggestions may be useful: (wind on the beam, sea state appropriate to wind)

Craft	Moderate	Gale
Offshore racer	none	5°
Motor sailer	5°	10°
Displacement power boat	5°	10°
Semi-displacement boat	5°	15°

In very severe conditions, leeway can become very marked; a total set of two and a half knots under the influence of windage, surface water drift and breaking seas has been observed, in Force eleven storms in the Bay of Biscay.

No satisfactory way of measuring leeway, other than guessing it, has yet been devised. Suggestions have included observing the angle between the trailing line of a towed log and the ship's fore-and-aft line; measuring the angle of the wake similarly; watching the progress of floating rubbish thrown over the side; and various instruments of differing impracticability. None of these approaches seems to offer much advantage over an educated guess.

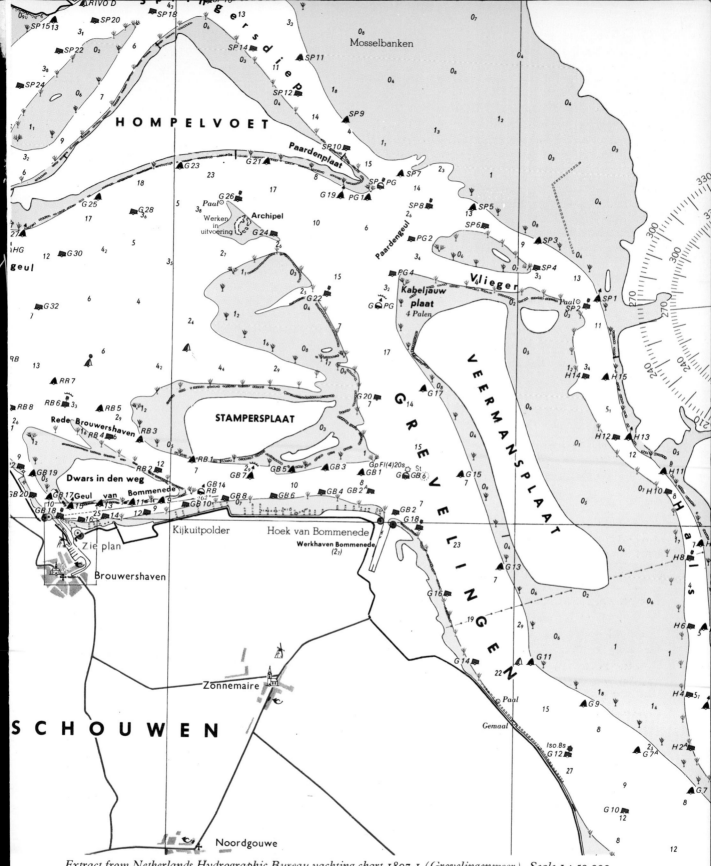

Extract from Netherlands Hydrographic Bureau yachting chart 1807.1 (Grevelingenmeer). Scale 1 : 50,000.

Reproduced from a portion of Chart No. 1807.1 by permission of Netherlands Hydrographic Bureau.

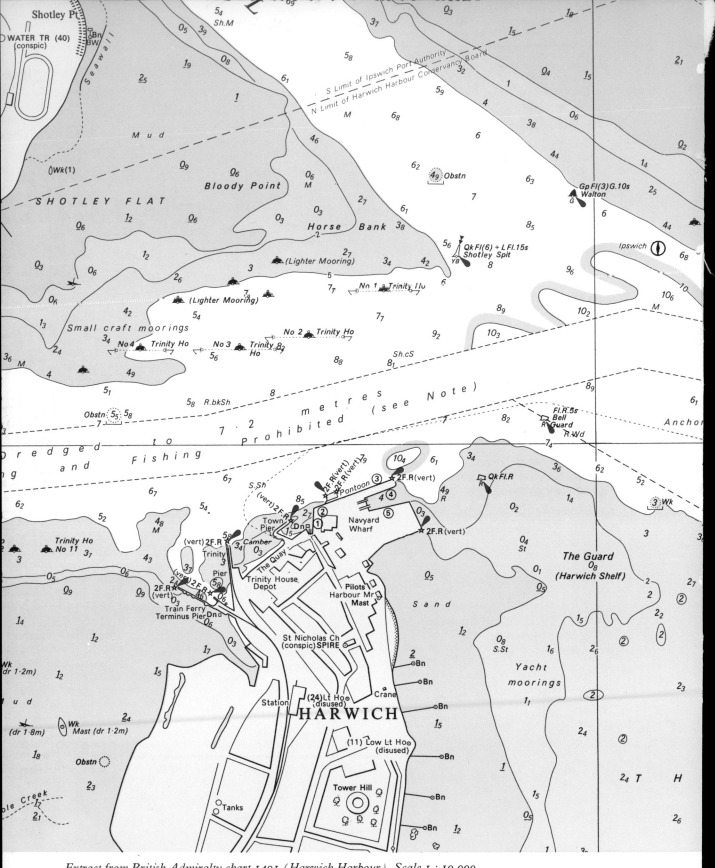

Extract from British Admiralty chart 1491 (Harwich Harbour). Scale 1 : 10,000.

Reproduced from a portion of BA Chart No. 1491 with the sanction of the Controller, HM Stationery Office and of the Hydrographer of the Navy.

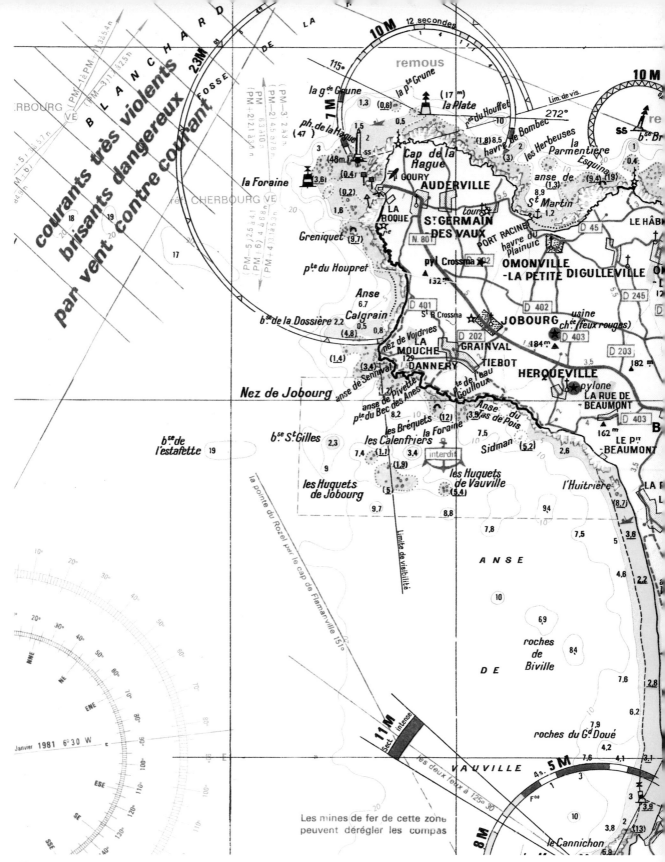

*Extract from a French commercial chart: Editions Cartographiques Maritimes chart 1014 (Iles Anglo-Normandes).
Scale 1 : 100,000.*

Reproduced from Chart No. 1014 by permission of Service Hydrographique de la Marine.

Extract from Brazilian Government chart 110 (Baia de Todos os Santos). Scale 1 : 65,000.

20   Dead reckoning accuracy

Whilst a carefully maintained dead reckoning position is the bedrock on which sound navigation is based, it is essential to understand very clearly the errors involved in the process. These are generally quite large and errors accumulate as time passes, so there may come a time when the position becomes so uncertain as to cause problems. The navigator would hope to reduce these uncertainties by making observations of objects on shore or in the heavens, but this is not always possible at the time the navigator would like them most.

Before dead reckoning can even be attempted, systematic errors in the equipment must be removed; the compass must be properly adjusted (or at least swung), and the log must be calibrated. The correct magnetic variation appropriate to the date and the ship's position must be used; on a long passage, the variation can alter markedly from beginning to end.

Each of the components used in plotting the DR position makes its own contribution to the error of the final position:

Compass and steering errors Random errors in the compass and in the steering of the yacht will result in her being to one side or the other of the chosen track.

Log error The random error in the log results in the vessel being either ahead or astern of the calculated position.

Tidal stream or current errors Errors in the estimation of the direction or the strength of the flow velocity will affect the final position.

Leeway estimation error Errors in estimating leeway will result in an across-the-track error rather like compass error. When the actual leeway is small, then any error in estimation will have little effect, but in bad conditions this factor may become significant.

It is possible to make separate allowances for these different errors but the process would be laborious. A more practical approach is to lump all the errors together in the form of a radial error, such that the boat is known to lie (with 95 per cent probability) within a circle centred on the DR position. As all the errors tend to increase with the distance travelled, it is convenient to express the radius of this circle as a proportion of the distance run since the last fix.

Table 1 offers some suggestions for 95 per cent DR errors under various conditions. Rough seas will tend to increase certain errors, and the speed of the craft will affect the relative influence of tidal stream or current errors. There may be circumstances which cause these errors to be smaller than the table indicates; if the passage is an out-and-home run, then certain heading errors will cancel out. On a longer passage, errors in assessing tidal streams will tend to diminish because of the cyclic nature of the flow.

Table 1 *95 per cent dead reckoning errors*

Error	Magnitude		Percentage	
	Calm	Rough	Calm	Rough
Five knot yacht				
Compass and steering	3°	5°	5	8
Log	2½ %	5 %	2½	5
Tidal stream or current	¾ kt	¾ kt	15	15
Leeway	2°	5°	3	8
Combined error			*16*	*19*
Ten knot yacht				
Compass and steering	3°	5°	5	8
Log	2½ %	5 %	2½	5
Tidal stream or current	¾ kt	¾ kt	7½	7½
Leeway	2°	5°	3	8
Combined error			*10*	*14*

20.1 *Dead reckoning – an example.*

Time	Course Ordered	Course Steered	Log Reading	Wind & Weather	Barometer	Remarks
14 30	—	—	81·2	SW5	1005	Position 240°. Lt. Vess 4mi. Co. 270C (port tack). Deviation 3°E Leeway 5° Tidal stream 1400-1500 112°T. 1·9 kts
1500	270	270	84·3	SW5	1004	Tidal stream 1500-1600 125 1·5 kts
1600	270	265	90·1	SW5	1003	Tidal stream 1600-1700 210 1·0 kts
1625	270	265	93·3	SW5	1003	Tacked to 175C Deviation 1°W Leeway still 5°
1700	175	175	96·5	SW5	1002	(Estimated position 241°. Lt. Vess 15·1mi

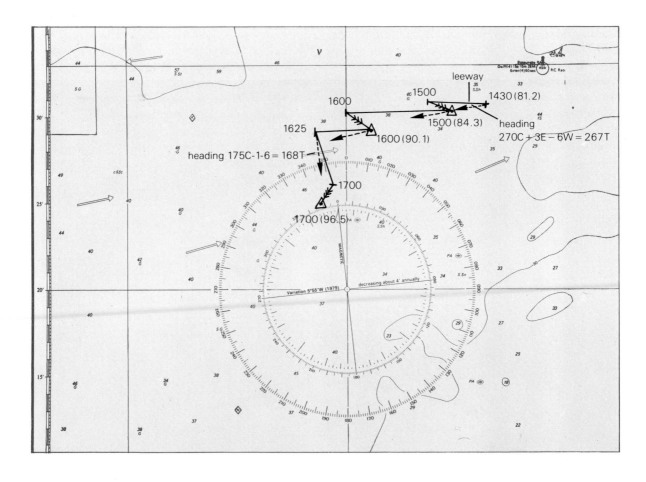

Experienced navigators may consider the figures in Table 1 to be far too pessimistic. They should firstly remember that the errors are the 95 per cent (20 : 1) errors and that the most likely error is about half as big. They might also reflect on how often they have found themselves very much further from their dead reckoning than they thought possible; a gloomy view of errors avoids nasty surprises.

Example of DR navigation

Figure 1 gives an extract from a deck log, together with the plotted dead reckoning and estimated positions. The reader may care to plot these figures as an exercise on a spare chart or plotting sheet, to confirm that the principles and techniques have been mastered.

However, mastering the techniques of DR navigation in the classroom or on the dining-room table is only part of the story. The problem takes on a different dimension at sea; the chart table is likely to be small and cramped; the motion may be violent; the navigator may be wet, cold, tired and possibly seasick; and the boat's actual progress through the water may be fitful and erratic, especially if under sail. The result of all these factors is that work at the chart-table becomes very slow and prone to blunders. The track on the chart soon begins to look like the ramblings of a drunken spider, and everything seems to take longer than you expect. In consequence it is all too easy for the navigator to lose confidence in what he is doing. Only by a firm effort of will can he maintain a grip on what is happening, and preserve his trust in the information he is using (a trust tempered by an understanding of the likely errors). And when anxiety does set in (as it inevitably will), the rest of the crew must never be allowed to see it.

Note: Experienced navigators will notice that the definition of dead reckoning given in this book differs from that in most text books – this is a deliberate step as I feel it reflects the actual situation exactly.

THE POSITION

21 The position line

The position line is one of the most important and useful concepts in navigation; it can be defined as follows:

A position line is a line on the surface of the earth on which the navigator knows, from some observation, his vessel must lie.

In the USA, the term 'line of position' (LOP) is used.

The importance of the position line concept is that it can be used to complement the other fundamental idea in navigation, the dead reckoning. The DR position is derived from a knowledge of the direction and distance the yacht has sailed, with allowances for external factors such as tidal stream and leeway; but the errors in the DR position grow rapidly with time (see page 65), so the position becomes more and more uncertain. If the navigator can observe some external object whose position he knows, he can use the measurements he makes to correct his DR position or reduce his uncertainty. It does not matter what object is observed, provided that the navigator knows where it is at the time he observes it; it can be on land, attached to the sea bed (like a buoy), in orbit round the earth (moon, navigation satellites), part of the solar system or a distant star. Equally, it does not matter how the observation is made, provided the navigator can estimate its accuracy; he can use visible light, radio waves (radio beacons, radar etc), or sound (echo sounder). The instruments he uses can range from the incredibly advanced (such as a navigational satellite receiver) to the centuries-old simplicity of a weight on a piece of line for measuring the depth of water; some position lines can be observed without any instruments at all.

Position lines can therefore be derived in many ways, the most likely of which to come the yacht navigator's way are described below.

Transits (Ranges) (Figure 1)

The simplest of all position lines can be obtained when the navigator sees that two objects, whose positions he knows, are in line with each other. All he has to do is to draw a line on the chart through the two positions, and he knows that he must lie somewhere on the extension of that line, which is known as a *transit* or *range*. A transit has the great

21.1 *The transit (range).*

advantage that it can be observed without any instruments at all (except, perhaps, binoculars), but the drawback is that transits only appear at variable and unpredictable intervals; the navigator should keep his eyes open to take advantage of any transits that appear, and train his watchkeepers to do the same. If a compass bearing is taken of two objects in transit, it can be used to check the accuracy of the compass.

Accuracy The accuracy of a transit depends upon the relative positions of the objects and the ship; it will be least when the two objects are close together and the ship is a long way away. However the transit is likely to be the most accurate position line that a navigator will find, and he should use them whenever possible.

Compass bearings (Figure 2)

A compass bearing of an object is taken by observing the object across a suitable compass card and noting the direction in which the object lies; it

21.2 *The compass bearing.*

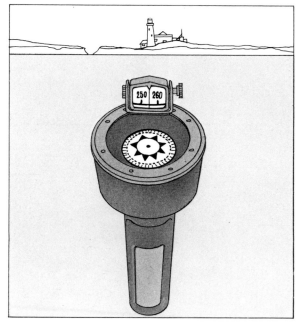

follows that the vessel must be on a line in the *opposite* direction from the object. For example, if the object is north of the ship, then the ship must be south of the object. Compass bearings are generally taken with a hand bearing compass (see page 27), but may also be taken with the steering compass if suitably sited, perhaps with the aid of an attachment known as an *azimuth ring*. Compass bearings must be corrected for variation and deviation (see pages 28–30); for the steering compass, deviation can be obtained from the deviation table (*Caution*: use the deviation that applies to the ship's head, not the deviation that applies to the observed bearing). Hand bearing compasses can be assumed to be free of deviation if used well away from magnetic influences; this may prove difficult in steel or ferro-cement yachts. Compass bearings are quick and easy to take, and are the most common type of position line in yacht navigation, though the accuracy can be poor in bad conditions.

Accuracy The 95 per cent error of a bearing taken with a good quality compass and properly corrected for variation (and deviation if appropriate) will be of the order of:

Good conditions $+ / - 2°$
Moderate conditions $+ / - 5°$
Rough conditions $+ / - 10°$

Relative bearings (Figure 3)

A *relative* bearing of an object is one that is taken using the ship's head as a reference, using a device known as a *pelorus*. This looks very like a compass card, but it is fixed on the fore-and-aft line of the ship, rather than north. A relative bearing is given as red or green (depending on whether the object is to port or starboard), followed by the number of degrees from ship's head; thus an object exactly on the port beam has a relative bearing of red 90 and an object almost right astern on the starboard side may have a relative bearing of green 175. (US practice is to measure relative bearings on a scale of 0°–360° from ship's head.)

Before the navigator can use a relative bearing as a position line, he has to convert it to a compass bearing; this is done by adding or subtracting the relative bearing to the ship's compass course – red bearings (on the port side) are subtracted and green bearings (starboard side) are added.

For example:	1	2
Ship's head	125	335
Relative bearing	R90	G175
Compass bearing	035	510 − 360 = 150

Having obtained a compass bearing, the navigator must correct it for variation and deviation in the same way as any other compass bearing (*Caution*: use the deviation that applies to the ship's head, not the deviation that applies to the compass bearing derived from the relative bearing).

21.3 *The relative bearing.*

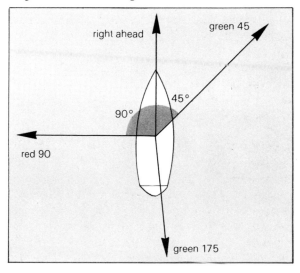

When taking relative bearings for navigational purposes, it is necessary to record ship's head at the same time as each of the relative bearings; the helmsman should be instructed to call out the exact heading at the moment that the bearing is taken. Given the marked tendency for yachts to yaw, even in a moderate seaway, the headings called out may not be the same for each bearing, or the same as the course the helmsman is steering.

Accuracy As a relative bearing involves the additional operation of recording the ship's compass heading at the moment of observation, the resulting position lines are somewhat less accurate than compass bearings taken directly. The 95 per cent errors of properly observed and corrected relative bearings will be of the order of:

Good conditions $+ / - 4°$
Moderate conditions $+ / - 8°$
Rough conditions $+ / - 15°$

Horizontal angle (Figure 4)
A position line can be obtained if the angle between two objects is measured. From simple geometry, it can be shown that the resulting position line is an arc of a circle. The advantage of such a position line from a horizontal angle is that it is substantially more accurate than a compass bearing, especially if a sextant (see pages 45–7) is used to measure the angle in question. It is not usual to plot a single position line of this kind as the work involved, though simple, is tedious. It is more usual to plot a *horizontal angle fix*, using two measured angles between three objects. Methods of plotting this type of fix, potentially the most accurate visual fix available, are given on pages 82–3.

21.4 *Horizontal angle position line.*

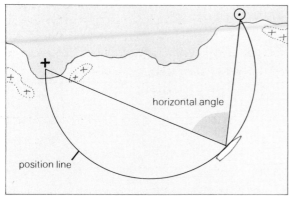

Range by narrow horizontal angle (Figure 5)
An alternative way of getting a position line from the angle between two objects is to use trigonometry to compute a range; for best results, the two objects should be at approximately the same distance from the vessel. A typical opportunity to use this type of position line is when both the left- and right-hand edges of a small island are visible at a distance; knowing the width of the island and the angle between the two edges, the range of the mid-point of the island can be calculated.

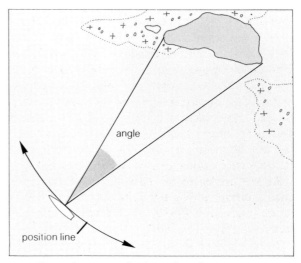

21.5 *Range by narrow horizontal angle.*

Calculation Using a calculator with trigonometric functions or trigonometric tables, the range is given by:

$$R = \frac{D}{2 \cdot \tan \cdot (A)} \quad \text{or} \quad \frac{D}{2} \cot \cdot (A)$$

where D is the distance between the objects
    A is the measured angle
    R is the range of the mid-point between the objects

A rule of thumb, accurate within 2 per cent for angles between 1° and 25° is:

Range (n miles) =
$$\frac{28 \times \text{distance between object (n miles)}}{\text{measured angle (degrees)}}$$

Accuracy The accuracy of the resulting position line will depend upon the accuracy with which the angle can be measured, and on the accuracy with which the distance between the two objects can be determined. Using a sextant, a 95 per cent accuracy of better than 5 per cent should be obtainable even in the case of small angles; 2 per cent might be a more typical figure. If the angle is measured by a less precise technique the accuracy will be substantially impaired.

Range by vertical sextant angle (Figure 6)

If the angle between the top and the bottom of an object of known height can be measured, then simple trigonometry makes it possible to calculate the distance of the object from the observer. Whilst this approach can be very useful, it is not always possible to see the base of an object (particularly from the low height of eye of a yacht's deck), as the base of the object will be below the sea horizon.

Another complication can be atmospheric refraction, which tends to bend rays of light and alter the measured angle. The tables published for finding range by vertical sextant angle vary in their scope from those intended for short-range work only to others that can give a useful range of a distant mountain peak; the table on pages 187–91 can be used for any type of observation, and includes corrections for atmospheric refraction.

As the angles to be measured are frequently small (perhaps only a few minutes of arc), an accurate measuring device, such as a sextant (see pages 45–7) must be used.

The height of shore objects is generally given with respect to mean high water springs or mean high water (see your chart title to find out which); depending on the state of the tide when an observation is made, the actual height of the object will probably be greater than the charted value; for accurate results, the charted height should be corrected to allow for the height of the tide. If this is not done, it will appear that the vessel is closer to the object than is actually the case; many navigators use this fact as a sort of in-built safety margin. When taking an angle of a lighthouse, the charted height refers to the height of the lantern itself, not the top of the structure.

21.6 Range by vertical sextant angle.

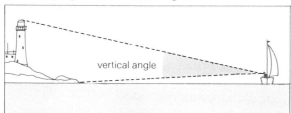

Calculation Most books of nautical tables and yachtsman's almanacs contain tables to convert angles to distances; an alternative table is given on pages 187–190 of this book. The formula on which this table is based is given on page 184. It is laborious, but could be used on a programmable calculator.

Accuracy The accuracy of a vertical sextant angle position line depends upon a comparison between the accuracy of the sextant observation and the angle actually measured; the smaller the measured angle, the less reliable the results. The 95 per cent accuracy of a vertical sextant angle observation by an average user is probably one minute for a metal sextant and five minutes for a plastic one. Thus, if the angle measured is 50 minutes of arc, the 95 per cent error of the resulting distance would be about 2 per cent if using a metal sextant, or 10 per cent if using a plastic sextant. It would be unwise to expect a 95 per cent error of less than 2 per cent under normal circumstances.

Lights dipping or raising (Figure 7)

A special case of the vertical angle position line is of great value to the navigator; it happens when the angle to measure is zero, i.e., when the top of the object is exactly on the horizon. It is of most value at night, when approaching or leaving a coastline. Most navigational lights can be seen when the actual lantern is below the horizon, as the beam is scattered by the air to give what is called the *loom* of the light – a bright patch over the position of the light. It is immediately obvious when the light itself comes over the horizon; the loom is replaced by clear, bright flashes. Approaching the coast, the transition from loom to bright flash is called *raising* the light; when the opposite happens on leaving the coast, the light is said to *dip*. Given the height of the light above sea level, a simple table can be used to obtain the distance of the light at the moment of raising or dipping. The observation is

21.7 Range by lights dipping or raising.

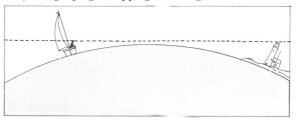

quick and simple, as it needs no instruments; it is merely necessary to know the height of the light and the height of eye of the observer.

The actual moment of raising or dipping a light can only be established in good visibility. It can be confirmed by changing the height of eye; if it is raised (by standing on the coachroof, for example), the light should be visible. Lowering the height of eye should make the light disappear, to be replaced by the loom.

Calculation Appropriate tables are printed in most books of nautical tables and yachtsman's almanacs; a version is given on page 192 of this book. The table is entered with the height of the light above sea level and the height of the observer's eye above sea level.

Accuracy Most lights will raise or dip at a range between ten and 25 miles, depending on the height of the light. The 95 per cent accuracy is about a quarter of a mile.

Important The raising or dipping of a light is one of the most valuable position lines available to the navigator making a landfall or taking a departure. It is simple and accurate, and the watch on deck should be trained to look out for the opportunity to take one.

Range by rangefinder or distance meter
(Figure 8)

Various optical devices for measuring distance are available. They are either based on the rangefinder principle of binocular vision, or on an image-splitting principle. In either event, such instruments are unlikely to be of much use to the navigator; the maximum accurate range of either type is little over a mile (perhaps less), and at this sort of range the 95 per cent error may be as much as 10 per cent. The reason for this poor performance is one of cost – the yacht market could not afford to pay for the very high quality optics needed by an accurate rangefinder that works up to five miles or so. Better results can be obtained from a sextant (even a plastic one) which can also be used in many other ways.

Sounding (Figure 9)

A sounding, or a line of soundings can provide a position line provided that the shape of the sea bottom is sufficiently distinctive. Soundings can

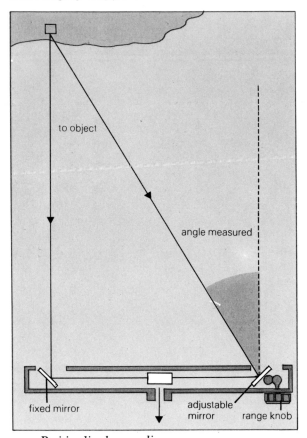

21.8 *Range by rangefinder.*

to object

angle measured

fixed mirror

adjustable mirror

range knob

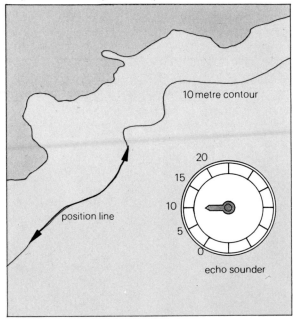

21.9 *Position line by sounding.*

10 metre contour

position line

echo sounder

be taken by an echo sounder or (in shallow water) by means of a lead and line (see page 38).

An example of a position line from a single sounding is the traditional indication of the approach of land after an ocean passage. The 100 fathom (180 metres) contour marks the edge of the continental shelf; whilst its distance off shore varies, it offers invaluable landfall information. It also gives a useful departure line when setting off on an ocean passage.

A similar position line may be obtained by crossing a particular depth contour, provided that the sea bed is sufficiently regular for the correct contour to be identified without ambiguity.

If the seabed is irregular, a position line can sometimes be obtained by running a line of soundings. This involves recording soundings at regular intervals whilst the ship proceeds in a straight line; after a sufficient interval (perhaps an hour), a selection of the soundings can be plotted on a piece of paper, using the same scale as the chart in use (Fig. 10). This line of soundings is lined up on the chart to correspond in direction with the course steered by the ship, and the paper is moved about the chart near the DR position, to try and find a match between the depths on the chart and the line of soundings on the paper. Again, it is important to be on your guard against ambiguities caused by an

21.10 *Running a line of soundings.*

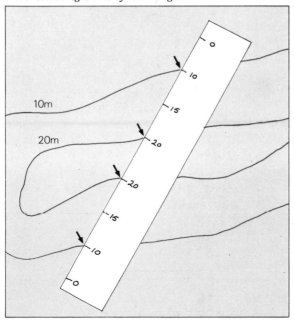

irregular bottom, and confirmatory information should be sought if at all possible.

Reduction to soundings A sounding taken in tidal waters will differ from the charted depth by reason of the rise of the tide; the sounding must be *reduced* by the height of the tide above chart datum. It is almost always sufficient to estimate this correction, because it is laborious and time-consuming to calculate for a slight improvement in accuracy. For those occasions when it is needed, the procedure is described on page 104.

Accuracy The 95 per cent error of an echo sounder will be about 2–4 per cent depending on the range in use (deep ranges will tend to be less accurate). A further error should be allowed if it has been necessary to reduce the sounding.

Bearing by radio direction finding
(see pages 110–4)

By using a suitable radio receiver and directional aerial, it is possible to take radio bearings of beacon transmitters to obtain a position line. The process, together with errors and corrections, is described on pages 112–4. Radio bearings are very useful when making a landfall or sailing out of sight of land, and they can be invaluable in poor visibility; but the accuracy is not particularly good, and can be distinctly poor in certain circumstances. Best results are obtained with radio bearings when they are used with caution, understanding and practice.

Accuracy The 95 per cent accuracy of a bearing from a properly installed and calibrated MFDF set, properly operated will be about:

Good conditions	5°
Moderate conditions	10°
Poor conditions	15°

Under certain conditions, MFDF bearings will be so unreliable as to be unusable, particularly near sunrise and sunset (see page 114).

Half convergency When taking MFDF bearings at long range, an allowance may be needed to convert the great circle bearing given by the set to a rhumb line bearing (see page 15). This correction is known as half convergency; it can be obtained from most books of tables, lists of radio signals or yachtsman's almanacs, or from the table on page 191. The correction is applied to the measured bearing *towards* the equator. An equation for calculator use is given on page 184.

Bearing by directional radio beacons

Certain types of radio beacon give directional information without the need for a specialized receiver; two of these systems, Consol and the radio lighthouse, are described on pages 122–3, which also describes VOR for which a special receiver is needed.

Another type of radio directional beacon, known as a *radio range*, is occasionally found (Fig. 11). Its function is not to provide a position line but rather a path along which a craft can travel. Radio ranges are commonly used in aviation but their use is much less common at sea. One example of a marine radio range is to be found at Boulogne (France), where the beacon lays down a path in the direction $101\frac{1}{2}°$ to guide shipping into the harbour. If the vessel lies to the north of the beam, a succession of morse letter 'A' (.–.–.–.–) can be heard. On the beam itself, the signal is a continuous note and to the south it becomes a succession of morse letter 'N' (–.–.–.–.). The beam width of the continuous note is 5°, so the radio range is not a precision aid by any means; however the effect of this wide beam becomes less as the beacon is approached so it still can provide valuable homing information.

21.11 *Radio range.*

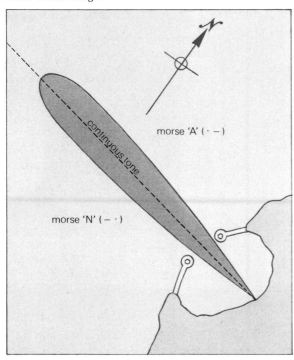

morse 'A' (· —)

continuous tone

morse 'N' (— ·)

Range differences and hyperbolic position lines

A number of radio aids to navigation have been devised which measure the difference in distance between pairs of special radio transmitters. These aids are described fully on pages 120–1. The position lines produced by these aids are families of hyperbolae which require the use of special charts over-printed with a lattice, or a specially programmed computer in some modern equipment. The various systems offer different coverage areas, accuracies and costs; they all tend to be expensive and all require special receivers and signal processors. In sailing yachts, the electrical power demand can also be significant.

Radar range

The use and limitations of radar are described on pages 115–9. From a navigational point of view, radar can provide two types of position line – the range of an object and its bearing. Of these, the range is very much the more accurate. In radar terms, the measurement of range involves the measurement of a time interval between the transmission of a radio pulse and the reception of an echo from the target; electronic techniques make this a very simple and accurate process. Bearings from a radar set are very much less accurate (see below). If at all possible, radar ranges should be used in preference to radar bearings.

Accuracy In normal yacht radar sets, the range of an echo is estimated, using fixed range rings as a guide; there are normally four range rings across the width of the screen. A practiced operator should be able to estimate a range to within about 2 per cent of the total range in use (95 per cent). Many radars now offer a device called a *variable range marker* as an optional extra; this device provides a single range ring which can be moved across the screen by means of a knob. A display then shows the exact range to which the range ring is set. Using the variable range marker, the 95 per cent error of a radar range should not exceed 1 per cent of the range in use.

Radar bearing

The use and limitations of radar are described on pages 115–9. A radar set can provide the navigator with the range and the bearing of an echo; of these two, the range is very much more accurate and should be used whenever possible in preference to a radar bearing. However, radar bearings can be used provided that their limitations are always borne in mind. These limitations arise from a number of factors, connected with the fact that the radar aerial has to rotate, at a fairly low speed, with respect to the ship's head. Because the rotation is with respect to ship's head, any bearing measured is a *relative bearing* (see page 69), and hence needs the addition of the ship's course to give a compass bearing; and because the rotation is slow, the effect of the yacht's yaw can be pronounced. Another factor leading to poor radar bearings is the relatively wide beam produced both by transmitting and receiving aerials (3° is typical). It is difficult under the best circumstances to measure a bearing with an accuracy smaller than the beam-width.

Accuracy Taking all factors into account, the 95 per cent accuracy of a radar bearing taken in good conditions is probably no better than 6°; in poor conditions this may increase to 15° or even more.

Astronomical position lines

A section of this book explains how to obtain astronomical position lines and how to assess the likely errors; it may help to relieve the mystique traditionally ascribed to astronomical navigation to stress that its major function is to provide the navigator with a position line (possibly when no other source of position lines is available). Whilst the techniques of astronomical navigation may appear unusual at first glance, the end result (the position line) is now familiar. The accuracy of such a position line is discussed on page 132.

Unusual position lines

The position lines so far described may be called conventional, in that most navigators know about them and will use them when the opportunity arises; however, position lines may be obtained from the most unusual of sources, if the navigator keeps his eyes open and his wits about him. A good navigator never lets a position line escape him; some of the following ideas may lead to very inaccurate position lines, but the good navigator will realize this, and make use of any information he can acquire with due allowance for its quality.

Sectored lights In many parts of the world (for example Scandinavia), navigational lights are often sectored, showing different colours over different arcs of the compass (Fig. 12); a position line can be obtained by observing the colour of a particular light or (more accurately) by observing the change from one colour to another.

Clouds In tropical waters it is common for the heating effect of the sun to cause clouds to form over land during the late forenoon. These clouds can often be seen for a considerable distance, marking for example the position of an island below the horizon. In temperate latitudes, similar effects can occur but are less predictable.

Waves and swell Experienced seamen can detect the disturbance of a wave train caused by the presence of land – this is one of the major clues used by Polynesian navigators.

Shipping lanes Commercial shipping tends to follow certain clearly defined routes, and the presence of merchant ships can often give valuable

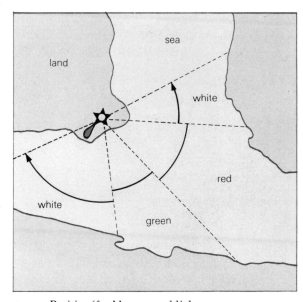

21.12 *Position 'fan' by sectored light.*

navigational information; the information can be even more precise if it is known that traffic separation schemes are in force, confining the ships to narrow traffic lanes.

Ferry routes The sighting of a ferry on a known route can tell the navigator a lot, especially if he knows the ferry's timetable as well.

Aircraft Similarly, a knowledge of the air routes within the vicinity of the yacht can also give useful indications of position.

Birds Certain birds feed at sea and roost on shore; they fly out from the land at dawn, and return to the land at dusk. If such birds can be recognized and their flight directions identified, then the direction of the nearest land is established.

Garbage In the absence of shipping, the floating garbage it leaves behind can be helpful; such garbage is sometimes marked at a distance by scavenging seabirds.

Sound The ears can offer useful information; a dull roar on an otherwise still day may indicate surf on a reef; a barking dog signals land. In fog, ships can sometimes hear echoes from their sirens reflected from cliffs; given the sort of sound signalling equipment on a yacht, it may only be possible to detect the echo of a cliff at half a mile or so, but that might still make all the difference between a safe passage and a stranding.

Rule of thumb Very roughly, the distance of an object detected by echo (in cables = 0.1 miles) is equal to the number of seconds between signal and echo; i.e., if an echo is heard five seconds after the signal, the object is five cables, or half a mile away.

Smell The nose is a very sensitive organ, and it may well happen that it will detect a smell which gives a clue to position. Typical smells that might be useful are fumes from an oil refinery or production platform, the smell of growing plants on shore, or rotting seaweed on the shoreline.

22   The transferred position line

A position line is only valid at the instant of observation, because the vessel moves away from the position line as time goes by; however, it is not always possible to obtain a position line at the exact moment that it is wanted, so it would be very helpful if we could extend the useful life of a position line in some way. This can be done by using the techniques of dead reckoning, and the result is known as a *transferred position line*.

Assume, in Figure 1, that a position line is observed at 0900 – a lighthouse (L) bears 015 degrees true. The vessel must lie somewhere along the position line, but it is not known where. Let us pick three of the infinite number of possible positions at random, A1, B1 and C1, and see what happens as the vessel proceeds on its way.

If the ship's course and speed are 090, seven knots, then one hour later (at 1000) it will be seven miles east of its original position. If that position had been A1 at 0900, then it will be A2 at 1000; if it had started from B1, then it would arrive at B2; and if C1 had been the 0900 position, then at 1000 the DR position would be C2.

The essential point to observe is that the line A2 B2 C2 is parallel to the original position line A1 B1 C1, and displaced from that line by a distance and direction exactly equal to the movement of the ship during the time interval since the original observation. Of course, the ship may not have actually been at A1, B1 or C1 at 0900, but whatever position was actually correct, the DR at 1000 must lie somewhere along the line A2 B2 C2, which is the original position line *transferred* by the movement of the ship in the interval.

An alternative way of looking at this very important concept is to imagine that the original position line has a physical existence, like a thin rod connecting the ship and the lighthouse at 0900; the ship can be imagined to pick up this rod and carry it along, keeping it parallel with its original direction. At any subsequent moment, the actual position of the ship must lie somewhere on this imaginary rod, the transferred position line (Fig. 2).

The original position line was established with reference to the earth's surface, and if it is to be transferred correctly then allowance must be made

22.1 *Principle of the transferred position line.*

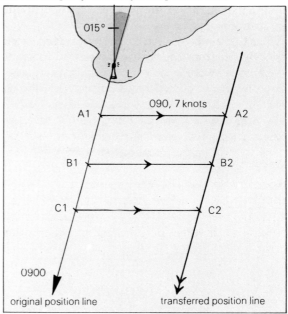

22.2 *Carrying the position line along.*

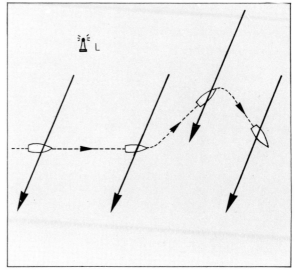

for the ship's progress over the ground; therefore full allowance must be made for such factors as tidal stream, current and leeway as well as the ship's course and speed. All the appropriate techniques of DR navigation must be used. The transferred position line is therefore an interesting combination of the two major concepts of position finding, dead reckoning and position line observation.

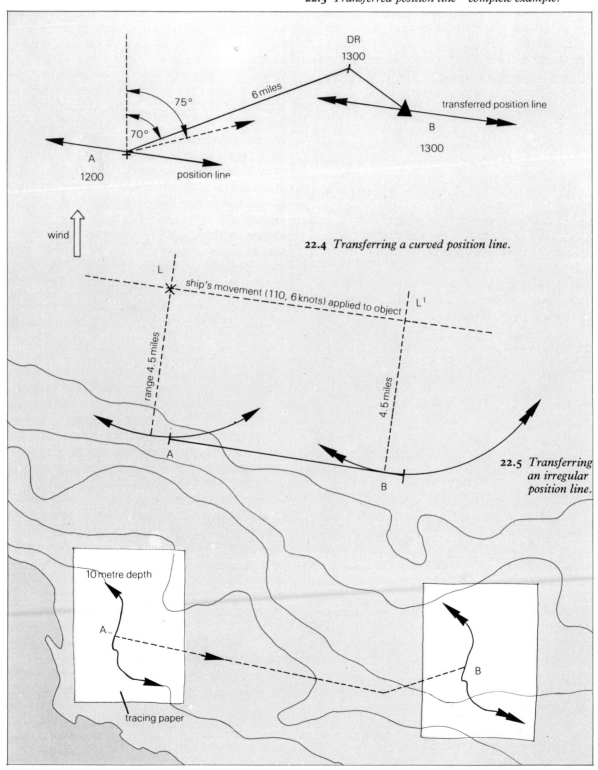

22.3 *Transferred position line – complete example.*

22.4 *Transferring a curved position line.*

22.5 *Transferring an irregular position line.*

Figure 3 shows the full process of DR navigation applied to a position line (this time assumed to be an astronomical position line). The starting point (initial DR position) is assumed to be at A; the vessel is steering 075 at six knots, and 5° of leeway is allowed because of the fresh southerly wind. The tidal stream is setting 120 at two knots. After one hour, the estimated position of the ship is at B, with the transferred position line running through it, parallel with the original. It is conventional to mark a transferred position line with a double arrow head.

The majority of position lines are straight lines, and can be transferred as has been described. If the position line is an arc of a circle (from a radar range, for example), then the simplest way to transfer it is to move the centre of the circle according to the DR (Fig. 4). A transferred position circle can then be struck from the new centre, using the same radius as the original. An irregular position line, such as a depth contour, can also be transferred (Fig. 5); in this case, the simplest technique is to make a tracing of the original line and then move the tracing paper appropriately, pricking the transferred line through onto the chart.

A transferred position line has just the same validity as any other position line. Due allowance must be made for the fact that a transferred position line is necessarily less accurate than the original line (see below), but apart from this there is no difference between them.

Accuracy A transferred position line will have a larger error than the original, because of the errors in the DR. The original position line would have its own 95 per cent error, the magnitude of which depends on the type of observation and the circumstances of the moment. As the line is transferred, the errors of the DR are added to the original error (Fig. 6). The navigator must keep an eye on the error of a transferred position line, which grows with time, and make his own decision on the line's usefulness.

22.6 *Transferred position line accuracy.*

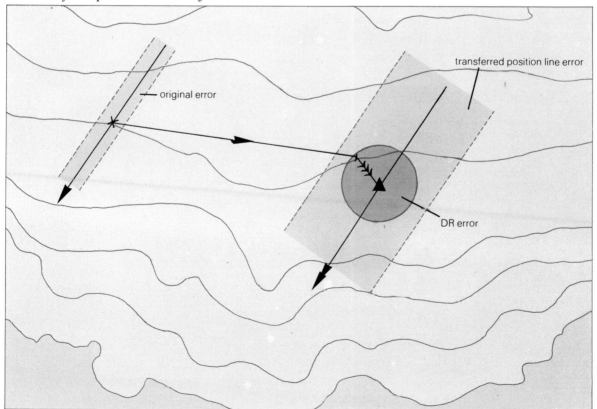

23 Using single position lines

Position lines are of restricted value in themselves, as they only give limited information about the position of the vessel; they are normally used in combination to provide a fix (see page 84). However, there are circumstances when a single position line can be of great use to a navigator.

Leading line A position line can be used to indicate a safe course for the vessel to follow. A common example is the use of a transit to indicate the safe approach to a harbour (Fig. 1). Beacons are often erected for this special purpose, and in more important harbours these beacons will be lit for use at night. Such lights may be sectored so as to show more brightly when on the transit (or range), and the lights are sometimes synchronized to aid identification. The nearer light or beacon is normally lower than the further. When steering a ship along a transit, any deviation from the correct line causes the transit to open; the ship should be turned towards the *nearer* beacon (*lower* light) to bring it back onto the correct line. A transit makes a convenient and accurate leading line, but any position line will do; Figure 2 shows the use of a compass bearing as a leading line.

23.1 *Leading line.*

23.2 *Compass leading line.*

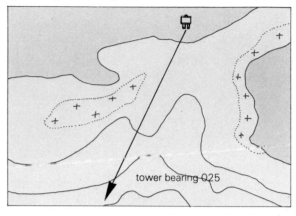

tower bearing 025

Clearing line Another way of using a position line is as a way of avoiding a danger. In Figure 3, a clearing bearing of 060 has been chosen to avoid a shoal. Provided that the bearing is 060 or less, it is known with certainty that the ship will pass clear of the shoal.

23.3 *Clearing line.*

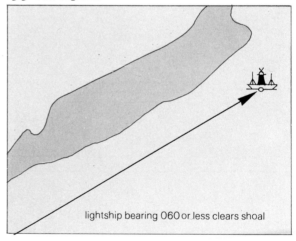

lightship bearing 060 or less clears shoal

Finding a channel or haven A transferred position line can be used to find a channel or haven when no other navigational information is available (Fig. 4). In the example, a single position line was obtained by means of the compass bearing of a headland. If this position line is transferred to pass through the destination, the ship can first run the required distance and then alter course along the transferred position line. Within the limits of accuracy of the position line, this will lead the ship to the desired point.

23.4 *Finding a haven with a transferred position line.*

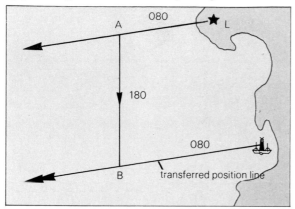

Track checking A single position line can be used to estimate a position relative to the desired track (Fig. 5). A position line which crosses the track at right angles (or nearly so) gives an indication of how far ahead or astern of the DR the ship actually is; a position line parallel (or nearly) to the track indicates the extent to which the ship has been set to port or starboard of the track. Astronomical position lines are often used for this purpose, when it may be possible to select the time of observation to yield the desired direction of position line.

23.5 *Track checking.*

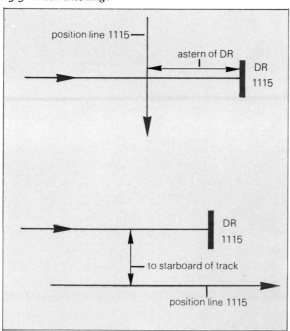

Danger approaching A single position line can be used to warn of approaching danger; when making a landfall, for example, it may be possible to select a limiting sounding (Fig. 6). Even though the position of the vessel may be in doubt, it is safe to continue the approach until the limiting sounding is reached; thereafter, the ship must be navigated with extreme caution until the true position can be established. A common strategy is to alter course to follow the position line, therefore using it as a clearing line.

23.6 *Danger limit line.*

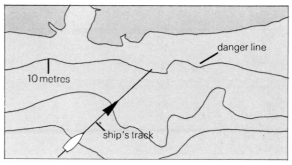

Danger circle A variation on the idea of a clearing line is so common as to be worth special mention; this is the danger circle (Fig. 7). In the example, it has been decided that it would be unsafe to go within a mile of the lighthouse (height 25 metres). This distance corresponds to a vertical angle of 47 minutes of arc on a sextant. Provided that the actual vertical angle observed is 47 minutes or less, it is certain that the ship is outside the danger circle. A similar technique can be used with radar. Provided that the echo of the lighthouse is not permitted to come inside the one-mile range ring, then the ship is at a safe distance.

23.7 *Danger circle.*

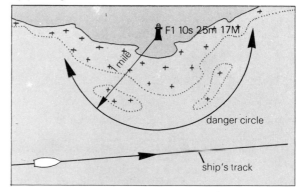

24 The fix

If dead reckoning navigation could be made perfect, then no other technique would ever be needed from start to finish of a passage. However, DR is far from perfect and the errors grow with time so that after a period the DR can become so vague as to be of little value. The navigator must continually seek to remove or reduce the error in his estimation of the ship's position by using observations to find out where he actually is. A position established by observation is called a *fix*.

A fix can be obtained in a variety of ways, of which the fix by intersection of position lines is by far the most common:

Pinpoint A pinpoint is established by passing very close to some object (e.g., a navigational buoy) whose position is known.

Electronic fix Certain electronic aids to navigation (Satnav, some Loran C sets) carry out internal processing on the position lines that they derive to present an output in the form of a fix (latitude and longitude).

Outside help A fix can sometimes be obtained from an outside source. A blue water yachtsman can often get a position from a merchant ship that he may happen to encounter, though it is by no means certain that such a position will be any more reliable than the yachtsman's own opinion – big ships make mistakes, too. Closer to shore, a more reliable position can sometimes be obtained from traffic surveillance and harbour control systems which use shore-based radar; the most common and practical means of communication with such bodies is by vhf radiotelephone. For example, the Dover Strait Information Service monitors traffic in the very crowded waters of the Dover Strait, using powerful and precise radar sets on the French and English coasts and vhf direction finding equipment. On request, the coastguards are able to identify your echo on their screen and tell you your position; they may also be able to offer advice on safe manoeuvres to avoid other shipping. A navigator who takes pride in his work would normally be reluctant to seek outside help, but there may be circumstances (especially in fog) when prudent seamanship would indicate that this was a sensible thing to do.

When coasting in fog, any position obtained by asking passers-by should be treated with grave suspicion; they may have less idea of where they are than you do.

Fixing by horizontal angles As mentioned on page 70, a circular position line can be obtained by measuring the angle between two objects. In practice, such a position line is rarely used on its own; the more common technique is to use two angles, taken at the same time, between three objects. This is known as a *horizontal angle fix*. The angles can be measured by subtracting the compass bearings of the objects, or (more accurately) with a sextant used horizontally.

There are two simple methods of plotting a horizontal angle fix. The first involves the use of tracing paper, or perhaps the surface of a clear protractor (Fig. 1). From a point on the paper (or the centre of the protractor), three lines are drawn such that the angles between them correspond with the measured angles. The paper or protractor is then moved over the surface of the chart until the three lines each pass through the appropriate object on the chart; the vessel is at the point where the lines originate.

24.1 *Horizontal angle fix.*

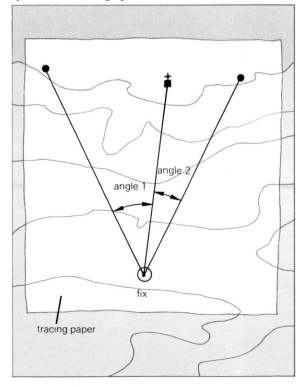

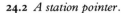

24.2 *A station pointer.*

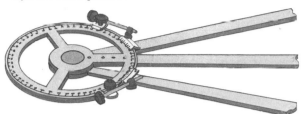

The second method of plotting a horizontal angle fix involves the use of an instrument known as a *station pointer* (Fig. 2). This consists of three arms, mounted on a graduated ring. The centre arm is fixed, whilst the two outer arms can be set to any angle required against the graduations of the ring. In use, the two angles are set up on the arms and the whole instrument is moved about the chart until the ruling edge of each arm passes through the appropriate object. The ship's position is then at the centre of the station pointer. Though more accurate than the tracing paper approach, a station pointer is expensive and cumbersome; they are rarely found in yachts.

Limitations and accuracy Under certain circumstances, a fix by horizontal angles can be ambiguous or inaccurate; to avoid such a situation, the objects chosen for observation should be selected to fufill one of the following conditions (Fig. 3):

a) All three objects are more or less in line with each other.

b) The middle object is closer to the ship than the outer two.

c) The ship lies inside the triangle formed by joining the three objects.

If one of these three conditions is observed, the accuracy of the resulting fix will be high. If the fix is plotted using the differences between compass bearings as input, the resulting fix will be more accurate than one obtained by plotting the compass bearings themselves, because the systematic errors (variation and deviation) will be eliminated. If a sextant is used for measuring the angles, then the resulting fix is likely to be the most accurate available by visual means; before the advent of precise radio aids, the method was widely used for the very accurate navigation needed in minesweeping. The 95 per cent error of the fix will depend upon the actual geometry of the case, but typical values might be:

a)

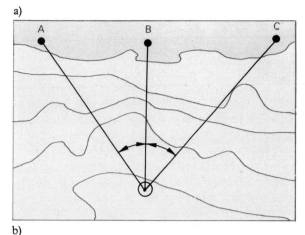

b)

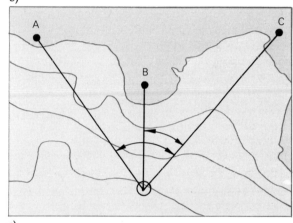

c)

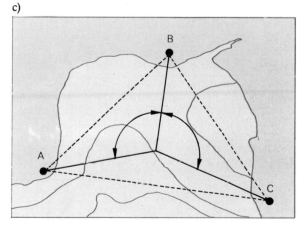

24.3 *Conditions for a satisfactory horizontal angle fix.*

Sextant angles	$\frac{1}{2}$ a per cent of mean distance between objects
Angles from compass bearings	$2\frac{1}{2}$ per cent of mean distance between objects

Fixing by intersecting position lines By far the most common type of fix in normal navigation is formed by the intersection of two (or more) position lines obtained at the same time. In Figure 4, two position lines, A and B, have been obtained at the same time. From the definition of a position line, it is known that the ship must lie somewhere on the line A; equally, she must also lie somewhere on the line B. The only place where these two facts can both be true is at the point where the position lines intersect; this is a fix. If the position lines did not intersect (i.e., they were parallel), then no fix is possible.

A fix can be obtained from the intersection of any two (or more) position lines, however derived. A transferred position line will serve if it has been transferred to the same time as the other observation(s).

It cannot be emphasized too strongly that a fix can be obtained from two or more position lines of any kind at all; an astronomical position line can cross a sounding, a radar range cross a visual bearing, a visual transit can cross an MFDF bearing. The sole requirements are:

1) The position lines must be taken simultaneously (or transferred to the same time).
2) The position lines must intersect.

Whilst any two intersecting position lines provide a fix, it is obvious that the number of position lines, the accuracy of each and the angle of intersection will all affect the quality of the resulting fix. These aspects are discussed on the facing page.

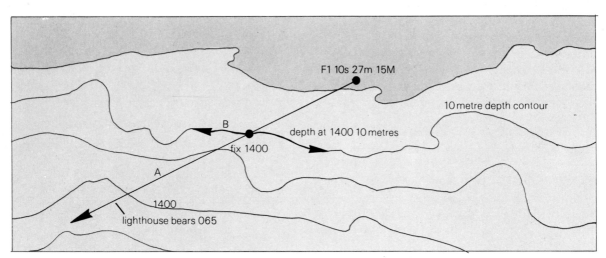

24.4 *Intersecting position line.*

25 Fix accuracy

Having plotted a fix by the intersection of position lines, the navigator needs to assess the quality of the fix and the reliance he can place on it by establishing its 95 per cent error. This will vary from fix to fix, and depends upon a number of factors:

The quality of the individual position lines (Fig. 1) Each position line will have its own 95 per cent error, of which the navigator should be aware. If each position line is regarded as a 'ridge of probability' rather than a line, then the intersection gives rise to a 'heap of probability'. If the 95 per cent errors of the position lines are approximately the same, then the resulting 'heap' will be circular, with a diameter roughly equal to the width of the 'ridges'. The 95 per cent error of the fix can therefore be taken as roughly the same as that of the position lines. If the errors of the position lines are different (Fig. 1b.), then the 'heap' is distorted in shape and the resulting error is greater in one direction than the other (see page 11).

25.1 Effect of individual position line errors: (a) similar errors; (b) differing errors.

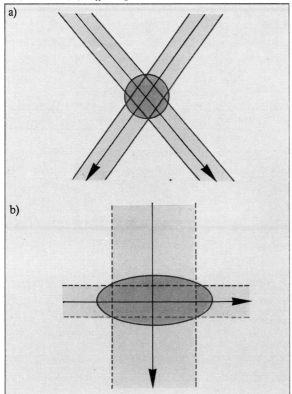

The angle of cut If two position lines of equal error cross at right angles, then the resulting heap is circular and as small as possible. As the angle of cut decreases, the 'heap' becomes more and more elliptical, giving rise to greater error in the fix in one direction. In practical terms, this effect may be ignored as long as the smaller angle of cut is more than 50° (Fig. 2).

Angles of cut less than 50° should be avoided. If their use is essential, then great care must be taken in assessing the resulting errors.

25.2 Effect of angle of cut.

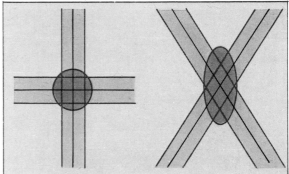

Number of position lines In practice it is wise to plot fixes with at least three position lines whenever possible. From a mathematical point of view, there is little improvement in the resulting error determination, but the plotting of three lines will generally detect any blunders that may have been made in observation or plotting (Figure 3). Three position lines will rarely intersect in a point, as they would if no errors were present. The size of the 'cocked hat' should be compared with the errors of the individual position lines; a blunder is likely if the size of the cocked hat is greater than the position line errors.

25.3 Detecting blunders with three position lines.

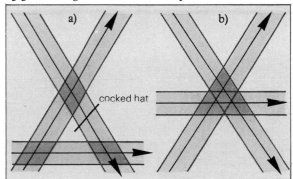

If compass bearings of three objects lying on a common circle are taken, the fix is ambiguous and should be rejected.

Simultaneous observations A fix requires that the position lines result from simultaneous observations. With a single observer, it is impossible to make two observations at once, though the time interval between them may be so short as to be of no significance. However, it may happen that a noticeable interval elapses between observations; in high speed craft in particular, the delay may

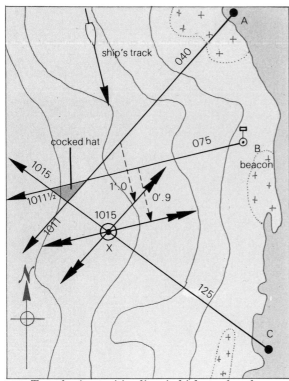

25.4 *Transferring position lines in high speed craft.*

cause inaccuracy. The solution is to transfer the earlier position lines by the distance that the craft has moved in the interval (Fig. 4).

Comparison with DR A fix should be examined for consistency with the dead reckoning position. Whilst the purpose of the fix is to reduce the errors that have accumulated in the reckoning, there should still be consistency between the two. If the 'heap' of the fix is not included within the larger 'heap' of the DR, then one or other must be wrong; a blunder has been detected, and both fix and DR should be re-worked until it has been found.

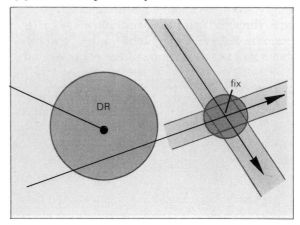

25.5 *Inconsistency between fix and DR.*

There is a temptation to accept the fix and ignore the (seemingly wrong) DR; it is a potentially dangerous practice to yield to this temptation (Fig. 5).

Practical points

When using the ideas of probability and 95 per cent errors for the first time, it can be helpful to draw the 'ridges' and 'heaps' of probability on the chart, although this may make the chart look messy. As experience is gained with this approach there is no need actually to mark the chart provided that the existence of the errors is never forgotten; the drawing of a shape around a fix, indicating the 95 per cent error, is probably always good practice as it reduces the demand on the navigator's memory and indicates to the rest of the crew what is going on.

There is no need to be over-precise in the assessment of errors; they are only estimations and are subject to random variation. Where 95 per cent errors for different observations are quoted in this book, they are merely suggestions based on the author's experience. Any navigator is entitled to disagree, but should remember that pessimism is generally safer than optimism.

Some navigators may feel that the errors suggested in this book are very large. They should perhaps remember that the figure quoted is the 95 per cent error, not the most likely error (probably half). The 95 per cent error is defined as the error that will only be exceeded on one occasion in twenty. The basis of this idea is discussed in the section on errors (see pages 9–13).

Choosing a position within a 'heap' of probability is influenced by circumstances (Fig. 6). In ordinary circumstances, the middle of the heap will serve as well as any other point; however, it may be wise to choose some other point to build in a margin of safety. It is sensible, for example, to choose the point closest to the nearest danger if it is desired to guarantee that the danger be cleared. In other circumstances it may be wise, in a sailing yacht, to assume a position to the leeward side of the 'heap', so that any errors result in his being to windward and he can be sure of retaining the advantage of the weather gauge. It is always worth avoiding a last-minute beat.

25.6 *Selecting a position within a fix error zone.*

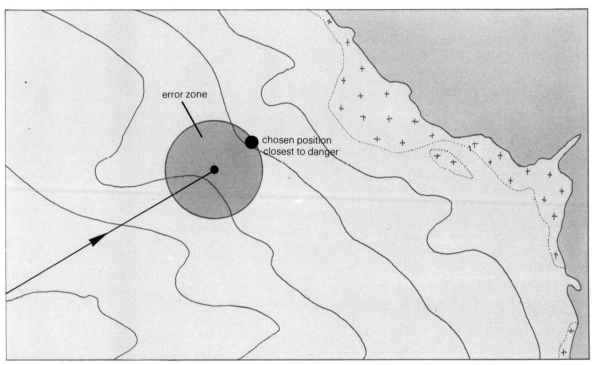

THE ENVIRONMENT

26 Global weather

The atmosphere exerts a pressure on the surface of the earth, but because of the energy input from the sun the atmosphere is warmer in some places (notably around the equator) and cooler in others (around the poles). Warm air is less dense than cold air, so in warmer areas the pressure is less and in cold areas it is greater. There is a tendency for air to move from high-pressure areas to fill low pressure areas, but because of the rotation of the earth such movements, the winds, are deflected to the right in the northern hemisphere and to the left in the southern hemisphere. The result is a pattern of pressure and wind belts across the globe shown in Figure 1.

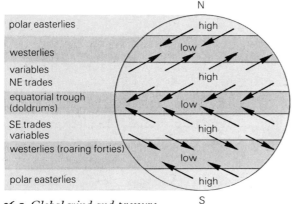

26.1 *Global wind and pressure.*

The effect of the land masses of the earth on this basic pattern is considerable. Not only are the belts of high and low pressure broken up into separate cells over the major oceans; the heating or cooling of large land masses also affects the barometric pressure. Pressure tends to be high over cold ground and low over warm ground. On a continental scale, such effects (known as *monsoons*) exert a major influence on the winds in the oceans that border them. Figures 2 and 3 show the major wind systems of the world for January and July. Note that the systems in tropical and temperate latitudes are shifted bodily north or south, depending on the declination of the sun; note also the influence of the monsoons.

The equatorial trough (doldrums)

This is an area of low pressure situated between the two belts of trade winds, generally north of the equator in the northern summer and south of it in the northern winter. The doldrums vary greatly in width both daily and seasonally, so that one vessel may hardly notice them, whilst another may be stuck for many days with light and baffling winds. Winds are generally light and variable, with occasional squally rain and thunderstorms.

The trade winds

The trade winds are two belts of remarkably steady and persistent winds on either side of the doldrums, and were so named for the very great assistance they gave to trading ships under sail. They blow with an average strength of force four, though the strength varies with the season and can reach force seven at times. The north-east trades blow in the northern hemisphere and the south-east trades in the southern; the trades can be suppressed by the monsoons in certain areas, notably the Indian Ocean, the west Pacific Ocean and the waters off West Africa. They are sometimes interrupted by tropical revolving storms (see pages 92–3).

In the trade winds, the weather is generally fair with an endless procession of small, puffy cumulus clouds across the sky. Rainfall is frequent in the west and visibility, except in the rain, is generally good.

The variables

Between the trade winds and the westerlies there lies a belt of light and variable winds associated with high pressure. In the northern hemisphere, the variables are sometimes called the horse latitudes.

The westerlies

On the poleward side of the variables lie the westerlies, regions where the wind is predominantly from the west, but very variable in character with the passage of a large number of depressions. Gales are frequent, especially in winter. Bad weather is so common in the southern hemisphere that the region is known as the roaring forties (south of 40°S). In the northern hemisphere, fog is common in the west.

The polar regions

Mainly un-navigable by reason of ice, such areas are avoided by all but the most intrepid yachtsmen.

26.2 *World winds – January.*

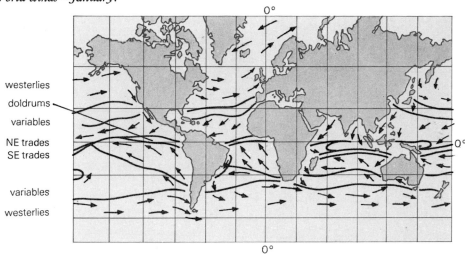

westerlies
doldrums
variables
NE trades
SE trades

variables
westerlies

26.3 *World winds – July.*

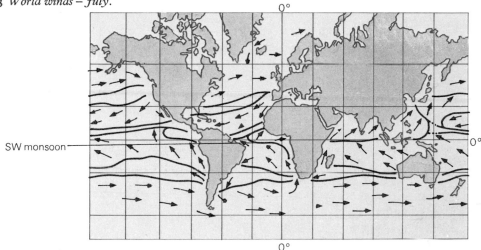

SW monsoon

26.4 *World ocean currents.*

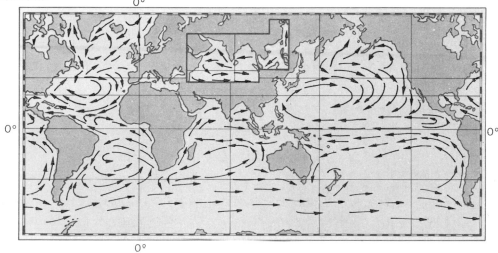

27 Depressions and fronts

Depressions (or *lows*) are areas of low pressure, generally oval in shape which form in middle latitudes and are largely responsible for strong winds and unsettled weather. They can vary greatly in size (from 100 miles to 2,000 miles diameter) and intensity (central pressure 950 mb to 1000 mb). They can move in any direction, but generally tend easterly, and the speed can range from 60 knots for a newly formed vigorous depression to almost zero. The average life of a depression is four to six days, after which they slow down and fill.

Buys Ballot's Law to find the centre of low pressure.

If you face the wind, the centre of low pressure will be between 90° and 135° on your right hand in the northern hemisphere, on your left hand in the southern hemisphere.

A depression has a series of *fronts* associated with it, and Figure 1 shows how both come into being. A front is the boundary between two kinds of air, say polar (cold) air and tropical (warm) air. The front is not stable, and it tends to kink; this causes a circulation of air to build up, with a consequent fall in pressure which forms the depression. As the system gathers momentum, the depression deepens and moves off, carrying the kinked front with it. The leading part of the front, which has cold air in front and warm air behind, is called a *warm front*, and the second front, between the warm air in front and the cold air behind, is called a *cold front*. The cold front tends to travel faster than the warm front, so it will eventually catch up with it to form an *occluded front*. An occluded front can be very vigorous, but it effectively 'pinches off' the kink in the front and the depression will soon start to fill.

The behaviour of fronts and depressions depends on the hemisphere; in the following description, the equivalents in square brackets apply to the southern hemisphere.

In the northern [southern] hemisphere, the winds blow round a depression in an anticlockwise [clockwise] direction. The wind direction generally follows the isobars, but is inclined inwards to the centre of low pressure by a few degrees; wind strength depends on the pressure

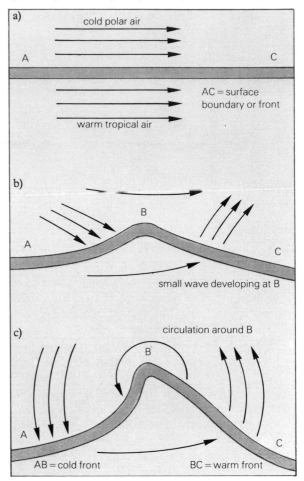

27.1 *The formation of a depression (northern hemisphere).*

a) cold polar air

A   C

AC = surface boundary or front

warm tropical air

b)

B

A

C

small wave developing at B

c) circulation around B

B

A

C

AB = cold front   BC = warm front

gradient, indicated by the spacing of the isobars (lines of equal pressure). The closer the isobars, the stronger the wind.

The passage of a warm front (Fig. 2) is characterized by the appearance of high, streaky clouds (mares tails) which progressively get lower and thicker, leading at first to drizzle and then rain. At the front itself, the wind will veer [back]. The rain will stop, the temperature will rise and the sky will remain overcast with moderate visibility. The cold front brings squalls, more rain and a fall in temperature. The wind will veer [back] further and the barometer will start to rise. Cold fronts are generally more active than warm fronts, and occluded fronts more active than either.

The pattern of events as a typical depression passes by is as follows:

27.2 *The passage of warm and cold fronts.*

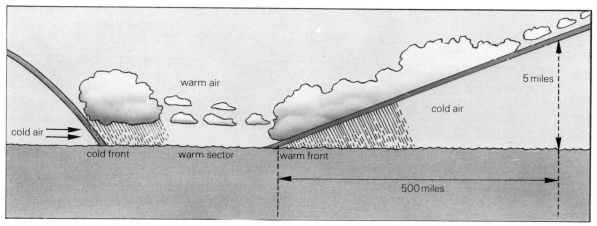

1) If the depression passes north [south] of you, moving from west to east, the first signs are high cirrus clouds and a falling barometer. The winds will shift to SW [NW] or S [N] and freshen as cloud builds up in the west. The clouds will lower until it starts to drizzle and then rain. At the warm front, the wind will veer [back], and the passage of the cold front will cause it to veer [back] even more to W or NW [SW], often with a sharp squall. Behind the depression the weather will be cool, bright and showery, though another depression may well be on its way.

2) If the depression passes south [north] of you, the passage is less eventful, as the fronts do not pass over your position. The barometer will fall, clouds will thicken and the wind will freshen. Prolonged periods of rain and unpleasant weather are possible. The winds in front of the depression will be E, and they will gradually back [veer] through NE [SE] to N [S] or NW [SW]. Sudden changes are unlikely.

Secondary depressions

It is not uncommon for a depression to calve off a secondary depression, which generally forms on the cold front. The secondary usually moves faster than the primary and can be a great deal more vicious, especially on the S [N] side. Secondary depressions can be dangerous, not least because they often come as a surprise to the forecasters as well as the sailors who have to endure them, bringing gales where none were expected (Fig. 3).

27.3 *Secondary depression.*

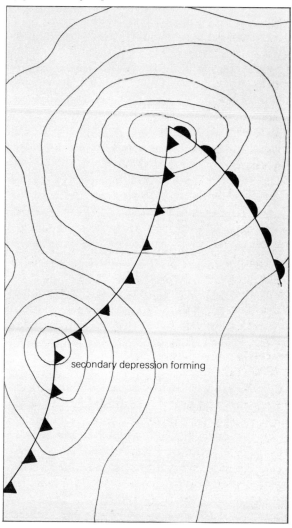

28 Tropical revolving storms

(Figures in square brackets refer to the southern hemisphere)

Tropical revolving storms occur in a number of regions, under different names. They resemble a depression in many ways, but are much smaller, more intense and quicker moving. They are intensely dangerous, and must be avoided by yachts if humanly possible, even to the extent of leaving the area or laying the boat up during the dangerous season.

A tropical revolving storm, which may be known as a hurricane, a typhoon, a cyclone or a willy-willy in different areas, is an area of intense

and move off in a WNW [WSW] direction. Sometimes they maintain this course until they strike land and exhaust themselves, but generally they recurve to the NE [SE] in latitude 20° or so. The speed of the storm usually starts at about ten knots, rising to 20–25 knots after recurving, though many go faster.

Generally speaking, when the progress of a storm is erratic, its speed is low. The storm is divided into the *dangerous semicircle* on the pole side of the expected track, and the *navigable semicircle* on the equatorial side. The term 'navigable' should not be taken too literally; it merely means that survival is a little more likely than in the other semicircle.

Area	Local name	Season	Average number per year
West Indies	hurricane	late May–mid Nov worst months Aug–Oct	8
E North Pacific	hurricane	June–October worst months Aug, Sept	7–8
W North Pacific	typhoon	June–November worst months Aug, Sept	22
N Indian Ocean	cyclone	May–Nov	6–8
S Indian Ocean	cyclone	December–April	6
Australia	willy-willy	December–March	1
(Queensland)	hurricane	December–March	2–3
S Pacific	hurricane	December–April	2

winds spiralling in towards an area of low pressure; the rotation is anti-clockwise [clockwise] in the northern [southern] hemisphere. Within 75 miles or so of the centre, gusts of 175 knots have been reported, with mountainous, confused seas and zero visibility because of torrential rain and blown spray. In the eye of the storm, winds are light or moderate and variable, but the earlier passage of the storm has left a huge, confused swell, which will soon be increased by the trailing half of the storm.

Tropical revolving storms can occur at any season, but they are mostly confined to the late summer season of the locality in question. The table above makes this clear.

The general path and progress of a tropical storm is shown in Figure 1, though each storm is highly individual and may vary wildly from the norm. They generally originate in latitude 7°–15°N [S]

Detecting the approach

In these days of weather satellites, the most common warning of tropical storms comes from weather broadcasts; however, if such a warning is not received, the navigator must be able to detect the approach of a storm and decide what to do about it.

Barometer The first warning will usually come from the barometer, which is normally remarkably constant in these regions. For most of the time, only a *diurnal variation*, a change in pressure between night and day, will be seen. If the diurnal variation is suppressed, or if the barometer falls three millibars (0.09 in) or more, trouble is about; if the barometer falls more than five millibars (0.15 in), a tropical storm is in the area.

Swell Even before the barometer begins to fall, a long, low swell from the direction of the storm may be seen.

Weather Sudden changes in wind direction or strength, unusual cloud formations and an unusual 'feel' to the weather can all indicate that something unpleasant is likely to happen.

What to do

The first essential is to decide the direction of the storm centre, its likely path and the relative position occupied by the ship. When the barometer has fallen by five millibars (0.15 in), and the wind has freshened to force six, the storm centre is about 200 miles away. Using Buys Ballot's Law, if you face the wind, the storm centre will be about 110° on your right [left] hand. Two such bearings taken a few hours apart will indicate how the storm is moving. It will rarely be moving towards the equator, and if below 20° latitude it is unlikely to have any east in its movement.

Northern hemisphere

If the wind veers, you are in the dangerous semicircle. Heave to on the starboard tack.

If the wind is steady or backs, you are either directly ahead of the storm or in the navigable semicircle. Run with the wind on the starboard quarter.

Southern hemisphere

If the wind backs, you are in the dangerous semicircle. Heave to on the port tack.

If the wind is steady or veers, you are either directly ahead of the storm or in the navigable semicircle. Run with wind on the port quarter.

In all cases, prepare for heavy weather.

28.1 *Typical storm paths.*

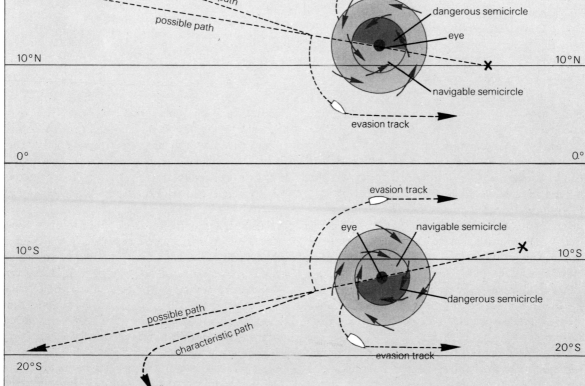

29 Local weather effects

There are a number of local effects which can modify the weather in a particular place.

Fog

Fog is caused by the cooling of the air by the surface with which it comes into contact to the point where the water vapour in the air condenses into droplets. Fog can occur in three main ways:
Advection fog is the most common type of fog found at sea, and is caused by relatively warm air blowing over cold sea; it is most common in late spring and early summer, when the contrast in temperature between sea and air is greatest. This type of fog is often associated with cold currents, such as the Labrador Current, the California Current and the Oya Shio, off Japan. Winds can remain quite strong during advection fog.
Frontal fog is sometimes formed in advance of a warm or occluded front in temperate or high latitudes; it is normally quite narrow in extent.
Radiation fog is formed over the land on clear, cold, still nights (generally when pressure is high); it can drift some ten to fifteen miles offshore. It is thickest during the late night and early morning, but is normally burned off by the sun or dissipated by heat from the relatively warm sea during the forenoon. This type of fog is associated with calms.

Sea breeze

The sea breeze is a local effect, extending no more than ten miles offshore, caused by the heating of the land by the sun until it is much warmer than the sea (Fig. 1). The heated air over the land rises, drawing in cooler air from the sea, to give rise to the onshore wind known as a sea breeze. Sea breezes are most common in tropical and subtropical latitudes, though they are found in temperate latitudes (with less force) in the summer. The sea breeze normally sets in during the late forenoon and reaches a peak some two to three hours after local noon; it will die away at about sunset.

The actual effect of the sea breeze will depend on the prevailing wind blowing at the time. A weak prevailing wind can be reduced or even reversed by the sea breeze, or it may merely be deflected towards the shore by the sea breeze effect. Whatever the effect, the sea breeze sets in earlier and lasts longer close inshore, so that is where a yacht wanting to take advantage of it ought to be. A sea breeze uninfluenced by any prevailing wind will average about force four (less in higher latitudes), but may reach force five or six at times.

Land breeze

The land breeze is the complement of the sea breeze; it occurs at night, when the land cools relative to the sea, and cold, dense air moves off the land, giving an off-shore breeze (Fig. 2). The land breeze is generally less marked than the sea breeze. It will set in at about midnight and disappear again at about dawn. As the effect is not as strong as the sea breeze effect, it is easier for a prevailing wind to mask any land breeze that may wish to blow.

Katabatic wind

Katabatic winds are akin to the land breeze, but can happen at any time of day and with considerable force. Where a coast is backed by snow-covered mountains, it is possible for cold air to accumulate (Fig. 3). It then needs only a small trigger for this mass of cold, dense air to slide down the mountain slopes and out to sea. These winds can reach gale force, they can arrive almost without warning and close inshore they can blow down at an angle rather than horizontally. For all these reasons, katabatic winds can be dangerous to small craft.

High coasts and cliffs

An onshore wind which meets high ground will tend to be deflected to blow parallel with the coast; near headlands and around islands, gusts and sudden wind shifts may be expected. If the wind is offshore, a narrow band of fluky wind can be expected in the lee. Squalls can be expected offshore if the air is colder than the sea.

Rivers and straits

A river or strait will tend to funnel the wind along its length, especially if the shore on either side is steep. The wind will increase in strength as the inlet narrows.

29.1 *The sea breeze.*

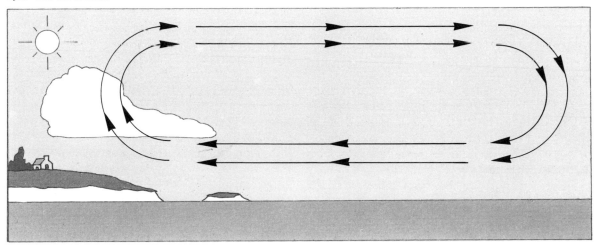

29.2 *The land breeze.*

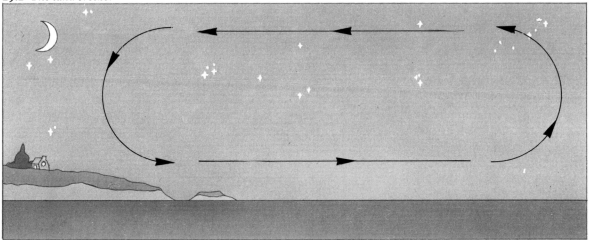

29.3 *Katabatic winds.*

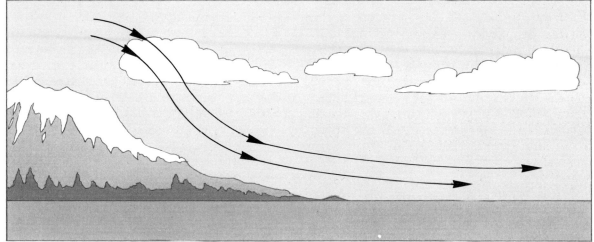

30 Land- and seamarks

For visual fixing, any conspicuous charted object such as a headland, a church, a water tower or a mountain can be used. But such marks are not always in the position where the navigator would like them, and in any case are hard to see at night. From the earliest times, landmarks and seamarks, including lights for night use, have been erected for the mariner.

Landmarks

The landmarks most commonly used for visual navigation by day are *lighthouses* from which lights are exhibited at night. They are located at key positions around the coast, and are painted conspicuously so they can be seen. In harbour approaches, *beacons* are often erected to mark a channel, possibly in pairs to act as leading lines. Beacons are sometimes fitted with a *topmark*, a special shape fitted to the top of the beacon, to distinguish one from another, and they may also carry lights.

A description of the construction and appearance of any landmark carrying a light is given in the *Light List* and the *Pilot* for the area. The *Pilot* also carries a description of any unlit beacon or object of navigational importance.

Seamarks

Seamarks are almost always floating objects moored to the seabed, though occasionally a tower or other construction is built offshore. *Buoys* are widely used to mark channels and as a landfall aid, whilst *lightships* (manned) or *lightfloats* (unmanned) mark more important or dangerous features. All lightships and most buoys carry lights, and lightships may also carry an MF radio beacon transmitter.

Radar reflectors and racons

A buoy is not a particularly large object, and the vast majority are now fitted with a radar reflector to assist in detection by radar; they are sometimes fitted to beacons as well. A *racon* is a device which makes an identifying mark on the radar screen, to label the object to which it is fitted.

Buoyage systems

Buoys are generally established according to an organized system, to help the navigator identify each buoy more easily and find out his position from them. Unfortunately there are several different systems in use around the world, in spite of great efforts from the International Association of Lighthouse Authorities (IALA) to get agreement for a unified system. The IALA system A has now been introduced in most European waters; many countries associated with the British Commonwealth use the Uniform Lateral system, whilst the United States has its own system, which is also found in waters where US influence is strong. Elsewhere, countries will use their own system of buoyage (or none).

A point of particular importance for intending transatlantic voyagers is the difference in American and European systems for lateral marking. In Europe, a buoy to be left to starboard in a channel (when approaching from seaward) is painted green, and a buoy to be left to port is painted red. American practice is the opposite.

A new buoyage scheme for the US, known as IALA system B, has been agreed; it is akin to the system A used in Europe, but maintaining the red-to-starboard principle. Implementation began in Spring 1982 and should be completed about 1988. IALA system A and B are shown on pages 43–4.

When using buoys for navigation, it should not be forgotten that they are moored by chains to the seabed, and can therefore move a little about their charted position. Small buoys used to mark a narrow channel into a yacht haven can be set over the bank they are intended to mark during the flood.

Lights

Lights, whether exhibited from lighthouses, lightships or buoys, are of the utmost value for pilotage at night, and indeed often make a coastline easier to traverse than in daytime.

A navigational light is described by various characteristics:

1) *Character* This describes the behaviour of a light, whether it is fixed, flashes or is coded in some other way. Figure 1 gives the possibilities, with the abbreviation to be found on the chart (older charts may not use the International abbreviations).

30.1 *Light characters.*

Fathoms and Metric Charts			
CLASS OF LIGHT	International abbreviations	Older form (where different)	Illustration Period shown ————
21 Fixed *(steady light)*	F		
22 Occulting *(total duration of light more than dark)*			
22 *Single-occulting*	Oc	Occ	
27 *Group-occulting* e.g.	Oc(2)	Gp Occ(2)	
(Ka) *Composite group-occulting* e.g.	Oc(2+3)	Gp Occ(2+3)	
23a Isophase *(light and dark equal)*	Iso		
23 Flashing *(total duration of light less than dark)*			
23 *Single-flashing*	Fl		
(Kb) *Long-flashing (flash 2s or longer)*	L Fl		
28 *Group-flashing* e.g.	Fl(3)	Gp Fl(3)	
(Kc) *Composite group-flashing* e.g.	Fl(2+1)	Gp Fl(2+1)	
24 Quick *(50 to 79–usually either 50 or 60–flashes per minute)*			
24 *Continuous quick*	Q	Qk Fl	
(Kd) *Group quick* e.g.	Q(3)	Qk Fl(3)	
25 *Interrupted quick*	IQ	Int Qk Fl	
(Ke) Very Quick *(80 to 159–usually either 100 or 120–flashes per minute)*			
(Ke) *Continuous very quick*	VQ	V Qk Fl	
(Kf) *Group very quick* e.g.	V Q(3)	V Qk Fl(3)	
(Kg) *Interrupted very quick*	IVQ	Int V Qk Fl	
(Kh) Ultra Quick *(160 or more–usually 240 to 300–flashes per minute)*			
(Kh) *Continuous ultra quick*	UQ		
(Ki) *Interrupted ultra quick*	IUQ		
30a Morse Code e.g.	Mo(K)		
29 Fixed and Flashing	F Fl		
26 Alternating e.g.	Al.WR	Alt.WR	

COLOUR		International abbreviations	Older form (where different)	RANGE in sea miles		International abbreviations	Older form
67	White	W *(may be omitted)*		*Single range* e.g.		15M	
66	Red	R					
64	Green	G		*2 ranges* e.g.		14/12M	14,12M
(Kj)	Yellow	Y					
65	Orange	Y	Or	*3 or more ranges* e.g.		22-18M	22,20,18M
63	Blue	Bu	Bl				
61	Violet	Vi					
ELEVATION Is given in metres (m) or feet (ft)				PERIOD in seconds e.g.		5s	5sec

2) *Colour* The colour of a light may be white (W) (which may be omitted), red (R), green (G), yellow or orange (Y), blue (Bu) or violet (Vi); the two last are not common. A light may show a single colour over the whole of its arc of visibility, or two or more colours over different arcs. Sometimes a light shows two colours in succession over the same arc, and is known as an alternating light. Al WR, for example, means a light that first shows white and then red.

3) *Period* This is the time in seconds for one complete cycle of the character.

4) *Elevation* The elevation of the light is the height of the lantern above the datum for heights (normally mean high water springs or mean high water). The higher a light, the further it can be seen (if it is bright enough). The geographical range of a light is the same as its dipping distance.

On a mountainous coast, a light may be set so high that it is often obscured by low cloud.

5) *Nominal range* This is a measure of the brightness of the light; it is the range under which the light will be seen (regardless of elevation) in specified conditions of visibility. A light which exhibits more than one colour may have a different nominal range for each colour.

Fog signals

Fog signals can be of great assistance to the navigator in thick weather, though the behaviour of sound in fog is rather unpredictable, and taking bearings of fog signals 'by ear' may not always work. Buoys are fitted with relatively simple, short-range signals, such as a bell or whistle operated by wave action, or a horn driven by gas. Lighthouses and lightships carry more elaborate apparatus designed to give greater range and clarity.

Diaphone A low-pitched sound, ending in a characteristic 'grunt'

Horn Something like a magnified car horn (or several)

Siren A high-pitched wail

Explosive A bang

A fog signal has a character just like a light, though the period is usually quite long – a minute is typical. Most of the more leisurely 'flashing' rhythms are used, as well as Morse code letters.

When listening for a fog signal that you expect to hear but cannot, bear in mind that the fog which is restricting your visibility may not be present at the lighthouse or lightship, therefore the reason for not hearing the signal could be that it has not been switched on.

31 Tidal theory

Tides are regular and periodic changes in sea level, caused by the gravitational attraction of the sun and moon.

Tidal streams are regular and periodic horizontal movements of water which take place as a consequence of the tides.

According to gravitational theory, any two bodies exert an attraction on each other. The earth attracts the moon, which keeps the moon in its orbit. By the same token, the moon attracts the earth. Most of the earth is rigid, and so responds very little to this force; earth tides do exist, but can only be detected with special instruments. However, the water of the oceans is not rigid, and so is able to respond to the forces exerted by the moon. The way in which this gives rise to a *tide-raising force* is shown in Figure 1. The force of gravity varies with distance; therefore the moon's gravity as seen at a point immediately below it (A) is greater than at places where the moon is on the horizon (B), and water at A will tend to 'pile up' under the moon. Similarly, the moon's gravity at a point diametrically opposite the moon (C) will be *less* than at B′, and the water will tend to lag behind. The net effect is that two humps of water are created, one under the moon and the other opposite it.

31.1 *The tide-raising force.*

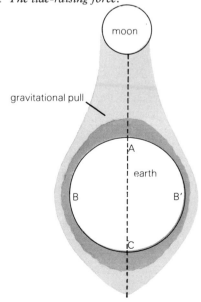

As the earth rotates, this would produce two tides in each lunar day (every 25 hours approximately), and is known as the *semi-diurnal* (i.e., half-daily) tide raising force. However, the moon is constantly changing position in the sky (specifically its declination is changing, page 137), and this also causes a *diurnal* (i.e., daily) force, which combines with the semi-diurnal force to produce the result shown in Figure 2. The relative magnitudes of the semi-diurnal and the diurnal forces can vary very greatly, to the extent that one or the other may disappear altogether.

31.2 *Diurnal and semi-diurnal effects.*

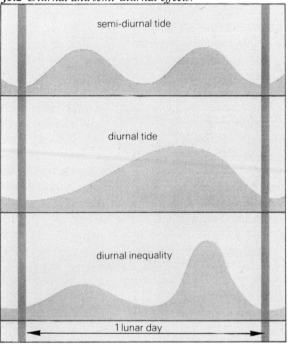

A further complication is the presence of the sun, which also causes tide-raising forces in exactly the same way as the moon. Although the sun is very massive, it is also a very long way away compared with the moon, and the sun's tides are relatively small. Their effect is to modify the tides caused by the moon, in a manner which depends upon their relative positions in the sky (Fig. 3). When the sun, moon and earth are more or less in line (i.e., at full moon and new moon), the tide-raising forces of the sun and the moon add together to produce a bigger tide than the average, a *spring tide*. When the sun and moon are at right

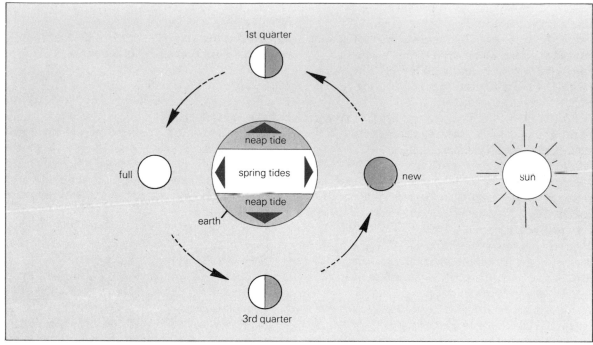

31.3 *Spring and neap tides.*

angles as seen from the earth, their respective tides act in opposition to each other, causing a smaller tide than the average, a *neap tide*. As the sun and moon are roughly in the same relative position every 28 days, there is a regular pattern of spring and neap tides; spring tides happen each fortnight, at new and full moon, while neap tides occur in the alternate weeks, when the moon is in its first or third quarter.

The actual tides as they exist

The foregoing explanation merely describes how the forces that cause the tide are generated. The actual tides are controlled almost entirely by geography. The periodic tide-raising forces set up waves which travel across oceans, alter in height as the depth changes and are reflected from coasts, with the end result that no two places on earth experience exactly the same tides. Some places experience very little tide – the Mediterranean, the Baltic and some Pacific islands have tides which may never exceed 0.6 metres (two feet), whilst places like the Severn estuary (England), Darwin (Australia) and the Bay of Fundy have tides averaging twelve metres (39 feet) or more. In the Atlantic Ocean, the diurnal effect is generally small, so there are two tides a day of roughly equal height; in the Pacific, the diurnal effect is very much more marked, leading to a pronounced *diurnal inequality* in many places, where one tide of the day is very much bigger than the other. Some places have very complicated tides indeed; Southampton owes its position as a major port to the fact that it has four high tides a day, because of the influence of the Isle of Wight. The shape of the sea bottom also affects the shape of the tidal 'wave' as it approaches the coast. As the water gets shallower, the wave increases in height and gets steeper, so the tide rises more quickly than it falls.

Tidal definitions

The following terms to describe various levels that the water can reach are illustrated in Figure 4:

Lowest astronomical tide (LAT) The lowest level to which the tide can predictably fall. Atmospheric effects can sometimes give rise to a lower level (see below). LAT is frequently used as chart datum to which depths are referred.

Mean low water springs (MLWS) The average height, throughout the year, of two consecutive low waters at spring tides.

Mean low water neaps (MLWN) The average

height, throughout the year, of two consecutive low waters at neap tides.

Mean level (ML) The average level of the sea calculated from a long series of observations.

Mean high water neaps (MHWN) The average height, throughout the year, of two consecutive high waters at neap tides.

Mean high water The average height throughout the year of high water, sometimes used as the reference datum for charted heights.

Mean high water springs (MHWS) The average height, throughout the year, of two consecutive high waters at spring tides. Sometimes called the spring rise. Charted heights of objects on shore are often referred to MHWS.

Highest astronomical tide (HAT) The highest level to which the tide can predictably rise.

Height of the tide The height of the tide at any instant above chart datum.

Range of the tide The difference in height between the levels of successive high and low waters.

Equinoctal tides Spring tides which occur near the equinoxes, when the moon is closest to the earth. These spring tides are greater than average.

Drying height The height of an object covered at MHWS, above chart datum.

Charted sounding The depth of the bottom in a particular position below chart datum.

Meteorological effects

Unusual weather conditions can cause marked variations in the tide:

1) A high barometric pressure reduces the depth of water, and *vice versa*. A change of ten milibars causes an approximate change of 0.1 metre (4 in) in sea level (or a change of 1 in in barometric pressure causes a change of 1 ft in level).

2) A prevailing wind can cause changes in tidal level; an on-shore wind tends to increase levels, and an off-shore wind to depress them.

3) In some areas (e.g., the southern North Sea), a storm surge can occur. Some sudden change in conditions, such as the passage of a vigorous depression, can set up oscillations in sea level; if these oscillations coincide with the tidal wave, tides considerably greater or less than predicted can occur.

31.4 *The definition of tidal levels.*

32 Tidal predictions

Tidal heights can be predicted for any time where data is available. The necessary information is published in *Tide Tables*, issued by charting authorities and oceanographical institutes. Many local tide tables are also published by boatyards, yacht equipment suppliers and others; where these are soundly based on the proper predictions they are reliable enough, but they tend to be a mixed bag. Tidal information given in almanacs specially designed for small craft is thoroughly reliable. The *Tide Tables* used for illustration in this book are published by the (British) Hydrographer of the Navy (NP 201). They are issued annually in three volumes to cover the entire world. Tables 1, 2 and 3 are reproductions of parts of the tables in Volume 1, *European Waters*. Tidal publications vary widely in layout around the world, but are easy enough to follow with a little careful study.

In the tables, detailed information of the times and heights of high and low water for each day of the year is given for a series of standard ports (Table 1). A pair of curves is also given for each standard port, showing the way in which the tidal height varies with time at springs and at neaps. These curves are used in predicting the height of the tide at times between high and low water (Table 2). Other ports in the general area of the standard port are known as secondary ports. For these, differences in the time and height of the tide are given, to be applied to those for the standard port (Table 3).

Pacific ports In many Pacific secondary ports, where the tide is largely diurnal in character, the method of time and height differences cannot be used, and an alternative method is needed. Voyagers in these areas should consult the instructions in the *Tide Tables* (Volume 3).

Local time The time zone to which the entries are referred is given at the top of the page (GMT for Dover in Table 1). Many countries operate summer time, and a suitable correction must be applied to obtain local time.

Times and heights of high and low water – standard ports

This information can be read directly from the standard port tables.

For example: High and low waters at Dover on 16 May 1983

HW 0048 6.4 m
LW 0818 0.8 m
HW 1321 6.3 m
LW 2039 0.9 m
Range 6.4–0.8 = 5.6 m (Springs)

Times and heights of high and low water – secondary ports

1) Extract the times of high and low water for the standard port; subtract the height of LW from the height of HW to get the range.
2) From the secondary port table, extract the time correction for high water and for low water; these may require interpolation, according to the actual times of high and low water.
3) Also from the secondary port table, extract the height correction for high and for low water. The figures given are for springs and for neaps, and may require interpolation. The range of the tide obtained in step 1 can be compared with the mean spring and neap ranges given in Table 2 to decide whether it is springs, neaps, or in between.
4) Apply the corrections obtained to find the times and heights of the tides at the secondary port.

For example:
To find the times and heights of the first high and low waters at Deal on 20 May 1983

Dover	HW0452	5.5 m	LW1217	1.7 m	range 5.5 − 1.7
					= 3.8 m
Differences	+0018*	−0.3 m	+0009*	0.0 m	
Deal (GMT)	0510	5.2 m	1226	1.7 m	range 3.5 m

*Interpolated figures from Table 3

Intermediate times and heights – standard ports

The problem of finding intermediate times and heights of the tide can take one of two forms:

1) What will be the height of the tide at a particular time?
2) At what time will the height of the tide reach a particular value?

Both of these problems are handled in a similar way, using the tidal curves illustrated in Table 2.

Table 1 *Admiralty* Tide Tables – *standard port.*

ENGLAND, SOUTH COAST - DOVER

LAT 51°07′N   LONG 1°19′E

TIME ZONE **GMT**   TIMES AND HEIGHTS OF HIGH AND LOW WATERS   YEAR **1983**

MAY

Day	TIME	M	Day	TIME	M
1 SU	0112	6.4	**16** M	0048	6.4
	0833	1.0		0818	0.8
	1331	6.1		1321	6.3
	2044	1.2		2039	0.9
2 M	0145	6.1	**17** TU	0137	6.2
	0905	1.2		0903	1.0
	1406	5.9		1413	6.1
	2119	1.4		2128	1.1
3 TU	0222	5.7	**18** W	0234	6.0
	0941	1.6		0956	1.3
	1447	5.6		1508	5.9
	2159	1.8		2224	1.3
4 W	0310	5.3	**19** TH	0339	5.7
	1023	1.9		1059	1.6
	1542	5.3		1612	5.7
	2247	2.1		2333	1.5
5 TH	0420	5.0	**20** F	0452	5.5
	1115	2.2		1217	1.7
	1657	5.1		1726	5.6
	2350	2.2			
6 F	0550	4.8	**21** SA	0052	1.5
	1224	2.4		0624	5.5
	1817	5.1		1337	1.6
				1850	5.7
7 SA	0110	2.2	**22** SU	0212	1.3
	0702	5.0		0738	5.7
	1342	2.2		1451	1.4
	1920	5.3		1955	5.9
8 SU	0226	1.9	**23** M	0321	1.1
	0755	5.2		0833	6.0
	1449	1.9		1555	1.2
	2009	5.6		2047	6.2
9 M	0327	1.6	**24** TU	0421	0.9
	0836	5.6		0918	6.1
	1545	1.6		1649	1.1
	2051	6.0		2131	6.4
10 TU	0417	1.3	**25** W	0513	0.8
	0912	5.9		1000	6.3
	1635	1.3		1734	1.0
	2129	6.2		2213	6.5
11 W	0505	1.0	**26** TH	0556	0.8
	0949	6.2		1040	6.3
	1722	1.1		1811	1.0
	2206	6.4		2255	6.6
12 TH	0549	0.9	**27** F	0631	0.9
	1027	6.4		1120	6.4
	1804	0.9		1842	1.0
	2244	6.5		2336	6.5
13 F	0628	0.8	**28** SA	0702	0.9
	1106	6.5		1200	6.4
	1841	0.8		1913	1.0
	2322	6.6			

JUNE

Day	TIME	M	Day	TIME	M
1 W	0158	5.8	**16** TH	0236	6.2
	0917	1.5		1000	1.2
	1423	5.8		1500	6.2
	2138	1.6		2227	1.0
2 TH	0242	5.5	**17** F	0332	6.0
	0956	1.8		1059	1.3
	1510	5.6		1556	6.0
	2221	1.8		2327	1.2
3 F	0341	5.2	**18** SA	0435	5.8
	1041	2.0		1204	1.5
	1609	5.4		1659	5.9
	2313	2.0			
4 SA	0451	5.1	**19** SU	0035	1.3
	1137	2.2		0549	5.7
	1716	5.4		1310	1.6
				1810	5.8
5 SU	0017	2.0	**20** M	0144	1.3
	0600	5.1		0659	5.7
	1242	2.2		1418	1.6
	1821	5.4		1917	5.9
6 M	0126	1.9	**21** TU	0251	1.3
	0657	5.3		0759	5.8
	1349	2.0		1521	1.5
	1917	5.6		2016	6.0
7 TU	0230	1.7	**22** W	0352	1.3
	0748	5.5		0851	5.9
	1451	1.8		1616	1.4
	2005	5.9		2107	6.1
8 W	0329	1.4	**23** TH	0442	1.2
	0834	5.8		0939	6.1
	1550	1.5		1702	1.4
	2050	6.1		2153	6.3
9 TH	0426	1.2	**24** F	0526	1.2
	0918	6.1		1023	6.2
	1645	1.3		1742	1.3
	2134	6.3		2238	6.3
10 F	0516	1.0	**25** SA	0603	1.2
	1002	6.3		1104	6.3
	1736	1.1		1815	1.3
	2217	6.5		2319	6.3
11 SA	0603	0.9	**26** SU	0636	1.2
	1047	6.5		1143	6.3
	1822	0.9		1852	1.2
	2304	6.5		2358	6.3
12 SU	0648	0.8	**27** M	0710	1.2
	1136	6.6		1219	6.3
	1907	0.8		1928	1.2
	2351	6.5			
13 M	0730	0.8	**28** TU	0032	6.2
	1228	6.6		0745	1.2
	1952	0.8		1252	6.3
				2005	1.2

JULY

Day	TIME	M	Day	TIME	M
1 F	0218	5.8	**16** SA	0310	6.2
	0931	1.6		1045	1.2
	1440	5.9		1529	6.3
	2156	1.6		2309	1.1
2 SA	0305	5.6	**17** SU	0404	6.0
	1009	1.8		1134	1.5
	1528	5.8		1624	6.1
	2238	1.7			
3 SU	0402	5.4	**18** M	0003	1.3
	1054	1.9		0505	5.8
	1623	5.6		1229	1.7
	2329	1.9		1729	5.9
4 M	0502	5.3	**19** TU	0104	1.6
	1147	2.1		0615	5.6
	1722	5.6		1334	1.9
				1839	5.7
5 TU	0028	1.9	**20** W	0213	1.7
	0601	5.3		0726	5.6
	1250	2.1		1443	1.9
	1821	5.6		1948	5.7
6 W	0133	1.8	**21** TH	0319	1.7
	0659	5.5		0827	5.7
	1358	2.0		1545	1.8
	1919	5.8		2049	5.8
7 TH	0239	1.7	**22** F	0414	1.6
	0757	5.7		0921	5.9
	1507	1.8		1637	1.6
	2013	5.9		2141	6.0
8 F	0346	1.5	**23** SA	0502	1.5
	0851	5.9		1007	6.1
	1614	1.5		1720	1.5
	2107	6.1		2226	6.1
9 SA	0448	1.2	**24** SU	0542	1.4
	0943	6.2		1048	6.2
	1715	1.2		1800	1.4
	2200	6.3		2305	6.2
10 SU	0546	1.1	**25** M	0618	1.3
	1035	6.4		1125	6.3
	1810	1.0		1836	1.3
	2252	6.5		2340	6.2
11 M	0639	0.9	**26** TU	0655	1.3
	1127	6.6		1158	6.4
	1902	0.8		1914	1.2
	2344	6.6			
12 TU	0731	0.8	**27** W	0012	6.2
	1217	6.7		0730	1.2
	1951	0.7		1229	6.4
				1951	1.2
13 W	0038	6.6	**28** TH	0042	6.2
	0822	0.8		0804	1.3
	1306	6.7		1300	6.4
	2042	0.6		2026	1.2

AUGUST

Day	TIME	M	Day	TIME	M
1 M	0308	5.7	**16** TU	0423	5.7
	1013	1.8		1136	1.9
	1524	5.9		1649	5.8
	2244	1.7			
2 TU	0402	5.5	**17** W	0015	1.9
	1059	2.0		0533	5.4
	1619	5.7		1238	2.2
	2336	1.9		1805	5.5
3 W	0502	5.4	**18** TH	0127	2.1
	1157	2.1		0655	5.3
	1722	5.6		1401	2.2
				1926	5.4
4 TH	0041	2.0	**19**	0246	2.1
	0608	5.4		0806	5.5
	1310	2.2		1518	2.1
	1832	5.5		2034	5.5
5 F	0154	1.9	**20** SA	0350	1.9
	0721	5.5		0905	5.7
	1430	2.0		1616	1.8
	1945	5.7		2131	5.7
6 SA	0314	1.7	**21** SU	0441	1.7
	0834	5.8		0952	6.0
	1552	1.6		1704	1.6
	2053	5.9		2214	5.9
7 SU	0430	1.4	**22** M	0525	1.5
	0935	6.1		1030	6.2
	1659	1.3		1746	1.4
	2152	6.0		2249	6.1
8 M	0533	1.1	**23** TU	0604	1.4
	1027	6.5		1102	6.4
	1758	0.9		1824	1.2
	2244	6.5		2318	6.2
9 TU	0634	0.9	**24** W	0639	1.2
	1115	6.7		1133	6.5
	1855	0.7		1859	1.1
	2333	6.7		2346	6.3
10 W	0728	0.7	**25** TH	0712	1.2
	1200	6.9		1203	6.5
	1947	0.5		1933	1.1
11 TH	0022	6.8	**26** F	0014	6.3
	0818	0.6		0742	1.2
	1245	6.9		1232	6.5
	2034	0.4		2004	1.1
12 F	0109	6.7	**27** SA	0045	6.3
	0901	0.7		0809	1.2
	1330	6.9		1302	6.5
	2118	0.5		2032	1.1
13 SA	0155	6.6	**28** SU	0116	6.2
	0939	0.9		0836	1.3
	1413	6.7		1330	6.4
	2157	0.7		2058	1.2

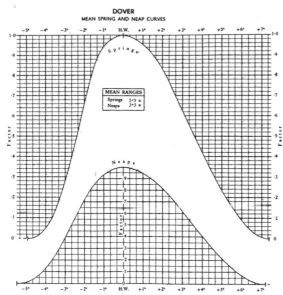

DOVER
MEAN SPRING AND NEAP CURVES

Table 2 *Admiralty* Tide Tables – *tidal curve, Dover*

1) Find the times and heights of the high and low waters either side of the time of interest, as described above. Subtract the LW height from the HW height to get the range of the tide.

2) *Case A* With the desired time as argument (related to the time of HW), find the corresponding factor. Use the spring or neap curve as appropriate, or if necessary use both curves and interpolate.

   Multiply the range of the tide (step 1) by the factor thus found, and add the result to the low water height. This is the height of the tide at the time chosen.

3) *Case B* Subtract the height of low water from the desired height, and divide the answer by the range, to establish the factor.

   Using this factor as argument, find the time (relative to HW) appropriate to it. There will in fact be two times, one for the rising tide and one for the falling tide. Choose whichever suits the case, and apply the result to the time of HW, to obtain the time required.

Note: If the tide happens to be greater than mean springs (or less than mean neaps), use the spring (or neap) factors.

   For example:

Case A What will be the height of the tide at Dover at 1115 GMT on 17 May 1983?

Dover LW 0903 1.0 m HW 1413 6.1 m range 5.1 m   (nearly springs)
Time required is 1115 GMT = 3 hours before HW Dover
Factor (from Table 2) = 0.28, so rise = 0.28 × 5.1 = 1.4 m
Tidal height at 1115 = 1.0 (LW height) + 1.4 = 2.4 m

Case B On 6th June 1983, at what time will the height of tide first rise to 3.5 metres at Dover?

Dover LW 0126 1.9 m HW 0657 5.3 m range 3.4 m   (neaps)
Height required = 3.5 m, so rise = 3.5 − 1.9 = 1.6 m
Factor = rise ÷ range = 1.6 ÷ 1.9 = 0.47 m
Interval (from Table 2) = 2 h 45 m before HW = 0412 GMT

Note: If this problem had specified a falling tide, this would have occurred 3 h 40 m after HW, or at 1037 GMT.

Intermediate times and heights – secondary ports

These are handled in exactly the same way as standard ports, but it is necessary to begin with tidal times, heights and range worked out for the secondary port. The tidal curve for the standard port is used to establish the factor.

Accuracy of tidal predictions

Whilst the basic predictions in the *Tide Tables* (particularly for standard ports) are generally very accurate, the effect of weather conditions can introduce considerable errors. Tidal figures should therefore not be regarded as particularly accurate, and a 95 per cent error of fifteen minutes (in time) and 0.5 m (1.6 feet) (in height) should not be thought unlikely. For smaller secondary ports, and in areas where the tide behaves curiously, the errors may be greater.

Reduction to soundings

When a sounding is taken, the depth actually measured will differ from the charted depth by the height of the tide; in order to compare the two, the sounding must be *reduced*. For this to be done, the height of the tide must be established at some point offshore. The range of the tide is smaller offshore

ENGLAND, SOUTH AND EAST COASTS

No.	PLACE	Lat. N.	Long. W.	TIME DIFFERENCES High Water (Zone G.M.T.)		Low Water		HEIGHT DIFFERENCES (IN METRES) MHWS	MHWN	MLWN	MLWS	M.L. Z0 m.	
81	**SHOREHAM**	(see page 18)		0500 and 1700	1000 and 2200	0000 and 1200	0600 and 1800	6·2	5·0	1·9	0·7		
75	Worthing	50 48	0 22	+0015	0000	+0010	−0005	−0·1	−0·2	0·0	0·0	⊙	
81	**SHOREHAM**	50 50	0 15	STANDARD PORT				See Table V				3·36	
82	Brighton	50 49	0 08	−0010	−0005	−0005	−0005	+0·3	+0·1	0·0	−0·1	3·49	
		N.	E.										
83	Newhaven	50 47	0 04	−0015	−0010	0000	0000	+0·4	+0·2	0·0	−0·2	3·61	
84	Eastbourne	50 46	0 17	−0010	−0005	+0015	+0020	+1·1	+0·6	+0·2	+0·1	3·77	
89	**DOVER**	(see page 22)		0000 and 1200	0600 and 1800	0100 and 1300	0700 and 1900	6·7	5·3	2·0	0·8		
85	Hastings	50 51	0 35	0000	−0010	−0030	−0030	+0·8	+0·5	+0·1	−0·1	3·85	
86	Rye (Approaches)	50 55	0 47	+0005	−0010	⊙	⊙	+1·0	+0·7	⊙	⊙	⊙	
86a	Rye (Harbour)	50 56	0 46	+0005	−0010	⊙	⊙	−1·4	−1·7	⊙	⊙	1·97	
87	Dungeness	50 54	0 58	−0010	−0015	−0020	−0010	+1·0	+0·5	+0·2	−0·1	4·03	
88	Folkestone	51 05	1 12	−0020	−0005	−0010	−0010	+0·4	+0·4	0·0	−0·1	3·74	
89	**DOVER**	51 07	1 19	STANDARD PORT				See Table V				3·70	
98	Deal	51 13	1 25	+0010	+0020	+0010	+0005	−0·6	−0·3	0·0	0·0	3·13	x
99	Richborough	51 18	1 21	+0015	+0015	+0030	+0030	−3·4	−2·6	−1·7	−0·7	1·42	c
102	Ramsgate	51 20	1 25	+0020	+0015	−0007	−0007	−1·8	−1·5	−0·8	−0·4	2·56	
103	**MARGATE**	(see page 26)		0100 and 1300	0700 and 1900	0100 and 1300	0700 and 1900	4·8	3·9	1·4	0·5		
102a	Broadstairs	51 21	1 27	−0020	−0008	+0007	+0010	−0·2	−0·2	−0·1	−0·1	⊙	
103	**MARGATE**	51 24	1 23	STANDARD PORT				See Table V				2·67	
104	Herne Bay	51 23	1 07	+0034	+0022	+0015	+0032	+0·4	+0·4	0·0	0·0	2·73	
105	Whitstable Approaches	51 22	1 02	+0042	+0029	+0025	+0050	+0·6	+0·6	+0·1	0·0	⊙	
108	**SHEERNESS**	(see page 30)		0200 and 1400	0800 and 2000	0200 and 1400	0700 and 1900	5·7	4·8	1·5	0·6		
	River Swale												
106	Grovehurst Jetty	51 22	0 46	−0007	0000	0000	+0016	0·0	0·0	0·0	−0·1	⊙	

Table 3 *Admiralty Tide Tables – secondary port differences.*

than it is on the coast, and to reduce soundings accurately a co-tidal chart is needed. For a rough rule of thumb, use three-quarters of the range within a few miles of the shore, and half the range further out. The *rule of twelfths* may be used to estimate heights between high and low water. This states that the tide will rise (or fall):

Range × one twelfth in the first hour

Range × two twelfths in the second hour
Range × three twelfths in the third and fourth hours

Range × two twelfths in the fifth hour
Range × one twelfth in the sixth hour.
Do not rely too heavily on the results.

Tables on pages 103, 104 and above reproduced from portions of ATT Vol. 1 with the sanction of the Controller, HM Stationery Office and of the Hydrographer of the Navy.

33   Tidal streams

Associated with the vertical rise and fall of the tides are horizontal movements of the water, known as *tidal streams*. Like the tides, they are of no significance in the deep oceans and become more significant as the coast is approached. Their strength depends very much upon the geography of the area, and in a few places can reach speeds of eight knots or more. They can also give rise to races, overfalls and bores (see below), and no craft, however large and powerful, can afford to ignore their effects.

Tidal streams, like the tides which give rise to them, are cyclic in nature; the water moves to and fro, but there is no net movement. Over a complete tide, the tidal streams cancel themselves out. Tidal streams take one of two main forms:

1) *Rectilinear*, in which the water flows in one direction for half the tide, and then reverses to flow in the opposite direction for the remaining half of the tide. The moment when the tidal stream stops and changes direction is known as *slack water*.

2) *Rotary*, in which the tidal stream constantly changes direction around the compass, often with no period of slack water.

Of these two types, rectilinear motion is most often found in narrow channels, estuaries, rivers and straits; rotary motion is generally to be found in open seas and wide bays.

Tidal streams are greatly affected by the detailed geography of the area, including the sea bed. In their turn, tidal streams can also affect the sea state; when wind and tide oppose each other, the sea becomes shorter, higher and more confused than it would otherwise be, and may be dangerous to small craft. The major tidal stream effects that the navigator should look for, to use to his advantage or to avoid, are:

1) A tidal stream flowing parallel to an indented coast can often be worked to advantage. The tidal stream runs more strongly past headlands, and less strongly within bays (Fig. 1). The tidal stream tends to set into and out of a bay, and there may be a back eddy in the tidal lee of a headland.

2) An irregular bottom or a shoal or shelf can deflect a tidal stream upwards, causing an area of disturbed seas, known as an *overfall*. In strong wind-against-tide situations, these areas can be dangerous (Fig. 2).

3) If a tidal stream is forced through a narrow channel, its speed increases dramatically, leading to a *race* (Fig. 3). If a race can be carried in calm weather, it can give a boat a very useful lift; passage against the tidal stream may be literally impossible. Because of the difficult seas caused by a race, they should be avoided, whichever way they are running, in bad weather.

4) In some rivers with narrow channels, the new flood in the lower reaches can fight with the old ebb still running further up. Eventually the flood wins, and sends a wave, known as a *bore*, surging up the river; this can be dangerous. The River Severn has perhaps the best-known example of a bore.

5) When a tidal stream flows through a channel fringed by wide, flat mud- or sand-banks, there is a tendency for the water to set onto the banks at the flood, and off the banks on the ebb (Fig. 4). This can be important for a yacht going out against the flood; if it hugs one bank to keep in shallow water (and hence less tidal stream), it might be set onto the bank and aground.

6) Areas where tidal streams converge or diverge (as at the junctions of rivers or estuaries) can lead to unpredictable tidal streams and confused seas.

Predicting tidal streams

In most parts of the world, tidal streams can be related to the tide at a nearby standard port. Slack water will be related to high water at the port, though generally the two times will not be the same; tidal streams tend to run a little longer (up to three hours) after the time of high water on the adjacent coast. For most areas it is possible to produce chartlets or tables of tidal streams, related to high water at a suitable standard port, and this is the method most often adopted. There are a few areas where this is not possible (for example, the Straits of Malacca), and special arrangements have to be made.

33.1 *Tidal streams along a coast.*

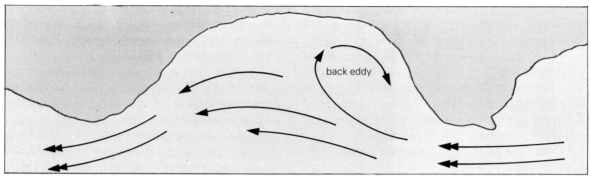

33.2 *Overfalls.*

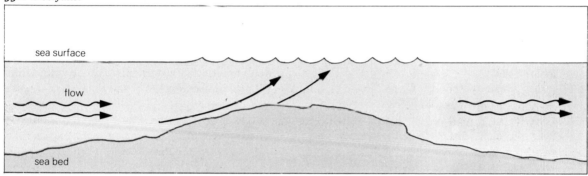

33.3 *A race.*

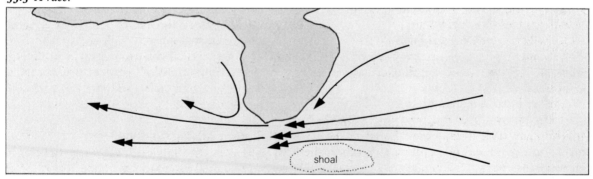

33.4 *Tidal streams setting across banks: (a) on the flood; (b) on the ebb.*

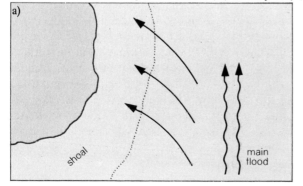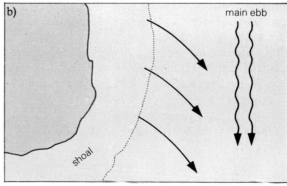

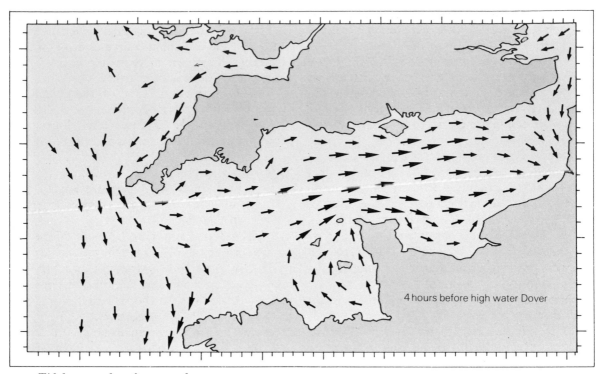

4 hours before high water Dover

33.5 *Tidal stream chart from an atlas.*

Table 1 *Extract from NOS* Tidal Current Tables.

TABLE 2. – CURRENT DIFFERENCES AND OTHER CONSTANTS, 1983

NO.	PLACE	METER DEPTH	POSITION		TIME DIFFERENCES				SPEED RATIOS		AVERAGE SPEEDS AND DIRECTIONS							
			Lat.	Long.	Min. before Flood	Flood	Min. before Ebb	Ebb	Flood	Ebb	Minimum before Flood		Maximum Flood		Minimum before Ebb		Maximum Ebb	
		ft	° ' N	° ' W	h. m.	h. m.	h. m.	h. m.			knots deg.		knots deg.		knots deg.		knots deg.	
	LONG ISLAND SOUND Time meridian, 75°W				on THE RACE, p.34													
	Connecticut River																	
2551	Lynde Point, channel east of........		41 16	72 20	+0 42	+0 50	+0 18	+0 29	0.3	0.2	0.0	- -	0.9	344	0.0	- -	0.7	161
2556	Saybrook Point, 0.2 mile northeast of		41 17.02	72 20.87	+0 35	+0 51	+0 47	+0 30	0.5	0.4	0.0	- -	1.5	355	0.0	- -	1.5	160
2561	Railroad drawbridge.................	15	41 19.00	72 20.77	+0 27	-0 26	+0 54	+1 06	0.4	0.3	0.0	- -	1.0	360	0.0	- -	1.0	198
						+0 35			0.2				0.6	359				
						+1 31			0.3				0.9	356				
2566	Eustasia Island, 0.6 mile ESE of.....		41 23.30	72 24.23	+1 53	+1 38	+1 23	+1 26	0.4	0.4	0.0	- -	1.1	290	0.0	- -	1.4	070
2571	Eddy Rock Shoal, west of............	15	41 26.57	72 27.78	+1 41	+2 16	+2 01	+1 20	0.3	0.2	0.0	- -	0.8	350	0.0	- -	0.6	155
2576	Higganum Creek, 0.5 mile ESE of......		41 30.02	72 32.62	+3 06	+2 52	+2 35	+3 01	0.3	0.3	0.0	- -	0.8	270	0.0	- -	1.0	080
2581	Wilcox Island Park, east of.........		41 34.33	72 38.88	+4 06	+3 36	+3 07	+3 35	0.3	0.3	0.0	- -	0.9	355	0.0	- -	1.0	160
2586	Rocky Hill......	9	41 39.82	72 37.73	+4 41	+3 37	+3 21	+3 30	0.2	0.2	0.0	- -	0.6	335	0.0	- -	0.8	135
2591	Hartford Jetty <42>.................	9	41 45.07	72 39.02	+5 45	+4 39	+3 22	+4 29	0.0	0.2	0.0	- -	0.1	290	0.0	- -	0.7	095
2596	Saybrook Breakwater, 1.5 miles SE of....		41 14.78	72 19.05	-1 30	-1 11	-0 55	-1 57	0.7	0.6	0.0	- -	1.9	260	0.0	- -	2.0	070
2601	Mulford Point, 3.1 miles northwest of	15	41 12.00	72 19.08	-0 06	-1 05	-0 05	-0 24	0.7	0.6	0.0	- -	1.9	269	0.0	- -	2.3	066
2606	Orient Point, 1 mile WNW of..........		41 10.02	72 15.11	-1 09	-2 02	-0 33	-1 15	0.5	0.9	0.0	- -	1.4	245	0.0	- -	3.1	055
						-0 59			0.3				0.8	255				
						-0 09			0.7				2.1	245				
2611	Rocky Point, 0.3 mile north of........	15	41 08.63	72 21.42	-0 27	-1 02	-1 01	-0 28	0.6	0.6	0.0	- -	1.8	279	0.0	- -	2.1	041
2616	Cornfield Point, 3 miles south of.......	7	41 12.9	72 22.4	-0 56	-0 17	-0 03	-0 20	0.6	0.4	0.0	- -	2.0	256	0.0	- -	1.7	094
2621	Cornfield Point, 1.1 miles south of.....	15	41 14.65	72 23.40	-1 01	-1 34	-1 02	-2 03	0.5	0.5	0.0	- -	1.4	293	0.0	- -	1.6	108
2626	Kesley Point, 2.1 miles southeast of.....		41 14.10	72 27.93	-0 35	-1 02	-0 54	-1 00	0.5	0.5	0.0	- -	1.5	260	0.0	- -	1.8	070
2631	Six Mile Reef, 1.5 miles north of......		41 12.66	72 28.87	-0 17	-0 12	-0 23	-0 41	0.3	0.4	0.0	- -	1.0	290	0.0	- -	1.3	095
2636	Six Mile Reef, 2 miles east of.........		41 10.83	72 26.90	-0 36	-0 12	-0 07	-0 35	0.6	0.6	0.0	- -	1.6	235	0.0	- -	2.1	040
2641	Horton Point, 1.4 miles NNW of........		41 06.30	72 27.40	+0 04	+0 08	-0 03	-0 18	0.5	0.6	0.0	- -	1.4	260	0.0	- -	2.0	040
2646	Kelsey Point, 1 mile south of..........		41 14	72 30	-1 32	-1 00	-1 03	-1 51	0.6	0.3	0.0	- -	2.0	249	0.0	- -	1.5	118
2651	Hammonasset Point, 1.2 miles SW of.....	15	41 14.22	72 34.00	-0 59	-1 15	-0 44	-1 31	0.3	0.4	0.0	- -	1.0	287	0.0	- -	1.0	106
2656	Hammonasset Point, 5 miles south of....		41 09.80	72 34.17	-0 03	-0 03	-0 24	-0 06	0.5	0.4	0.0	- -	1.4	284	0.0	- -	1.5	090
2661	Mattituck Inlet, 1 mile northwest of....	15	41 01.68	72 34.22	-0 21	-0 15	-0 08	-0 26	0.3	0.3	0.0	- -	0.9	241	0.0	- -	1.0	053
2666	Sachem Head, 1 mile SSE of...........		41 13.65	72 42.30	-0 38	-0 36	-0 35	-1 02	0.4	0.4	0.0	- -	1.1	255	0.0	- -	1.0	065
2671	Sachem Head 6.2 miles south of.......	15	41 08.73	72 42.30	+0 29	+0 24	-0 12	-0 04	0.2	0.3	0.0	- -	0.6	260	0.0	- -	0.9	065
2676	Roanoke Point, 5.6 miles north of......	15	41 04.37	72 42.53	-0 02	-0 02	-0 15	-0 24	0.2	0.2	0.0	- -	0.7	255	0.0	- -	0.9	050
2681	Roanoke Point, 2.3 miles NNW of.......		41 00.92	72 42.97	-1 19	-0 22	-0 10	-0 29	0.3	0.2	0.0	- -	0.9	270	0.0	- -	0.7	070
2686	Sachem Head, 1 mile south of..........		41 14	72 43	-0 46	+0 03	-0 33	-0 38	0.3	0.3	0.0	- -	0.9	278	0.0	- -	1.2	084
2691	Herod Point, 2.8 miles north of........	15	41 00.97	72 49.93	-0 29	-0 17	-0 27	-0 06	0.2	0.2	0.1	020	0.4	290	0.1	020	0.6	090
2696	Herod Point, 6.5 miles north of........	15	41 04.65	72 49.80	-0 27	+0 06	+0 12	-0 07	0.3	0.2	0.0	- -	0.9	254	0.0	- -	0.7	070
2701	New Haven Harbor entrance <12>......		41 14	72 55	-1 11	-1 34	-0 37	-1 15	0.4	0.2	0.0	- -	1.4	319	0.0	- -	0.9	152
2706	City Point, 1.3 miles northeast of......		41 17.83	72 54.42	+0 11	+0 30	+0 33	+0 08	0.1	0.1	0.0	- -	0.3	015	0.0	- -	0.4	215
2711	Oyster River Pt., 1.3 miles SSE of <1>..		41 12.87	72 58.00	- - -	-0 15	- - -	-0 47	0.1	0.1	0.0	- -	0.3	255	0.0	- -	0.3	060
2716	Pond Point, 4.2 miles SSE of..........		41 08.60	72 58.08	-0 20	+0 04	-0 04	-0 14	0.2	0.2	0.0	- -	0.6	265	0.0	- -	0.6	065
2721	Stratford Shoal, 6 miles east of.......		41 04.52	72 58.43	+0 01	-0 02	-0 07	-0 09	0.2	0.2	0.0	- -	0.6	265	0.0	- -	0.6	060
2726	Sound Beach, 2.2 miles north of........		41 00.33	72 58.45	-0 03	-0 06	-0 15	-0 25	0.3	0.3	0.0	- -	0.9	270	0.0	- -	0.9	075
2731	Charles Island, 0.8 mile SSE of.......		41 10.77	73 02.63	-0 15	-0 36	-0 30	-0 54	0.1	0.1	0.0	- -	0.4	250	0.0	- -	0.4	070
	Housatonic River																	
2736	Milford Point, 0.2 mile west of......	10	41 10.35	73 06.82	-0 06	+0 01	+0 15	-0 55	0.4	0.3	0.0	- -	1.2	330	0.0	- -	1.2	135
2741	Railroad drawbridge, above..........	5	41 12.53	73 06.67	+0 34	+0 13	+0 29	-0 55	0.4	0.4	0.0	- -	1.1	350	0.0	- -	1.3	185
2746	Fowler Island, 0.1 mile NNW of......	5	41 14.40	73 06.23	+0 48	+0 10	+0 30	+0 48	0.4	0.4	0.0	- -	1.1	040	0.0	- -	1.1	270

Endnotes can be found at the end of Table 2.

Having established the time of high water at the appropriate standard port, there are two ways of finding the tidal stream at any location:

1) By using a *Tidal Stream Atlas*, which gives a chartlet for each hour of the tide, with arrows showing the direction and numbers giving the spring and neap rate of the tidal stream (Fig. 5). Similar chartlets are printed in many yachting almanacs.

2) The chart of the area may also carry tidal stream information, either in the form of a table giving rates and directions for certain positions, or by means of feathered arrows (on older charts). When using a table, the navigator should not forget that the directions given refer to the true compass (not the magnetic). Two rates are given, for springs and neaps, and interpolation should be used if required.

3) Some charting authorities publish tidal stream or tidal current tables, rather than atlases.

Tidal stream estimates from any source should be made as carefully as possible, interpolating if required.

Accuracy of tidal stream predictions

However carefully tidal stream predictions are made, the only thing that can be said about them with confidence is that they will be wrong. In tidal waters, errors in estimating tidal stream are without doubt the dominant source of error in dead reckoning. There are three main reasons for the poor quality of the predictions:

1) The information upon which the predictions are based is very much more sparse than the information used for *Tide Tables*. It generally relates to one short period of time which may not be typical.

2) The predictions are only accurate (!) for the exact position in which they were made; a position only a few metres away may experience a different tidal stream.

3) Tidal streams appear to be more affected by meteorological effects than the actual tide itself.

The navigator should always be aware that his tidal stream estimates may be grossly in error, and he should always try to check them. Passing close to a navigational buoy, an anchored fishing boat or a fishing float can give a valuable clue; on a cross-tide leg, a back bearing of the mark just left can show if the tidal stream is being under- or overestimated (it seems a fact of life that underestimation is much more common); or a careful comparison of a fix with the estimated position may show that something is wrong.

34 Medium frequency direction finding

Medium frequency direction finding (MFDF) is by far the most important radio aid to navigation for the yachtsman. Although the accuracy is generally poor, the equipment required can be relatively cheap and easy to use, and there are generally enough radio beacons in well-travelled areas to provide useful position lines.

MFDF is used in two principal ways; as the radio waves employed follow the curvature of the earth, they can be received at a considerable distance (200 miles or more in some circumstances), and so form a useful landfall aid. Secondly, as radio waves are relatively little affected by the weather they can provide positional information in poor visibility.

Principles

MFDF equipment consists of a suitable receiver in the ship, connected to an antenna with directional properties. The principle of such an antenna is shown in Figure 1; when the antenna (which often consists of a coil of wire wound around a ferrite rod) is pointing directly towards the transmitter, the signal received is at a minimum, and when the antenna is rotated through a right angle, the received signal is at a maximum. A bearing of the transmitter is taken by rotating the antenna until a minimum (a null) is found, and noting the direction in which the antenna is pointing. As the antenna has a directional response resembling a figure-eight, the bearing obtained is ambiguous; to put it simply, the simple MFDF antenna does not tell you if the transmitter is in front of you or behind you. This 180° ambiguity is known as the *sense ambiguity*. In most circumstances it will cause the navigator no difficulty, but various means are available for its resolution (see below).

34.1 *A directional antenna.*

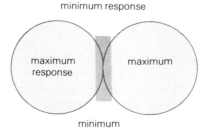

minimum response

maximum response | maximum

minimum

Most MFDF antennae for the yacht market are of this simple type, generally with a magnetic compass attached to allow the direct reading of magnetic bearings (Fig. 2). More expensive equipment can offer improved facilities. A sense antenna may be fitted to provide a way of resolving the sense ambiguity described above, and an array of two loops at right angles to each other can be used to indicate bearings automatically, with the sense ambiguity resolved; such an automatic direction finder (ADF) can offer a very much improved performance, but with a substantial cost and space penalty.

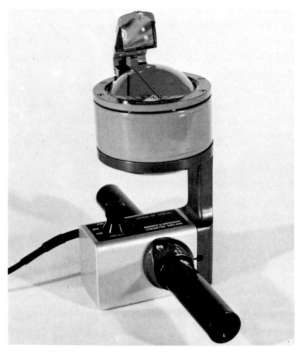

34.2 *MFDF antenna with compass.*

Receivers for use with MFDF antennae must be properly designed for the purpose; they must be fitted with quick and accurate means of tuning to the frequency of the desired beacon; they must have good selectivity and sensitivity to pick out a weak beacon signal in the presence of interference; and certain types of radio beacon require the use of a device within the receiver known as a beat frequency oscillator (BFO).

The actual procedure for taking radio bearings will vary according to the equipment in use. The manufacturers instructions should be followed carefully; the successful use of MFDF equipment depends very much upon experience, and every opportunity should be taken to practice.

Radio beacons
In principle, radio bearings can be taken of any radio transmission that the MFDF set is capable of receiving; in practice, almost all radio bearings are taken of specially established transmitters known as radiobeacons. It is sometimes also possible to take bearings of broadcast transmitters carrying entertainment programmes.

Marine radiobeacons
Marine radiobeacons are established by lighthouse authorities around the coast, especially for use by mariners. They are generally established at lighthouses, on lightships or at other positions of navigational importance. The details of each beacon are listed in the appropriate *List of Radio Signals* (*Light List* in the USA). It is common practice to group together a number of beacons in the same area onto a common frequency; each beacon in the group will transmit at a different time, to allow several bearings of different beacons to be obtained without having to re-tune the receiver. Marine radio-beacons generally operate on a six-minute cycle, with each beacon occupying one minute of the cycle. The *sequence number* of the beacon indicates which slot it occupies in each cycle; Table 1 translates the sequence number into the actual time (minutes past each hour) that each beacon transmits. Some modern MFDF sets incorporate a clock which keeps track of the current sequence number, but this should never be used as the sole means of identification; the Morse identification transmitted by the beacon should always be checked before using a bearing.

Aero radiobeacons
Radiobeacons are widely used by aircraft, and suitably sited aero radiobeacons can be useful at sea; details of such beacons are given in the *List of Radio Signals* (*Light List* in the USA). Aero beacons are generally powerful, and each one operates continuously on its own frequency.

Aeromarine radiobeacons
Aeromarine beacons are established in areas where radio aids tend to be few and far between, and are designed to suit the needs both of the seaman and the aviator. They generally have similar characteristics to aero radiobeacons.

Broadcast transmitters
It is sometimes possible to use broadcast transmitters for radio bearings, but there are difficulties. One of these is the problem of finding out exactly where the transmitter is sited; this information is not easy to obtain and transmitters can be sited at some distance from the studios which originate the broadcast.

34.3 *Synchronized broadcast transmitters.*

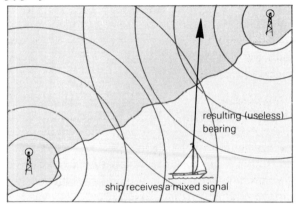

resulting (useless) bearing

ship receives a mixed signal

A more fundamental difficulty arises with the growing practice of synchronizing transmitters to improve the coverage of broadcast stations. This means that two or more transmitters carry the same programme on the same frequency. If any attempt is made to take a bearing, then part of the signal may come from one transmitter and part from another; the resulting bearing will be seriously in error (Fig. 3). However, the powerful signal from a broadcast transmitter can be very useful if it is known not to be synchronized (e.g., when situated on an island or in some other remote area of population).

Table 1 *Sequence numbers and times of marine radiobeacons*

Sequence	Time (minutes past the hour)									
1	00	06	12	18	24	30	36	42	48	54
2	01	07	13	19	25	31	37	43	49	55
3	02	08	14	20	26	32	38	44	50	56
4	03	09	15	21	27	33	39	45	51	57
5	04	10	16	22	28	34	40	46	52	58
6	05	11	17	23	29	35	41	47	53	59

35   Taking MFDF bearings

The actual process of taking MFDF bearings will vary according to the equipment being used; however, the following sequence illustrates the process for the most common type of equipment – the hand-held antenna with magnetic compass attached.

1) From the chart, identify suitable radio-beacons in the vicinity of the DR position.
2) From the *List of Radio Signals* (or other suitable document), extract the following information (Table 1):
   a) The frequency of the beacon
   b) The Morse identification code
   c) The sequence number
   d) The maximum range
   e) The mode of emission (A1, A2, A2* etc).
3) When possible, choose beacons which are close to your position; in any event, do not use beacons beyond their listed maximum range.
4) Tune the receiver (and, if necessary, the antenna) to the given frequency, and adjust the set in accordance with the mode of emission. The maker's handbook will explain how to do this.
5) Listen for the beacon at the time indicated by its sequence number; move the antenna about and adjust the tuning if necessary to get a clear signal.
6) Make a positive identification of the beacon by reading the Morse identity code transmitted several times at the beginning of its sequence.
7) When the beacon transmits a long dash, turn the antenna until the signal goes through a minimum (a null). This null is best detected by ear, but some sets provide a meter indication and/or a dimming light as well.
8) Move the antenna through the null several times, and observe the compass reading of the minimum signal. If the null is diffuse or difficult to detect, the resulting bearing should be used with caution.
9) Re-check the identification at the end of the sequence.
10) Plot the resulting position line; if taking bearings at long range, apply the half-convergency correction (see below). This is not necessary for bearings of beacons within 50 miles.

Sense ambiguity

With simple equipment, there is no way of resolving the sense ambiguity within the set itself, so that bearings may be wrong by 180°. In most situations, no ambiguity exists; for a beacon on the coast, the reciprocal bearing probably lies inland, for example. However, where doubt exists, as in Figure 1, two steps may be taken to resolve it:

1) An unambiguous bearing of another radio-beacon may indicate which of the two reciprocal bearings is correct.
2) Otherwise, a second bearing of the original beacon should be taken after sufficient time for the bearing to have made a noticeable change. The sense in which the bearing has changed, clockwise or anticlockwise, will always allow you to decide on which side of the beacon you lie.

Automatic direction finding

ADF equipment will automatically swing to the bearing of the beacon, with sense ambiguities resolved, as soon as the beacon begins to transmit (the reading may be unsteady during the Morse identification). ADF sets are normally very easy to use, but two cautions should be observed:

1) As with all MFDF bearings, it is vital to identify the beacon by means of its Morse identification.
2) An ADF will indicate a bearing of the beacon relative to the ship's head. This relative bearing must be added to or subtracted from the magnetic ship's head to obtain a magnetic bearing to plot on the chart.

Errors in MFDF

Whilst MFDF is an invaluable aid for yachts, it is subject to numerous (and sometimes large) errors. These errors must be properly understood if MFDF is to become a trusted tool in the navigator's box of tricks.

Systematic errors

1) *DF compass deviations*. If the MFDF set has a magnetic compass attached, this can suffer from deviations, like any other compass. In wood, glass fibre or aluminium boats, it should be possible to find, by experiment, locations where the DF compass is not deviated; look out

RADIOBEACONS AND RADIO DIRECTION–FINDING STATIONS

(Atlantic Coast) UNITED STATES

RC	**Highland Lt, Cape Cod**[1]				42°02′23″N	70°03′43″W	**5849**
	286	A2*					

No	Name	Ident	Range	Seq	Fog	Clear
5849	Highland Lt	**HI**	100	1	Cont	Cont
5841	Nantucket Sh	**NS**	100	2	Cont	Cont
5779	Montauk Pt	**Y**	20	3	Cont	Cont
5747	Ambrose	**T**	125	4	Cont	Cont
5893	Great Duck I	**GD**	50	5	Cont	Cont
5885	Manana I	**MI**	100	6	Cont	Cont

1) Located 352° 52m from the Lt

RC	**Cape Cod Canal Breakwater**[1]				41°46′29″N	70°29′51″W	**5853**
	U	318	A2*	20 n miles	H24		

1) Located 224° 815 m from Lt J0372

RC Marker	**Scituate Harbour**				42°12′00″N	70°43′12″W	**5855**
	SH	295	A2*	10 n miles			

RC	**Boston Lt Buoy B**				42°22′40″N	70°47′00″W	**5857**
	BH	304	A2*	30 n miles	H24		

Aero RC	**Lynnfield**				42°27′08″N	70°57′50″W	**5861**
	SEW	382	A2*	100 n miles	H24		

RC	**Eastern Point Lt, Gloucester Harbour**				42°34′49″N	70°39′54″W	**5865**
	EP	325	A2*	10 n miles	H24		

RC	**Portland Lt Buoy P**				43°31′36″N	70°05′30″W	**5869**
	PH	301	A2*	30 n miles	H24		

RC	**Halfway Rock Lt**				43°39′20″N	70°02′15″W	**5877**
	HR	291	A2*	10 n miles	H24		

RC Marker	**The Cuckolds Lt**				43°46′46″N	69°39′02″W	**5881**
	CU	320	A2*	10 n miles	H24		

RC	**Manana Island Fog Signal Station**				43°45′48″N	69°19′38″W	**5885**
	MI—Grouped with 5849						

RC	**Matinicus Rock Lt**				43°47′00″N	68°51′22″W	**5889**
	MR	314	A2*	20 n miles	H24		

Table 1 *Extract from* List of Radio Signals (Light List).

for instruments, radios, cameras or other magnetic equipment. The hand-held type of MFDF equipment can only be used with difficulty in steel or concrete boats; the crossed-loop type of set is much more satisfactory.

2) *Siting error.* A relatively small error may be introduced by the actual siting of the aerial within the vessel. This error is generally unimportant, and can be minimized by placing the aerial on the centreline of the ship.

3) *Quadrantal error.* This is the most important of the systematic errors of MFDF, and arises because some of the structure of the boat itself can act as an aerial, causing a distortion of the incoming signal from the beacon. It is called quadrantal error, because it does not affect signals coming from the bow or the stern, or from either beam. The error is at a maximum for signals on either bow or either quarter (Fig. 2). Quadrantal error can be minimized by making sure there are no continuous loops of metal around the boat; guardrails are the most common offenders, and the loop should be broken by insulators or a rope lanyard in at least two places.

Simple hand-held equipment does not permit the correction of these systematic errors. They should be minimized by careful siting of the set,

35.1 *Resolving sense ambiguity.*

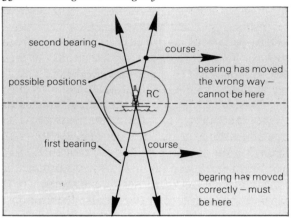

and the errors measured by 'swinging' the MFDF; this involves comparing MFDF bearings of a suitable beacon with visual bearings taken at the same time. A correction table can then be drawn up.

Random errors

1) *Night effect* Radio waves from a beacon may reach the receiving antenna by two paths – the ground wave which follows the surface of the earth, or the sky wave which is reflected from the ionosphere. The reception of sky wave signals can cause substantial errors in MFDF bearings. The effect of sky waves on MFDF are most marked at night, and especially within two hours of sunset or sunrise. Sky wave effects can often be detected by erratic and fluttering signals and a poor null. Such bearings should be used cautiously (if at all), and bearings close to sunrise or sunset should be avoided altogether.

2) *Land effect* The velocity of a radio wave depends to some extent on the nature of the surface over which it travels. This has the effect of causing the wave to be refracted where it passes from land to sea (Fig. 3). The angle of refraction is zero for a wave that crosses the coast at right angles, and can be six or seven degrees for a wave crossing at a grazing angle (the refraction is always towards the land). Marine radiobeacons are normally sited in such a way that land effects are unimportant, but aero or aero-marine beacons may not be. Similar effects may

be seen with radio waves that have to cross mountains between the transmitter and the receiver.

Random errors in MFDF can be very large – six or seven degrees for land effect and tens of degrees for night effect. Land effect can usually be avoided by choosing beacons which do not have to cross land on their way to your antenna; night effect can almost always be detected by the poor quality of the null. This is why it is better to detect the null by ear rather than by a meter or lamp.

The 95 per cent error of a properly installed and calibrated MFDF set will probably be of the order of 5° in good conditions, 10° in moderate conditions and 15° (or more) in bad conditions.

35.2 *Quadrantal error.*

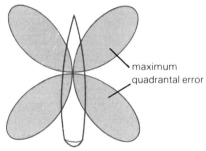

Half convergency

Radio waves follow a great circle path, and as is shown on page 15, a great circle and a rhumb line (line of constant bearing) do not in general coincide. To obtain the compass bearing of a distant MFDF station, a correction must be applied to the measured bearing; this correction is called the *half convergency*. It can be computed with a calculator by using the equation ($\frac{1}{2}$d. long sin [mid lat]), or the table on page 191 may be used. Half convergency is always applied towards the equator. It need not be applied for beacons less than 50 miles away, or for a beacon which lies almost due north or south.

35.3 *Coastal refraction.*

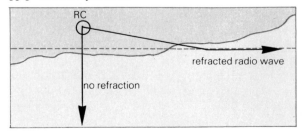

36 The principles of radar

Radar is a method of using radio waves to detect distant objects and displaying their position relative to the radar-equipped vessel on a display screen. It will work equally well by day or by night, in clear weather or in fog, but large seas or heavy rain or snow may affect its performance. In merchant ships, radar has become an indispensable aid to navigation and collision avoidance; the less elaborate sets suitable for fitting in yachts offer a much reduced, but still useful, performance.

A radar set works by transmitting short, powerful pulses of radio energy from a directional antenna. When these pulses, moving away at the speed of light, strike a solid object, part of the energy is reflected back towards the transmitter. A receiving antenna detects the very small returning signal, called for obvious reasons an 'echo'. The range of the reflecting object can be calculated by the time interval between the transmitted pulse and the returning echo, using the fact that radio waves travels at about 162,000 nautical miles a second; the direction of the reflecting object is given by the direction in which the transmitting and receiving antennae are pointing. These antennae (which may be combined in one antenna) are caused to rotate (Fig. 1).

36.1 *Principles of radar.*

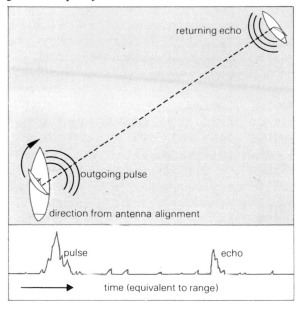

A typical small radar set will operate at 10,000 MHz, which corresponds to a wavelength of three centimetres (one and a quarter inches). The transmitted pulse will have a power of between three and ten kW, but will last for less than a microsecond (one millionth of a second); the pulses will be repeated about 1,000 or 2,000 times a second. At the same time, the antenna array rotates at twenty or thirty revolutions per minute. The maximum range of the set will be sixteen miles or more, but the range at which any particular object will be detected depends upon its size, the material from which it is made and its height above sea level; the height of the radar antenna is also an important factor in detection range.

The received echoes are displayed on a screen known as a plan position indicator (PPI). A radial line, known as a trace, rotates around the screen in synchronism with the antennae; a returning echo causes the trace to brighten at a distance from the centre which is proportional to the range of the object, causing a bright mark (or 'paint') on the screen. As the aerials (and the trace) sweep round, a picture of detectable objects is built up, rather like a map centred on the ship's position.

The bearing of an object can be measured by means of a radial cursor and a scale around the edge of the PPI; range can either be estimated using fixed 'range rings' at known increments of range, or measured more exactly by means of a unit which produces a variable range ring under the operator's control. When the range ring is moved to coincide with an object, its range can be read on a display attached to the unit.

Adjustment of a radar set

Each make or model of radar has its own procedures for switching on and adjustment, and these will be described in detail in the maker's handbook. For best results, you should follow the maker's instructions carefully; however, the following general points may be of some help in getting a good picture.

1) *Brightness* As its name suggests, this controls the brightness of the picture; it should be set so that the picture is clear, but without any tendency to smear across the screen.

2) *Gain* This controls the sensitivity of the receiver. If it is set too low, echoes will be lost

because the receiver misses them; if set too high, echoes can be obscured or lost in excessive 'noise' (a speckled effect on the screen). A suitable setting of the gain control is one which just leaves faint speckling on the screen.

3) *Tuning* Like any other receiver, the radar receiver must be tuned to the correct frequency. If it is not, echoes may be lost. The tuning control should be varied until maximum response is apparent on the PPI.

4) *Sea clutter* This control is designed to minimize the effect of waves close to the ship, which 'clutter' the centre of the screen with a host of unwanted echoes. The sea clutter control reduces the gain of the receiver at short ranges, without affecting the gain at longer ranges. It should only be used when necessary, and even then it should be used with care; too much control can cause small echoes nearby, such as navigational buoys and other yachts, to be lost.

5) *Rain clutter* Heavy rain, snow or hail, and sometimes storm clouds, can show up on the PPI as blotches with soft edges, rather like cotton wool in appearance. The rain clutter control can be used to help reveal small echoes which might otherwise be obscured. It should be adjusted to give best results, and turned off when not in use

Factors affecting radar detection range

The range at which any particular object will be detected by a radar set depends upon a number of factors:

1) *Antenna height* As radar waves travel in straight lines, a high antenna has a more distant radar horizon than one low down; when installing a set, the antenna should be mounted as high as topweight and other considerations permit.

2) *Transmitter power* Greater power in the transmitted pulse will lead to stronger echoes and hence longer detection ranges, but the power of most radars is adequate for the purpose for which they are intended.

3) *Receiver sensitivity* The inherent sensitivity of any radar receiver is adequate, but will only be achieved if the various controls, especially gain and tuning, are properly adjusted.

4) *Target height* A high target, such as a cliff, will

be picked up at a longer range than a low one, because the radar energy can see it further round the curvature of the earth (Fig. 2).

5) *Target size* A big target will reflect more energy than a small one, and hence will be detected at a greater range.

6) *Target material* Some materials reflect radar energy better than others; steel and stone reflect well, wood, fibreglass and sand reflect badly. It is possible to enhance the echo of an object by fitting a *radar reflector* (Fig. 3); this is often done to navigational buoys, and a radar reflector is an essential piece of safety equipment for the small yacht, especially if made of wood or fibreglass.

7) *Atmospheric conditions* Heavy rain and high seas can both cause clutter on the screen which obscures echoes; the proper adjustment of the clutter controls will reduce this problem, but not cure it entirely. Another atmospheric effect which can occur (though very rarely) is anomalous propagation, in which the radar waves travel very much further round the curvature of the earth than normal, leading to unusually

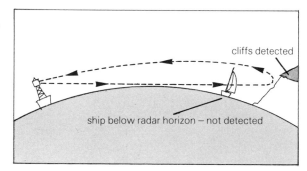

36.2 *Effect of target height.*

long range detection of large targets such as land.

All these various factors are combined into Table 1, which gives typical figures of performance for a yacht radar in proper adjustment and under good conditions. These figures are only representative, and wide variations may be found in practice; however, they may serve as a guide as to what to expect.

Caution When sailing in thick and heavy weather, it is not safe to assume that commercial shipping will detect you on their radar, even if you have

36.3 *Radar reflector.*

taken the seamanlike precaution of rigging a good radar reflector. Quite apart from questions of good or bad watchkeeping, the echo of a yacht will be small, and can very easily be lost in sea clutter. A radar reflector helps, but if the sea clutter on the other ship's radar is extensive, it may reach beyond the detection range of your yacht, even with a radar reflector. In these circumstances, you are very unlikely to be picked up on radar.

Table 1 *Typical detection ranges for a yacht radar (antenna height ten metres, 3kW transmitter power)*

	miles
Bold, high land	25
Large ships	11
Medium ships	8
Fishing vessels	3
Yachts with radar reflector	$2\frac{1}{2}$–3
Yachts without radar reflector	1
Navigational buoys with reflectors	$2\frac{1}{2}$
Dinghy (wood or fibreglass)	$\frac{1}{2}$
Withy (thin wooden channel marker)	$\frac{1}{2}$**

** Withies show up remarkably well on radar, and can be very useful when navigating in fog.

37 Using radar

A radar set in a yacht can be used in any one of four ways, and it is possible to switch rapidly from one to another if the circumstances require. The four main tasks are:

1) Landfall – detecting land at long range.
2) Coastal navigation, either in fog or as a supplement to visual navigation.
3) Lookout – the detection of approaching shipping
4) Collision avoidance in thick weather.

1) *Landfall* Radar can be a very valuable landfall aid, as the set can often pick up land which is well beyond visual range, even in relatively clear conditions. However, the actual detection range will depend upon the antenna height of the set and the nature of the coast. A mountainous coastline with high cliffs may well be detected at the maximum range of which the set is capable, while low-lying, sandy coasts may not appear on the PPI until quite close.

Another factor in making a landfall is the nature of the coastline; at long range, a low-lying coast may be below the radar horizon, whilst high ground in the hinterland may be above it, and hence be detected. The identification of a feature on the radar may not be easy, though examination of the height contours on the chart can indicate which areas are likely to be detected first.

2) *Coastal navigation* Radar is a very useful aid to coastal navigation in all conditions. In fog, it may be the most accurate and reliable aid available, but even in good visibility radar can help the navigator a great deal. When used to supplement visual navigation, radar's biggest contribution is its ability to provide range information. If an object is conspicuous both to the eye and the radar, a simultaneous radar range and visual bearing can be taken to provide a reliable fix.

In poor visibility, radar becomes the primary navigational aid. The most important thing to remember is that radar provides accurate ranges, but very inaccurate bearings (see below). When collecting position lines to form a fix, it is very much better to use two or three

ranges of radar-conspicuous objects than to use radar bearings (Fig. 1).

A radar picture is not easy to interpret correctly, and every opportunity should be taken to practise blind pilotage when conditions are good, to build up skill and confidence for the occasion when the visibility closes in. It is best to avoid the temptation to conn the ship by eye off the radar screen; rather, use the radar to fix the ship at frequent intervals, and make careful allowance for such factors as tidal stream. If at all possible, a blind passage should be meticulously planned in advance.

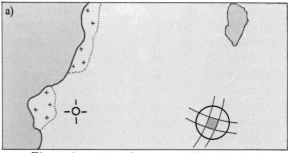

37.1 Fixes using: (a) radar ranges; (b) radar bearings.

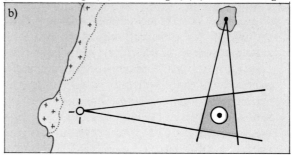

The identification of navigational marks is not always easy. If a coastline is at some little distance, parts of it may paint on the screen, while other lower-lying regions do not appear at all. And, whilst the display on the PPI may look like a map, it is formed from the view as seen by the radar antennae; a nearby bluff, for example, may obscure part of the coastline behind, so that the appearance of the coast alters as the ship moves past it (Fig. 2). It can also be hard to pick out navigational buoys on the screen from small craft nearby, or to distinguish the echo of a light vessel from merchant ships. Some important marks carry a

37.2 *Effect of a change of viewpoint on radar pictures.*

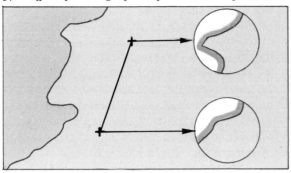

Racon, a radar transponder which 'labels' an echo so that it can be identified. These can be very helpful where they exist, but it is good practice to fix the ship on the chart frequently, and use the fix to identify new radar objects as they come into range. This process also helps to avoid the momentary confusion which often occurs when the ship alters course; as the radar picture is related to the ship's head (in the 12 o'clock position), it revolves as the ship turns and changes appearance radically.

3) *Lookout* For detecting the presence of nearby ships, radar is at its most valuable in poor conditions – in fog obviously, but also when high seas or blown spray make a visual lookout difficult. However, radar should only be regarded as an aid to lookout; echoes may be lost if the set wanders off tune or if the clutter controls are not used properly. Never rely exclusively on a radar lookout, but use it rather to supplement and extend the visual lookout being kept by the watch on deck.

4) *Collision Avoidance* **The use of a small, yacht-type radar for collision avoidance at close quarters is extremely dangerous, and should be avoided if at all possible.**
Commercial shipping uses radar for collision avoidance as a routine measure, but with equipment and skills denied to the average yachtsman. Even so, in spite of special training, north-stabilized and true-motion radar, plotting aids and computer-controlled collision avoidance systems, so-called 'radar-assisted collisions' still occur. The relatively primitive radar typically fitted in a yacht is totally unsuited for this task and the operator is most

unlikely to have the training or experience to make safe decisions on the basis of the information he sees. The main reason for this situation is the fact that the radar picture is related to ship's head – i.e. the bow of the ship is always represented at the 12 o'clock position. Even on autopilot, yachts are not steered perfectly and in a seaway they can yaw considerably. Thus the relative bearing of the target ship on the radar can change from sweep to sweep, making it very difficult to estimate its actual bearing; allied to the poor bearing accuracy inherent in the radar to begin with, it is clear that it is almost impossible to decide if the bearing of the target is constant or not, which defines the risk of collision. The difficulties are at their most apparent when the two ships are end-on (or nearly so) to each other, which is the most dangerous situation to be in. It is only too easy to misinterpret the radar picture and alter course the wrong way – towards the ship you are trying to avoid.
Never assume that the other ship can see you on his radar, just because you can see him on yours.
If you are forced into the position of having to use radar for collision avoidance, take steps to keep clear as early as possible. Try to prevent other ships coming within a mile of you – two miles is better. Have the best radar watchkeeper on board at the set, and keep the deck watch informed about what is happening; if a mistake is made, it will be they who have to get you out of it.

Radar errors
Radar is most accurate in measuring ranges, especially if a variable range marker unit is fitted. Bearings are very much less accurate, partly because of the beam width of the antenna (typically 3°) and partly because of the tendency for small craft to yaw. The 95 per cent errors might typically be:

Range	
with range rings	2 per cent of range in use
with variable range marker	1 per cent of range in use

Bearing	
good conditions	± 6°
bad conditions	± 15°

38 Hyperbolic radio aids to navigation

Following their initial introduction in the Second World War, a number of radio aids to navigation are available which use a common principle of measuring the difference in range between a number of transmitting stations. In general, the cost and complexity of these navigation systems put them beyond the reach of the average yachtsman, but they may sometimes be found in larger craft. Modern developments in electronics may reduce the cost of some systems, especially Loran C, to the point where they come into much wider use in yachts, though the present coverage of Loran C is inadequate in Europe.

These navigation systems are known as *hyperbolic* aids because the position lines that the equipment produces take the form of a series of hyperbolae. The principle of these aids is shown in Figure 1. Two radio transmitters are arranged to send out a short pulse of energy at exactly the same moment, and these pulses are picked up by a receiver in the craft; because the speed of light (and radio waves) is constant, the difference in the time that the two pulses are received in the craft gives the difference in the range (or distance) of the two transmitters. If the pulses arrive together, then the two transmitters are equi-distant and the craft must lie somewhere on the perpendicular bisector of the base-line (the line joining the two transmitters). In all other cases, it can be shown that the craft lies on a hyperbolic position line with the nearer transmitter as its focus. In practice, a number of transmitters are grouped in such a way as to provide a number of hyperbolic position lines which intersect to provide a fix. A special chart with an overprinted 'lattice' is used for plotting fixes (Fig. 2) The three hyperbolic systems available for general navigation are Loran C, Decca and Omega, all of which require special receivers and signal processing equipment; the earlier Loran A system is now obsolescent.

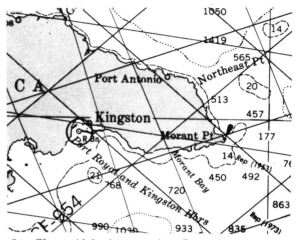

38.2 *Chart with lattice overprint (Omega).*

Loran C

One of the first hyperbolic aids to be developed was called Loran (LOng RAnge Navigation), and Loran C is an improved version of this original system. It operates on LF (low frequency) and has a maximum range of about 1500 nautical miles at night, and rather less by day. Receiver operation is automatic, and time differences can be read directly from a numerical display for plotting on a Loran C lattice chart. Modern receivers sometimes incorporate a microprocessor which can translate time differences into latitude and longitude; this is an obvious advantage, as it eliminates the need to carry the special lattice charts otherwise needed for plotting position lines.

The accuracy of a Loran C position line depends upon a number of factors, including the position of the craft within the lattice and the ionospheric conditions which can affect the transmission of the radio signals. In favourable circum-

38.1 *Principle of hyperbolic radio aids.*

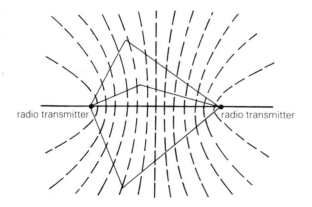

radio transmitter — radio transmitter

stances at short range, the 95 per cent accuracy can be less than a quarter of a mile; the error increases with distance to perhaps one or two miles at a range of 1000 miles from the baseline.

The major drawback of Loran C, which is in many ways an excellent aid, is that it has been installed for military rather than civil use; hence the coverage of the world by Loran C shows gaps which are annoying from the yachtsman's point of view (Fig. 3). The most notable omission is the area south of the Dover Strait, which excludes the

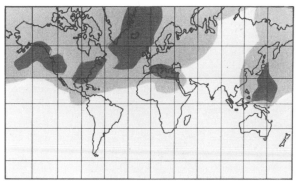

38.3 *Loran C coverage (1981).*

most important yachting areas of England and France.

Decca

Decca is a short-range, high accuracy hyperbolic system working in the low frequency band, which is widely used by commercial and military users both at sea and in the air. Decca equipment was only available on hire from the Decca Navigator Company, but they have recently (1982) introduced a yacht version for sale. Some 'pirate' Decca receivers have been put on the market, but these should be viewed with caution.

Decca is not quite as easy to use as Loran C because it is necessary to guard against an ambiguity known as 'lane slippage'; but with a careful study of the handbook and a little practice, it will provide fixes of the highest quality. The maximum range of a particular Decca chain is about 250

miles from the master station (less at night), and chains are generally arranged to provide an overlap of coverage.

The accuracy of Decca is very high; close to the base line, the 95 per cent error may be less than 100 yards (90 metres), and at 100 miles it will be between a half and one mile, depending upon the position of the craft within the lattice. At long ranges ionospheric effects can become important and errors may be as much as ten times greater at times, particularly during winter nights. Because of these effects and also the need for lane identification, great care should be taken when entering the Decca coverage, especially at night, to make quite sure that the Decca receiver is properly set up and telling the truth.

The accuracy of Decca has caused problems in the past; fishing vessels use the system a great deal to find their grounds, and have developed a habit of running to and from the grounds along a particular Decca line as shown on their equipment. There have been a number of stem-to-stem collisions between boats travelling in opposite directions along the same Decca line!

Omega

Omega is a VLF (very low frequency) hyperbolic system recently introduced by the United States Navy. Eight stations, operating on a basic frequency of 10.2 kilohertz, provide between them a virtually world-wide coverage.

To offset the advantage of global coverage, Omega is not particularly accurate; a 95 per cent accuracy of one mile by day and two miles by night is as much as one can expect, though various ways of providing automatic corrections for varying conditions have been tried. One approach is for a fixed Omega receiver to detect variations in the received signal, which are then broadcast as corrections for Omega users in the vicinity.

Another drawback with Omega is that it cannot recover the position of the vessel after the equipment has been switched off. Whilst operating, the Omega receiver will provide position lines continuously, but if switched off (or after a breakdown) it must be told by the navigator exactly where it is within the lattice.

39 Other radio aids

There are several other radio aids which can be used by yachts although for various reasons they are limited in their scope. They are all designed to give a vessel the bearing of the transmitting beacon without using the directional type of antenna needed for MFDF.

Consol

Consol is a system originally developed in Germany during the Second World War under the title *Elektra Sonne*; it is now obsolescent and many of the stations have been closed down. A similar system, called Consolan, was installed on the eastern seaboard of the United States but this, too, is now closed down.

Consol is described technically as a collapsed hyperbolic system, and the effect is to produce a radial fan of signals from the transmitter, rather like the spokes of a wheel (Fig. 1). The only equipment required by the ship is a beacon-band receiver fitted with a BFO (beat frequency oscillator).

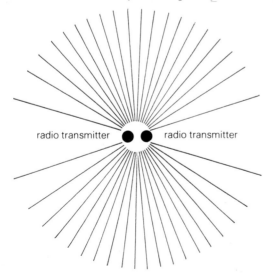

radio transmitter   radio transmitter

39.1 *Consol collapsed lattice.*

After tuning the receiver to the correct frequency, the operator will hear the identification of the station in Morse, followed by a series of 60 Morse symbols (dots or dashes). The sequence will begin with a series of either dots or dashes; at some point the signal will fade out, and then re-appear with the opposite symbol. For example, the sequence

may begin with dots, fade out and then return as dashes (or *vice versa*). The operator counts the number of symbols he can hear before the fade-out (known as the equisignal), and then the number of symbols that he hears after the equisignal. It is normal for a number of symbols to be lost in the equisignal, so the operator must then work out his final count, making use of the knowledge that there were 60 symbols altogether in the sequence.

For example:

Before equisignal	20 dots	5 dashes
After equisignal	36 dashes	50 dots
Total heard	56	55
Missed in equisignal	4	5
Correction (half)	2	$2\frac{1}{2}$
Final count	22 dots	$7\frac{1}{2}$ dashes

The final count is expressed as the number of symbols heard *before* the equisignal; it is also necessary to note which symbol this was, a dot or a dash, as this affects the position line. Having established the count, the position line can then be plotted on a special chart with a printed overlay of the Consol counts. Alternatively, tables have been published which convert the count into true bearings, which can be plotted on a normal chart; when working at long range, it may be necessary to correct these bearings for half convergency (see page 191). As the pattern repeats itself a number of times around the horizon, a reliable dead reckoning position may be needed to resolve any ambiguity in the bearing.

Consol is delightfully simple to use, and can be effective over 1000 miles or more; a major advantage is that no special equipment is needed, though best results require practice. However, the accuracy is not particularly good; a 95 per cent error of 1° to 2° can be expected by day, and double this at night. Bearings at about 400 miles (where the ground wave and the first sky wave of the signal mix together) may be considerably more in error.

Radio lighthouse

The radio lighthouse is a system, still in the experimental stage, which offers the prospect of a radio aid thoroughly suitable for yachts and small craft in coastal waters. It is in principle very much like Consol, but operates in the international marine mobile band on VHF (very high frequency). As with Consol, it is only necessary to tune the vessel's own VHF receiver to the correct channel, identify the radio lighthouse by its callsign, and then count the symbols that follow (the signal differs in detail from the Consol signal). The resulting count can then be translated into a true bearing of the transmitter by means of special tables.

Unlike Consol, the radio lighthouse is intended to be a short-range aid – of the order to twenty miles, depending on the heights of the transmitting and receiving antennae. The suggestion is that it should be sited with important lighthouses or lightships to provide adequate cover of coastal waters, with sufficient beacons within range to allow for reliable fixing. If expectations are met and the radio lighthouse is put into service, it would offer yachts a far more suitable aid in coastal waters than MFDF. In 1982, there were a number of experimental installations in European waters.

The accuracy of the radio lighthouse is probably better than 2° on 95 per cent of occasions, and the system is much less subject to propagation errors because of the short ranges involved and the high frequency of the transmissions. Like Consol, it has the advantage that no special equipment is needed, though it seems likely that special receivers which make the process quicker and easier by automatic tuning and counting will appear on the market.

VOR

VOR (vhf omni-range) is a radio aid widely used by aircraft. If VOR beacons are suitably sited, they can also be used by small craft within VHF range of the shore. The VOR set carried in the vessel picks up the signal from the beacon, and translates this automatically into a continuous reading of the magnetic bearing of the station from the craft; by switching channels, another VOR beacon within range can be used to provide a fix.

It is only in certain areas where VOR beacons happen to be suitably sited for marine use that yachts can use the system; it is most popular in the waters of the United States. The range of these beacons is limited by low antenna height in small craft.

ASTRONOMICAL NAVIGATION

40 The principles of astronomical navigation

Many navigators, even some with considerable experience, are under the impression that astronomical navigation is difficult. On the contrary, finding one's position by observation of heavenly bodies is no more difficult and time-consuming than (for example) the use of MF direction finding. To be sure, a special instrument (a sextant) is needed with associated books of tables, and good results will need practice; but the end result is a system for observing position lines of very high quality anywhere on the surface of the earth, provided only that the sky is not totally obscured. Unless the trans-oceanic navigator is prepared to invest in one of the modern electronic systems, then astronomical navigation is the only method available; in any case, the 'electronic navigator' would need a back-up system. It is not always appreciated that astronomical navigation can be just as useful for coastal work. It may be, for example, that a distant headland is in sight, so the navigator has one position line from its compass bearing; if the sun is shining, he may be able to get another position line to give him his distance off.

The principle of astronomical navigation is extremely straightforward; it can even be thought of as a special case of obtaining a position line by vertical sextant angle (see page 71), extended to cover the case of an object of infinite height. By measuring the height of the object, i.e. the angle between the object and the horizon, it is possible to calculate a distance, and hence obtain a position line.

The first step is to associate some point on the surface of the earth with the position of the heavenly body in the sky. This can be done by joining the centre of the earth with the body in question; the position where this imaginary line meets the surface of the earth is known as the *geographical position* (GP) of the body (Fig. 1). It is the point where the body would be seen vertically overhead (in the zenith, as astronomers say). As the earth rotates on its axis and revolves around the sun, the geographical position is constantly moving (at speeds of up to 900 n miles an hour), but it can be established for any second during the year by using the tables in the *Nautical Almanac* (see page 137).

40.1 *The geographical position.*

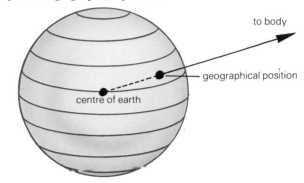

40.2 *The relationship between altitude and geographical position.*

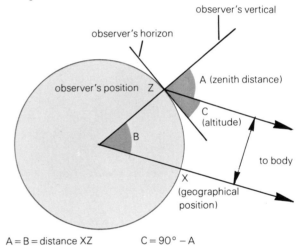

$A = B = $ distance XZ $C = 90° - A$

The whole basis of astronomical navigation is that the angle of a heavenly body above the horizon is directly related to the distance of the geographical position (Fig. 2). Because the body is a very long way away from the earth (the sun is 93,000,000 miles away), it can be assumed that rays of light reaching the earth are parallel. The argument then runs as follows:

1) By simple geometry, the angle A, between the observer's zenith (the point directly above his head) and the object, is equal to the angle B, the angle at the centre of the earth between the observers position and the geographical position of the body.

2) By definition, the angle B is equivalent to the distance on the surface of the earth between X (the GP of the body) and Z (the position of the observer) (see page 15).

40.3 *Plotting the position line at high altitudes.*

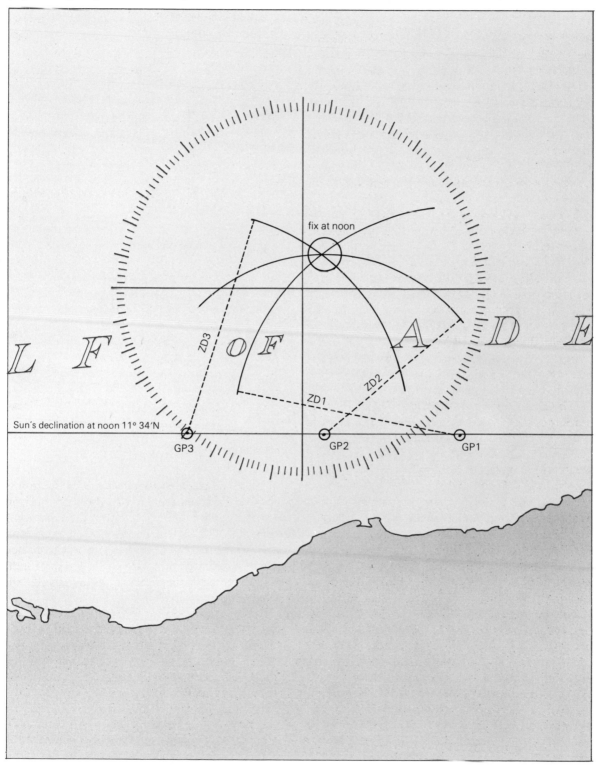

3) Therefore, the angle A, measured in minutes of arc, is equal to the distance between X and Z in nautical miles.

4) In a small craft, there is no practical way of measuring the angle A directly; however it is easy to observe the angle C, the angle between the body and the horizon directly below it.

5) The angles A and C must add together to give 90°, the total angle between the horizon and the zenith; therefore the angle C equals 90° minus angle A.

The angle A is known as the *zenith distance* of the body, and the angle C is known as the *altitude*.

A simple numerical example may help to make the theory clear; assume that the altitude of a body is measured as 30°:

Altitude (angle C) 30°
Zenith distance (angle A) $90° - 30° = 60°$
Therefore distance X to Z $60° \times 60 = 3600$ n miles

Provided that the GP (from the *Nautical Almanac*) can be plotted on the same chart as the observer's DR position, then the position line can easily be drawn by setting a pair of compasses to the zenith distance and striking an arc from the GP; however, this is not always practicable, because as the example above shows, the distance involved can be considerable. The lowest altitude at which a body can reliably be observed is about 15°, which implies a zenith distance of 4500 nautical miles; even if it were possible to plot such a position line on a chart, the pencil line would be several miles thick (at the scale of the chart), and the potential accuracy of the method would be totally lost. This difficulty is overcome by the *intercept method*, described on pages 147–9.

There are certain rare occasions when the GP of the body and the position lines can be drawn directly. These occasions arise when the body (almost always the sun) passes close overhead, i.e. near noon in tropical latitudes. In such circumstances, the GP of the sun will be close to the ship and can be plotted. Having established the zenith distance, the position circle can be plotted directly (Fig. 3). If the process is repeated a few minutes later, when the sun's GP has moved sufficiently, a second position circle can be drawn; the intersection of these two circles gives a fix. A possible ambiguity exists, because two circles intersect in two points, but knowledge of the DR position should be able to resolve this difficulty. Otherwise, a third observation will settle the matter definitely.

An astronomical position line of this kind is not easy to observe, as the altitude is very great (85° or more).

41   Taking sextant altitudes

Astronomical navigation involves the measurement of the altitude of a heavenly body by means of a sextant. The principle and construction of this remarkable instrument are described on pages 45–7; this section deals with its use in measuring altitudes. At first, the beginner is likely to find this quite difficult, but the technique can soon be mastered with a little practice. It is rather like learning to ride a bicycle – hard at first, but it soon becomes almost second nature.

The basic idea is simple enough (Fig. 1). Holding the sextant vertically, the navigator looks at the horizon directly below the body through the plain (unsilvered) section of the horizon glass; he then adjusts the index arm until the reflected image of the body is co-incident with the horizon. When the object and the horizon are exactly in line (with the sextant held truly vertical), the graduated scale and micrometer show the sextant altitude of the body. For most sights, the navigator needs to record the exact time, so the geographical position of the body can be established from the *Nautical Almanac*.

Preparation Remove the sextant carefully from its box and check that it does not seem to have suffered accidental damage since it was last used, and that the mirrors, shades, lenses and scales are clean. Every sextant should be fitted with a lanyard; put the lanyard round your neck immediately to protect it from dropping. If the sextant is supplied with a choice of telescopes, then ship the star telescope (bell shaped); this telescope, which gives an upright image and a wide field of view, is the most generally suitable for use in a yacht.

The index error of the sextant should be checked every time the instrument is used. The easiest way is to look at the horizon with the arm set to zero. The micrometer should then be adjusted until the direct and the reflected images of the horizon form a continuous unbroken line (Fig. 2). The reading of the sextant is then the index error. The error may be *on the arc* (Fig. 3a), in which case it has to be *subtracted* from the measured angle; if the error is *off the* arc (Fig. 3b), it must be *added*.

41.1 *Taking sextant altitudes. (below left)*
41.2 *Checking the index error. (below)*

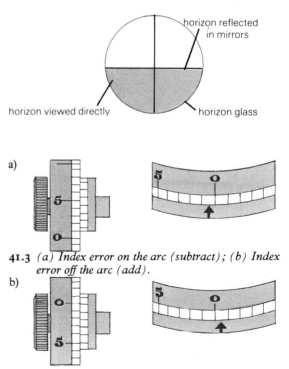

41.3 *(a) Index error on the arc (subtract); (b) Index error off the arc (add).*

Position To take an observation, the navigator must find a position where he has a clear view of both the object and the horizon (not always easy in a sailing yacht). He must also make sure that he is safe; he needs both hands to operate the sextant, and must make sure that there is no risk of being thrown off balance. Apart from the risk of personal injury or damage to the sextant, it is not unknown for navigators to be lost overboard whilst taking sights. A safety harness is a seamanlike precaution.

Apart from getting a clear view of the body and the horizon, the navigator should choose a position according to the state of the horizon. If it appears to be hazy, then a low position brings the sea horizon closer and makes it look sharper. In a seaway, a high position should be chosen to take the eye (if possible) above the tops of nearby waves, which obscure the true horizon.

Having found a safe and suitable position, the navigator should try to 'lock' his legs and the lower part of his body to the boat, leaving the head, arms and upper body free to move to compensate for the motion of the boat; it is often helpful to brace the body against the safety line. If the motion is so violent that the use of the sextant is difficult, it may be possible to improve conditions by altering course or, if necessary, heaving to.

Finding the object It can be quite difficult to find the object in the sextant's field of view, particularly if the object is faint, like a star. There are three ways of tackling the problem:

1) Set the sextant to zero, and look directly at the object. *Caution*: when looking at the sun, adjust the shades to reduce the light and prevent damage to the eyes. Then bring the sextant slowly down to the horizontal, at the same time moving the index arm so as to keep the object in the silvered part of the horizon glass (Fig. 4).

2) An alternative method, which some navigators find easier for faint objects, is to use the sextant upside down (Fig. 5). This time, the object is kept in the *clear* part of the horizon glass, and the arm is adjusted until the horizon appears in the silvered part. The sextant can now be reversed and used normally.

3) Stars and planets are almost always observed at dawn and dusk, when there is sufficient light to give a clear horizon; this means that the sky is

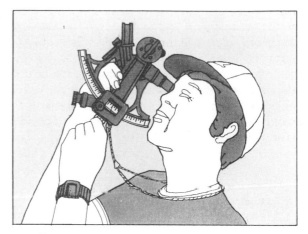

41.4 *Bringing an object down to the horizon.*

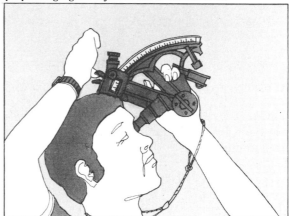

41.5 *Bringing the horizon up to the object.*

still bright and faint stars may only be visible through the sextant telescope. The only way to find such objects is to predict their position in the sky from the DR position; the sextant is set to the predicted altitude and swept across the appropriate bearing until the object is seen. The way of predicting the position of a star is given on page 159.

Use of shades Both the horizon and the index glasses are fitted with shades or filters to cut down the light of the sun. Both should be used when finding the sun; thereafter the horizon glass need only be shaded if the sun is low and the horizon bright. The shades on the index glass should always be used unless the sun is veiled by thin cloud. They should be adjusted to give a clear image which can be viewed without strain; it is a mistake to have too bright an image of the sun.

Measuring the altitude Having found the object in the field of view, it is now possible to take the exact altitude by lining the object up with the horizon. The altitude will be correct only if the sextant is vertical. This can be ensured by rocking the sextant slightly from side to side (Fig. 6). The object will swing from side to side like the bob of a pendulum. The sextant is vertical when the 'bob' is at its lowest point.

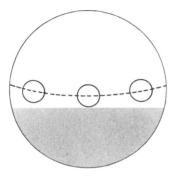

41.6 *Rocking the sextant to ensure that it is vertical.*

It is generally better not to chase the altitude of the body by continual adjustment of the index arm, but rather to set the sextant to an altitude and let the body move. If the body is in the eastern half of the sky, it is rising. Set an altitude a little greater than the actual position and wait until the body rises to the altitude you have set. If the body is in the western sky, it is sinking so the sextant should be set to a lower altitude. Then watch the body as it approaches the horizon and note the time when they are in line.

Stars and planets are effectively points of light, and the altitude is taken by putting this point onto the horizon (Fig. 7a). The sun and the moon both have sensible diameters, and the sextant altitude is taken on the top or the bottom edge – known as the *upper* and *lower limbs*. For the sun, it is conventional to take the lower limb, though the upper can be used if desired (Fig. 7b). With the moon, it is necessary to use whichever limb is visible, depending on the phase (Fig. 7c).

Recording the results When taking sights, it is almost always necessary to record the exact time on the ship's chronometer or master watch. This is most conveniently done by recruiting another crew member as 'scribe', to record the watch times and matching sextant altitudes. The single-

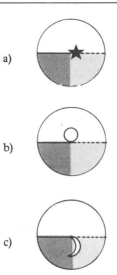

41.7 *Bringing (a) a star (b) the sun and (c) the moon to the horizon.*

handed navigator must devise some suitable alternative, such as a stopwatch or digital wristwatch to carry his time around with him.

It is not wise to rely on a single observation of a body; a series should be taken and averaged, to reduce the errors that may arise. A useful technique is to take either three or five observations at equal intervals of altitude (say, five minutes of arc). It is then only necessary to average the times, as the average altitude is equal to the middle value of the set. It is also possible to examine the time intervals between the observations; if these are equal, it tends to indicate that the observations are good.

For example:

Altitude	Time	Interval
34°20′.0	10 h 14 m 02 s	
		32 seconds
34°25′.0	10 h 14 m 34 s	
		29 seconds
34°30′.0	10 h 15 m 03 s	
Average 34°25′.0	10 h 14 m 33 s	

In this example, the intervals between the observations (32 and 29 seconds) are more or less equal, so the set of observations is probably acceptable.

Of course, conditions may be such that only one hurried sight is possible, as the sun peeps momentarily through overcast. Any sight is better than no sight at all, but it must be remembered that a single observation is not as reliable as the average of a consistent set.

42 Sextant altitude corrections

The angle actually measured on the sextant is known as the *sextant altitude* of the body; a number of corrections must be applied to this angle to get the *observed altitude* (Ho), which is the basis of the position line to be derived.

Index error The index error of a sextant is the zero error of the instrument, caused by the two mirrors not being exactly parallel. It should be checked every time the sextant is used, as described on the previous page.

The index error is applied to the sextant altitude; index error on the arc is subtracted, and index error off the arc is added (see examples below).

Dip The angle measured by a sextant is that between the body and the sea horizon; however, as Figure 1 shows, the sea horizon is always below the true horizontal, by an amount which depends on the height of eye of the observer. The correction for *dip* is given in the *Nautical Almanac* (Table 1), using height of eye as an argument. This table, like other altitude correction tables, is arranged as a *critical entry* table; the correction given applies to all values of height of eye between the two values immediately above and below the correction. For example, a dip correction of $-4'.2$ applies to any height of eye from 5.5 metres up to (but not including) 5.8 metres. The dip correction is *always subtracted* to give the *apparent altitude*.

42.1 *Dip of the sea horizon.*

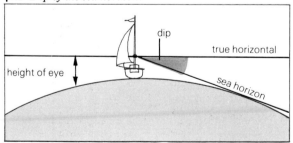

Refraction As the rays of light from the body observed pass through the various layers of atmosphere, they are bent or refracted, by an amount which depends mainly on the altitude of the body (Fig. 2). This correction, which is always negative, is incorporated in the various correction tables with other corrections.

42.2 *Refraction.*

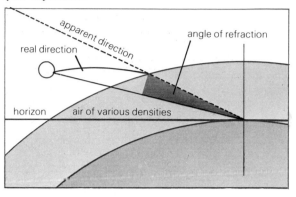

Semidiameter Semidiameter is the somewhat curious name given by astronomers to the radius of the sun or the moon. A correction must be applied to the measured altitude to allow for the fact that the observation was made on either the upper or lower limb of the sun or moon, whereas the altitude required is of its centre. Semidiameter depends on the size of the body and its distance from the earth. For lower limb observations, semidiameter is added, for upper limb observations it is subtracted. This correction is incorporated in the sun and moon correction tables (Tables 1 and 2).

Parallax This correction is only of importance for observations of the moon, and it arises because the moon is relatively close to the earth – close enough for the diameter of the earth to affect the observations (Fig. 3). It depends upon various factors, chiefly the altitude and the distance of the moon. A special correction is given in the moon correction tables (Table 2), which require a quantity called horizontal parallax (HP) as argument.

42.3 *Parallax.*

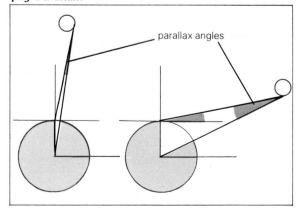

Table 1 *Sun, star and planet corrections.*

A2 ALTITUDE CORRECTION TABLES 10°-90°—SUN, STARS, PLANETS

OCT.—MAR. SUN APR.—SEPT.

App. Alt.	Lower Limb	Upper Limb	App. Alt.	Lower Limb	Upper Limb
9 34	+10.8	−21.5	9 39	+10.6	−21.2
9 45	+10.9	−21.4	9 51	+10.7	−21.1
9 56	+11.0	−21.3	10 03	+10.8	−21.0
10 08	+11.1	−21.2	10 15	+10.9	−20.9
10 21	+11.2	−21.1	10 27	+11.0	−20.8
10 34	+11.3	−21.0	10 40	+11.1	−20.7
10 47	+11.4	−20.9	10 54	+11.2	−20.6
11 01	+11.5	−20.8	11 08	+11.3	−20.5
11 15	+11.6	−20.7	11 23	+11.4	−20.4
11 30	+11.7	−20.6	11 38	+11.5	−20.3
11 46	+11.8	−20.5	11 54	+11.6	−20.2
12 02	+11.9	−20.4	12 10	+11.7	−20.1
12 19	+12.0	−20.3	12 28	+11.8	−20.0
12 37	+12.1	−20.2	12 46	+11.9	−19.9
12 55	+12.2	−20.1	13 05	+12.0	−19.8
13 14	+12.3	−20.0	13 24	+12.1	−19.7
13 35	+12.4	−19.9	13 45	+12.2	−19.6
13 56	+12.5	−19.8	14 07	+12.3	−19.5
14 18	+12.6	−19.7	14 30	+12.4	−19.4
14 42	+12.7	−19.6	14 54	+12.5	−19.3
15 06	+12.8	−19.5	15 19	+12.6	−19.2
15 32	+12.9	−19.4	15 46	+12.7	−19.1
15 59	+13.0	−19.3	16 14	+12.8	−19.0
16 28	+13.1	−19.2	16 44	+12.9	−18.9
16 59	+13.2	−19.1	17 15	+13.0	−18.8
17 32	+13.3	−19.0	17 48	+13.1	−18.7
18 06	+13.4	−18.9	18 24	+13.2	−18.6
18 42	+13.5	−18.8	19 01	+13.3	−18.5
19 21	+13.6	−18.7	19 42	+13.4	−18.4
20 03	+13.7	−18.6	20 25	+13.5	−18.3
20 48	+13.8	−18.5	21 11	+13.6	−18.2
21 35	+13.9	−18.4	22 00	+13.7	−18.1
22 26	+14.0	−18.3	22 54	+13.8	−18.0
23 22	+14.1	−18.2	23 51	+13.9	−17.9
24 21	+14.2	−18.1	24 53	+14.0	−17.8
25 26	+14.3	−18.0	26 00	+14.1	−17.7
26 36	+14.4	−17.9	27 13	+14.2	−17.6
27 52	+14.5	−17.8	28 33	+14.3	−17.5
29 15	+14.6	−17.7	30 00	+14.4	−17.4
30 46	+14.7	−17.6	31 35	+14.5	−17.3
32 26	+14.8	−17.5	33 20	+14.6	−17.2
34 17	+14.9	−17.4	35 17	+14.7	−17.1
36 20	+15.0	−17.3	37 26	+14.8	−17.0
38 36	+15.1	−17.2	39 50	+14.9	−16.9
41 08	+15.2	−17.1	42 31	+15.0	−16.8
43 59	+15.3	−17.0	45 31	+15.1	−16.7
47 10	+15.4	−16.9	48 55	+15.2	−16.6
50 46	+15.5	−16.8	52 44	+15.3	−16.5
54 49	+15.6	−16.7	57 02	+15.4	−16.4
59 23	+15.7	−16.6	61 51	+15.5	−16.3
64 30	+15.8	−16.5	67 17	+15.6	−16.2
70 12	+15.9	−16.4	73 16	+15.7	−16.1
76 26	+16.0	−16.3	79 43	+15.8	−16.0
83 05	+16.1	−16.2	86 32	+15.9	−15.9
90 00			90 00		

STARS AND PLANETS

App. Alt.	Corrn
9 56	−5.3
10 08	−5.2
10 20	−5.1
10 33	−5.0
10 46	−4.9
11 00	−4.8
11 14	−4.7
11 29	−4.6
11 45	−4.5
12 01	−4.4
12 18	−4.3
12 35	−4.2
12 54	−4.1
13 13	−4.0
13 33	−3.9
13 54	−3.8
14 16	−3.7
14 40	−3.6
15 04	−3.5
15 30	−3.4
15 57	−3.3
16 26	−3.2
16 56	−3.1
17 28	−3.0
18 02	−2.9
18 38	−2.8
19 17	−2.7
19 58	−2.6
20 42	−2.5
21 28	−2.4
22 19	−2.3
23 13	−2.2
24 11	−2.1
25 14	−2.0
26 22	−1.9
27 36	−1.8
28 56	−1.7
30 24	−1.6
32 00	−1.5
33 45	−1.4
35 40	−1.3
37 48	−1.2
40 08	−1.1
42 44	−1.0
45 36	−0.9
48 47	−0.8
52 18	−0.7
56 11	−0.6
60 28	−0.5
65 08	−0.4
70 11	−0.3
75 34	−0.2
81 13	−0.1
87 03	0.0
90 00	

Additional Corrn — 1980

VENUS

Jan. 1-Feb. 26
App. Alt.	Additional Corrn
42	+0.1

Feb. 27-Apr. 13
| 47 | +0.2 |

Apr. 14-May 9
| 46 | +0.3 |

May 10-May 25
| 11 | +0.4 |
| 41 | +0.5 |

May 26-June 3
6	+0.5
20	+0.6
31	+0.7

June 4-June 26
4	+0.6
12	+0.7
22	+0.8

June 27-July 6
6	+0.5
20	+0.6
31	+0.7

July 7-July 21
| 11 | +0.4 |
| 41 | +0.5 |

July 22-Aug. 17
| 46 | +0.3 |

Aug. 18-Oct. 2
| 47 | +0.2 |

Oct. 3-Dec. 31
| 42 | +0.1 |

MARS

Jan. 1-Apr. 28
| 41 | +0.2 |
| 75 | +0.1 |

Apr. 29-Dec. 31
| 60 | +0.1 |

DIP

Ht. of Eye (m)	Corrn	Ht. of Eye (ft)
2.4	−2.8	8.0
2.6	−2.9	8.6
2.8		9.2
3.0	−3.0	9.8
3.2	−3.1	10.5
3.4	−3.2	11.2
3.6	−3.3	11.9
3.8	−3.4	12.6
4.0	−3.5	13.3
4.3	−3.6	14.1
4.5	−3.7	14.9
4.7	−3.8	15.7
5.0	−3.9	16.5
5.2	−4.0	17.4
5.5	−4.1	18.3
5.8	−4.2	19.1
6.1	−4.3	20.1
6.3	−4.4	21.0
6.6	−4.5	22.0
6.9	−4.6	22.9
7.2	−4.7	23.9
7.5	−4.8	24.9
7.9	−4.9	26.0
8.2	−5.0	27.1
8.5	−5.1	28.1
8.8	−5.2	29.2
9.2	−5.3	30.4
9.5	−5.4	31.5
9.9	−5.5	32.7
10.3	−5.6	33.9
10.6	−5.7	35.1
11.0	−5.8	36.3
11.4	−5.9	37.6
11.8	−6.0	38.9
12.2	−6.1	40.1
12.6	−6.2	41.5
13.0	−6.3	42.8
13.4	−6.4	44.2
13.8	−6.5	45.5
14.2	−6.6	46.9
14.7	−6.7	48.4
15.1	−6.8	49.8
15.5	−6.9	51.3
16.0	−7.0	52.8
16.5	−7.1	54.3
16.9	−7.2	55.8
17.4	−7.3	57.4
17.9	−7.4	58.9
18.4	−7.5	60.5
18.8	−7.6	62.1
19.3	−7.7	63.8
19.8	−7.8	65.4
20.4	−7.9	67.1
20.9	−8.0	68.8
21.4	−8.1	70.5

Ht. of Eye	Corrn
m	
1.0	−1.8
1.5	−2.2
2.0	−2.5
2.5	−2.8
3.0	−3.0
See table ←	
m	
20	−7.9
22	−8.3
24	−8.6
26	−9.0
28	−9.3
30	−9.6
32	−10.0
34	−10.3
36	−10.6
38	−10.8
40	−11.1
42	−11.4
44	−11.7
46	−11.9
48	−12.2
ft.	
2	−1.4
4	−1.9
6	−2.4
8	−2.7
10	−3.1
See table ←	
ft.	
70	−8.1
75	−8.4
80	−8.7
85	−8.9
90	−9.2
95	−9.5
100	−9.7
105	−9.9
110	−10.2
115	−10.4
120	−10.6
125	−10.8
130	−11.1
135	−11.3
140	−11.5
145	−11.7
150	−11.9
155	−12.1

This quantity is given in the daily pages of the almanac for each hour of the year; it is extracted from the tables at the same time as the other ephemeral data (see page 156).

A number of other factors also affect the correction of apparent altitude to true altitude, but these are included in the various correction tables and need not concern the navigator.

Refraction, semidiameter, parallax and various other factors are combined as appropriate into tables for correcting apparent altitude (i.e., sextant altitude corrected for index error and dip) into *observed altitude*. Samples of these tables are given in Tables 1 and 2; the originals are given in the *Nautical Almanac* (NP 314). Other almanacs and books of nautical tables may include altitude correction tables on a different basis; if using these, the instructions given should be studied and followed carefully.

Stars and planets (Table 1)

The correction for stars and planets is solely for refraction, and is always negative. It is the sole correction for all stars and the planets Jupiter and Saturn. For Venus and Mars, there are small additional corrections depending on the date, caused by parallax and phase. The Venus correction can be almost 1′, but the Mars correction can safely be ignored by all except the very precise navigator.

The sun (Table 1)

The sun correction table is somewhat more complicated, because of the need to include corrections for semidiameter and parallax. The table is in two parts, for October to March and for April to September; in each section the total correction is given for the lower limb (always positive) and the upper limb (always negative).

The moon (Table 2)

Because the moon is so close to the earth, the correction table for the moon is the most complicated of all – though still not difficult to use; if in doubt, the instructions are printed beside the table in the almanac.

The table is in two parts. The first correction is taken from the upper part, using the apparent altitude as argument. First find the appropriate column (each one appropriate to a 5° 'band' of altitudes), and then find the correction in the column according to the exact altitude (to the nearest 10′ of arc). Then, follow *the same column* down to the lower part of the table, and find the second correction using the horizontal parallax as argument and the sub-columns L or U, depending on whether the lower or upper limb was observed. Both corrections are always *added* to apparent altitude, but 30′ must be subtracted from the result if the upper limb was observed.

Additional correction tables

The tables illustrated cover apparent altitudes between 10° and 90°; in practice, because of the variable nature of refraction, it is not wise to take altitudes below about 15° if they can be avoided. However, if there is no choice but to use a low altitude sight, then special correction tables are supplied in the almanac. Particularly at low altitudes, it may also be necessary to correct for temperature and barometric pressure (both affecting refraction). A special table is supplied for this purpose, though it can be ignored for almost all normal sights; only if the temperature is very different from 10°C (50°F), or the barometric pressure very different from 1010 millibars (29.8 inches), is the correction liable to amount to much. Above altitudes of 25°, the correction is insignificant anyway.

Accuracy of true altitude

The accuracy of the measured altitude (corrected as described) is the dominant factor in assessing astronomical position lines; all other sources of error are insignificant by comparison. Typical 95 per cent errors for a practised observer using a good sextant might be:

Good conditions	1 mile (1 minute of arc)
Moderate conditions	2 miles (2 minutes of arc)
Poor conditions	10 miles (10 minutes of arc)

The novice should not expect to do so well, but accuracy will come with practice.

Table 2 *Moon corrections.*

ALTITUDE CORRECTION TABLES 0°–35°—MOON

App. Alt.	0°–4° Corrⁿ	5°–9° Corrⁿ	10°–14° Corrⁿ	15°–19° Corrⁿ	20°–24° Corrⁿ	25°–29° Corrⁿ	30°–34° Corrⁿ	App. Alt.
00	0° 33.8	5° 58.2	10° 62.1	15° 62.8	20° 62.2	25° 60.8	30° 58.9	00
10	35.9	58.5	62.2	62.8	62.1	60.8	58.8	10
20	37.8	58.7	62.2	62.8	62.1	60.7	58.8	20
30	39.6	58.9	62.3	62.8	62.1	60.7	58.7	30
40	41.2	59.1	62.3	62.8	62.0	60.6	58.6	40
50	42.6	59.3	62.4	62.7	62.0	60.6	58.5	50
00	1° 44.0	6° 59.5	11° 62.4	16° 62.7	21° 62.0	26° 60.5	31° 58.5	00
10	45.2	59.7	62.4	62.7	61.9	60.4	58.4	10
20	46.3	59.9	62.5	62.7	61.9	60.4	58.3	20
30	47.3	60.0	62.5	62.7	61.9	60.3	58.2	30
40	48.3	60.2	62.5	62.7	61.8	60.3	58.2	40
50	49.2	60.3	62.6	62.7	61.8	60.2	58.1	50
00	2° 50.0	7° 60.5	12° 62.6	17° 62.7	22° 61.7	27° 60.1	32° 58.0	00
10	50.8	60.6	62.6	62.6	61.7	60.1	57.9	10
20	51.4	60.7	62.6	62.6	61.6	60.0	57.8	20
30	52.1	60.9	62.7	62.6	61.6	59.9	57.8	30
40	52.7	61.0	62.7	62.6	61.5	59.9	57.7	40
50	53.3	61.1	62.7	62.6	61.5	59.8	57.6	50
00	3° 53.8	8° 61.2	13° 62.7	18° 62.5	23° 61.5	28° 59.7	33° 57.5	00
10	54.3	61.3	62.7	62.5	61.4	59.7	57.4	10
20	54.8	61.4	62.7	62.5	61.4	59.6	57.4	20
30	55.2	61.5	62.8	62.5	61.3	59.6	57.3	30
40	55.6	61.6	62.8	62.4	61.3	59.5	57.2	40
50	56.0	61.6	62.8	62.4	61.2	59.4	57.1	50
00	4° 56.4	9° 61.7	14° 62.8	19° 62.4	24° 61.2	29° 59.3	34° 57.0	00
10	56.7	61.8	62.8	62.3	61.1	59.3	56.9	10
20	57.1	61.9	62.8	62.3	61.1	59.2	56.9	20
30	57.4	61.9	62.8	62.3	61.0	59.1	56.8	30
40	57.7	62.0	62.8	62.2	60.9	59.1	56.7	40
50	57.9	62.1	62.8	62.2	60.9	59.0	56.6	50

H.P.	L U	L U	L U	L U	L U	L U	L U	H.P.
54.0	0.3 0.9	0.3 0.9	0.4 1.0	0.5 1.1	0.6 1.2	0.7 1.3	0.9 1.5	54.0
54.3	0.7 1.1	0.7 1.2	0.7 1.2	0.8 1.3	0.9 1.4	1.1 1.5	1.2 1.7	54.3
54.6	1.1 1.4	1.1 1.4	1.1 1.4	1.2 1.5	1.3 1.6	1.4 1.7	1.5 1.8	54.6
54.9	1.4 1.6	1.5 1.6	1.5 1.6	1.6 1.7	1.6 1.8	1.8 1.9	1.9 2.0	54.9
55.2	1.8 1.8	1.8 1.8	1.9 1.9	1.9 1.9	2.0 2.0	2.1 2.1	2.2 2.2	55.2
55.5	2.2 2.0	2.2 2.0	2.3 2.1	2.3 2.1	2.4 2.2	2.4 2.3	2.5 2.4	55.5
55.8	2.6 2.2	2.6 2.2	2.6 2.3	2.7 2.3	2.7 2.4	2.8 2.4	2.9 2.5	55.8
56.1	3.0 2.4	3.0 2.5	3.0 2.5	3.0 2.5	3.1 2.6	3.1 2.6	3.2 2.7	56.1
56.4	3.4 2.7	3.4 2.7	3.4 2.7	3.4 2.7	3.4 2.8	3.5 2.8	3.5 2.9	56.4
56.7	3.7 2.9	3.7 2.9	3.8 2.9	3.8 2.9	3.8 3.0	3.8 3.0	3.9 3.0	56.7
57.0	4.1 3.1	4.1 3.1	4.1 3.1	4.1 3.1	4.2 3.1	4.2 3.2	4.2 3.2	57.0
57.3	4.5 3.3	4.5 3.3	4.5 3.3	4.5 3.3	4.5 3.3	4.5 3.4	4.6 3.4	57.3
57.6	4.9 3.5	4.9 3.5	4.9 3.5	4.9 3.5	4.9 3.5	4.9 3.5	4.9 3.6	57.6
57.9	5.3 3.8	5.3 3.8	5.2 3.8	5.2 3.7	5.2 3.7	5.2 3.7	5.2 3.7	57.9
58.2	5.6 4.0	5.6 4.0	5.6 4.0	5.6 4.0	5.6 3.9	5.6 3.9	5.6 3.9	58.2
58.5	6.0 4.2	6.0 4.2	6.0 4.2	6.0 4.2	6.0 4.1	5.9 4.1	5.9 4.1	58.5
58.8	6.4 4.4	6.4 4.4	6.4 4.4	6.3 4.4	6.3 4.3	6.3 4.3	6.2 4.2	58.8
59.1	6.8 4.6	6.8 4.6	6.7 4.6	6.7 4.6	6.7 4.5	6.6 4.5	6.6 4.4	59.1
59.4	7.2 4.8	7.1 4.8	7.1 4.8	7.1 4.8	7.0 4.7	7.0 4.7	6.9 4.6	59.4
59.7	7.5 5.1	7.5 5.0	7.5 5.0	7.5 5.0	7.4 4.9	7.3 4.8	7.2 4.7	59.7
60.0	7.9 5.3	7.9 5.3	7.9 5.2	7.8 5.2	7.8 5.1	7.7 5.0	7.6 4.9	60.0
60.3	8.3 5.5	8.3 5.5	8.2 5.4	8.2 5.4	8.1 5.3	8.0 5.2	7.9 5.1	60.3
60.6	8.7 5.7	8.7 5.7	8.6 5.7	8.6 5.6	8.5 5.5	8.4 5.4	8.2 5.3	60.6
60.9	9.1 5.9	9.0 5.9	9.0 5.9	8.9 5.8	8.8 5.7	8.7 5.6	8.6 5.4	60.9
61.2	9.5 6.2	9.4 6.1	9.4 6.1	9.3 6.0	9.2 5.9	9.1 5.8	8.9 5.6	61.2
61.5	9.8 6.4	9.8 6.3	9.7 6.3	9.7 6.2	9.5 6.1	9.4 5.9	9.2 5.8	61.5

DIP

Ht. of Eye	Corrⁿ	Ht. of Eye	Ht. of Eye	Corrⁿ	Ht. of Eye
m		ft.	m		ft.
2.4	−2.8	8.0	9.5	−5.5	31.5
2.6	−2.9	8.6	9.9	−5.6	32.7
2.8	−3.0	9.2	10.3	−5.7	33.9
3.0	−3.1	9.8	10.6	−5.8	35.1
3.2	−3.2	10.5	11.0	−5.9	36.3
3.4	−3.3	11.2	11.4	−6.0	37.6
3.6	−3.4	11.9	11.8	−6.1	38.9
3.8	−3.5	12.6	12.2	−6.2	40.1
4.0	−3.6	13.3	12.6	−6.3	41.5
4.3	−3.7	14.1	13.0	−6.4	42.8
4.5	−3.8	14.9	13.4	−6.5	44.2
4.7	−3.9	15.7	13.8	−6.6	45.5
5.0	−4.0	16.5	14.2	−6.7	46.9
5.2	−4.1	17.4	14.7	−6.8	48.4
5.5	−4.2	18.3	15.1	−6.9	49.8
5.8	−4.3	19.1	15.5	−7.0	51.3
6.1	−4.4	20.1	16.0	−7.1	52.8
6.3	−4.5	21.0	16.5	−7.2	54.3
6.6	−4.6	22.0	16.9	−7.3	55.8
6.9	−4.7	22.9	17.4	−7.4	57.4
7.2	−4.8	23.9	17.9	−7.5	58.9
7.5	−4.9	24.9	18.4	−7.6	60.5
7.9	−5.0	26.0	18.8	−7.7	62.1
8.2	−5.1	27.1	19.3	−7.8	63.8
8.5	−5.2	28.1	19.8	−7.9	65.4
8.8	−5.3	29.2	20.4	−8.0	67.1
9.2	−5.4	30.4	20.9	−8.1	68.8
9.5		31.5	21.4		70.5

MOON CORRECTION TABLE

The correction is in two parts; the first correction is taken from the upper part of the table with argument apparent altitude, and the second from the lower part, with argument H.P., in the same column as that from which the first correction was taken. Separate corrections are given in the lower part for lower (L) and upper (U) limbs. All corrections are to be **added** to apparent altitude, *but 30′ is to be subtracted from the altitude of the upper limb.*

For corrections for pressure and temperature see page A4.

For bubble sextant observations ignore dip, take the mean of upper and lower limb corrections and subtract 15′ from the altitude.

App. Alt. = Apparent altitude = Sextant altitude corrected for index error and dip.

43   Time, longitude and hour angle

As explained earlier, one of the fundamental pieces of information needed in astronomical navigation is the geographical position of the heavenly body being observed – this is the position on the surface of the earth from which the body appears to be vertically overhead. Because the earth itself is both rotating on its axis and moving in an orbit around the sun, the geographical position moves very quickly. By using the *Nautical Almanac*, the geographical position of the body can be established for any particular time throughout the year, but to make proper use of this information it is necessary to understand the somewhat unfamiliar relationship between time, longitude and the related quantity known as hour angle.

Figure 1 shows the earth, viewed from a point in space directly above the south pole. The sun is shining from what can be considered a fixed direction, while the earth is rotating clockwise. If we imagine a gigantic clock face, graduated into 24 one-hour divisions, fixed to the sun, and also imagine an hour hand attached to the earth, then this hour hand will sweep through the 24 hours of the day as the earth rotates on its axis. The time thus measured is *solar time*, the time that would be shown (in daylight) on a sundial.

Figure 1 also shows that the time of day, measured by the sun, depends upon the longitude of the observer. The datum for measuring time is the same as the datum for measuring longitude, the Greenwich meridian. If an observer is west of the Greenwich meridian, his time is *earlier* than

that at Greenwich; if he is east of the Greenwich meridian his time is *later*. There is an exact relationship between time and longitude. As the earth rotates through 360° in 24 hours (or 15° in one hour), a time difference of one hour is the same as a longitude difference of 15°.

The situation is complicated by the fact that the earth also travels in an orbit around the sun, with a period of one year. The earth moves faster in some parts of its orbit than in others, and this makes the sun an irregular timepiece; each day, from noon to noon or midnight to midnight, has a slightly different length. To overcome this difficulty, the astronomers have invented the *mean sun*, an imaginary body which clocks off a regular day of 24 hours exactly (Fig. 2). At different times of the year, the true sun can be up to a quarter of an hour fast or slow on the mean sun – a quantity known as the *equation of time*. This quantity is not often used in astronomical navigation, but is given on the daily pages of the *Nautical Almanac* if needed.

In Figure 2, the imaginary clock face has now been fixed with relationship to the mean sun, and the hour hand at the Greenwich meridian now sweeps out *Greenwich mean time*. The hour hand of an observer in a different longitude shows his *local mean time*, which is, of course, related to Greenwich mean time by his longitude, at the rate of one hour of time for 15° of longitude. For example:

GMT 12 h 00 m 00 s longitude 30°W LMT 10 h 00 m 00 s
17 h 30 m 00 s ″ 75°E ″ 22 h 30 m 00 s

43.1 *Time and longitude.*

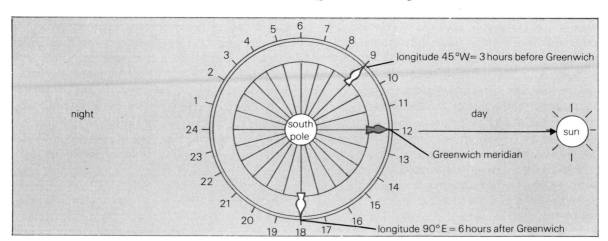

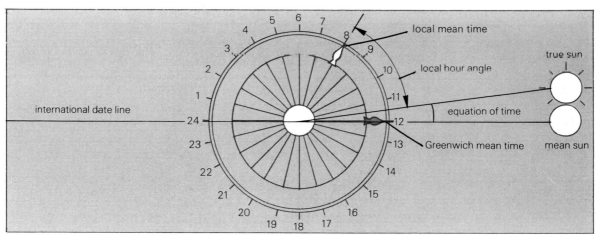

43.2 *The mean sun and hour angle.*

It may happen that the combination of Greenwich mean time and the observer's longitude puts him on the opposite side of the midnight mark of the clock face, which means that the date changes. For example:

GMT 01 h 00 m 00 s longitude 45°W LMT 22 h 00 m 00 s
    5 May   *the previous day*
                                          4 May

    17 h 30 m 00 s   150°E   03 h 30 m 00 s
    12 August   *the next day*
                                         13 August

One curious effect of the relationship between time and longitude is that, if nothing were done, a traveller who went round the world would find that the date on his calendar would be different from the date being kept at his starting point – he would apparently have gained or lost a day, depending on which way round the world he went. To correct for this, the *international date line* has been established, running more or less along the meridian of 180° east or west (with diversions to keep island groups on the same side). The date on the eastern side of the line is one day behind the date on the western side (as is the day of the week). A vessel crossing the date line has to adjust its calendar appropriately; crossing from east to west, add a day – from west to east, subtract a day.

Local mean time depends upon the longitude, but it would be very inconvenient if every place within a country kept a different time. National governments therefore establish a *civil time*, which is the official time to be kept in that country (big countries like Australia or the United States need several civil times as they span a lot of longitude). Civil time is generally (but not always) an exact number of hours ahead of or behind GMT; details are given in the *Nautical Almanac*. Many countries also keep some form of daylight saving time in summer – generally one hour ahead of the normal civil time. This is called *summer time*.

For convenience, a similar scheme is adopted by ships at sea. The world is divided up into 24 zones, each 15° wide in longitude, centred on the Greenwich meridian; the time kept in each zone is an appropriate number of hours ahead or behind Greenwich (Fig. 3). Thus, between $7\frac{1}{2}$°W and $7\frac{1}{2}$°E, GMT is kept, between $7\frac{1}{2}$°W and $22\frac{1}{2}$°W, zone + 1 is kept, and so on. The sign given to the zone indicates how many hours must be added to or subtracted from the local zone time to get back to GMT.

It is very often necessary to convert from civil time or zone time to GMT, as all entries in the *Nautical Almanac* are referred to GMT. In making this conversion, the navigator must always be alert to the possibility of the date at Greenwich being different from the date he is keeping; this could result in his looking up data in the almanac for the wrong day. Each such conversion should contain a check of the *Greenwich date*. For example:

Zone date and time   24 May 04 h 45 m
Zone kept   −6 hours
Greenwich date and time 23 May 22 h 45 m

43.3 *Time zones.*

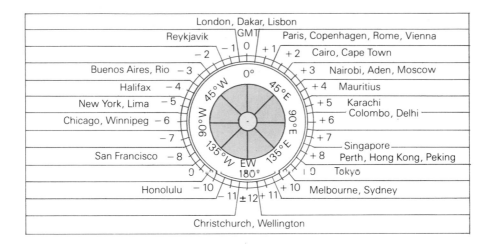

Hour angle

As can be seen in Figure 2, the true sun is not in line with the mean sun – the difference between them being the equation of time. Another way of considering this is to say that the sun has a longitude which changes continually as the earth rotates; the same thing can be said of any heavenly body. For convenience, the longitude of heavenly bodies is not used in navigation; it is replaced by a very similar quantity known as *Greenwich hour angle*. The Greenwich hour angle of a body is the angle, measured westwards, between the meridian of Greenwich and the meridian over which the body stands. Unlike longitude, the Greenwich hour angle starts at 0° when the body is on the Greenwich meridian, and increases throughout (roughly) 24 hours to 360°, when it is once more on the Greenwich meridian. The Greenwich hour angle of important heavenly bodies is tabulated for each hour in the daily pages of the *Nautical Almanac*.

The navigator generally is more interested in the angle between his own meridian and the body, rather than the Greenwich meridian. He can obtain this angle, known as the *local hour angle*, by combining the GHA from the nautical almanac with his longitude, using the rule:

> GHA to LHA – add easterly longitude
> subtract westerly longitude.

For example:

GHA	27°15'.9
Long E	14°11'.5 (E long, so add)
LHA	41°27'.4

GHA	331°11'.2
Long W	72°54'.0 (W long, so subtract)
LHA	258°17'.2

If the combination of GHA and longitude results in a negative number, add 360°; if the result exceeds 360°, then subtract 360° from the answer.

For example:

GHA	345°
Long E	44°
LHA	389° − 360° = 29°

GHA	35°
Long W	102°
LHA	−67° + 360° = 353°

Keeping GMT

To establish the GP of a body, GMT must be known. A modern quartz timepiece, with a periodic check from a radio time signal, will suit admirably but it is wise to have a back-up timepiece as well. A quartz wristwatch will be quite suitable, even if it belongs to another member of the crew. This, too, should be checked regularly against time signals.

44 The geographical position – declination and Greenwich hour angle

The geographical position of any body of navigational importance can be established for any second of GMT throughout the year by using the *Nautical Almanac*. Various almanacs exist, mostly published by the national authorities of various countries. The *Nautical Almanac* used in this book is the one published jointly by the British Nautical Alamanac Office and the United States Naval Observatory; the British publication is known as N.P. 314. Almanacs are normally published at least a year in advance, to cope with the needs of vessels making extended passages.

The data from this almanac is now used by a dozen other countries, with necessary changes for language and so on.

The *Nautical Almanac* defines the geographical positions of bodies by using two quantities which correspond closely with latitude and longitude – *declination* and *Greenwich hour angle* respectively.

The declination of a body is exactly equivalent to the latitude of the geographical position; it is expressed in degrees, minutes and decimals either north or south of the equator.

The longitude of the geographical position is expressed as its Greenwich hour angle (GHA). The only real difference between them is that longitude is given either east or west of the Greenwich meridian; GHA is given in degrees, minutes and decimals *west* of the Greenwich meridian. It is possible (though not often necessary) to convert GHA to longitude by the following process:

GHA between 0° and 180° – longitude west = GHA

GHA between 180° and 360° – longitude east = 360° − GHA

Both the declination and the Greenwich hour angle for the navigationally important objects are given for each hour throughout the year on the daily pages of the *Nautical Almanac* (Table 1). Each page opening gives the data needed by a navigator for three days, with the hours of GMT down the left-hand side of each page. The daily pages contain much information apart from declination and GHA; these items will be described as they are needed.

Finding the declination

Declination is the easier of the two quantities to obtain, as it changes relatively slowly.

Stars The declination of the 57 most commonly used stars is given in the right-hand column of the left page (Table 1). This value can be used without correction at any time during the three days to which the daily page refers.

Sun, Venus, Mars, Jupiter, Saturn Each of these bodies has its own column for both GHA and declination. Using the correct day and the hour of GMT, extract the value of declination for the hour, not forgetting to note whether it is north or south. Also, glance down the column to see if the declination is increasing in magnitude or decreasing; this is needed for the correction of declination for minutes of GMT described below. Then record the value d, given at the foot of the column; if the declination is increasing in magnitude, give d a + sign, otherwise call it − . d gives the rate of change of declination in one hour.

Moon The declination of the moon is obtained in the same way as that of the sun and planets, except that d is given for each hour rather than a three-day period.

Correcting declination The declination is constantly changing, as expressed by the value of d; the value given in the *Nautical Almanac* is only correct at the exact hour of GMT, so a correction must be applied for the minutes past the hour of the observation. In the case of the sun and the planets, d is small and a mental interpolation is quite accurate enough – for 15 minutes past the hour, use $\frac{1}{4}d$, 30 minutes past $\frac{1}{2}d$, 45 minutes past $\frac{3}{4}d$ and so on. For the moon, d can be quite large (up to 10′ per hour) and a more accurate interpolation is needed. A table of increments and corrections is provided at the back of the almanac, for correcting both GHA and declination. To obtain the d correction, find the section of the table corresponding to the minutes of GMT (Table 2). In the columns headed 'v or d', search for the appropriate value of d (small type). The correction to apply is given beside it in larger type.

Whether d is interpolated by eye or by means of the increments and corrections table, the value found should be added or subtracted from the declination found in the daily pages, according to the sign given to d earlier.

Table 1 Almanac *daily page*.

1980 MAY 3, 4, 5 (SAT., SUN., MON.)

G.M.T.	ARIES G.H.A.	VENUS −4.2 G.H.A.	Dec.	MARS +0.4 G.H.A.	Dec.	JUPITER −1.8 G.H.A.	Dec.	SATURN +1.0 G.H.A.	Dec.	STARS Name	S.H.A.	Dec.
3 00	221 02.7	136 57.5	N27 38.3	68 30.5	N13 28.6	68 13.2	N12 30.5	48 49.7	N 5 55.3	Acamar	315 37.9	S40 23.2
01	236 05.2	151 58.2	38.4	83 32.4	28.3	83 15.6	30.4	63 52.2	55.3	Achernar	335 46.1	S57 20.2
02	251 07.7	166 58.8	38.4	98 34.3	28.0	98 18.1	30.4	78 54.8	55.4	Acrux	173 36.9	S62 59.6
03	266 10.1	181 59.5	·· 38.5	113 36.1	·· 27.7	113 20.5	·· 30.4	93 57.3	·· 55.4	Adhara	255 32.5	S28 57.0
04	281 12.6	197 00.2	38.6	128 38.0	27.4	128 22.9	30.4	108 59.9	55.4	Aldebaran	291 18.6	N16 28.0
05	296 15.1	212 00.8	38.6	143 39.8	27.0	143 25.3	30.3	124 02.4	55.4			
06	311 17.5	227 01.5	N27 38.7	158 41.7	N13 26.7	158 27.7	N12 30.3	139 04.9	N 5 55.5	Alioth	166 42.3	N56 04.2
07	326 20.0	242 02.2	38.7	173 43.5	26.4	173 30.1	30.3	154 07.5	55.5	Alkaid	153 18.3	N49 24.8
S 08	341 22.5	257 02.9	38.8	188 45.4	26.1	188 32.6	30.3	169 10.0	55.5	Al Na'ir	28 15.5	S47 03.3
A 09	356 24.9	272 03.5	·· 38.9	203 47.2	·· 25.8	203 35.0	·· 30.2	184 12.6	·· 55.6	Alnilam	276 12.2	S 1 13.0
T 10	11 27.4	287 04.2	38.9	218 49.1	25.5	218 37.4	30.2	199 15.1	55.6	Alphard	210 20.8	S 8 34.5
U 11	26 29.8	302 04.9	39.0	233 50.9	25.2	233 39.8	30.2	214 17.6	55.6			
R 12	41 32.3	317 05.6	N27 39.0	248 52.8	N13 24.8	248 42.2	N12 30.2	229 20.2	N 5 55.6	Alphecca	126 32.0	N26 46.9
D 13	56 34.8	332 06.3	39.1	263 54.6	24.5	263 44.6	30.1	244 22.7	55.7	Alpheratz	358 09.9	N28 58.6
A 14	71 37.2	347 07.0	39.1	278 56.4	24.2	278 47.1	30.1	259 25.3	55.7	Altair	62 32.7	N 8 48.9
Y 15	86 39.7	2 07.7	·· 39.2	293 58.3	·· 23.9	293 49.5	·· 30.1	274 27.8	·· 55.7	Ankaa	353 40.9	S42 24.8
16	101 42.2	17 08.4	39.2	309 00.1	23.6	308 51.9	30.1	289 30.4	55.7	Antares	112 56.9	S26 23.3
17	116 44.6	32 09.1	39.3	324 02.0	23.3	323 54.3	30.0	304 32.9	55.8			
18	131 47.1	47 09.8	N27 39.0	339 03.8	N13 22.9	338 56.7	N12 30.0	319 35.4	N 5 55.8	Arcturus	146 18.4	N19 17.1
19	146 49.6	62 10.5	39.4	354 05.7	22.6	353 59.1	30.0	334 38.0	55.8	Atria	108 20.9	S68 59.4
20	161 52.0	77 11.2	39.4	9 07.5	22.3	9 01.5	30.0	349 40.5	55.8	Avior	234 28.4	S59 27.1
21	176 54.5	92 11.9	·· 39.5	24 09.3	·· 22.0	24 03.9	·· 29.9	4 43.0	·· 55.9	Bellatrix	278 59.3	N 6 19.8
22	191 57.0	107 12.6	39.5	39 11.2	21.7	39 06.4	29.9	19 45.6	55.9	Betelgeuse	271 28.8	N 7 24.1
23	206 59.4	122 13.3	39.6	54 13.0	21.3	54 08.8	29.9	34 48.1	55.9			
4 00	222 01.9	137 14.0	N27 39.6	69 14.8	N13 21.0	69 11.2	N12 29.9	49 50.7	N 5 55.9	Canopus	264 07.7	S52 41.4
01	237 04.3	152 14.7	39.7	84 16.7	20.7	84 13.6	29.8	64 53.2	56.0	Capella	281 12.1	N45 58.7
02	252 06.8	167 15.4	39.7	99 18.5	20.4	99 16.0	29.8	79 55.7	56.0	Deneb	49 48.6	N45 12.3
03	267 09.3	182 16.2	·· 39.7	114 20.4	·· 20.1	114 18.4	·· 29.8	94 58.3	·· 56.0	Denebola	182 59.1	N14 41.0
04	282 11.7	197 16.9	39.8	129 22.2	19.7	129 20.8	29.7	110 00.8	56.0	Diphda	349 21.5	S18 05.8
05	297 14.2	212 17.6	39.8	144 24.0	19.4	144 23.2	29.7	125 03.4	56.0			
06	312 16.7	227 18.3	N27 39.9	159 25.9	N13 19.1	159 25.6	N12 29.7	140 05.9	N 5 56.1	Dubhe	194 22.2	N61 51.7
07	327 19.1	242 19.1	39.9	174 27.7	18.8	174 28.0	29.7	155 08.4	56.1	Elnath	278 44.8	N28 35.4
08	342 21.6	257 19.8	39.9	189 29.5	18.5	189 30.5	29.6	170 11.0	56.1	Eltanin	90 57.5	N51 29.3
S 09	357 24.1	272 20.5	·· 40.0	204 31.4	·· 18.1	204 32.9	·· 29.6	185 13.5	·· 56.1	Enif	34 11.9	N 9 46.9
U 10	12 26.5	287 21.3	40.0	219 33.2	17.8	219 35.3	29.6	200 16.0	56.2	Fomalhaut	15 51.9	S29 43.6
N 11	27 29.0	302 22.0	40.0	234 35.0	17.5	234 37.7	29.6	215 18.6	56.2			
D 12	42 31.5	317 22.8	N27 40.1	249 36.8	N13 17.2	249 40.1	N12 29.5	230 21.1	N 5 56.2	Gacrux	172 28.5	S57 00.3
A 13	57 33.9	332 23.5	40.1	264 38.7	16.9	264 42.5	29.5	245 23.7	56.2	Gienah	176 18.0	S17 26.0
Y 14	72 36.4	347 24.2	40.2	279 40.5	16.5	279 44.9	29.5	260 26.2	56.3	Hadar	149 23.1	S60 16.7
15	87 38.8	2 25.0	·· 40.2	294 42.3	·· 16.2	294 47.3	·· 29.4	275 28.7	·· 56.3	Hamal	328 29.6	N23 22.0
16	102 41.3	17 25.7	40.2	309 44.1	15.9	309 49.7	29.4	290 31.3	56.3	Kaus Aust.	84 17.0	S34 23.5
17	117 43.8	32 26.5	40.2	324 46.0	15.6	324 52.1	29.4	305 33.8	56.3			
18	132 46.2	47 27.3	N27 40.3	339 47.8	N13 15.2	339 54.5	N12 29.4	320 36.3	N 5 56.4	Kochab	137 17.9	N74 14.3
19	147 48.7	62 28.0	40.3	354 49.6	14.9	354 56.9	29.3	335 38.9	56.4	Markab	14 03.6	N15 05.7
20	162 51.2	77 28.8	40.3	9 51.4	14.6	9 59.3	29.3	350 41.4	56.4	Menkar	314 41.8	N 4 00.6
21	177 53.6	92 29.5	·· 40.4	24 53.3	·· 14.3	25 01.7	·· 29.3	5 43.9	·· 56.4	Menkent	148 36.5	S36 16.4
22	192 56.1	107 30.3	40.4	39 55.1	13.9	40 04.1	29.2	20 46.5	56.4	Miaplacidus	221 44.9	S69 38.5
23	207 58.6	122 31.1	40.4	54 56.9	13.6	55 06.5	29.2	35 49.0	56.5			
5 00	223 01.0	137 31.8	N27 40.4	69 58.7	N13 13.3	70 08.9	N12 29.2	50 51.6	N 5 56.5	Mirfak	309 17.0	N49 47.4
01	238 03.5	152 32.6	40.5	85 00.5	13.0	85 11.4	29.1	65 54.1	56.5	Nunki	76 29.3	S26 19.2
02	253 05.9	167 33.4	40.5	100 02.4	12.6	100 13.8	29.1	80 56.6	56.5	Peacock	53 58.8	S56 47.7
03	268 08.4	182 34.2	·· 40.5	115 04.2	·· 12.3	115 16.2	·· 29.1	95 59.2	·· 56.6	Pollux	243 58.7	N28 04.5
04	283 10.9	197 35.0	40.5	130 06.0	12.0	130 18.6	29.1	111 01.7	56.6	Procyon	245 26.2	N 5 16.4
05	298 13.3	212 35.7	40.6	145 07.8	11.7	145 21.0	29.0	126 04.2	56.6			
06	313 15.8	227 36.5	N27 40.6	160 09.6	N13 11.3	160 23.4	N12 29.0	141 06.8	N 5 56.6	Rasalhague	96 29.6	N12 34.4
07	328 18.3	242 37.3	40.6	175 11.5	11.0	175 25.8	29.0	156 09.3	56.7	Regulus	208 10.2	N12 03.8
08	343 20.7	257 38.1	40.6	190 13.3	10.7	190 28.2	28.9	171 11.8	56.7	Rigel	281 36.6	S 8 13.7
M 09	358 23.2	272 38.9	·· 40.6	205 15.1	·· 10.3	205 30.6	·· 28.9	186 14.4	·· 56.7	Rigil Kent.	140 25.5	S60 45.2
O 10	13 25.7	287 39.7	40.6	220 16.9	10.0	220 33.0	28.9	201 16.9	56.7	Sabik	102 41.2	S15 42.0
N 11	28 28.1	302 40.5	40.7	235 18.7	09.7	235 35.4	28.8	216 19.4	56.7			
D 12	43 30.6	317 41.3	N27 40.7	250 20.5	N13 09.4	250 37.8	N12 28.8	231 22.0	N 5 56.8	Schedar	350 09.7	N56 25.5
A 13	58 33.1	332 42.1	40.7	265 22.3	09.0	265 40.2	28.8	246 24.5	56.8	Shaula	96 55.8	S37 05.3
Y 14	73 35.5	347 42.9	40.7	280 24.1	08.7	280 42.6	28.8	261 27.0	56.8	Sirius	258 56.2	S16 41.6
15	88 38.0	2 43.7	·· 40.7	295 25.9	·· 08.4	295 45.0	·· 28.7	276 29.6	·· 56.8	Spica	158 57.5	S11 03.6
16	103 40.4	17 44.5	40.7	310 27.8	08.0	310 47.4	28.7	291 32.1	56.8	Suhail	223 11.0	S43 21.5
17	118 42.9	32 45.3	40.8	325 29.6	07.7	325 49.8	28.7	306 34.6	56.9			
18	133 45.4	47 46.2	N27 40.8	340 31.4	N13 07.3	340 52.2	N12 28.6	321 37.2	N 5 56.9	Vega	80 55.8	N38 45.8
19	148 47.8	62 47.0	40.8	355 33.2	07.1	355 54.6	28.6	336 39.7	56.9	Zuben'ubi	137 33.0	S15 57.6
20	163 50.3	77 47.8	40.8	10 35.0	06.7	10 57.0	28.6	351 42.2	57.0			
21	178 52.8	92 48.6	·· 40.8	25 36.8	·· 06.4	25 59.4	·· 28.5	6 44.8	·· 57.0		S.H.A.	Mer. Pass.
22	193 55.2	107 49.4	40.8	40 38.6	06.1	41 01.8	28.5	21 47.3	57.0	Venus	275 12.1	14 50
23	208 57.7	122 50.3	40.8	55 40.4	05.7	56 04.2	28.5	36 49.8	57.0	Mars	207 13.0	19 21
Mer. Pass.	9 10.4	v 0.7	d 0.0	v 1.8	d 0.3	v 2.4	d 0.0	v 2.5	d 0.0	Jupiter	207 09.3	19 20
										Saturn	187 48.8	20 37

138

1980 MAY 3, 4, 5 (SAT., SUN., MON.)

G.M.T.	SUN G.H.A.	Dec.	MOON G.H.A.	v	Dec.	d	H.P.
	o ' o '		o '	'	o '	'	'
3 00	180 47.1 N15 39.2		328 25.9	10.8	S17 39.5	4.5	55.7
01	195 47.1	39.9	342 55.7	10.7	17 44.0	4.5	55.8
02	210 47.2	40.7	357 25.4	10.6	17 48.5	4.3	55.8
03	225 47.3 ··	41.4	11 55.0	10.6	17 52.8	4.3	55.8
04	240 47.3	42.1	26 24.6	10.6	17 57.1	4.2	55.8
05	255 47.4	42.9	40 54.2	10.5	18 01.3	4.1	55.8
06	270 47.5 N15 43.6		55 23.7	10.4	S18 05.4	4.0	55.9
07	285 47.5	44.3	69 53.1	10.4	18 09.4	3.9	55.9
S 08	300 47.6	45.1	84 22.5	10.4	18 13.3	3.8	55.9
A 09	315 47.7 ··	45.8	98 51.9	10.3	18 17.1	3.8	55.9
T 10	330 47.7	46.5	113 21.2	10.3	18 20.9	3.6	55.9
U 11	345 47.8	47.3	127 50.5	10.2	18 24.5	3.5	56.0
R 12	0 47.8 N15 48.0		142 19.7	10.2	S18 28.0	3.5	56.0
D 13	15 47.9	48.7	156 48.9	10.2	18 31.5	3.4	56.0
A 14	30 48.0	49.5	171 18.1	10.1	18 34.9	3.2	56.0
Y 15	45 48.0 ··	50.2	185 47.2	10.0	18 38.1	3.2	56.0
16	60 48.1	50.9	200 16.2	10.0	18 41.3	3.1	56.1
17	75 48.2	51.6	214 45.2	10.0	18 44.4	2.9	56.1
18	90 48.2 N15 52.4		229 14.2	9.9	S18 47.3	2.9	56.1
19	105 48.3	53.1	243 43.1	9.9	18 50.2	2.8	56.1
20	120 48.3	53.8	258 12.0	9.9	18 53.0	2.7	56.1
21	135 48.4 ··	54.6	272 40.9	9.8	18 55.7	2.5	56.2
22	150 48.5	55.3	287 09.7	9.7	18 58.2	2.5	56.2
23	165 48.5	56.0	301 38.4	9.7	19 00.7	2.4	56.2
4 00	180 48.6 N15 56.7		316 07.1	9.7	S19 03.1	2.3	56.2
01	195 48.6	57.5	330 35.8	9.7	19 05.4	2.2	56.3
02	210 48.7	58.2	345 04.5	9.6	19 07.6	2.1	56.3
03	225 48.8 ··	58.9	359 33.1	9.6	19 09.7	1.9	56.3
04	240 48.8 15 59.6		14 01.6	9.6	19 11.6	1.9	56.3
05	255 48.9 16 00.3		28 30.2	9.5	19 13.5	1.8	56.3
06	270 48.9 N16 01.1		42 58.7	9.4	S19 15.3	1.6	56.4
07	285 49.0	01.8	57 27.1	9.4	19 16.9	1.6	56.4
08	300 49.1	02.5	71 55.5	9.4	19 18.5	1.5	56.4
S 09	315 49.1 ··	03.2	86 23.9	9.4	19 20.0	1.3	56.4
U 10	330 49.2	04.0	100 52.3	9.3	19 21.3	1.3	56.5
N 11	345 49.2	04.7	115 20.6	9.3	19 22.6	1.1	56.5
D 12	0 49.3 N16 05.4		129 48.9	9.2	S19 23.7	1.1	56.5
A 13	15 49.4	06.1	144 17.1	9.3	19 24.8	0.9	56.5
Y 14	30 49.4	06.8	158 45.4	9.2	19 25.7	0.8	56.5
15	45 49.5 ··	07.5	173 13.6	9.2	19 26.5	0.8	56.6
16	60 49.5	08.3	187 41.7	9.1	19 27.3	0.6	56.6
17	75 49.6	09.0	202 09.8	9.1	19 27.9	0.5	56.6
18	90 49.6 N16 09.7		216 37.9	9.1	S19 28.4	0.4	56.6
19	105 49.7	10.4	231 06.0	9.1	19 28.8	0.3	56.7
20	120 49.7	11.1	245 34.1	9.0	19 29.1	0.2	56.7
21	135 49.8 ··	11.8	260 02.1	9.0	19 29.3	0.1	56.7
22	150 49.9	12.6	274 30.1	8.9	19 29.4	0.1	56.7
23	165 49.9	13.3	288 58.0	8.9	19 29.3	0.1	56.8
5 00	180 50.0 N16 14.0		303 25.9	8.9	S19 29.2	0.3	56.8
01	195 50.0	14.7	317 53.9	8.8	19 28.9	0.3	56.8
02	210 50.1	15.4	332 21.7	8.9	19 28.6	0.5	56.8
03	225 50.1 ··	16.1	346 49.6	8.8	19 28.1	0.6	56.9
04	240 50.2	16.8	1 17.4	8.9	19 27.5	0.6	56.9
05	255 50.2	17.6	15 45.3	8.7	19 26.9	0.8	56.9
06	270 50.3 N16 18.3		30 13.0	8.8	S19 26.1	0.9	56.9
07	285 50.3	19.0	44 40.8	8.8	19 25.2	1.1	57.0
08	300 50.4	19.7	59 08.6	8.7	19 24.1	1.1	57.0
M 09	315 50.4 ··	20.4	73 36.3	8.7	19 23.0	1.2	57.0
O 10	330 50.5	21.1	88 04.0	8.7	19 21.8	1.4	57.0
N 11	345 50.5	21.8	102 31.7	8.7	19 20.4	1.4	57.0
D 12	0 50.6 N16 22.5		116 59.4	8.6	S19 19.0	1.6	57.1
A 13	15 50.7	23.2	131 27.0	8.7	19 17.4	1.7	57.1
Y 14	30 50.7	23.9	145 54.7	8.6	19 15.7	1.8	57.1
15	45 50.8 ··	24.6	160 22.3	8.6	19 13.9	1.9	57.1
16	60 50.8	25.4	174 49.9	8.6	19 12.0	2.0	57.2
17	75 50.9	26.1	189 17.5	8.6	19 10.0	2.1	57.2
18	90 50.9 N16 26.8		203 45.1	8.6	S19 07.9	2.2	57.2
19	105 51.0	27.5	218 12.7	8.5	19 05.7	2.4	57.2
20	120 51.0	28.2	232 40.2	8.6	19 03.3	2.5	57.3
21	135 51.1 ··	28.9	247 07.8	8.5	19 00.8	2.5	57.3
22	150 51.1	29.6	261 35.3	8.5	18 58.3	2.7	57.3
23	165 51.1	30.3	276 02.8	8.5	18 55.6	2.8	57.4
	S.D. 15.9 d 0.7		S.D. 15.3	15.4			15.6

Lat.	Twilight Naut.	Civil	Sunrise	Moonrise 3	4	5	6
o	h m	h m	h m	h m	h m	h m	h m
N 72	////	////	01 23	01 45	■	■	■
N 70	////	////	02 12	00 14	01 53	03 05	03 24
68	////	00 13	02 43	24 56	00 56	01 58	02 35
66	////	01 35	03 05	24 22	00 22	01 22	02 04
64	////	02 10	03 23	23 57	24 56	00 56	01 40
62	00 11	02 35	03 37	23 38	24 36	00 36	01 22
60	01 24	02 55	03 50	23 22	24 19	00 19	01 07
N 58	01 57	03 10	04 00	23 09	24 06	00 06	00 53
56	02 20	03 24	04 09	22 57	23 54	24 42	00 42
54	02 38	03 35	04 17	22 47	23 43	24 32	00 32
52	02 53	03 45	04 25	22 38	23 34	24 24	00 24
50	03 06	03 54	04 31	22 30	23 26	24 16	00 16
45	03 31	04 12	04 45	22 13	23 08	23 59	24 44
N 40	03 51	04 27	04 56	21 59	22 54	23 45	24 32
35	04 06	04 39	05 06	21 47	22 42	23 33	24 22
30	04 19	04 49	05 15	21 37	22 31	23 23	24 12
20	04 39	05 06	05 29	21 19	22 13	23 05	23 56
N 10	04 54	05 20	05 42	21 04	21 57	22 50	23 43
0	05 07	05 32	05 53	20 49	21 42	22 35	23 30
S 10	05 18	05 43	06 05	20 35	21 27	22 21	23 16
20	05 28	05 54	06 17	20 20	21 11	22 06	23 03
30	05 37	06 06	06 31	20 02	20 53	21 48	22 47
35	05 42	06 12	06 39	19 52	20 42	21 38	22 37
40	05 47	06 19	06 48	19 41	20 30	21 26	22 27
45	05 52	06 27	06 58	19 27	20 16	21 12	22 14
S 50	05 58	06 37	07 11	19 10	19 59	20 55	21 59
52	06 00	06 41	07 17	19 03	19 51	20 47	21 52
54	06 03	06 45	07 24	18 54	19 41	20 38	21 44
56	06 06	06 50	07 31	18 44	19 31	20 28	21 35
58	06 08	06 56	07 39	18 33	19 20	20 17	21 25
S 60	06 12	07 02	07 48	18 20	19 06	20 04	21 13

Lat.	Sunset	Twilight Civil	Naut.	Moonset 3	4	5	6
o	h m	h m	h m	h m	h m	h m	h m
N 72	22 40	////	////	02 28	■	■	■
N 70	21 46	////	////	04 00	04 07	04 46	06 19
68	21 14	////	////	04 40	05 05	05 53	07 07
66	20 51	22 25	////	05 07	05 39	06 28	07 38
64	20 33	21 47	////	05 28	06 04	06 54	08 01
62	20 18	21 21	////	05 45	06 23	07 14	08 19
60	20 06	21 01	22 35	05 59	06 39	07 31	08 34
N 58	19 55	20 45	22 00	06 12	06 53	07 44	08 47
56	19 46	20 31	21 36	06 22	07 04	07 56	08 58
54	19 37	20 20	21 17	06 31	07 15	08 07	09 08
52	19 30	20 10	21 02	06 40	07 24	08 16	09 17
50	19 23	20 01	20 49	06 47	07 32	08 24	09 24
45	19 09	19 42	20 23	07 03	07 49	08 42	09 41
N 40	18 58	19 27	20 04	07 16	08 03	08 56	09 54
35	18 48	19 15	19 48	07 28	08 15	09 08	10 06
30	18 39	19 05	19 35	07 37	08 26	09 19	10 16
20	18 25	18 48	19 15	07 54	08 44	09 37	10 33
N 10	18 12	18 34	19 00	08 09	09 00	09 53	10 47
0	18 00	18 22	18 47	08 23	09 14	10 07	11 01
S 10	17 49	18 10	18 36	08 37	09 29	10 22	11 15
20	17 36	17 59	18 25	08 51	09 45	10 38	11 30
30	17 22	17 47	18 16	09 08	10 03	10 56	11 47
35	17 14	17 41	18 11	09 18	10 13	11 06	11 56
40	17 05	17 34	18 06	09 29	10 25	11 18	12 07
45	16 54	17 25	18 00	09 43	10 39	11 32	12 20
S 50	16 42	17 16	17 55	09 59	10 57	11 50	12 36
52	16 36	17 12	17 52	10 06	11 05	11 58	12 44
54	16 29	17 07	17 50	10 15	11 14	12 07	12 52
56	16 22	17 02	17 47	10 24	11 24	12 17	13 01
58	16 14	16 57	17 44	10 35	11 36	12 28	13 11
S 60	16 04	16 51	17 41	10 48	11 49	12 42	13 23

Day	SUN Eqn. of Time 00h	12h	Mer. Pass.	MOON Mer. Pass. Upper	Lower	Age	Phase
	m s	m s	h m	h m	h m	d	
3	03 08	03 11	11 57	02 11	14 36	18	
4	03 14	03 17	11 57	03 02	15 28	19	◐
5	03 20	03 22	11 57	03 55	16 21	20	

Finding the Greenwich hour angle The GHA of a body changes very much more quickly than the declination, so the correction is a little more involved. The GHA is normally made up of three components:

The value for the exact hour from the daily tables.

An increment for minutes and seconds past the hour.

A further small (v) correction for irregularity.

Sun The GHA for the exact hour is given on the daily page. The increment for minutes and seconds is found in the table of increments and corrections (Table 2). In the 'box' appropriate to the minutes, find the seconds in the left-hand column; the increment is then found in the column headed 'Sun, Planets'. This should always be *added* to the GHA found in the daily pages. There is no v correction for the sun.

Planets The GHA for the hour is found in the appropriate column of the daily page and the increment for minutes and seconds is given in the table of increments and corrections, exactly as for the sun. However, a v correction must also be applied, using the value of v to be found at the foot of the column. If v is small, the correction may be interpolated mentally, otherwise the table of increments and corrections may be used. The procedure is exactly the same as for the d correction of declination. NOTE The v correction for Venus is sometimes negative.

Moon The procedure is the same as for the planets, except that v is given for each hour, and the increment is given in a separate column of the table of increments and corrections.

Stars The *Nautical Almanac* gives details of 173 stars (including 57 selected stars most commonly used for navigation). It would clearly be impractical to list the GHA of each star for each hour of the year. Instead, the almanac makes use of the fact that stars are virtually fixed in their places. The almanac lists the GHA of a fixed point in the night sky, known as the first point of Aries (or just Aries); to this must be added a quantity called the *sidereal hour angle*, which gives the angles between the star itself and Aries (Fig. 1). The GHA of a star is therefore obtained by combining:

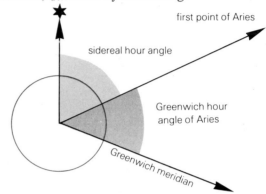

44.1 *GHA Aries and sidereal hour angle.*

1) The GHA of Aries for the hour (daily page)
2) The increment for minutes and seconds, using the Aries column of the table of increments and corrections.
3) The sidereal hour angle (SHA) of the star, from the star column of the daily page.

For example: To illustrate the use of the *Nautical Almanac*, the GHA and declination of the sun, moon, Venus and Aldebaran are given for 3 May 1980, 05 h 42 m 27 s.

	Sun	Moon	Venus	Aldebaran	
GHA 05 h	255°47′.4	40°54′.2 v = 10′.5	212°00′.8 v = 0.7	296°15′.1	(Aries)
Incr. 42 m 27 s	10°36′.8	10°07′.7	10°36′.8	10°38′.5	
v correction	–	7′.4	0′.5	–	
SHA	–	–	–	291°18′.6	
GHA	266°24′.2	51°09′.3	222°38′.1	598°12′.2	
				−360°	
				238°12′.2	
Dec 05 h	N15°42′.9 d = +0.7	S18°01′.3 d = +4.1	N27°38′.6 d = 0	N16°28′.0	
d correction	+0′.5	+2′.9	0.0	–	
Dec	N15°43′.4	S18°04′.2	N27°38′.6	N16°28′.0	

Table 2 *Increments and corrections*

INCREMENTS AND CORRECTIONS

42ᵐ

42ᵐ s	SUN PLANETS ° '	ARIES ° '	MOON ° '	v or Corrⁿ d		v or Corrⁿ d		v or Corrⁿ d	
00	10 30.0	10 31.7	10 01.3	0.0	0.0	6.0	4.3	12.0	8.5
01	10 30.3	10 32.0	10 01.5	0.1	0.1	6.1	4.3	12.1	8.6
02	10 30.5	10 32.2	10 01.8	0.2	0.1	6.2	4.4	12.2	8.6
03	10 30.8	10 32.5	10 02.0	0.3	0.2	6.3	4.5	12.3	8.7
04	10 31.0	10 32.7	10 02.3	0.4	0.3	6.4	4.5	12.4	8.8
05	10 31.3	10 33.0	10 02.5	0.5	0.4	6.5	4.6	12.5	8.9
06	10 31.5	10 33.2	10 02.7	0.6	0.4	6.6	4.7	12.6	8.9
07	10 31.8	10 33.5	10 03.0	0.7	0.5	6.7	4.7	12.7	9.0
08	10 32.0	10 33.7	10 03.2	0.8	0.6	6.8	4.8	12.8	9.1
09	10 32.3	10 34.0	10 03.4	0.9	0.6	6.9	4.9	12.9	9.1
10	10 32.5	10 34.2	10 03.7	1.0	0.7	7.0	5.0	13.0	9.2
11	10 32.8	10 34.5	10 03.9	1.1	0.8	7.1	5.0	13.1	9.3
12	10 33.0	10 34.7	10 04.2	1.2	0.9	7.2	5.1	13.2	9.4
13	10 33.3	10 35.0	10 04.4	1.3	0.9	7.3	5.2	13.3	9.4
14	10 33.5	10 35.2	10 04.6	1.4	1.0	7.4	5.2	13.4	9.5
15	10 33.8	10 35.5	10 04.9	1.5	1.1	7.5	5.3	13.5	9.6
16	10 34.0	10 35.7	10 05.1	1.6	1.1	7.6	5.4	13.6	9.6
17	10 34.3	10 36.0	10 05.4	1.7	1.2	7.7	5.5	13.7	9.7
18	10 34.5	10 36.2	10 05.6	1.8	1.3	7.8	5.5	13.8	9.8
19	10 34.8	10 36.5	10 05.8	1.9	1.3	7.9	5.6	13.9	9.8
20	10 35.0	10 36.7	10 06.1	2.0	1.4	8.0	5.7	14.0	9.9
21	10 35.3	10 37.0	10 06.3	2.1	1.5	8.1	5.7	14.1	10.0
22	10 35.5	10 37.2	10 06.5	2.2	1.6	8.2	5.8	14.2	10.1
23	10 35.8	10 37.5	10 06.8	2.3	1.6	8.3	5.9	14.3	10.1
24	10 36.0	10 37.7	10 07.0	2.4	1.7	8.4	6.0	14.4	10.2
25	10 36.3	10 38.0	10 07.3	2.5	1.8	8.5	6.0	14.5	10.3
26	10 36.5	10 38.2	10 07.5	2.6	1.8	8.6	6.1	14.6	10.3
27	10 36.8	10 38.5	10 07.7	2.7	1.9	8.7	6.2	14.7	10.4
28	10 37.0	10 38.7	10 08.0	2.8	2.0	8.8	6.2	14.8	10.5
29	10 37.3	10 39.0	10 08.2	2.9	2.1	8.9	6.3	14.9	10.6
30	10 37.5	10 39.2	10 08.5	3.0	2.1	9.0	6.4	15.0	10.6
31	10 37.8	10 39.5	10 08.7	3.1	2.2	9.1	6.4	15.1	10.7
32	10 38.0	10 39.7	10 08.9	3.2	2.3	9.2	6.5	15.2	10.8
33	10 38.3	10 40.0	10 09.2	3.3	2.3	9.3	6.6	15.3	10.8
34	10 38.5	10 40.2	10 09.4	3.4	2.4	9.4	6.7	15.4	10.9
35	10 38.8	10 40.5	10 09.7	3.5	2.5	9.5	6.7	15.5	11.0
36	10 39.0	10 40.7	10 09.9	3.6	2.6	9.6	6.8	15.6	11.1
37	10 39.3	10 41.0	10 10.1	3.7	2.6	9.7	6.9	15.7	11.1
38	10 39.5	10 41.3	10 10.4	3.8	2.7	9.8	6.9	15.8	11.2
39	10 39.8	10 41.5	10 10.6	3.9	2.8	9.9	7.0	15.9	11.3
40	10 40.0	10 41.8	10 10.8	4.0	2.8	10.0	7.1	16.0	11.3
41	10 40.3	10 42.0	10 11.1	4.1	2.9	10.1	7.2	16.1	11.4
42	10 40.5	10 42.3	10 11.3	4.2	3.0	10.2	7.2	16.2	11.5
43	10 40.8	10 42.5	10 11.6	4.3	3.0	10.3	7.3	16.3	11.5
44	10 41.0	10 42.8	10 11.8	4.4	3.1	10.4	7.4	16.4	11.6
45	10 41.3	10 43.0	10 12.0	4.5	3.2	10.5	7.4	16.5	11.7
46	10 41.5	10 43.3	10 12.3	4.6	3.3	10.6	7.5	16.6	11.8
47	10 41.8	10 43.5	10 12.5	4.7	3.3	10.7	7.6	16.7	11.8
48	10 42.0	10 43.8	10 12.8	4.8	3.4	10.8	7.7	16.8	11.9
49	10 42.3	10 44.0	10 13.0	4.9	3.5	10.9	7.7	16.9	12.0
50	10 42.5	10 44.3	10 13.2	5.0	3.5	11.0	7.8	17.0	12.0
51	10 42.8	10 44.5	10 13.5	5.1	3.6	11.1	7.9	17.1	12.1
52	10 43.0	10 44.8	10 13.7	5.2	3.7	11.2	7.9	17.2	12.2
53	10 43.3	10 45.0	10 13.9	5.3	3.8	11.3	8.0	17.3	12.3
54	10 43.5	10 45.3	10 14.2	5.4	3.8	11.4	8.1	17.4	12.3
55	10 43.8	10 45.5	10 14.4	5.5	3.9	11.5	8.1	17.5	12.4
56	10 44.0	10 45.8	10 14.7	5.6	4.0	11.6	8.2	17.6	12.5
57	10 44.3	10 46.0	10 14.9	5.7	4.0	11.7	8.3	17.7	12.5
58	10 44.5	10 46.3	10 15.1	5.8	4.1	11.8	8.4	17.8	12.6
59	10 44.8	10 46.5	10 15.4	5.9	4.2	11.9	8.4	17.9	12.7
60	10 45.0	10 46.8	10 15.6	6.0	4.3	12.0	8.5	18.0	12.8

43ᵐ

43ᵐ s	SUN PLANETS ° '	ARIES ° '	MOON ° '	v or Corrⁿ d		v or Corrⁿ d		v or Corrⁿ d	
00	10 45.0	10 46.8	10 15.6	0.0	0.0	6.0	4.4	12.0	8.7
01	10 45.3	10 47.0	10 15.9	0.1	0.1	6.1	4.4	12.1	8.8
02	10 45.5	10 47.3	10 16.1	0.2	0.1	6.2	4.5	12.2	8.8
03	10 45.8	10 47.5	10 16.3	0.3	0.2	6.3	4.6	12.3	8.9
04	10 46.0	10 47.8	10 16.6	0.4	0.3	6.4	4.6	12.4	9.0
05	10 46.3	10 48.0	10 16.8	0.5	0.4	6.5	4.7	12.5	9.1
06	10 46.5	10 48.3	10 17.0	0.6	0.4	6.6	4.8	12.6	9.1
07	10 46.8	10 48.5	10 17.3	0.7	0.5	6.7	4.9	12.7	9.2
08	10 47.0	10 48.8	10 17.5	0.8	0.6	6.8	4.9	12.8	9.3
09	10 47.3	10 49.0	10 17.8	0.9	0.7	6.9	5.0	12.9	9.4
10	10 47.5	10 49.3	10 18.0	1.0	0.7	7.0	5.1	13.0	9.4
11	10 47.8	10 49.5	10 18.2	1.1	0.8	7.1	5.1	13.1	9.5
12	10 48.0	10 49.8	10 18.5	1.2	0.9	7.2	5.2	13.2	9.6
13	10 48.3	10 50.0	10 18.7	1.3	0.9	7.3	5.3	13.3	9.6
14	10 48.5	10 50.3	10 19.0	1.4	1.0	7.4	5.4	13.4	9.7
15	10 48.8	10 50.5	10 19.2	1.5	1.1	7.5	5.4	13.5	9.8
16	10 49.0	10 50.8	10 19.4	1.6	1.2	7.6	5.5	13.6	9.9
17	10 49.3	10 51.0	10 19.7	1.7	1.2	7.7	5.6	13.7	9.9
18	10 49.5	10 51.3	10 19.9	1.8	1.3	7.8	5.7	13.8	10.0
19	10 49.8	10 51.5	10 20.2	1.9	1.4	7.9	5.7	13.9	10.1
20	10 50.0	10 51.8	10 20.4	2.0	1.5	8.0	5.8	14.0	10.2
21	10 50.3	10 52.0	10 20.6	2.1	1.5	8.1	5.9	14.1	10.2
22	10 50.5	10 52.3	10 20.9	2.2	1.6	8.2	5.9	14.2	10.3
23	10 50.8	10 52.5	10 21.1	2.3	1.7	8.3	6.0	14.3	10.4
24	10 51.0	10 52.8	10 21.3	2.4	1.7	8.4	6.1	14.4	10.4
25	10 51.3	10 53.0	10 21.6	2.5	1.8	8.5	6.2	14.5	10.5
26	10 51.5	10 53.3	10 21.8	2.6	1.9	8.6	6.2	14.6	10.6
27	10 51.8	10 53.5	10 22.1	2.7	2.0	8.7	6.3	14.7	10.7
28	10 52.0	10 53.8	10 22.3	2.8	2.0	8.8	6.4	14.8	10.7
29	10 52.3	10 54.0	10 22.5	2.9	2.1	8.9	6.5	14.9	10.8
30	10 52.5	10 54.3	10 22.8	3.0	2.2	9.0	6.5	15.0	10.9
31	10 52.8	10 54.5	10 23.0	3.1	2.2	9.1	6.6	15.1	10.9
32	10 53.0	10 54.8	10 23.3	3.2	2.3	9.2	6.7	15.2	11.0
33	10 53.3	10 55.0	10 23.5	3.3	2.4	9.3	6.7	15.3	11.1
34	10 53.5	10 55.3	10 23.7	3.4	2.5	9.4	6.8	15.4	11.2
35	10 53.8	10 55.5	10 24.0	3.5	2.5	9.5	6.9	15.5	11.2
36	10 54.0	10 55.8	10 24.2	3.6	2.6	9.6	7.0	15.6	11.3
37	10 54.3	10 56.0	10 24.5	3.7	2.7	9.7	7.0	15.7	11.4
38	10 54.5	10 56.3	10 24.7	3.8	2.8	9.8	7.1	15.8	11.5
39	10 54.8	10 56.5	10 24.9	3.9	2.8	9.9	7.2	15.9	11.5
40	10 55.0	10 56.8	10 25.2	4.0	2.9	10.0	7.3	16.0	11.6
41	10 55.3	10 57.0	10 25.4	4.1	3.0	10.1	7.3	16.1	11.7
42	10 55.5	10 57.3	10 25.6	4.2	3.0	10.2	7.4	16.2	11.7
43	10 55.8	10 57.5	10 25.9	4.3	3.1	10.3	7.5	16.3	11.8
44	10 56.0	10 57.8	10 26.1	4.4	3.2	10.4	7.5	16.4	11.9
45	10 56.3	10 58.0	10 26.4	4.5	3.3	10.5	7.6	16.5	12.0
46	10 56.5	10 58.3	10 26.6	4.6	3.3	10.6	7.7	16.6	12.0
47	10 56.8	10 58.5	10 26.8	4.7	3.4	10.7	7.8	16.7	12.1
48	10 57.0	10 58.8	10 27.1	4.8	3.5	10.8	7.8	16.8	12.2
49	10 57.3	10 59.0	10 27.3	4.9	3.6	10.9	7.9	16.9	12.3
50	10 57.5	10 59.3	10 27.5	5.0	3.6	11.0	8.0	17.0	12.3
51	10 57.8	10 59.6	10 27.8	5.1	3.7	11.1	8.0	17.1	12.4
52	10 58.0	10 59.8	10 28.0	5.2	3.8	11.2	8.1	17.2	12.5
53	10 58.3	11 00.1	10 28.3	5.3	3.8	11.3	8.2	17.3	12.5
54	10 58.5	11 00.3	10 28.5	5.4	3.9	11.4	8.3	17.4	12.6
55	10 58.8	11 00.6	10 28.7	5.5	4.0	11.5	8.3	17.5	12.7
56	10 59.0	11 00.8	10 29.0	5.6	4.1	11.6	8.4	17.6	12.8
57	10 59.3	11 01.1	10 29.2	5.7	4.1	11.7	8.5	17.7	12.8
58	10 59.5	11 01.3	10 29.5	5.8	4.2	11.8	8.6	17.8	12.9
59	10 59.8	11 01.6	10 29.7	5.9	4.3	11.9	8.6	17.9	13.0
60	11 00.0	11 01.8	10 29.9	6.0	4.4	12.0	8.7	18.0	13.1

45 Latitude by meridian altitude

There are some circumstances when it is particularly easy to obtain a position line from the observation of a body. The most generally useful of these 'short cut' observations is that for obtaining latitude by *meridian altitude*; this observation is made at local noon, when the sun is either due north or due south of the observer, depending on his latitude. This sight has a long and distinguished history; it was first used by the Portuguese navigators in the late 15th century, and has been in daily use by mariners all over the world to this day. It has the great virtues of providing a latitude without the need for special tables (except the *Nautical Almanac*), and without the need for precise GMT. This section only discusses meridian altitude of the sun; other bodies are not often used.

Principle The sun rises every day in the eastern sky and crosses the heavens to set in the western sky. At noon, local time, the sun is either due north or due south of the observer (i.e. it has the same longitude). The altitude of the sun at this moment can be simply processed to give a latitude, as shown in Figure 1. This is a cross-section of the earth through the meridian of longitude on which both the sun and the observer stand. The altitude of the sun can be converted to the zenith distance ($= 90° -$ Alt.); the zenith distance is the distance from the observer to the geographical position or, in this special case, the difference in latitude between the observer and the GP. However, the latitude of the GP is known – it is equal to the declination of the sun at that moment. Thus, by combining zenith distance with declination, it is possible to derive latitude. The sun's declination changes slowly, so it does not matter if the precise GMT of the observation is not known.

45.1 *Noon altitude and latitude.*

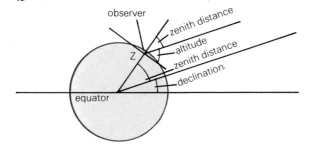

The actual crossing of the meridian is known as *meridian passage*, and the time at which this will happen is given in the *Nautical Almanac*. Meridian passage can happen in a number of different ways, as shown in Figure 2, depending on whether the sun is on the same side of the equator as the observer or not, and on whether the sun is closer to the equator than the observer, or further away. The rules for combining zenith distance and declination vary according to the circumstances; these rules become obvious if a diagram like one of those in Figure 2 is drawn for each case. Otherwise, the precepts given in the description of the method given below will always give the correct answer.

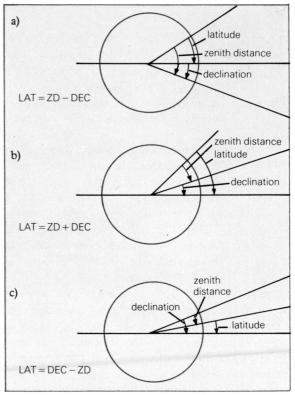

45.2 *Latitude and declination: (a) contrary name; (b) same name, declination less than latitude; (c) same name, declination greater than latitude.*

Preparation Meridian passage can be observed merely by watching the sun as it rises until it gets to its highest point in the sky, which is the moment of meridian passage. However, it is much more convenient to be able to predict the time of meridian passage to within a few minutes, to avoid wasting time and running the risk of missing the moment.

On the daily page of the nautical almanac, a figure is given for the meridian passage of the sun for each day (p. 139). This can be taken as the local mean time of meridian passage. The GMT of meridian passage can be obtained from this figure by applying a correction for the DR longitude, converted to time; easterly longitude is subtracted, westerly longitude added.

For example:

3 May 1980, a ship in DR longitude 12°15′W wishes to find the approximate time of meridian passage:

LMT mer pass	11 h 57 m	daily page
Long W in time		
(15° = 1 hr)	00 h 45 m	add W long
GMT	12 h 42 m	

Notes 1) It may be convenient to convert the GMT thus found to zone time, i.e., ship's clock time. In the above example, the ship would probably be keeping zone +1, so ship's time of meridian passage would be 11 h 42 m (+1).

2) It is quite easy to convert longitude to time by mental arithmetic, because

15° = 1 hour
1° = 4 minutes
15′ = 1 minute

A table for converting arc (angles) to time is given just before the table of increments and corrections in the *Nautical Almanac*.

Observing meridian altitude Come on deck about a quarter of an hour before the predicted time of meridian passage, and find the sun, putting it exactly on the horizon. Thereafter, observe the sun again at intervals of about a minute; if a gap has appeared between the lower limb of the sun and the horizon, increase the sextant altitude with the micrometer. The micrometer should *only* be adjusted in one direction – to increase the measured altitude. At noon, the sun will appear to 'hang' in the sky for several minutes, and then begin to fall. Do not adjust the sextant to follow the fall – it is the highest altitude reached that is required. Note the GMT of meridian passage (to the nearest minute or so), for later use in obtaining declination.

Calculating latitude The sextant altitude of meridian passage is converted to latitude by following these steps:

1) Convert sextant altitude to true altitude, as described on pages 130–3. Name the true altitude north or south to agree with its bearing at noon.

2) Obtain the True Zenith Distance (TZD) (= 90° − true altitude), and name it *opposite* to true altitude.

3) Find the declination of the sun for the GMT of the observation (see page 137); be sure to note the name (N or S) of the declination.

4) Combine the TZD and the declination:
same names – Add TZD and declination to give latitude of *same* name.
contrary names – Subtract smaller quantity from the greater to obtain latitude; name the latitude as the greater of TZD or declination.

Normally there is no difficulty in naming the latitude, as the DR position makes it obvious; however it may be possible for confusion to arise near to the equator. Following the rules given above will always cope with the situation, as the following examples show:

True altitude	80°N	80°N
TZD	10°S	10°S
Declination	9°N	11°N
Latitude (name as greater)	1°S	1°N

The following example shows the complete working of a sight for noon latitude by meridian altitude.

3 May 1980 12 h 45 m GMT: a ship in DR position 41°30′N, 12°15′W observes meridian altitude. Sextant altitude 64°22′.5 bearing south, index error + 1′.5, height of eye 3 metres.

Sextant altitude	64°22′.5	
Index error	+ 1′.5	
	64°24′.0	
Dip	− 3′.0	
Apparent altitude	64°21′.0	
Correction	+ 15′.5	
True altitude	64°36′.5 S	(rule 1)
True zenith distance		
(90° − TA)	25°23′.5 N	(rule 2)
Declination (12 h)		
N15°48′.0 + (d)0′.5	15°48′.5 N	(see page 137)
Latitude at 1245 GMT	41°12′.0 N	(rule 4)

46 Noon longitude by equal altitudes

Noon longitude by equal altitudes is a particularly simple way of establishing longitude once a day (at local noon), which requires only a sextant, the *Nautical Almanac* and an accurate source of GMT. In conjunction with an observation of meridian passage for latitude, it offers the ocean navigator a daily position with very little effort; for much of any ocean passage, a daily position will be quite sufficient.

The principle of this type of sight is very simple. At meridian passage, the observer and the sun's geographical position have the same longitude. If the exact GMT of meridian passage can be established, then the observer's longitude is equal to the GHA of the sun (which is another way of expressing the longitude of the GP). It is not possible to obtain the GMT of meridian passage by direct observation, as the sun's altitude is changing very slowly at meridian passage and it appears to 'hang' in the sky for several minutes. The procedure adopted is to observe the altitude of the sun while it is still changing quite rapidly, at some suitable time before noon, and note the GMT. The sun will then rise to meridian passage (when a latitude would normally be obtained), and then sinks; the navigator notes the exact GMT at which the sun reaches the same altitude as the observation before noon. The GMT of meridian passage is half way between the two GMTs observed (Fig. 1).

The observations
The first step in observing the longitude by this method is to work out the predicted time of meridian passage (pages 142–3); this time will also be needed for the latitude sight at noon. Then work out the best time for the forenoon altitude by the following rule of thumb:

Combine the DR latitude and the declination (degrees only), by adding if contrary name and subtracting the smaller from the larger if names are the same. Make the first observation the same number of minutes before predicted meridian passage.

For example:

Latitude	45°N
Dec	15°N
Combined	30°N

Therefore make the first observation 30 minutes before meridian passage.

Latitude	30°S
Dec	10°N
Combined	40°

First observation made 40 minutes before meridian passage.

Note: If by following this rule, the result comes to more than an hour (60 minutes) before noon, avoid using this method if possible; the simplifying assumptions that it makes start to break down, and longitudes may be significantly in error.

When the predicted time arrives, take a sextant altitude of the sun and record this with the precise

46.1 *Principle of noon longitude by equal altitudes.*

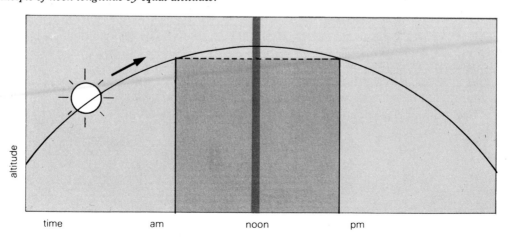

GMT of the observation; there is no need to apply any correction to the sextant altitude thus obtained. If there is cloud in the sky, it would be a prudent precaution to make several observations at intervals, in case the sun is intermittently obscured in the afternoon. With several sights to play with, you would be unlucky not to match up at least one of the forenoon sights.

Afternoon observation If the ship has not changed latitude since the first observation, nor the sun changed declination, it is merely necessary to set the same altitude on the sextant as was observed in the forenoon, observe the sun as it sinks and then note the exact GMT at which it touches the horizon; as with the forenoon observation, there is no need to apply any correction for index error, dip, refraction or semidiameter, provided the height of eye is the same for both observations.

If, as is more generally the case, the ship has changed her latitude in the interval between the sights and/or the sun has changed its declination, then a correction must be applied to the sextant altitude for the second observation.

Ship movement The difference in latitude between the DR of the forenoon sight and the (predicted) DR of the afternoon sight must be worked out. This difference in latitude (in minutes of arc) must be *added* to the first sextant altitude if the ship is moving *towards* the sun, and subtracted if the ship is moving away.

Change in declination The rate of change of declination, in minutes of arc per hour, is given in the *Nautical Almanac*; it is the quantity d at the foot of the sun column. Given this value and the total time between the two observations, it is possible to work out a correction to be applied to the sextant, to be *added* if the sun is moving *towards* the ship, and subtracted if it is moving away.

For example:

On 3 May 1980, a ship in DR latitude 52°N wishes to observe noon longitude by equal altitudes. Declination is 16°N, so the chosen time to observe is (52 − 16 =) 36 minutes before meridian passage. Ship's course 180 (true), speed 6 knots. From the *Nautical Almanac*, d for 3 May is 0.7 and the sun is moving north (the northerly declination is increasing). Total time between observations 2 × 36 m = 1 hr 12 m or 1.2 hours.

The ship movement correction in this case is 7′.2 (1.2 hours on course 180 at 6 knots); the ship is north of the sun and moving south, so this correction must be added to the sextant altitude.

The declination correction is 0′.8 (d of 0′.7 for 1.2 hours); the sun is south of the ship and moving north, so this correction too must be added.

The total correction is therefore 8′.0, to be added to the sextant altitude of the forenoon observation.

Having made the observations before and after noon, the two times recorded are used to work out the GMT of meridian passage by simple averaging, thus:

GMT of first sight	10 h 59 m 49 s
GMT of second sight	12 h 11 m 59 s
Added together	23 h 11 m 48 s
Divide by 2 = GMT mer pass	11 h 35 m 54 s

The actual longitude is found by looking out the sun's GHA for the GMT thus found:

GHA 11 h	345°47′.8
Increment 35 m 54 s	8°58′.5
GHA (= longitude west)	354°46′.3

Or, subtracting from 360°, long = 5°13′.7 East

Note: Unlike longitude, GHA is always measured west of the Greenwich meridian. To convert GHA to longitude, the rule is:

If GHA is less than 180°, longitude west = GHA

If GHA is more than 180°, longitude east = 360° − GHA

A complete example is given on the following page.

Complete example: The example below completes that on page 143, which showed how the latitude was worked out from meridian passage. The additional information needed for longitude by equal altitude is that the ship is in DR position 41°30′N, 12°15′W, steering north at 7 knots. The predicted time of meridian passage is 3 May 1980 12 h 45 m GMT. Latitude − declination = 41° − 16° = 25°.

First observation 58°17′.1 at   12 h 17 m 47 s GMT

This observation was taken about 25 minutes before meridian passage, so the second will be approximately 25 minutes after, a total interval of 50 minutes.

Ship movement correction
(50 m at 7 knots)   − 6′.0
(− ve as ship is moving due north away from the sun)
Declination correction
(50 m at d = 0′.7)   + 0′.6
(+ ve as sun is moving north towards the ship)
Total correction   − 5′.4
So sextant altitude for pm
sight   58°17′.1 − 5′.4
                  = 58°11′.7

The second observation with this sextant altitude was made at:

	13 h 07 m 27 s GMT
First observation	12 h 17 m 47 s GMT
(add)	25 h 25 m 14 s
meridian passage	
(divide by two)	12 h 42 m 37 s GMT
GHA for 12 h on	
3 May	0°47′.8
Increment 42 m 37 s	10°39′.3
Therefore longi-	
tude = (add)	11°27′.1 W

Notes: 1) This method is not suitable for use when the sun is low in the sky at noon, i.e. in winter, especially in higher latitudes.

2) It is also unsuitable for high-speed craft, where latitude corrections may become large. Its use should be confined to vessels travelling at ten knots or less.

3) If the sky clouds over in the afternoon, it may not be possible to complete the observation; in this case, the forenoon observation can be worked out as a general position line (see pages 156–7) and thus not wasted, though the angle of cut with the noon latitude may be rather acute.

4) In an emergency it is possible to get some idea of longitude even without a sextant. In a slow-moving craft (such as a liferaft), it may be possible to record the GMT at which the sun clears the eastern horizon in the morning, and touches the western horizon in the evening; the mean of these two times is (rather approximately) the longitude.

47 The general position line; intercepts

The astronomical position lines so far described rely on the special circumstance that the body is on the same meridian as the observer, that is, the LHA of the body is 0°. For the sun, this happens at local noon, and offers two simple and excellent solutions to the position line problem – for latitude and for longitude. However it is not generally so simple to convert a sextant altitude and time into a position line; the process is still not difficult, but requires some new ideas, new techniques and new tables. For the general solution of astronomical position lines, this book uses the *Sight Reduction Tables for Air Navigation* (in Britain, AP 3270; in the US, Pub. 249). This publication is in three volumes; volumes 2 and 3 are used for general solutions and volume 1 deals with star sights (see pages 158–60).

At first glance, the general astronomical position line is easy enough to work out; the GHA and declination of the body at the moment of observation define the geographical position (see pages 137–41), whilst the true sextant altitude (converted to true zenith distance) (see page 124) gives the distance of the ship from the GP. The position line is therefore a circle with radius equal to the true zenith distance, centred on the GP. The difficulty that arises is purely one of scale; the zenith distance may be several thousand miles, and it is quite impossible to plot a position line as described with any pretence at accuracy; on a chart or globe of suitable scale to take to sea, even the thickness of a pencil line may represent tens of miles on the surface.

Except in very rare circumstances (see page 126), the direct plotting of GP and zenith distance is quite impracticable. Instead, a mathematical trick known as an *intercept* is brought into play, to allow the position line to be plotted directly on the chart in use, at a practical scale. The intercept is derived by following this argument (and see Fig. 1):

1) Choose a convenient position close to the ship's actual (but unknown) position.
2) Calculate the distance between this chosen position and the GP of the body.
3) Compare this distance with the true distance

measured on the sextant. The difference in the distances is known as the *intercept*, and it shows by how much the true distance from the GP is more or less than the calculated value from the chosen position.

4) Another quantity, the bearing of the GP (known as the *azimuth* of the body), must also be obtained, either by taking a compass bearing of the body observed, or from the tables.
5) Given the intercept and the azimuth, the position line can be plotted, as shown in Figure 2. The position line is technically part of a circle, but because the GP is so far away, the line can be assumed to be straight, running in a direction at right angles to the azimuth.

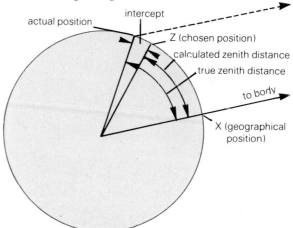

47.1 *Principle of the intercept method.*

47.2 *Plotting a position line using the intercept.*

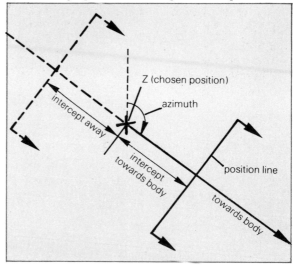

The function of all the various methods of *sight reduction* is to provide the answers for step 2 (distance to the GP from the chosen position) and step 4 (the azimuth of the body). These are both problems in spherical trigonometry, though the navigator need not let this fact dismay him. In these modern days of microelectronics, the problems are easily solved by calculator or computer (see page 165); otherwise, various methods have been developed over the years to give the practical seaman an easy route to the answers he needs. The primary method chosen for this book is the use of the *Sight Reduction Tables for Air Navigation* (AP 3270, Pub. 249). Other methods are described on pages 164–5.

Sight Reduction Tables for Air Navigation (AP 3270, Pub. 249) As the name implies, these tables were devised for use by aviators. They are also very suitable for use in yachts, because, at the price of an unimportant loss of precision, they are quick and easy to use. Volume 1 deals only with certain stars, and is used on pages 158–60. Volumes 2 and 3 provide general solutions to the two problems for all bodies with a declination of less than 30° north or south; this includes the sun, moon and planets, and 27 of the most important navigational stars. For normal use, this is quite sufficient. Specimen pages from Volume 3 are shown on pages 149 and 151.

The tables must be entered with three quantities:

1) Latitude of the chosen position; this must be a whole number of degrees. It selects the page at which the tables are opened.

2) Declination of the body – the degrees part only; this selects the column within the page. Detailed selection of the page and column also depends on the actual value of the declination (0–14° or 15°–29°), and on whether the declination has the same or contrary name to the latitude; page and column headings make this clear.

3) The local hour angle, which is a combination of the Greenwich hour angle from the *Nautical Almanac* and the chosen longitude. This quantity must be a whole number of degrees. It selects the line on the page where the solutions lie.

There are two outputs from the tables:

1) The calculated altitude (Hc). This is the altitude that would be observed if the ship were exactly at the chosen position; it can be compared directly with the observed altitude (Ho) to obtain the intercept. The tables give altitude rather than zenith distance to avoid an additional calculation without affecting the answer. The calculated altitude is given to the nearest minute of arc.

2) The azimuth angle (Z); this can be converted to azimuth (the true bearing of the GP) by following the precepts given at the top and foot of the page, depending on LHA and latitude.

The use of the tables is very slightly complicated by the need for interpolation, as described below.

The chosen position Having made an observation and extracted the body's GHA and declination from the *Nautical Almanac*, the next step is to choose the position for entry to the *Sight Reduction Tables*. The choice of position is somewhat confined, unlike some other methods, by the special requirements of the tables.

Latitude: The chosen latitude should be the whole number of degrees closest to the DR latitude. Thus if the DR latitude is 50°17′N, choose 50°N; if the DR latitude is 34°46′S, choose 35°S.

Longitude: The longitude must be chosen so that it is close to the DR longitude; also it must have a value which, when combined with the GHA of the body, yields an LHA which is a whole number of degrees. Easterly longitude is added, westerly longitude is subtracted from GHA to give LHA. Thus, if the DR longitude is 17°30′W and the GHA is 332°17′.2:

GHA	332°17′.2
Long W (chosen)	17°17′.2
LHA	315°

or, for DR longitude 112°30′E, GHA 17°22′.3:

GHA	17°22′.3
Long E (chosen)	112°37′.7
LHA	130°

Entering the tables

1) Choose the page according to chosen latitude, same or contrary name and declination range (0°–14° or 15°–29°).

2) Find the line appropriate to the LHA, either on the extreme left or extreme right of the page; it may be necessary to turn over the page to find the LHA required.

3) Find the intersection of the line of LHA and

N. Lat. {LHA greater than 180°……. Zn=Z; LHA less than 180°………. Zn=360−Z}

DECLINATION (15°-29°) SAME NAME AS LATITUDE

LAT 50°

LHA	15° Hc	d	Z	16° Hc	d	Z	17° Hc	d	Z	18° Hc	d	Z	19° Hc	d	Z
	° ′	′	°	° ′	′	°	° ′	′	°	° ′	′	°	° ′	′	°
0	55 30	+60	180	56 00	-60	180	57 00	+60	180	58 00	+60	180	59 00	+60	180
1	54 59	60	178	55 59	60	178	56 59	60	178	57 59	60	178	58 59	60	178
2	54 58	60	177	55 58	60	177	56 58	60	177	57 58	60	176	58 58	60	176
3	54 55	60	175	55 55	60	175	56 55	60	175	57 55	59	175	58 54	60	175
4	54 51	60	173	55 51	60	173	56 51	59	173	57 50	60	173	58 50	60	173
5	54 46	+60	172	55 46	+59	171	56 45	+60	171	57 45	+60	171	58 45	+59	171
6	54 40	59	170	55 39	60	170	56 39	59	170	57 38	60	169	58 38	59	169
7	54 32	60	168	55 32	59	168	56 31	60	168	57 31	59	168	58 30	59	167
8	54 24	59	167	55 23	60	166	56 23	59	166	57 22	59	166	58 21	59	166
9	54 15	59	165	55 14	59	165	56 13	59	164	57 12	59	164	58 11	59	164
10	54 04	+59	163	55 03	+59	163	56 02	+59	163	57 01	+58	162	57 59	+59	162
11	53 53	58	162	54 51	59	161	55 50	58	161	56 48	59	161	57 47	58	160
12	53 40	58	160	54 38	59	160	55 37	58	159	56 35	58	159	57 33	58	159
13	53 26	59	159	54 25	58	158	55 23	58	158	56 21	58	157	57 19	57	157
14	53 12	58	157	54 10	58	157	55 08	57	156	56 05	58	156	57 03	57	155
15	52 56	+58	156	53 54	+58	155	54 52	+57	155	55 49	+57	154	56 46	+57	154
16	52 40	57	154	53 37	57	154	54 34	58	153	55 32	56	152	56 28	57	152
17	52 23	57	152	53 20	56	152	54 16	57	151	55 13	57	151	56 10	56	150
18	52 04	57	151	53 01	57	150	53 58	56	150	54 54	56	149	55 50	56	149
19	51 45	56	150	52 41	57	149	53 38	56	148	54 34	56	148	55 30	55	147
20	51 25	+56	148	52 21	+56	147	53 17	+56	147	54 13	+55	146	55 08	+56	146
21	51 04	56	147	52 00	56	146	52 56	55	145	53 51	55	145	54 46	55	144
22	50 43	55	145	51 38	55	145	52 33	55	144	53 28	55	143	54 23	54	143
23	50 20	55	144	51 15	55	143	52 10	55	143	53 05	54	142	53 59	54	141
24	49 57	55	142	50 52	54	142	51 46	54	141	52 40	54	140	53 34	54	140
25	49 33	+54	141	50 27	+55	140	51 22	+54	140	52 16	+53	139	53 09	+53	138
26	49 08	55	140	50 03	53	139	50 56	54	138	51 50	53	138	52 43	53	137
27	48 43	54	138	49 37	53	138	50 30	53	137	51 23	53	136	52 16	53	136
28	48 17	54	137	49 11	53	136	50 04	52	136	50 56	53	135	51 49	52	134
29	47 51	53	136	48 44	52	135	49 36	53	134	50 29	52	134	51 21	52	133
30	47 23	+53	135	48 16	+52	134	49 08	+53	133	50 01	+51	132	50 52	+52	132
31	46 56	52	133	47 48	52	133	48 40	52	132	49 32	51	131	50 23	51	130
32	46 27	52	132	47 19	52	131	48 11	51	131	49 02	51	130	49 53	51	129
33	45 58	52	131	46 50	51	130	47 41	51	129	48 32	51	129	49 23	51	128
34	45 29	51	130	46 20	51	129	47 11	51	128	48 02	50	127	48 52	51	127
35	44 59	+51	128	45 50	+51	128	46 41	+50	127	47 31	+50	126	48 21	+50	125
36	44 28	51	127	45 19	51	127	46 10	50	126	47 00	50	125	47 50	49	124
37	43 58	50	126	44 48	50	125	45 38	50	125	46 28	49	124	47 17	49	123
38	43 26	50	125	44 16	50	124	45 06	50	124	45 56	49	123	46 45	49	122
39	42 54	50	124	43 44	50	123	44 34	49	122	45 23	49	122	46 12	48	121
40	42 22	+50	123	43 12	+49	122	44 01	+49	121	44 50	+49	121	45 39	+48	120
41	41 50	49	122	42 39	49	121	43 28	49	120	44 17	48	119	45 05	48	119
42	41 17	49	121	42 06	48	120	42 54	49	119	43 43	48	118	44 31	47	118
43	40 43	49	120	41 32	48	119	42 20	49	118	43 09	47	117	43 56	48	116
44	40 10	48	119	40 58	48	118	41 46	48	117	42 34	48	116	43 22	47	115
45	39 35	+49	118	40 24	+48	117	41 12	+47	116	41 59	+48	115	42 47	+47	114
46	39 01	48	117	39 49	48	116	40 37	47	115	41 24	47	114	42 11	47	113
47	38 27	47	116	39 14	48	115	40 02	47	114	40 49	47	113	41 36	46	112
48	37 52	47	115	38 39	48	114	39 27	46	113	40 13	47	112	41 00	46	111
49	37 16	48	114	38 04	47	113	38 51	47	112	39 38	46	111	40 24	46	110
50	36 41	+47	113	37 28	+47	112	38 15	+47	111	39 02	+46	110	39 48	+46	110
51	36 05	47	112	36 52	47	111	37 39	46	110	38 25	46	109	39 11	46	109
52	35 29	47	111	36 16	47	110	37 03	46	109	37 49	46	108	38 35	45	108
53	34 53	47	110	35 40	46	109	36 26	46	108	37 12	46	108	37 58	45	107
54	34 17	46	109	35 03	46	108	35 49	46	107	36 35	46	107	37 21	45	106
55	33 40	+47	108	34 27	+46	107	35 13	+45	107	35 58	+46	106	36 44	+45	105
56	33 03	47	107	33 50	45	106	34 35	46	106	35 21	45	105	36 06	45	104
57	32 26	47	106	33 13	45	106	33 58	46	105	34 44	45	104	35 29	45	103
58	31 49	46	105	32 35	46	105	33 21	45	104	34 06	45	103	34 51	45	102
59	31 12	46	105	31 58	45	104	32 43	46	103	33 29	44	102	34 13	45	101
60	30 35	+45	104	31 20	+46	103	32 06	+45	102	32 51	+45	101	33 36	+44	101
61	29 57	46	103	30 43	45	102	31 28	45	101	32 13	45	101	32 58	44	100
62	29 20	45	102	30 05	45	101	30 50	45	101	31 35	45	100	32 20	44	99
63	28 42	45	101	29 27	45	100	30 12	45	100	30 57	44	99	31 41	45	98
64	28 04	45	100	28 49	45	100	29 34	45	99	30 19	44	98	31 03	44	97
65	27 26	+45	100	28 11	+45	99	28 56	+45	98	29 41	+44	97	30 25	+44	96
66	26 48	45	99	27 33	45	98	28 18	44	97	29 02	45	96	29 47	44	96
67	26 10	45	98	26 55	44	97	27 39	45	96	28 24	44	96	29 08	44	95
68	25 31	45	97	26 16	45	96	27 01	44	96	27 45	45	95	28 30	44	94
69	24 53	45	96	25 38	45	96	26 23	44	95	27 07	44	94	27 51	44	93

LHA	20° Hc	d	Z	21° Hc	d	Z	22° Hc	d	Z	23° Hc	d	Z	24° Hc	d	Z
	° ′	′	°	° ′	′	°	° ′	′	°	° ′	′	°	° ′	′	°
0	60 00	+60	180	61 00	+60	180	62 00	+60	180	63 00	+60	180	64 00	+60	180
1	59 59	60	178	60 59	60	178	61 59	60	178	62 59	60	178	63 59	60	178
2	59 58	59	176	60 57	60	176	61 57	60	176	62 57	60	176	63 57	60	176
3	59 54	60	174	60 54	60	174	61 54	60	174	62 54	60	174	63 54	60	174
4	59 50	60	173	60 50	59	172	61 49	60	172	62 49	60	172	63 49	60	172
5	59 44	+60	171	60 44	+60	170	61 44	+59	170	62 43	+60	170	63 43	+59	170
6	59 37	60	169	60 37	59	169	61 36	60	168	62 36	59	168	63 35	59	168
7	59 29	60	167	60 29	59	167	61 28	59	166	62 27	59	166	63 26	59	166
8	59 20	59	165	60 19	59	165	61 18	59	164	62 17	59	164	63 16	59	164
9	59 10	58	163	60 08	59	163	61 07	59	163	62 06	58	162	63 04	59	162
10	58 58	+58	162	59 56	+59	161	60 55	+58	161	61 53	+58	160	62 51	+59	160
11	58 45	58	160	59 43	59	159	60 42	58	159	61 40	57	158	62 37	58	158
12	58 31	58	158	59 29	58	158	60 27	58	157	61 25	57	156	62 22	58	156
13	58 16	58	156	59 14	57	156	60 11	58	155	61 09	57	155	62 06	57	154
14	58 00	58	155	58 58	57	154	59 55	57	153	60 52	56	153	61 48	57	152
15	57 43	+57	153	58 40	+57	152	59 37	+56	152	60 33	+57	151	61 30	+56	150
16	57 25	57	151	58 22	56	151	59 18	56	150	60 14	56	149	61 10	56	149
17	57 06	56	150	58 02	56	149	58 58	56	148	59 54	56	148	60 50	55	147
18	56 46	56	148	57 42	56	147	58 38	55	147	59 33	55	146	60 23	55	145
19	56 25	56	146	57 21	55	146	58 16	55	145	59 11	54	144	60 05	55	143
20	56 04	+55	145	56 59	+54	144	57 53	+55	143	58 48	+54	143	59 42	+54	142
21	55 41	55	143	56 36	54	143	57 30	54	142	58 24	54	141	59 18	53	140
22	55 17	55	142	56 12	54	141	57 06	53	140	57 59	54	139	58 53	52	139
23	54 53	54	140	55 47	54	140	56 41	53	139	57 34	53	138	58 27	52	137
24	54 28	54	139	55 22	53	138	56 15	53	137	57 08	52	136	58 00	52	136
25	54 02	+54	137	54 56	+52	137	55 48	+53	136	56 41	+52	135	57 33	+51	134
26	53 36	53	136	54 29	52	135	55 21	52	134	56 13	51	134	57 04	52	133
27	53 09	52	135	54 01	52	134	54 53	52	133	55 45	51	132	56 36	50	131
28	52 41	52	133	53 33	52	133	54 25	51	132	55 16	50	131	56 06	51	130
29	52 13	51	132	53 04	51	131	53 55	51	130	54 46	50	129	55 36	50	128
30	51 44	+51	131	52 35	+51	130	53 26	+50	129	54 16	+50	128	55 06	+49	127
31	51 14	51	129	52 05	50	129	52 55	50	128	53 45	50	127	54 35	49	126
32	50 44	51	128	51 35	50	127	52 25	49	126	53 14	49	125	54 03	49	124
33	50 14	50	127	51 04	49	126	51 53	49	125	52 42	49	124	53 31	48	123
34	49 43	49	126	50 32	49	125	51 21	49	124	52 10	49	123	52 59	48	122
35	49 11	+49	125	50 00	+49	124	50 49	+49	123	51 38	+48	122	52 26	+47	121
36	48 39	49	123	49 28	49	122	50 17	48	122	51 05	47	121	51 52	48	120
37	48 06	49	122	48 55	48	121	49 43	48	120	50 31	48	119	51 19	47	118
38	47 34	48	121	48 22	48	120	49 10	48	119	49 58	47	118	50 45	46	117
39	47 00	48	120	47 48	48	119	48 36	47	118	49 23	47	117	50 10	46	116
40	46 27	+48	119	47 15	+47	118	48 02	+47	117	48 49	+46	116	49 35	+46	115
41	45 53	47	118	46 40	47	117	47 27	47	116	48 14	46	115	49 00	46	114
42	45 18	48	117	46 06	47	116	46 53	46	115	47 39	46	114	48 25	45	113
43	44 44	47	116	45 31	46	115	46 17	47	114	47 04	45	113	47 49	45	112
44	44 09	47	115	44 56	46	114	45 42	46	113	46 28	45	112	47 13	45	111
45	43 34	+46	114	44 20	+46	113	45 06	+46	112	45 52	+45	111	46 37	+45	110
46	42 58	46	113	43 44	46	112	44 30	46	111	45 16	45	110	46 01	44	109
47	42 22	46	112	43 08	46	111	43 54	45	110	44 39	45	109	45 24	45	108
48	41 46	46	111	42 32	46	110	43 18	45	109	44 03	44	108	44 47	45	107
49	41 10	46	110	41 56	45	109	42 41	45	108	43 26	44	107	44 10	44	106
50	40 34	+45	109	41 19	+45	108	42 04	+45	107	42 49	+44	106	43 33	+44	105
51	39 57	45	108	40 42	45	107	41 27	45	106	42 12	44	105	42 56	44	104
52	39 20	45	107	40 05	45	106	40 50	45	105	41 35	43	104	42 18	44	103
53	38 43	45	106	39 28	45	105	40 13	44	104	40 57	44	103	41 41	43	102
54	38 06	45	105	38 51	44	104	39 35	44	103	40 19	44	102	41 03	43	102
55	37 29	+44	104	38 13	+45	103	38 58	+44	102	39 42	+43	102	40 25	+43	101
56	36 51	45	103	37 36	44	102	38 20	44	102	39 04	43	101	39 47	43	100
57	36 14	44	102	36 58	44	102	37 42	44	101	38 26	43	100	39 09	43	99
58	35 36	44	102	36 20	44	101	37 04	44	100	37 48	43	99	38 31	43	98
59	34 58	44	101	35 42	44	100	36 26	44	99	37 10	43	98	37 53	43	97
60	34 20	+44	100	35 04	+44	99	35 48	+44	98	36 32	+43	97	37 15	+42	96
61	33 42	44	99	34 26	44	98	35 10	43	97	35 53	43	96	36 36	43	96
62	33 04	44	98	33 48	44	97	34 32	43	97	35 15	43	96	35 58	42	95
63	32 26	44	97	33 10	43	97	33 53	43	96	34 36	43	95	35 19	43	94
64	31 47	44	97	32 31	44	96	33 15	43	95	33 58	43	94	34 41	42	93
65	31 09	+44	96	31 53	+43	95	32 36	+44	94	33 20	+42	93	34 02	+43	92
66	30 31	43	95	31 14	44	94	31 58	43	93	32 41	43	92	33 24	42	92
67	29 52	44	94	30 36	43	93	31 19	43	93	32 02	43	92	32 45	43	91
68	29 14	43	93	29 57	44	93	30 41	43	92	31 24	43	91	32 07	42	90
69	28 35	44	93	29 19	43	92	30 02	43	91	30 45	43	90	31 28	43	89

LHA	25° Hc	d	Z	26° Hc	d	Z	27° Hc	d	Z	28° Hc	d	Z	29° Hc	d	Z	LHA
	° ′	′	°	° ′	′	°	° ′	′	°	° ′	′	°	° ′	′	°	
0	65 00	+60	180	66 00	+60	180	67 00	+60	180	68 00	+60	180	69 00	+60	180	360
1	64 59	60	178	65 59	60	178	66 59	60	178	67 59	60	178	68 59	60	178	359
2	64 57	60	176	65 57	60	176	66 57	60	175	67 57	60	175	68 57	60	175	358
3	64 54	59	174	65 53	60	173	66 53	60	173	67 53	60	173	68 53	59	173	357
4	64 49	59	172	65 48	60	171	66 48	59	171	67 47	60	171	68 47	59	170	356
5	64 42	+60	169	65 42	+59	169	66 41	+59	169	67 40	+60	168	68 40	+59	168	355
6	64 34	60	167	65 34	59	167	66 33	59	167	67 32	59	166	68 31	59	166	354
7	64 25	59	165	65 24	59	165	66 23	59	164	67 22	58	164	68 20	59	163	353
8	64 15	58	163	65 13	59	163	66 12	58	162	67 10	59	162	68 09	58	161	352
9	64 03	58	161	65 01	58	161	65 59	58	160	66 57	58	159	67 55	58	159	351
10	63 50	+58	159	64 48	+57	159	65 45	+58	158	66 43	+58	157	67 41	+57	156	350
11	63 35	58	157	64 33	57	157	65 30	57	156	66 27	57	155	67 24	57	154	349
12	63 20	57	155	64 17	57	155	65 14	57	154	66 11	56	153	67 07	56	152	348
13	63 03	57	153	64 00	56	153	64 56	56	152	65 52	56	151	66 48	56	150	347
14	62 45	56	151	63 41	56	151	64 37	56	150	65 33	56	149	66 29	55	148	346
15	62 26	+56	150	63 22	+55	149	64 17	+56	148	65 13	+54	147	66 07	+55	146	345
16	62 06	55	148	63 01	55	147	63 56	55	146	64 51	54	145	65 45	54	144	344
17	61 45	55	146	62 40	54	145	63 34	54	144	64 28	54	143	65 22	54	142	343
18	61 23	54	144	62 17	54	143	63 11	54	142	64 05	53	141	64 58	53	140	342
19	61 00	54	143	61 54	53	142	62 47	53	141	63 40	53	140	64 33	52	139	341
20	60 36	+53	141	61 29	+53	140	62 22	+53	139	63 15	+52	138	64 07	+52	137	340
21	60 11	53	139	61 04	53	138	61 57	52	137	62 49	51	136	63 40	51	135	339
22	59 45	53	138	60 38	52	137	61 30	51	136	62 21	51	135	63 12	51	133	338
23	59 19	52	136	60 11	52	135	61 03	51	134	61 54	50	133	62 44	50	132	337
24	58 52	51	135	59 43	51	134	60 34	51	133	61 25	50	131	62 15	49	130	336
25	58 24	+51	133	59 15	+51	132	60 06	+50	131	60 56	+49	130	61 45	+49	129	335
26	57 56	50	132	58 46	50	131	59 36	50	130	60 26	49	128	61 15	48	127	334
27	57 26	51	130	58 17	49	129	59 06	49	128	59 55	49	127	60 44	48	126	333
28	56 57	49	129	57 46	49	128	58 35	49	127	59 24	48	126	60 12	47	124	332
29	56 26	49	127	57 15	49	126	58 04	48	125	58 52	48	124	59 40	47	123	331
30	55 55	+49	126	56 44	+48	125	57 32	+48	124	58 20	+47	123	59 07	+47	122	330
31	55 24	48	125	56 12	48	124	57 00	48	123	57 48	46	121	58 34	46	120	329
32	54 52	48	123	55 40	48	122	56 28	46	121	57 14	47	120	58 01	45	119	328
33	54 19	48	122	55 07	47	121	55 54	47	120	56 41	46	119	57 27	45	118	327
34	53 47	47	121	54 34	47	120	55 21	46	119	56 07	45	118	56 52	45	117	326
35	53 13	+47	120	54 00	+47	119	54 47	+46	118	55 33	+45	117	56 18	+44	115	325
36	52 40	46	119	53 26	46	118	54 12	46	116	54 58	45	115	55 43	44	114	324
37	52 06	46	117	52 52	46	116	53 38	45	115	54 23	44	114	55 07	44	113	323
38	51 31	46	116	52 17	46	115	53 03	45	114	53 48	44	113	54 32	43	112	322
39	50 56	46	115	51 42	45	114	52 27	45	113	53 12	44	112	53 56	43	111	321
40	50 21	+46	114	51 07	+45	113	51 52	+44	112	52 36	+44	111	53 20	+43	110	320
41	49 46	45	113	50 31	45	112	51 16	44	111	52 00	43	110	52 43	43	109	319
42	49 10	45	112	49 55	45	111	50 40	43	110	51 23	44	109	52 07	42	108	318
43	48 34	45	111	49 19	44	110	50 03	44	109	50 47	43	108	51 30	42	107	317
44	47 58	45	110	48 43	44	109	49 27	43	108	50 10	43	107	50 53	42	106	316
45	47 22	+44	109	48 06	+44	108	48 50	+43	107	49 33	+42	106	50 15	+42	105	315
46	46 45	44	108	47 29	44	107	48 13	43	106	48 56	42	105	49 38	42	104	314
47	46 09	43	107	46 52	44	106	47 36	42	105	48 18	43	104	49 01	41	103	313
48	45 32	43	106	46 15	43	105	46 58	43	104	47 41	42	103	48 23	41	102	312
49	44 54	44	105	45 38	43	104	46 21	42	103	47 03	42	102	47 45	41	101	311
50	44 17	+43	104	45 00	+43	103	45 43	+42	102	46 25	+42	101	47 07	+41	100	310
51	43 40	43	103	44 23	42	102	45 05	43	101	45 48	41	100	46 29	41	99	309
52	43 02	43	102	43 45	43	101	44 28	42	100	45 10	41	99	45 51	41	98	308
53	42 24	43	101	43 07	43	101	43 50	41	100	44 31	42	99	45 13	41	98	307
54	41 46	43	101	42 29	42	100	43 11	42	99	43 53	42	98	44 35	40	97	306
55	41 08	+43	100	41 51	+42	99	42 33	+42	98	43 15	+41	97	43 56	+41	96	305
56	40 30	43	99	41 13	42	98	41 55	42	97	42 37	41	96	43 18	40	95	304
57	39 52	43	98	40 35	42	97	41 17	41	96	41 58	41	95	42 39	41	94	303
58	39 14	42	97	39 56	42	96	40 38	42	95	41 20	41	94	42 01	40	93	302
59	38 36	42	96	39 18	42	95	40 00	41	95	40 41	41	94	41 22	41	93	301
60	37 57	+43	96	38 40	+41	95	39 21	+42	94	40 03	+41	93	40 44	+40	92	300
61	37 19	42	95	38 01	42	94	38 43	41	93	39 24	41	92	40 05	41	91	299
62	36 40	43	94	37 23	41	93	38 04	42	92	38 46	41	91	39 27	40	90	298
63	36 02	42	93	36 44	42	92	37 26	41	91	38 07	41	90	38 48	41	90	297
64	35 23	43	92	36 06	41	91	36 47	42	91	37 29	41	90	38 10	40	89	296
65	34 45	+42	92	35 27	+42	91	36 09	+41	90	36 50	+41	89	37 31	+40	88	295
66	34 06	42	91	34 48	42	90	35 30	42	89	36 12	40	88	36 52	41	87	294
67	33 28	42	90	34 10	42	89	34 52	41	88	35 33	41	87	36 14	41	87	293
68	32 49	42	89	33 31	42	88	34 13	41	88	34 54	41	87	35 35	41	86	292
69	32 11	42	89	32 53	42	88	33 35	41	87	34 16	41	86	34 57	41	85	291

S. Lat. {LHA greater than 180°……. Zn=180−Z; LHA less than 180°………. Zn=180+Z}

DECLINATION (15°-29°) SAME NAME AS LATITUDE

70

Table 1 *Extract from AP3270 (USA, Pub. 249).*

the column corresponding to the number of degrees in the declination. Write down the three quantities, Hc, *d*, and Z.

4) Enter the correction table (Table 5, also supplied on a loose card), to correct the calculated altitude for the minutes of declination. *d* across the top of the table finds the correct column; run down the column to the line appropriate to the number of minutes in the declination.

5) Apply the correction just obtained to the calcu- lated altitude, with the same sign as *d*.

This results in the calculated altitude which is compared with the true altitude to give the intercept.

6) Take the value of Z given in the table, and process it as directed by the instructions at top and bottom of the page; this give the azimuth of the body.

All that remains is the plotting of the position line, which is described on page 152.

TABLE 5.—Correction to Tabulated Altitude for Minutes of Declination

d / ′	1	2	3	4	5	6	7	8	9	10	11	12	13	14	15	16	17	18	19	20	21	22	23	24	25	26	27	28	29	30	31	32	33	34	35	36	37	38	39	40	41	42	43	44	45	46	47	48	49	50	51	52	53	54	55	56	57	58	59	60	d / ′
0	0	0	0	0	0	0	0	0	0	0	0	0	0	0	0	0	0	0	0	0	0	0	0	0	0	0	0	0	0	0	0	0	0	0	0	0	0	0	0	0	0	0	0	0	0	0	0	0	0	0	0	0	0	0	0	0	0	0	0	0	0
1	0	0	0	0	0	0	0	0	0	0	0	0	0	0	0	0	0	0	0	0	0	0	0	0	0	0	0	0	0	0	1	1	1	1	1	1	1	1	1	1	1	1	1	1	1	1	1	1	1	1	1	1	1	1	1	1	1	1	1	1	1
2	0	0	0	0	0	0	0	0	0	0	0	0	0	0	0	1	1	1	1	1	1	1	1	1	1	1	1	1	1	1	1	1	1	1	1	1	1	1	1	1	1	1	1	1	2	2	2	2	2	2	2	2	2	2	2	2	2	2	2	2	2
3	0	0	0	0	0	0	0	0	0	0	1	1	1	1	1	1	1	1	1	1	1	1	1	1	1	1	1	1	1	2	2	2	2	2	2	2	2	2	2	2	2	2	2	2	2	2	2	2	2	2	3	3	3	3	3	3	3	3	3	3	3
4	0	0	0	0	0	0	0	1	1	1	1	1	1	1	1	1	1	1	1	1	1	1	2	2	2	2	2	2	2	2	2	2	2	2	2	2	2	3	3	3	3	3	3	3	3	3	3	3	3	3	3	3	4	4	4	4	4	4	4	4	4
5	0	0	0	0	0	0	1	1	1	1	1	1	1	1	1	1	1	2	2	2	2	2	2	2	2	2	2	2	2	2	3	3	3	3	3	3	3	3	3	3	3	4	4	4	4	4	4	4	4	4	4	4	4	4	5	5	5	5	5	5	5
6	0	0	0	0	0	1	1	1	1	1	1	1	1	1	2	2	2	2	2	2	2	2	2	2	2	3	3	3	3	3	3	3	3	3	4	4	4	4	4	4	4	4	4	4	4	5	5	5	5	5	5	5	5	5	6	6	6	6	6	6	6
7	0	0	0	0	1	1	1	1	1	1	1	1	2	2	2	2	2	2	2	2	2	3	3	3	3	3	3	3	3	4	4	4	4	4	4	4	4	4	5	5	5	5	5	5	5	5	5	6	6	6	6	6	6	6	6	7	7	7	7	7	7
8	0	0	0	1	1	1	1	1	1	1	1	2	2	2	2	2	2	2	3	3	3	3	3	3	3	3	4	4	4	4	4	4	4	5	5	5	5	5	5	5	5	6	6	6	6	6	6	6	7	7	7	7	7	7	7	7	8	8	8	8	8
9	0	0	0	1	1	1	1	1	1	2	2	2	2	2	2	2	3	3	3	3	3	3	3	4	4	4	4	4	4	4	5	5	5	5	5	5	6	6	6	6	6	6	6	7	7	7	7	7	7	8	8	8	8	8	8	8	9	9	9	9	9
10	0	0	0	1	1	1	1	1	2	2	2	2	2	2	2	3	3	3	3	3	4	4	4	4	4	4	4	5	5	5	5	5	6	6	6	6	6	6	6	7	7	7	7	7	8	8	8	8	8	8	8	9	9	9	9	9	10	10	10	10	10
11	0	0	1	1	1	1	1	1	2	2	2	2	2	3	3	3	3	3	3	4	4	4	4	4	5	5	5	5	5	6	6	6	6	6	6	7	7	7	7	7	8	8	8	8	8	8	9	9	9	9	9	10	10	10	10	10	10	11	11	11	11
12	0	0	1	1	1	1	1	2	2	2	2	2	3	3	3	3	3	4	4	4	4	4	5	5	5	5	5	6	6	6	6	6	7	7	7	7	7	8	8	8	8	8	9	9	9	9	9	10	10	10	10	10	11	11	11	11	11	12	12	12	12
13	0	0	1	1	1	1	2	2	2	2	2	3	3	3	3	3	4	4	4	4	5	5	5	5	5	6	6	6	6	6	7	7	7	7	8	8	8	8	8	9	9	9	9	10	10	10	10	10	11	11	11	11	11	12	12	12	12	13	13	13	13
14	0	0	1	1	1	1	2	2	2	2	3	3	3	3	4	4	4	4	4	5	5	5	5	6	6	6	6	7	7	7	7	7	8	8	8	8	9	9	9	9	10	10	10	10	10	11	11	11	11	12	12	12	12	13	13	13	13	14	14	14	14
15	0	0	1	1	1	2	2	2	2	2	3	3	3	4	4	4	4	4	5	5	5	6	6	6	6	6	7	7	7	8	8	8	8	8	9	9	9	10	10	10	10	10	11	11	11	12	12	12	12	12	13	13	13	14	14	14	14	14	15	15	15
16	0	1	1	1	1	2	2	2	2	3	3	3	3	4	4	4	5	5	5	5	6	6	6	6	7	7	7	7	8	8	8	9	9	9	9	10	10	10	10	11	11	11	11	12	12	12	13	13	13	13	14	14	14	14	15	15	15	15	16	16	16
17	0	1	1	1	1	2	2	2	3	3	3	3	4	4	4	5	5	5	5	6	6	6	7	7	7	7	8	8	8	8	9	9	9	10	10	10	10	11	11	11	12	12	12	12	13	13	13	14	14	14	14	15	15	15	16	16	16	16	17	17	17
18	0	1	1	1	2	2	2	2	3	3	3	4	4	4	4	5	5	5	6	6	6	7	7	7	8	8	8	8	9	9	9	10	10	10	10	11	11	11	12	12	12	13	13	13	14	14	14	14	15	15	15	16	16	16	16	17	17	17	18	18	18
19	0	1	1	1	2	2	2	3	3	3	3	4	4	4	5	5	5	6	6	6	7	7	7	8	8	8	9	9	9	10	10	10	10	11	11	11	12	12	12	13	13	13	14	14	14	15	15	15	16	16	16	16	17	17	17	18	18	18	19	19	19
20	0	1	1	1	2	2	2	3	3	3	4	4	4	5	5	5	6	6	6	7	7	7	8	8	8	9	9	9	10	10	10	11	11	11	12	12	12	13	13	13	14	14	14	15	15	15	16	16	16	17	17	17	18	18	18	19	19	19	20	20	20
21	0	1	1	1	2	2	2	3	3	4	4	4	5	5	5	6	6	6	7	7	7	8	8	8	9	9	9	10	10	10	11	11	12	12	12	13	13	13	14	14	14	15	15	15	16	16	16	17	17	18	18	18	19	19	19	20	20	20	21	21	21
22	0	1	1	1	2	2	3	3	3	4	4	4	5	5	6	6	6	7	7	7	8	8	8	9	9	10	10	10	11	11	11	12	12	12	13	13	14	14	14	15	15	15	16	16	16	17	17	18	18	18	19	19	19	20	20	21	21	21	22	22	22
23	0	1	1	2	2	2	3	3	3	4	4	5	5	5	6	6	7	7	7	8	8	8	9	9	10	10	10	11	11	12	12	12	13	13	13	14	14	15	15	15	16	16	16	17	17	18	18	18	19	19	20	20	20	21	21	21	22	22	23	23	23
24	0	1	1	2	2	2	3	3	4	4	4	5	5	6	6	6	7	7	8	8	8	9	9	10	10	10	11	11	12	12	12	13	13	14	14	14	15	15	16	16	16	17	17	18	18	18	19	19	20	20	20	21	21	22	22	22	23	23	24	24	24
25	0	1	1	2	2	2	3	3	4	4	5	5	5	6	6	7	7	8	8	8	9	9	10	10	10	11	11	12	12	12	13	13	14	14	15	15	15	16	16	17	17	18	18	18	19	19	20	20	20	21	21	22	22	22	23	23	24	24	25	25	25
26	0	1	1	2	2	3	3	3	4	4	5	5	6	6	6	7	7	8	8	9	9	10	10	10	11	11	12	12	13	13	13	14	14	15	15	16	16	16	17	17	18	18	19	19	20	20	20	21	21	22	22	23	23	23	24	24	25	25	26	26	26
27	0	1	1	2	2	3	3	4	4	4	5	5	6	6	7	7	8	8	9	9	9	10	10	11	11	12	12	13	13	14	14	14	15	15	16	16	17	17	18	18	18	19	19	20	20	21	21	22	22	22	23	23	24	24	25	25	26	26	27	27	27
28	0	1	1	2	2	3	3	4	4	5	5	6	6	7	7	7	8	8	9	9	10	10	11	11	12	12	13	13	14	14	14	15	15	16	16	17	17	18	18	19	19	20	20	21	21	21	22	22	23	23	24	24	25	25	26	26	27	27	28	28	28
29	0	1	1	2	2	3	3	4	4	5	5	6	6	7	7	8	8	9	9	10	10	11	11	12	12	13	13	14	14	14	15	15	16	16	17	17	18	18	19	19	20	20	21	21	22	22	23	23	24	24	25	25	26	26	27	27	28	28	29	29	29
30	0	1	2	2	2	3	4	4	4	5	6	6	6	7	8	8	8	9	10	10	10	11	12	12	12	13	14	14	14	15	16	16	16	17	18	18	18	19	20	20	20	21	22	22	22	23	24	24	24	25	26	26	26	27	28	28	28	29	30	30	30
31	1	1	2	2	3	3	4	4	5	5	6	6	7	7	8	8	9	9	10	10	11	11	12	12	13	13	14	14	15	16	16	17	17	18	18	19	19	20	20	21	21	22	22	23	23	24	24	25	25	26	26	27	27	28	28	29	29	30	30	31	31
32	1	1	2	2	3	3	4	4	5	5	6	6	7	7	8	9	9	10	10	11	11	12	12	13	13	14	14	15	15	16	17	17	18	18	19	19	20	20	21	21	22	22	23	23	24	25	25	26	26	27	27	28	28	29	29	30	30	31	31	32	32
33	1	1	2	2	3	3	4	4	5	6	6	7	7	8	8	9	9	10	10	11	12	12	13	13	14	14	15	15	16	16	17	18	18	19	19	20	20	21	21	22	23	23	24	24	25	25	26	26	27	28	28	29	29	30	30	31	31	32	32	33	33
34	1	1	2	2	3	3	4	5	5	6	6	7	7	8	8	9	10	10	11	11	12	12	13	14	14	15	15	16	16	17	18	18	19	19	20	20	21	22	22	23	23	24	24	25	26	26	27	27	28	28	29	29	30	31	31	32	32	33	33	34	34
35	1	1	2	2	3	4	4	5	5	6	6	7	8	8	9	9	10	10	11	12	12	13	13	14	15	15	16	16	17	18	18	19	19	20	20	21	22	22	23	23	24	24	25	26	26	27	27	28	29	29	30	30	31	32	32	33	33	34	34	35	35
36	1	1	2	2	3	4	4	5	5	6	7	7	8	8	9	10	10	11	11	12	13	13	14	14	15	16	16	17	17	18	19	19	20	20	21	22	22	23	23	24	25	25	26	26	27	28	28	29	29	30	31	31	32	32	33	34	34	35	35	36	36
37	1	1	2	2	3	4	4	5	6	6	7	7	8	9	9	10	10	11	12	12	13	14	14	15	15	16	17	17	18	18	19	20	20	21	22	22	23	23	24	25	25	26	27	27	28	28	29	30	30	31	31	32	33	33	34	35	35	36	36	37	37
38	1	1	2	3	3	4	4	5	6	6	7	8	8	9	10	10	11	11	12	13	13	14	15	15	16	16	17	18	18	19	20	20	21	22	22	23	23	24	25	25	26	27	27	28	28	29	30	30	31	32	32	33	34	34	35	35	36	37	37	38	38
39	1	1	2	3	3	4	5	5	6	6	7	8	8	9	10	10	11	12	12	13	14	14	15	16	16	17	18	18	19	20	20	21	21	22	23	23	24	25	25	26	27	27	28	29	29	30	31	31	32	32	33	34	34	35	36	36	37	38	38	39	39
40	1	1	2	3	3	4	5	5	6	7	7	8	9	9	10	11	11	12	13	13	14	15	15	16	17	17	18	19	19	20	21	21	22	23	23	24	25	25	26	27	27	28	29	29	30	31	31	32	33	33	34	35	35	36	37	37	38	39	39	40	40
41	1	1	2	3	3	4	5	5	6	7	8	8	9	10	10	11	12	12	13	14	14	15	16	16	17	18	18	19	20	20	21	22	23	23	24	25	25	26	27	27	28	29	29	30	31	31	32	33	33	34	35	36	36	37	38	38	39	40	40	41	41
42	1	1	2	3	4	4	5	6	6	7	8	8	9	10	10	11	12	13	13	14	15	15	16	17	18	18	19	20	20	21	22	22	23	24	24	25	26	27	27	28	29	29	30	31	32	32	33	34	34	35	36	36	37	38	38	39	40	41	41	42	42
43	1	1	2	3	4	4	5	6	6	7	8	9	9	10	11	11	12	13	14	14	15	16	16	17	18	19	19	20	21	22	22	23	24	24	25	26	27	27	28	29	29	30	31	32	32	33	34	34	35	36	37	37	38	39	39	40	41	42	42	43	43
44	1	1	2	3	4	4	5	6	7	7	8	9	10	10	11	12	12	13	14	15	15	16	17	18	18	19	20	21	21	22	23	23	24	25	26	26	27	28	29	29	30	31	32	32	33	34	34	35	36	37	37	38	39	40	40	41	42	43	43	44	44
45	1	2	2	3	4	4	5	6	7	8	8	9	10	10	11	12	13	14	14	15	16	16	17	18	19	20	20	21	22	22	23	24	25	26	26	27	28	28	29	30	31	32	32	33	34	34	35	36	37	38	38	39	40	40	41	42	43	44	44	45	45
46	1	2	2	3	4	5	5	6	7	8	8	9	10	11	12	12	13	14	15	15	16	17	18	18	19	20	21	21	22	23	24	25	25	26	27	28	28	29	30	31	31	32	33	34	34	35	36	37	38	38	39	40	41	41	42	43	44	44	45	46	46
47	1	2	2	3	4	5	5	6	7	8	9	9	10	11	12	13	13	14	15	16	16	17	18	19	20	20	21	22	23	24	24	25	26	27	27	28	29	30	31	31	32	33	34	34	35	36	37	38	38	39	40	41	42	42	43	44	45	45	46	47	47
48	1	2	2	3	4	5	6	6	7	8	9	10	10	11	12	13	14	14	15	16	17	18	18	19	20	21	22	22	23	24	25	26	26	27	28	29	30	30	31	32	33	34	34	35	36	37	38	38	39	40	41	42	42	43	44	45	46	46	47	48	48
49	1	2	2	3	4	5	6	7	7	8	9	10	11	11	12	13	14	15	16	16	17	18	19	20	20	21	22	23	24	24	25	26	27	28	29	29	30	31	32	33	33	34	35	36	37	38	38	39	40	41	42	42	43	44	45	46	47	47	48	49	49
50	1	2	2	3	4	5	6	7	8	8	9	10	11	12	12	13	14	15	16	17	18	18	19	20	21	22	22	23	24	25	26	27	28	28	29	30	31	32	32	33	34	35	36	37	38	38	39	40	41	42	42	43	44	45	46	47	48	48	49	50	50
51	1	2	3	3	4	5	6	7	8	8	9	10	11	12	13	14	14	15	16	17	18	19	20	20	21	22	23	24	25	26	26	27	28	29	30	31	31	32	33	34	35	36	37	37	38	39	40	41	42	42	43	44	45	46	47	48	48	49	50	51	51
52	1	2	3	3	4	5	6	7	8	9	10	10	11	12	13	14	15	16	16	17	18	19	20	21	22	23	23	24	25	26	27	28	29	29	30	31	32	33	34	35	36	36	37	38	39	40	41	42	42	43	44	45	46	47	48	49	49	50	51	52	52
53	1	2	3	4	4	5	6	7	8	9	10	11	11	12	13	14	15	16	17	18	19	19	20	21	22	23	24	25	26	26	27	28	29	30	31	32	33	34	34	35	36	37	38	39	40	41	42	42	43	44	45	46	47	48	49	49	50	51	52	53	53
54	1	2	3	4	4	5	6	7	8	9	10	11	12	13	14	14	15	16	17	18	19	20	21	22	22	23	24	25	26	27	28	29	30	31	32	32	33	34	35	36	37	38	39	40	40	41	42	43	44	45	46	47	48	49	50	50	51	52	53	54	54
55	1	2	3	4	5	6	6	7	8	9	10	11	12	13	14	15	16	16	17	18	19	20	21	22	23	24	25	26	27	28	28	29	30	31	32	33	34	35	36	37	38	38	39	40	41	42	43	44	45	46	47	48	49	50	50	51	52	53	54	55	55
56	1	2	3	4	5	6	7	7	8	9	10	11	12	13	14	15	16	17	18	19	20	21	21	22	23	24	25	26	27	28	29	30	31	32	33	34	35	35	36	37	38	39	40	41	42	43	44	45	46	47	48	49	49	50	51	52	53	54	55	56	56
57	1	2	3	4	5	6	7	8	9	10	10	11	12	13	14	15	16	17	18	19	20	21	22	23	24	25	26	27	28	28	29	30	31	32	33	34	35	36	37	38	39	40	41	42	43	44	45	46	47	48	48	49	50	51	52	53	54	55	56	57	57
58	1	2	3	4	5	6	7	8	9	10	11	12	13	14	14	15	16	17	18	19	20	21	22	23	24	25	26	27	28	29	30	31	32	33	34	35	36	37	38	39	40	41	42	43	44	44	45	46	47	48	49	50	51	52	53	54	55	56	57	58	58
59	1	2	3	4	5	6	7	8	9	10	11	12	13	14	15	16	17	18	19	20	21	22	23	24	25	26	27	28	29	30	30	31	32	33	34	35	36	37	38	39	40	41	42	43	44	45	46	47	48	49	50	51	52	53	54	55	56	57	58	59	59

Table 2 *Extract from AP3270 (USA, Pub. 249).*

48 Plotting the position line

The whole purpose of the sight reduction process is to produce three pieces of information which allow the position line to be plotted; they are:

The chosen position

The intercept, towards or away from the body

The azimuth

The basic method of plotting the position line is shown in Figure 1. First, the chosen position is marked, with the name of the body observed; if several bodies are observed at the same time (as for example in a set of star sights), then *each sight will have its own chosen position.*

The next step is to lay off the azimuth -either towards the body or away from it (the reciprocal of the azimuth), according to the way the intercept was named. If the true altitude was greater than the calculated altitude, then the ship was actually closer to the GP than the chosen position, and the

48.1 *Plotting the position line.*

intercept is *towards*; a smaller true altitude than calculated altitude means that the ship was further from the GP than the chosen position, and the intercept is marked *away*.

The intercept is now marked along the azimuth line, to give a point (A) which is at the correct true distance from the geographical position – it is a point on the position line.

The final step is to draw the position line itself. To be exact, the position line is a circle with its centre at the GP, but because this circle has, in general, a very large radius, the position line can be regarded as being a straight line in the area immediately surrounding the ship. The position line can be drawn through point A, at right angles to the azimuth. The line can be made as long or as short as desired, and it is conventional to mark it at each end with an arrow-head pointing towards the GP, as shown; the reason for this is explained below.

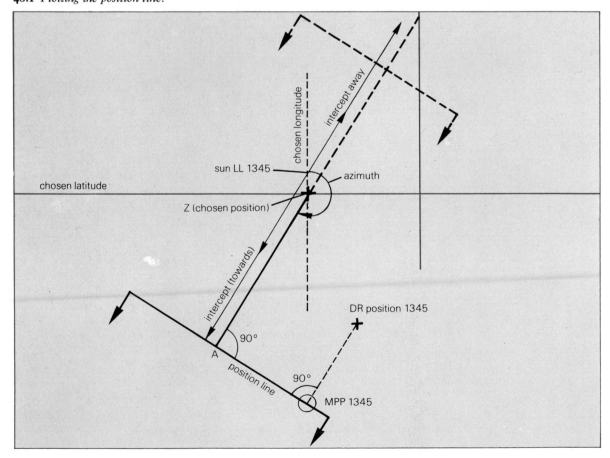

Most probable position When a single position line only is available, the navigator will wish to revise his DR to take into account the new information given by the position line. Provided that the position line is considered reliable, the MPP is usually selected at the point on the position line closest to the DR, as shown in Figure 2.

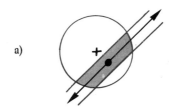

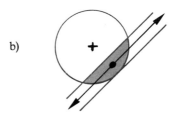

48.2 *Most probable position.*

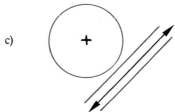

Fixes An astronomical position line is exactly the same, from a position finding point of view, as any other position line; it can be used for fixing in just the same way. A fix requires the intersection of two (or more) position lines related to the same time. Position lines from the simultaneous observation of two bodies suitably placed in azimuth can yield a fix, or one of the position lines could be derived from a sounding or a radio bearing or any other source. Figure 3 illustrates the plotting of a fix from simultaneous observations of the sun and moon; note that each body has its own chosen position. Using AP 3270 (Pub. 249), the chosen latitudes will be the same, but the longitudes differ. It very often happens that only one position line can be obtained at a particular time, and another becomes available later. The most common example is the use of the sun; one observation

48.3 *Astronomical fix from simultaneous observations of sun and moon.*

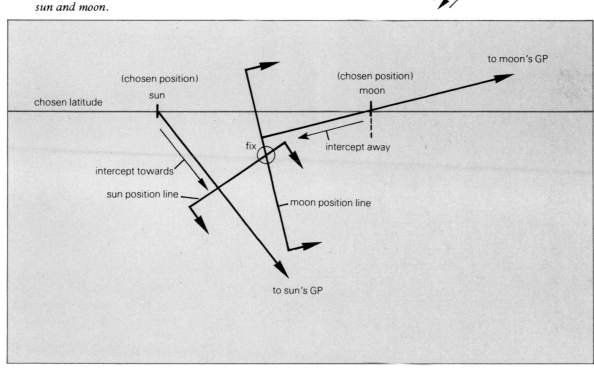

yields a position line, but it is not possible to get another position line from the sun which will intersect the first until sufficient time has passed for the sun's azimuth to change. This time interval is likely to be several hours, by which time the ship will have moved from the first position line. This problem is solved by use of the transferred position line idea (see pages 77–79). Figure 4 illustrates one of the classic fixes using the sun – a morning observation when the sun was still rising in the east, followed by a meridian altitude at local noon; the first position line is transferred to the same time as the second, the so-called *sun run-mer alt* fix. If the noon latitude sight cannot be taken for any reason, the same procedure can be followed using a second sun observation at a convenient time, the *sun-run-sun* fix.

Plotting without a chart It may well happen that no chart of a suitable scale for plotting sights is available; ocean charts, for example, are generally on such a small scale that it is impossible to plot positions and intercepts accurately. The three most practical ways of making up a suitable chart of the locality in which the vessel lies are:

1) Use a plotting sheet; these are blank 'charts' specially printed for this very purpose, covering various bands of latitude. These sheets carry a fixed longitude scale and various scales of latitude, and are used like an ordinary chart.

2) Latitude and longitude graduations can be taken from any chart of a suitable scale that covers the same latitude as the DR, and transferred to a sheet of paper.

3) Latitude and longitude scales can be manufactured on a sheet of paper; first choose an appropriate scale for latitude (for example one centimetre to one minute of latitude), and then make the longitude scale by using the equation:

Minutes of longitude = minutes of latitude × cos (lat). Table 1 gives the cosines of angles between 0° and 75°, for use if a calculator is not available.

Reducing errors with multiple position lines
When three or more position lines are drawn, they will very rarely meet in a point, giving rise to a 'cocked hat' (Fig. 5). In establishing the most probable position, it is possible to reduce certain errors in the position lines by *bisecting the external*

48.4 *Sun-run-mer alt fix.*

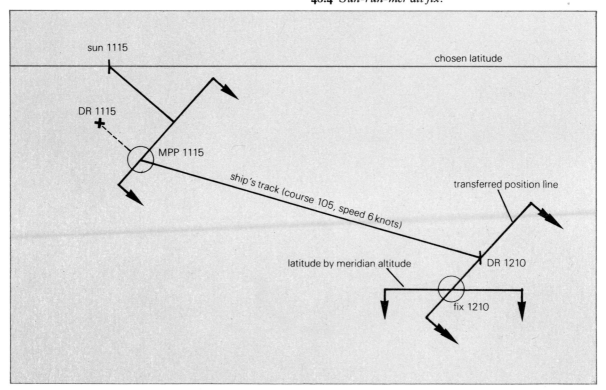

angles, as shown. Note that under certain circumstances, the MPP can lie *outside* the cocked hat (Fig. 5b). This process reduces any systematic errors in the observations considerably, and also helps to reduce the random errors to some extent.

48.5 *Reducing errors with a 'cocked hat'.*

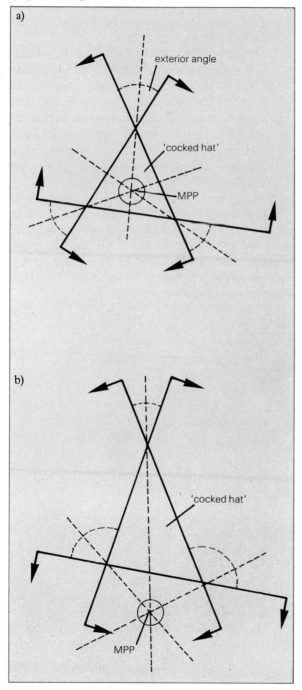

a)

exterior angle

'cocked hat'

MPP

b)

'cocked hat'

MPP

Table 1 Scale conversion table for longitude

Lat°		Lat°		Lat°		Lat°		Lat°	
0	1.000	1	1.000	2	0.999	3	0.999	4	0.998
5	0.996	6	0.995	7	0.993	8	0.990	9	0.988
10	0.985	11	0.982	12	0.978	13	0.974	14	0.970
15	0.966	16	0.961	17	0.956	18	0.951	19	0.946
20	0.940	21	0.934	22	0.927	23	0.921	24	0.914
25	0.906	26	0.899	27	0.891	28	0.883	29	0.875
30	0.866	31	0.857	32	0.848	33	0.839	34	0.829
35	0.819	36	0.809	37	0.799	38	0.788	39	0.777
40	0.766	41	0.755	42	0.743	43	0.731	44	0.719
45	0.707	46	0.695	47	0.682	48	0.669	49	0.656
50	0.643	51	0.629	52	0.616	53	0.602	54	0.588
55	0.574	56	0.559	57	0.545	58	0.530	59	0.515
60	0.500	61	0.485	62	0.469	63	0.454	64	0.438
65	0.423	66	0.407	67	0.391	68	0.375	69	0.358

49 General position line – summary and proforma

This section summarizes the steps that must be followed to obtain a general astronomical position line. Reference is made to the pages where the detailed procedures for each step are described. Also given is a proforma which can be used as a model for the navigator's own observations, with a worked example.

The basic procedure can be summarized as follows:

1) Select the body to be observed and the approximate time. Check the sextant and measure its index error (see page 127). Make sure that the watch to be used for recording time has recently been compared with GMT.

2) Make the observation(s) and record the time and sextant altitude for each. Time is required to the nearest second, altitude to the nearest 0.2 minutes of arc. If making a series of observations of the same body, average the results (see page 129).

3) On the sight form, record:
   a) The DR position   1
   b) The body (and limb) observed   2
   c) The height of eye   3
   d) The index error   4
   e) The date and approximate zone time   5
   f) The watch error on GMT   6
   g) The (averaged) watch time   7
   h) The (averaged) sextant altitude   8

4) Work out the Greenwich date and time, by applying the zone number to the zone time. 9
   Find the GMT of the observation by applying the watch error to the watch time.   10

5) Open the *Nautical Almanac* to the daily page appropriate to the *Greenwich date*; for the hour of GMT, record:
   a) The GHA of the body (GHA Aries for a star)   11
   b) v (moon, planets) or SHA (star)   12
   c) Declination (and name)   13
   d) d (not for star) and sign by inspection 14
   e) Horizontal parallax (HP) for the moon 15

6) Open the *Nautical Almanac* to the section of the increments and corrections table for the minutes of GMT. Record:

   a) The increment to GHA for the minutes and seconds of GMT. Use the correct column   16
   b) The v correction, if appropriate   17
   c) The d correction (or estimate mentally) 18
      This has the same sign as given to d.

7) Combine the above figures to obtain the exact GHA and declination for the instant of observation:
   a) Add together GHA, the increment and the v correction or SHA to obtain GHA   19
   b) Add or subtract the d correction according to its sign to obtain declination. 20

8) Choose a position for entry to the tables:
   a) Latitude – the nearest whole number of degrees to the DR.   21
   b) Longitude – the nearest longitude to the DR that will make the LHA a whole number of degrees (see page 148).   22
   Then apply the chosen longitude to the GHA to obtain LHA (add E long, subtract W long). 23

9) Choose volume 2 or volume 3 of the *Sight Reduction Tables* (AP 3270, Pub. 249) according to the chosen latitude; find the page in the correct volume according to:
   The chosen latitude.
   Whether latitude and declination have the same or contrary names.
   The range of declination (0–14° or 15°–29°). This will narrow the choice of pages to two, one of which will have the LHA in either the extreme left or extreme right hand column.
   From the selected page, in the column with the degrees of declination and the line with LHA, record:
   a) The quantity labelled Hc   24
   b) The quantity d (not the same as d in the *Nautical Almanac*)   25
   c) The azimuth angle, Z

10) Work out the azimuth of the body by following the precepts given at the top or bottom of the page.   26

11) Enter the Interpolation table (Table 5, also supplied on a loose card), with d across the top and the nearest minute of declination down the side. Record the altitude correction, with the same sign as d, and apply it to Hc, to give the calculated altitude.   27

12) Now find the observed altitude (Ho) as follows:
 a) Apply index error to the sextant altitude.
 b) From the altitude correction tables (at the front of the *Nautical Almanac*, also on a loose card), find the dip appropriate to the height of eye; apply this to obtain apparent altitude **28**
 c) Enter the correction table appropriate to the body with apparent altitude to get the altitude correction for refraction, semi-diameter etc. (The moon has its own tables). Apply the correction to apparent altitude to get observed altitude. **29**

13 Subtract the lesser of true and calculated altitude from the other to obtain the intercept. Name this 'towards' if the true altitude is greater, otherwise name it 'away'. **30**

14) The position line may now be plotted on the chart, laying off the intercept towards or away from the azimuth, from the chosen position (see page 147) (Fig. 1).

49.1 *Astronomical position line plotted.*

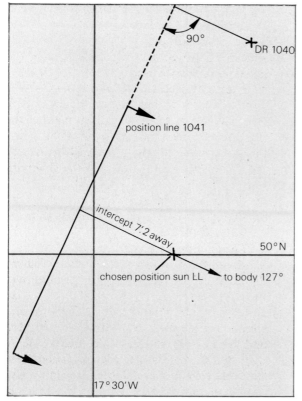

Pro forma and example

DR 50°15′N, 17°10′W **1**	Chosen lat 50°N **21** HE 3 m **3**
Body **2**	Sun LL
Zone date/time **5**	3 May 1980 09 h 40 m
Zone	+1 h
Greenwich date **9**	3 May 1980 10 h 40 m
Watch time **7**	10 h 41 m 17 s
Watch error **6**	01 m 02 s slow (+)
GMT **10**	10 h 42 m 19 s
GHA hrs **11** *v* **12**	330°47′.7 *v* −
Incr m,s **16**	10°34′.8
v Cor or SHA **17**	−
GHA **19**	341°22′.5
Chos long **22**	17°22′.5 W
LHA **23**	324°
Dec **13** *d* **14**	N15°46′.5 *d* + 0′.7
d Cor **18**	+0′.5
Dec **20**	N15°47′.0 SAME as lat
Hc **24** *d* **25**	44°28′ *d* + 51′
Cor	+40′
Calc alt **27**	45°08
Z	127°
Azimuth (Zn) **26**	127°
Sext alt **8**	44°47′.2
Index error **4**	+1′.2
	44°48′.4
Dip **28**	−3′.0
App alt	44°45′.4
Cor **29**	+15′.0
Moon cor (HP =) **15**	
Moon cor **2**	
True alt	45°00′.8
Calc alt	45°08′
Intercept **30**	7′.2 AWAY from 127°
Chos pos	50°N, 17°22′.5W
	(see Fig. 1 for the plotted position line)

50 Star sight using seven selected stars (AP 3270 Vol 1 [US Pub. 229])

The *Sight Reduction Tables for Air Navigation* (AP 3270, Pub. 249), in the interests of saving space and weight, are confined to declinations between 0° and 30°N or S. Whilst this allows reduction of sun, moon and planet sights, there are only 27 of the main navigational stars with declinations in this range. To make better use of the navigational stars, volume 1 of the sight reduction tables provides solutions for seven selected stars for all combinations of latitude and LHA Aries. The stars selected are chosen on the basis of the most favourable distribution in altitude and azimuth.

The great advantage of a fix derived from star sights is that several can be observed at (more or less) the same time to provide a number of position lines; not only does this give an immediate fix without the need to transfer a position line, but it also gives confidence in the fix if three or more position lines intersect closely. However, it is not easy to take star sights from the deck of a yacht unless conditions are very good. Even so, considerable practice is needed to get good results.

To observe the altitude of a star, you must be able to see both the star and the horizon. In practical terms, this confines the time at which such sights can be taken to a few minutes after sunset and a few minutes before sunrise. Exactly how long is available to make the observations depends on the latitude; in the tropics, it can be very short.

Predicting twilight The first step in observing stars is to predict the time at which they will be visible. This is generally accepted as being when the sun is 6° below the horizon, a time known as civil twilight. This is given on the daily pages of the *Nautical Almanac* (Table 1). The procedure is as follows:

1) In the civil twilight column appropriate to either dawn or dusk, select the local mean time of civil twilight for the DR latitude; interpolate by eye if necessary.
2) To the LMT thus obtained, apply the DR longitude (add W long, subtract E long) to obtain the GMT of civil twilight.
3) Correct the GMT according to the zone being kept on board, to obtain the time of civil twilight by the ship's clock. This is the

Lat.	Twilight		Sunrise	Moonrise			
	Naut.	Civil		3	4	5	6
°	h m	h m	h m	h m	h m	h m	h m
N 72	////	////	01 23	01 45	▬	▬	
N 70	////	////	02 12	00 14	01 53	03 05	03 24
68	////	00 13	02 43	24 56	00 56	01 58	02 35
66	////	01 35	03 05	24 22	00 22	01 22	02 04
64	////	02 10	03 23	23 57	24 56	00 56	01 40
62	00 11	02 35	03 37	23 38	24 36	00 36	01 22
60	01 24	02 55	03 50	23 22	24 19	00 19	01 07
N 58	01 57	03 10	04 00	23 09	24 06	00 06	00 53
56	02 20	03 24	04 09	22 57	23 54	24 42	00 42
54	02 38	03 35	04 17	22 47	23 43	24 32	00 32
52	02 53	03 45	04 25	22 38	23 34	24 24	00 24
50	03 06	03 54	04 31	22 30	23 26	24 16	00 16
45	03 31	04 12	04 45	22 13	23 08	23 59	24 44
N 40	03 51	04 27	04 56	21 59	22 54	23 45	24 32
35	04 06	04 39	05 06	21 47	22 42	23 33	24 22
30	04 19	04 49	05 15	21 37	22 31	23 23	24 12
20	04 39	05 06	05 29	21 19	22 13	23 05	23 56
N 10	04 54	05 20	05 42	21 04	21 57	22 50	23 43
0	05 07	05 32	05 53	20 49	21 42	22 35	23 30
S 10	05 19	05 43	06 05	20 33	21 27	22 21	23 16
20	05 28	05 54	06 17	20 20	21 11	22 06	23 03
30	05 37	06 06	06 31	20 02	20 53	21 48	22 47
35	05 42	06 12	06 39	19 52	20 42	21 38	22 37
40	05 47	06 19	06 48	19 41	20 30	21 26	22 27
45	05 52	06 27	06 58	19 27	20 16	21 12	22 14
S 50	05 58	06 37	07 11	19 10	19 59	20 55	21 59
52	06 00	06 41	07 17	19 03	19 51	20 47	21 52
54	06 03	06 45	07 24	18 54	19 41	20 38	21 44
56	06 06	06 50	07 31	18 44	19 31	20 28	21 35
58	06 08	06 56	07 39	18 33	19 20	20 17	21 25
S 60	06 12	07 02	07 48	18 20	19 06	20 04	21 13

Lat.	Sunset	Twilight		Moonset			
		Civil	Naut.	3	4	5	6
°	h m	h m	h m	h m	h m	h m	h m
N 72	22 40	////	////	02 28	▬		
N 70	21 46	////	////	04 00	04 07	04 46	06 19
68	21 14	////	////	04 40	05 05	05 53	07 07
66	20 51	22 25	////	05 07	05 39	06 28	07 38
64	20 33	21 47	////	05 28	06 04	06 54	08 01
62	20 18	21 21	////	05 45	06 23	07 14	08 19
60	20 06	21 01	22 35	05 59	06 39	07 31	08 34
N 58	19 55	20 45	22 00	06 12	06 53	07 44	08 47
56	19 46	20 31	21 36	06 22	07 04	07 56	08 58
54	19 37	20 20	21 17	06 31	07 15	08 07	09 08
52	19 30	20 10	21 02	06 40	07 24	08 16	09 17
50	19 23	20 01	20 49	06 47	07 32	08 24	09 24
45	19 09	19 42	20 23	07 03	07 49	08 42	09 41
N 40	18 58	19 27	20 04	07 16	08 03	08 56	09 54
35	18 48	19 15	19 48	07 28	08 15	09 08	10 06
30	18 39	19 05	19 35	07 37	08 26	09 19	10 16
20	18 25	18 48	19 15	07 54	08 44	09 37	10 33
N 10	18 12	18 34	19 00	08 09	09 00	09 53	10 47
0	18 00	18 22	18 47	08 23	09 14	10 07	11 01
S 10	17 49	18 10	18 36	08 37	09 29	10 22	11 15
20	17 36	17 59	18 25	08 51	09 45	10 38	11 30
30	17 22	17 47	18 16	09 08	10 03	10 56	11 47
35	17 14	17 41	18 11	09 18	10 13	11 06	11 56
40	17 05	17 34	18 06	09 29	10 25	11 18	12 07
45	16 54	17 25	18 00	09 43	10 39	11 32	12 20
S 50	16 42	17 16	17 55	09 59	10 57	11 50	12 36
52	16 36	17 12	17 52	10 06	11 05	11 58	12 44
54	16 29	17 07	17 50	10 15	11 14	12 07	12 52
56	16 22	17 02	17 47	10 24	11 24	12 17	13 01
58	16 14	16 57	17 44	10 35	11 36	12 28	13 11
S 60	16 04	16 51	17 41	10 48	11 49	12 42	13 23

Day	SUN			MOON			
	Eqn. of Time 00^h	12^h	Mer. Pass.	Mer. Pass. Upper	Lower	Age	Phase
	m s	m s	h m	h m	h m	d	
3	03 08	03 11	11 57	02 11	14 36	18	
4	03 14	03 17	11 57	03 02	15 28	19	◐
5	03 20	03 22	11 57	03 55	16 21	20	

Table 1 *Extract from sunrise, sunset and twilight table.*

approximate time at which observations will be possible.

For example: DR position 50°N, 17°30′W on 4 May 1980
Required, the time of dawn civil twilight

LMT	03 h 54 m
Long W 17°30′ (in time)	01 h 10 m (see page 143)
GMT	05 h 04 m
Zone in force	+1
Zone time of civil twilight	04 h 04 m (+1)

Predicting the star position The next step is to predict the approximate altitudes and azimuths of the selected stars. This is necessary because the sky at civil twilight is still very light and the stars are barely visible (or not visible at all) to the naked eye. The only reliable way of finding the stars you are looking for is to search the correct part of the sky with the sextant telescope. If the sky is dark enough for the stars to be plainly visible to the naked eye, then it is almost certain that the horizon is too dark for accurate observation.

1) Using the LMT of civil twilight (step 1 of the previous example), enter the Aries column on the opposite page to obtain the LHA of Aries at civil twilight; add the increment for the minutes of LMT (see page 140) and round off the result to the nearest whole degree of LHA Aries.

2) Enter AP 3270 volume 1 with arguments latitude (nearest whole degree to the DR lat) and LHA.

3) Extract the names, altitudes and azimuths of the seven selected stars. Note which stars are printed in capital letters (bright stars) and which three are marked with asterisks (the best three of the seven selected).

For example: Following on from the previous example, we have LMT of civil twilight at 03 h 54 m

LHA Aries 03 h	267°09′.3
Incr 54 m	13°32′.2
LHA Aries (to nearest degree)	281°
Latitude	50°N

	Alt (Hc)	Az (Zn)
*Mirfak	18°39′	032
Alpheratz	27°26′	077
*ALTAIR	46°36′	156
Rasalhague	49°55′	207
*ARCTURUS	29°09′	266
Alkaid	44°01′	299
Kochab	56°00′	336

Note It will be helpful when searching for the stars

to convert the azimuths to magnetic bearings by applying variation, so that the compass can be used to help find them.

Making the observations Come on deck with the sextant and watch about a quarter of an hour before the predicted time of civil twilight, and begin searching for the first star to be observed; at dawn, avoid the temptation to start too early, before the horizon has become firm.

Select the order in which you will look for the stars on the following basis:

At dawn, look in the lighter (eastern) part of the sky before the western sky; look for faint stars before bright ones.

At dusk, look in the darker (eastern) sky before the western sky; look for bright stars before faint ones.

Having decided which star to look for, set its predicted altitude on the sextant and sweep the sky on the compass bearing established from the predicted azimuth. By searching slowly and carefully from side to side and up and down, the star should appear within the field of the sextant telescope. Provided the bearing and altitude are approximately as predicted, the chances of observing the wrong star are small. Bring the star to the horizon in the usual way, and record the time. If the duration of twilight is short, as it is in the tropics, it may only be possible to take one sight of each star. Star sights should not be hurried, but it is important not to waste time.

Sights during the night If the horizon is bright, it is sometimes possible to take star sights throughout the night; this generally is possible when the moon is near full. Use the sextant without the telescope fitted, and avoid using the moon itself or any star close to it. The position line resulting from such an observation is likely to have a 95 per cent error of five miles or more, so it should be used with caution.

Reduction and plotting Reduction of the sights follow a similar, but rather simpler course as the general position line described on page 152. The following summary and Figure 1 should make the process plain.

1) The following steps must be applied to each star individually, so that each has its own chosen position, LHA Aries and calculated altitude.

2) For the GMT of the observation, find the GHA Aries. **1**

3) Choose a longitude close to the DR to make the LHA Aries a whole number, and choose the latitude as a whole number of degrees nearest the DR. **2**

4) Enter volume 1 of the tables with lat and LHA Aries for each star, and extract the calculated altitude (Hc) and azimuth (Zn). **3**

5) Correct the sextant altitude and compare the true altitude with the calculated altitude to obtain the intercept. **4**

6) Plot the position lines in the normal way. See page 154 for advice on reducing errors in a 'cocked hat'.

The fix is plotted in Figure 1; the final position, after bisecting the exterior angles (see page 155) is 50°07′.2N, 17°27′.5W.

Precession and nutation AP 3270 Volume 1 is published for a particular year; in other years, variations in the orbit of the earth, known as precession and nutation, introduce errors into the final fix. A table is supplied with the volume to correct this if desired; except at the end of the life of the tables, this correction does not matter very much. Full instructions are given with the correction table.

50.1 *Plotting the fix*

DR 50°10′N, 17°30′W   Chosen lat 50°N   HE 2 m

Body:	Mirfak	Altair	Arcturus	
ZD/Time	4 May 1980	0410 (+1)		
Zone		+1		
Greenwich date	4 May 1980	0510		
Watch time	05 h 07 m 22 s	05 h 08 m 31 s	05 h 09 m 54 s	
Watch error	12 s	12 s	12 s fast	
GMT	05 h 07 m 10 s	05 h 08 m 19 s	05 h 09 m 42 s	
GHA Aries	297°14′.2	297°14′.2	297°14′.2	
Incr	1°47′.8	2°05′.1	2°25′.9	
GHA	299°02′.0	299°19′.3	299°40′.1	1
Chos long	17°02′.0W	17°19′.3W	17°40′.1W	2
LHA Aries	282°	282°	282°	
Hc	19°00′	46°51′	28°30′	3
Zn	032	157	266	
Sext alt	19°02′.3	46°45′.1	28°25′.6	
Index error	+1′.1	+1′.1	+1′.1	
	19°03′.4	46°46′.2	28°26′.7	
Dip	−2′.5	−2′.5	−2′.5	
App alt	19°00′.9	46°43′.7	28°24′.2	
Correction	−2′.8	−0′.9	−1′.8	
Obs alt	18°58′.1	46°42′.8	28°22′.4	
Intercept	1′.9 from	8′.2 from	7′.6 from	4
Azimuth	032	157	266	
Chos pos	50°N	50°N	50°N	
	17°02′.0W	17°19′.3W	17°40′.1W	

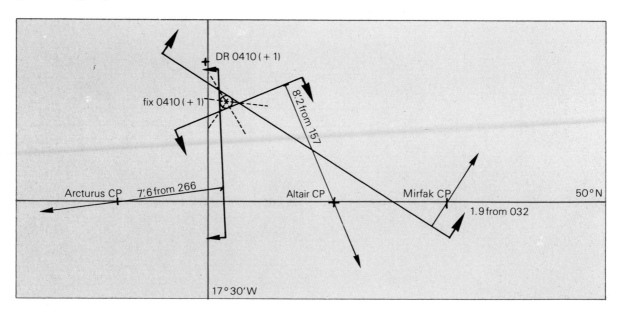

51 Latitude by polaris. Compass checking

Latitude by Polaris

Scientific astronomical navigation began when Arab travellers first used their astrolabes to find their latitude by observing the Pole Star (Polaris). This historical and very easy observation for latitude can still be very useful in the northern hemisphere, although Polaris is not a very bright star and is therefore quite hard to observe.

The value of Polaris is that it lies very close to the axis of the earth, and it is permanently (almost) over the north pole; in other words, it has a declination of (about) 90°N (Fig. 1). The important consequence is that the altitude of Polaris is 90° at the north pole, 0° from the equator, and in between the altitude is equal to the latitude of the observer. In actual fact, the declination of Polaris is about 89°10′N, so the GP of the star moves around the pole in a circle of about 50 miles radius. Various small corrections must therefore be applied to the altitude to obtain latitude; these are given in the Pole Star tables at the end of the *Nautical Almanac*.

Observing Polaris Polaris is not a very bright star, so it can sometimes be difficult to find before the horizon has gone. Set the sextant to the DR latitude and search in the north, and Polaris should appear within the telescope field. Take the altitude, and note GMT to the nearest minute. If Polaris cannot be found at twilight, it is a good subject for night-time observation, because the altitude changes very slowly, and hence the navigator can take his time over the sight; a bright, clear night with a moon is best, and the sextant telescope should be removed. The 95 per cent error of such a sight will be greater than at twilight, probably five miles or more.

Calculating the latitude The latitude is obtained by following these steps:

1) Using the GMT of the observation and the DR longitude, work out the LHA Aries.
2) Correct the sextant altitude for index error, dip and refraction to obtain observed altitude.
3) Enter the Pole Star tables in the *Nautical Almanac* to find the three corrections to be applied. The table is divided into columns, each covering a band of 10° of LHA Aries.
   a) Find the appropriate column according to LHA Aries.
   b) Within the column, find the first correction for LHA Aries, interpolating by eye.
   c) In the same column, find the second correction for the DR latitude in the second table.
   d) Still in the same column, find the correction for the month in the third table.
   e) Add all three corrections to the observed altitude and subtract 1° from the answer, to obtain latitude.

For example: In DR position 51°30′N, 3°45′E at 20 h 42 m GMT, 5 May 1980, the sextant altitude of Polaris is 50°58′.2. I.E. +2′.2, H.E. 3 m

Aries GHA 20 h	163°50′.3
Incr 42 m	10°31′.7
GHA Aries	174°22′.0
Long E	3°45′
LHA Aries	178°07′
Sext alt	50°58′.2
Index error	+2′.2
	51°00′.4
Dip	−3′.0
App alt	50°57′.4
Cor	−0′.8
Observed alt	50°56′.6
a_0	1°39′.5
a_1	0′.6
a_2	1′.0
Subtract 1° from sum to give latitude	51°37′.7N

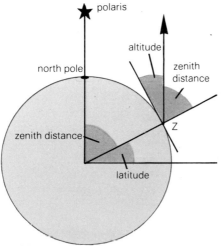

51.1 *Position of Polaris.*

POLARIS (POLE STAR) TABLES, 1980
FOR DETERMINING LATITUDE FROM SEXTANT ALTITUDE AND FOR AZIMUTH

L.H.A. ARIES	0°–9°	10°–19°	20°–29°	30°–39°	40°–49°	50°–59°	60°–69°	70°–79°	80°–89°	90°–99°	100°–109°	110°–119°
	a_0	a_0	a_0	a_0	a_0	a_0	a_0	a_0	a_0	a_0	a_0	a_0
0	0 17.5	0 13.3	0 10.6	0 09.4	0 09.7	0 11.5	0 14.7	0 19.4	0 25.2	0 32.0	0 39.7	0 48.0
1	17.0	13.0	10.4	09.3	09.8	11.7	15.1	19.9	25.8	32.8	40.5	48.8
2	16.5	12.7	10.2	09.3	09.9	12.0	15.5	20.4	26.5	33.5	41.3	49.7
3	16.1	12.4	10.1	09.3	10.0	12.3	16.0	21.0	27.1	34.3	42.1	50.5
4	15.7	12.1	09.9	09.3	10.2	12.6	16.4	21.5	27.8	35.0	43.0	51.4
5	0 15.2	0 11.8	0 09.8	0 09.3	0 10.4	0 12.9	0 16.9	0 22.1	0 28.5	0 35.8	0 43.8	0 52.2
6	14.8	11.5	09.7	09.4	10.6	13.3	17.3	22.7	29.2	36.6	44.6	53.1
7	14.4	11.3	09.6	09.4	10.8	13.6	17.8	23.3	29.9	37.3	45.4	53.9
8	14.1	11.0	09.5	09.5	11.0	14.0	18.3	23.9	30.6	38.1	46.3	54.8
9	13.7	10.8	09.4	09.6	11.2	14.3	18.8	24.6	31.3	38.9	47.1	55.7
10	0 13.3	0 10.6	0 09.4	0 09.7	0 11.5	0 14.7	0 19.4	0 25.2	0 32.0	0 39.7	0 48.0	0 56.5

Lat.	a_1	a_1	a_1	a_1	a_1	a_1	a_1	a_1	a_1	a_1	a_1	a_1
0	0.5	0.6	0.6	0.6	0.6	0.5	0.5	0.4	0.3	0.3	0.2	0.2
10	.5	.6	.6	.6	.6	.5	.5	.4	.4	.3	.3	.2
20	.5	.6	.6	.6	.6	.6	.5	.5	.4	.4	.3	.3
30	.6	.6	.6	.6	.6	.6	.5	.5	.5	.4	.4	.4
40	0.6	0.6	0.6	0.6	0.6	0.6	0.6	0.5	0.5	0.5	0.5	0.5
45	.6	.6	.6	.6	.6	.6	.6	.6	.6	.5	.5	.5
50	.6	.6	.6	.6	.6	.6	.6	.6	.6	.6	.6	.6
55	.6	.6	.6	.6	.6	.6	.6	.6	.7	.7	.7	.7
60	.6	.6	.6	.6	.6	.6	.7	.7	.7	.7	.8	.8
62	0.7	0.6	0.6	0.6	0.6	0.6	0.7	0.7	0.8	0.8	0.8	0.8
64	.7	.6	.6	.6	.6	.6	.7	.7	.8	.8	.9	0.9
66	.7	.6	.6	.6	.6	.7	.7	.8	.8	0.9	0.9	1.0
68	0.7	0.6	0.6	0.6	0.6	0.7	0.7	0.8	0.9	1.0	1.0	1.0

Month	a_2	a_2	a_2	a_2	a_2	a_2	a_2	a_2	a_2	a_2	a_2	a_2
Jan.	0.7	0.7	0.7	0.7	0.7	0.7	0.7	0.7	0.7	0.7	0.6	0.6
Feb.	.6	.7	.7	.7	.7	.8	.8	.8	.8	.8	.8	.8
Mar.	.5	.5	.6	.6	.7	.7	.8	.8	.8	.9	.9	.9
Apr.	0.3	0.4	0.4	0.5	0.6	0.6	0.7	0.7	0.8	0.9	0.9	0.9
May	.2	.3	.3	.4	.4	.5	.5	.6	.7	.8	.8	.9
June	.2	.2	.2	.2	.3	.3	.4	.5	.5	.6	.7	.7
July	0.2	0.2	0.2	0.2	0.2	0.3	0.3	0.3	0.4	0.5	0.5	0.6
Aug.	.4	.3	.3	.3	.2	.2	.3	.3	.3	.3	.4	.4
Sept.	.5	.5	.4	.4	.3	.3	.3	.3	.3	.3	.3	.3
Oct.	0.7	0.7	0.6	0.5	0.5	0.4	0.4	0.3	0.3	0.3	0.3	0.3
Nov.	0.9	0.8	.8	.7	.7	.6	.5	.5	.4	.4	.3	.3
Dec.	1.0	1.0	0.9	0.9	0.8	0.8	0.7	0.6	0.6	0.5	0.4	0.4

Lat.	AZIMUTH											
0	0.4	0.3	0.1	0.0	359.8	359.7	359.6	359.4	359.4	359.3	359.2	359.2
20	0.4	0.3	0.1	0.0	359.8	359.7	359.5	359.4	359.3	359.2	359.2	359.1
40	0.5	0.3	0.2	0.0	359.8	359.6	359.4	359.3	359.1	359.0	359.0	358.9
50	0.6	0.4	0.2	0.0	359.7	359.5	359.3	359.1	359.0	358.8	358.8	358.7
55	0.7	0.5	0.2	0.0	359.7	359.5	359.2	359.0	358.9	358.7	358.6	358.6
60	0.8	0.5	0.2	359.9	359.7	359.4	359.1	358.9	358.7	358.5	358.4	358.4
65	0.9	0.6	0.3	359.9	359.6	359.3	358.9	358.7	358.4	358.3	358.1	358.1

Latitude = Apparent altitude (corrected for refraction) − 1° + a_0 + a_1 + a_2

The table is entered with L.H.A. Aries to determine the column to be used; each column refers to a range of 10°. a_0 is taken, with mental interpolation, from the upper table with the units of L.H.A. Aries in degrees as argument; a_1, a_2 are taken, without interpolation, from the second and third tables with arguments latitude and month respectively. a_0, a_1, a_2 are always positive. The final table gives the azimuth of *Polaris*.

Table 1 *Extract from Pole Star tables.*

Compass checking

The prudent navigator will wish to check his compass at regular intervals, to make sure that no unexpected error has crept in. When coasting, it is generally easy enough to find transits of shore objects for this purpose (see page 34), but away from land, this is not possible. However, it is possible to find the true bearing of any heavenly body (i.e. its azimuth) at any time, and this can be compared with its compass bearing to find the compass error (allowing for variation).

The body most commonly observed for compass checking is the sun. The easiest way of finding its bearing is to use a shadow pin (Fig. 2); some compasses are fitted with one, or it may be possible to improvise a short, vertical pin over the pivot of

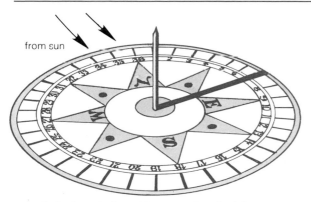

51.2 *A shadow pin for taking an azimuth of the sun.*

the compass card. The shadow of the pin reaches across the card to indicate the *reciprocal* of the sun's bearing; subtract 180° to get the bearing. In the absence of a shadow pin, the bearing of the sun when it is high in the sky demands some form of azimuth ring on the compass, fitted with a mirror (Fig. 3). This is rarely available in a yacht, so the most common time for checking a compass is near rising and setting, when the sun is low in the sky. Even so, some form of pelorus (see page 32) may be needed if the compass is unfavourably sited.

Having measured the sun's bearing (or that of any other identified body, for that matter), it is necessary to establish its azimuth. Over the years, a large number of different ways of doing this have been devised, such as special tables and diagrams; however, the yacht navigator need only bother with the two or three that are most convenient:

51.3 *Azimuth ring.*

1) *Sight Reduction Tables for Air Navigation* One of the two quantities required for the general astronomical position line is the azimuth. The GMT at which the bearing was taken is converted to LHA and declination. Entering these quantities, together with latitude, into the tables will give the azimuth. GMT is only needed to the nearest minute.

2) An alternative, though slightly more involved process is to use the azimuth or ABC tables published in most yacht almanacs and nautical tables. Layouts vary for these tables, and the instructions given in each volume should be followed. This method also requires LHA, declination and latitude.

3) The simplest method, and the most generally useful, is to take the bearing of the sun at sunrise or sunset, when its altitude is 0°. *Note:* Due to refraction, the true altitude of the sun is 0° when the lower limb is approximately half the sun's diameter above the horizon. The sun's azimuth can then be determined by the method of *amplitudes*. A table of amplitudes (one is given on page 193) is entered with latitude and declination; the result given is the bearing of the sun, either east (on rising) or west (on setting) from true north (declination N) or true south (declination S).

For example: 5 May 1980, in DR position 27°S, 122°W, the sun at sunset bore 280° by steering compass. Variation 6°E. Required, the compass error:

Lat	27°S
Dec (from *Nautical Almanac*)	16°N
Amplitude (from table on page 193)	N72°W
True bearing	360° − 72° = 288
Magnetic bearing	288° − 6°E = 282M
Compass bearing	280C
So compass error	2°E

Identifying planets

When observing planets, which are normally very bright and distinctive when compared with stars, the *Nautical Almanac* gives advice on identification. Normally no confusion is likely.

52 Sight reduction – alternative methods

Over the years, many different ways of calculating the zenith distance (or the calculated altitude) and azimuth have been published, all designed in one way or another to simplify the navigator's task. Most of these have been superseded by the tables for rapid sight reduction which are now published; however, it is as well for the navigator to have at least a glancing knowledge of other methods, in case he finds himself on a vessel which does not carry the tables he is used to using.

Alternative Nautical Almanacs

Various yachting and small ship almanacs are published, containing (amongst many other things) the ephemeral data for astronomical bodies. These generally follow a different layout from the *Nautical Almanac* used in this book; the purpose of this is to save space in the volume, by providing discrete values of GHA and declination at wider intervals and relying more on interpolation tables. As a result, such almanacs are slightly more difficult to use, and the values obtained can be somewhat less accurate, though entirely sufficient for yacht navigation. Anyone who has mastered the methods described in this book should have no difficulty in using such tables by following the instructions given with them. The advantage, of course, is that it is possible to carry most of the information that the yachtsman needs on all aspects of navigation within the covers of one volume.

Certain pre-programmed navigational calculators are able to provide ephemeral data on the sun for a number of years at the touch of a button.

Alternative methods of sight reduction

Sight reduction tables for marine navigation These tables are published in six volumes, by the British Admiralty as NP 401 and by the US Defense Mapping Agency Hydrographic/Topographic Center as Pub. No. 229. Each volume covers a 16° band of latitude for all possible combinations of local hour angle and declinations to 90° (same or contrary name). Calculated altitudes (Hc) are given to the nearest 0.1 minute of arc, and azimuth angles (Z) to the nearest 0.1 degree.

The tables are identical in principle to the *Sight Reduction Tables for Air Navigation* (AP 3270 Pub. 249) used in this book, although the layout is different. The only difference in use is a slightly more involved table for interpolating for the minutes and decimals of declination, required to maintain the extra precision offered by the main tables. Once this interpolation table has been mastered, the method is just as quick and easy as the air tables.

The advantages of this method over the air tables are:
1) Calculated altitudes are given to 0.1 minutes of arc, rather than to one minute (though this improved precision will rarely benefit the yacht navigator in normal conditions).
2) Solutions can be found for all bodies, rather than just those with declinations less than 30°.

The disadvantages are:
1) For world-wide coverage, six volumes are required, rather than the three volumes of AP 3270 (Pub. 249). This will increase cost and stowage requirements, but may be of little significance for a yacht which only sails in a limited area.
2) There is no equivalent to AP 3270 (Pub. 249) Volume 1 (seven selected stars), so choosing suitable stars and reducing their observations is more difficult.

The haversine method This was the most widely used method of sight reduction used at sea before the widespread introduction of rapid sight reduction tables; it requires tables of natural and log haversines and log cosines (haversine $(A) = \frac{1}{2}(1 - \text{cosine } A)$), which are often to be found in small craft almanacs and always in books of nautical tables; some tables contain natural and log versines rather than haversines, but the method is the same.

The 'raw ingredients' for the haversine method are the same as for any other – latitude, declination and local hour angle, but there is no need to choose a position; the DR position can be used directly. The procedure is then as follows:
1) From the tables, extract:
   a) The log haversine of the LHA
   b) The log cosine of the DR latitude
   c) The log cosine of the declination
   Add them together; discard the tens figure in the sum (the second figure to the left of the decimal point).

2) Find the sum thus obtained in the log haversine table, and extract the natural haversine that corresponds with it.

3) Combine the DR latitude and the declination (same names, subtract smaller from greater, contrary names add). Look up the natural haversine of this angle.

4) Add this natural haversine to the natural haversine found in step 2.

5) Look up the result of this addition in the natural haversine table. The angle to which it corresponds is the calculated zenith distance of the body.

6) Subtract the CZD from 90° to get the calculated altitude.

7) Use the ABC tables to find the azimuth.

8) Compare the calculated altitude with the true altitude to obtain the intercept, and plot the position line *from the DR position*.

Other short methods There is a host of other short methods for reducing a sight – Ageton, Driesenstock, Sadler and many more, each with their own adherents. If you find one you like, stick with it, but you should always be aware that some have limitations.

Computers and calculators Sight reduction is a problem admirably suited to computers or calculators. Various specialized calculators are available specifically for this problem; some of them also contain the data needed to work out the GHA and declination of the sun. An ordinary calculator needs to be of the scientific type (i.e. with trigonometric functions), and should also be programmable; a simple calculator can be used, but so many key-strokes are needed that a blunder is very likely. The equations for calculated altitude and azimuth, given DR latitude, declination and LHA, are on page 185.

PASSAGE MAKING

53 Passage planning

The amount of planning and preparation that a navigator makes before undertaking a passage will depend very much on his temperament. Some will make very detailed preparations indeed, on the basis that plans and calculations made in peace and comfort ashore will be much more useful and easy that similar work at sea, where he may have to cope with the motion of the boat, tiredness, possibly seasickness, and all of the host of factors which make navigation at sea difficult and liable to blunders. Another navigator may take the attitude that, whilst some preparation is obviously essential, detailed plans are bound to be changed by circumstances and are therefore a waste of time. The balance probably lies somewhere between these two extremes.

The following check-list is divided into essential items and useful ones; it does not include items which are the province of the skipper, rather than the navigator – crew considerations, provisions and fuel, customs clearances and the like. There is one factor amongst these that can have particular importance for the navigator. When going foreign, many countries require a yacht to enter at a particular port or ports for customs and immigration formalities; this obviously affects the route chosen.

Essential

1) *Books and charts* Make sure that you have all the books and charts that you are going to need, and that they are up to date. Small scale charts are needed for planning, medium scale for the actual conduct of the passage and large-scale harbour plans for the arrival. You should carry charts to cover *anywhere* you might conceivably find yourself, even if diverted by heavy weather; there is nothing more unnerving than being blown off the chart into the unknown. Harbour plans of any possible port of refuge are also needed, though in an emergency it is possible to make up a sketch plan of a port from information in the *Pilot* and the *Light List*, which will be sufficiently accurate for a cautious approach.

2) *The route* Using the *Pilot* and the charts, choose the route to be followed. For ocean passages, this will rarely be direct (see page 182), but for shorter passages, the most direct route is generally best. However, diversions should be made to give a good offing to dangerous or uncomfortable areas, or to approach some prominent navigational mark that can give a position check. Traffic separation schemes must either be followed correctly, crossed at right angles or avoided entirely. One can also plan to take advantage of a fair tide or avoid a foul one, at least in the early stages of a passage. After twelve hours or so, such planning is less valuable, as circumstances will almost certainly have changed.

Having chosen the route, plot it carefully on the passage charts and note the course and distance for each leg. Examine the tracks drawn on the chart minutely to make absolutely sure that they do not take the ship into some hitherto unnoticed danger. Plot and record any clearing lines that may be needed to keep the ship clear of dangers.

3) *Navigational aids* Make a note of the lights, radio beacons and other navigational aids which may be used during the passage, and consider the route afresh to make sure that you will make the best use of them.

4) *Tides* Work out from the tide tables the times of high and low water for the departure port around the proposed time of departure, the times of high water for the standard port to which tidal stream predictions are referred, and the times and heights of high and low water for the destination for a suitable period either side of the anticipated time of arrival. Consider that there may be times when the depth of water may make it impossible or unsafe to enter the destination port – a factor all too easily overlooked at the end of an exhausting and difficult passage.

If using a tidal stream atlas, it is helpful to write the actual times beside each chartlet, so that the appropriate one can be found at a glance.

5) *Refuges* Imagine all the difficult circumstances that may arise on passage, and consider a suitable course of action for each – whether to run for shelter, stand off until conditions improve or make for some harbour of refuge.

The actual decision will have to be made at the time, but thought in advance makes the decision much easier.

6) *Tools* Check the tools of your trade – pencils, erasers, dividers, parallel rulers and protractors – make sure they are present and in good order. Also check the compasses (is the steering compass corrected?), log, MFDF equipment and sextant (if carried). Make sure they are in working order and that spare, fresh batteries are carried. A torch (flashlight) with spare batteries is invaluable in case of electrical trouble.

These points must be checked particularly carefully when sailing in someone else's boat. Many navigators carry their own tools around with them from boat to boat.

7) *Weather forecast* Immediately before sailing, a detailed weather forecast, including a synoptic chart, should be obtained. This will form the basis upon which subsequent broadcast forecasts can be interpreted

Useful

8) *Lists* Lists of courses and distances, lights and other objects of navigational interest can be prepared and pinned up over the chart table, for use both by the navigator and the rest of the crew. A particularly useful list is one of frequencies, callsigns and sequence numbers of all radio beacons in the vicinity (this can also be written on the chart by the position of each beacon).

9) *Tidal streams* Details of tidal streams at key points in the passage (e.g. turning marks) can be noted on the chart – especially the times at which the tidal stream starts to run fair or foul.

10) *Dipping ranges* The range at which lights on the route will be raised or dipped can be worked out (page 192), and drawn as a circle on the chart; it is then only necessary to take a bearing of the light as it dips to obtain an instant fix (see pages 71–72).

54   On passage

Departure

On clearing the harbour, the first step is to take a *departure fix*, as a starting point for the dead reckoning, which begins at once. This fix is often a pinpoint (see page 82) on the outer buoy of the harbour approach channel. The fix should be marked on the chart and in the log, with the time and log reading. From this time on, the navigator must insist that the watch on deck keep a careful record of courses sailed and distances run in the log book, so that the dead reckoning can be maintained.

Coasting

Whilst coasting, or travelling parallel to a coast which is in sight, the DR should be plotted at regular intervals – at least once an hour. At the same time, fixes by observations of shore objects should be taken whenever the opportunity offers – again, once an hour is a good target to aim for. On each occasion, the DR and the fix should be compared, to detect any gross errors which may have occurred in either.

Whilst coasting, it can be difficult to identify shore marks positively as they come into view. As new objects appear, they can be *shot up*, by fixing the ship with position lines from objects already identified, and at the same time taking a compass bearing of the unidentified object. This bearing can then be plotted in reverse from the fix obtained; the resulting line will pass through (or close to) the unidentified object.

Keep an eye open for any transits (ranges) that may come into view (see page 68). Not only is a transit an easy and accurate position line; it also offers an opportunity to check the steering compass, which should be done as often as possible.

Monitoring

One of the navigator's basic functions is to monitor what is happening to the boat. Not only does this mean being aware of planned or spontaneous changes of course or speed; it also means watching the crew (especially the helmsman), to make sure that what the watch on deck write in the log is correct. Like any other equipment, helmsmen need to be calibrated (see pages 52–3), and the accuracy of log entries must also be assessed. Checking should be done unobtrusively, to avoid offence.

There are very many occasions, especially when racing, when the dominant requirement is boat speed, rather than the slavish holding of a particular course. These are circumstances that the navigator must accept, merely insisting that the small but frequent course changes are properly entered in the log book. In racing yachts, it is not uncommon for log entries to be required every fifteen minutes, as well as on all course changes. Cruising yachts need not be quite so meticulous, but hourly log readings should be entered even in mid-Atlantic. The deck watch will not mind – it breaks the monotony of a long watch, and gives someone a chance to warm up and put the kettle on.

Because of the relatively detached position the navigator often enjoys, he may be best placed to keep an eye on changes outside the boat itself. The watch on deck, preoccupied by sailing the boat, keeping a lookout and adjusting the sails, may be slow to appreciate the significance of a gradual wind shift or a changing sky; and a watch fresh on deck after leaving their bunks have nothing to compare what they see now with what has happened in the past few hours. A navigator outside the watch system provides a valuable continuity that is hard to manage in any other way.

Tactics (sailing vessels)

Beating When beating to windward, the cardinal principle is to keep the destination in the wind's eye (Fig. 1). First take the making tack, the tack which points up best towards the mark; when the mark is upwind, work up towards it with a series of relatively short tacks; in this way, you will always be well placed to take any advantage of wind shifts as they occur. Do not tack too often, especially when the mark is some distance away, but make the tacks shorter as you get closer.

If you have reason to believe that a wind shift is coming, then keep over towards the direction from where the new wind will come (Fig. 2). When the shift comes, you will be in a good position to make use of it; however, do not gamble too heavily, in case the shift never comes.

When beating, an old adage which rarely lets

54.1 *Tactics when beating.*

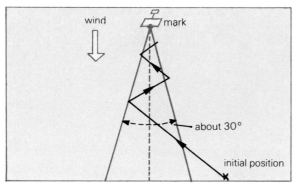

wind

mark

about 30°

initial position

54.2 *Making the best of an anticipated wind-shift.*

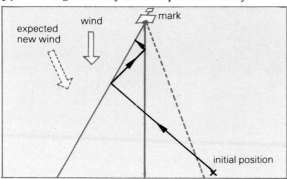

expected new wind

wind

mark

initial position

54.3 *Tacking downwind.*

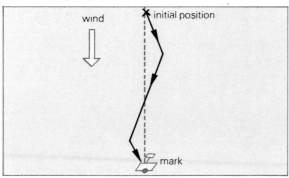

wind

initial position

mark

54.4 *Lee-bowing the tide.*

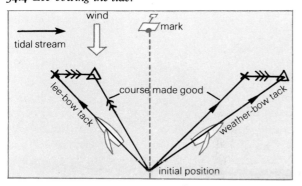

wind

tidal stream

mark

lee-bow tack

course made good

weather-bow tack

initial position

you down says 'always tack when headed off'. If the header heralds a permanent wind-shift, then you are using it straight away; if the header is only temporary, it is simple enough to tack back if desired.

Off the wind It is almost always wise to work a little way to windward as the opportunity offers, to protect yourself against a last-minute header.

Running A dead run is a slow and uncomfortable point of sailing, and one which causes the helmsman a lot of worry. It will almost always pay to luff up a little, put the wind on the quarter and go onto a broad reach. It means that you have further to travel, as you must *tack downwind* to reach your objective (Fig. 3), but the increase in speed and comfort makes it worth while. Exactly how far one should luff up depends on the boat, the wind strength and the sea, but 10° to 15° would probably be about right. As when beating, it is necessary to watch for wind shifts and gybe when needed.

Light airs The principle here is for the helmsman to keep the boat moving, in almost any direction. Some progress is better than no progress, and the small distances travelled mean that the navigator's life is not made too difficult by the variable courses steered.

If the speed of the boat through the water is not sufficient to stem the tide, then kedge immediately, and keep the kedge down until you are sure that you can do better without it. Many a race has been won with judicious use of the kedge anchor.

The foregoing remarks are, of course, addressed to the racing yachtsman; in light airs, the cruising man sensibly puts on the engine.

Beating across the tide On a beat where the tide is running at right angles (or nearly so) to the track, then the tack which puts the tide on the lee bow gets you towards the destination more quickly than the other (Fig. 4). If the tidal stream is constant, the lee-bow tack offers no advantage as one has to go on the other tack sometime or other and lose what you have gained. If, however, the tidal stream is going to slacken or even reverse its direction, then the lee-bow tack does indeed pay. Ideally, you would tack at the turn of the tide, to lee-bow the new tidal stream, or perhaps when you reach a position where the tidal stream has weakened.

55 Navigating at night, in fog and in heavy weather

Navigating at night

Navigation during the hours of darkness is often thought to be difficult but, if anything, the reverse is true. The process of keeping the dead reckoning is unchanged, and many types of position line can be obtained in exactly the same way as during the day – soundings, radio bearings, radar, and advanced electronic aids all work equally well in darkness or in daylight, though in one or two cases with reduced accuracy due to changes in the ionosphere. It is only visual observations that change; as twilight falls, visible objects gradually slide into the gloom, to be replaced by a pattern of twinkling, blinking lights – a pattern which may be easier to understand than the often meagre view of a distant coastline by day.

Whilst night navigation is not difficult, it does require a little preparation. The chart table must be fitted with a suitable light – not so bright as to dazzle the navigator and disturb the watch below, but bright enough to read the chart easily; a map light on a flexible stalk is almost ideal, though the addition of a dimmer improves it. A torch (flashlight) and batteries are needed in case the main lights fail. An illuminated magnifying glass is a valuable aid for anyone whose reading vision is not what it was.

The hand bearing compass must also be illuminated; most are fitted either with a luminous capsule or a built-in bulb and battery. If neither is fitted, or if the lamp fails, a pocket torch will be needed to light up the compass card to read off the bearing of a light.

Night vision In the dark, the human eye makes certain physiological adjustments to improve its performance in low light conditions. These adjustments take time – at least twenty minutes – so the navigator should avoid destroying his own or anyone else's night vision by flashing bright lights around. It is thought that red light damages night adaption relatively little, so some people prefer to use red lights at the chart table or wear red goggles.

In low light, the most sensitive part of the eye is not at the centre of the field of view, but at the edge (*peripheral vision*). If you are looking for an object in the dark, it is a mistake to stare; rather, keep the eyes moving all around and keep alert for the object in the corner of your eye.

Binoculars Suitable binoculars can make it easier to see things at night. The prime quality needed is light-gathering power, which is found in binoculars with large diameter lenses at the far end (the objective lens). 50 mm diameter is about the largest diameter that is readily available. The second factor is magnification and the allied question of field of view. On the unsteady platform of a yacht, too much magnification makes the binocular impossible to hold sufficiently still to be useful. The best compromise is a magnification of seven times; therefore the most suitable specification for marine binoculars is 7 × 50 mm.

Identifying lights The first step that must be taken on seeing a light is to identify it beyond question. This means watching for the character and colour of the light, and timing it *with a stop watch*. Timing the period of a light by counting or guessing is potentially dangerous, as the light may thereby be wrongly identified. Match the character, colour and period with those of lights printed on the chart to make the identification; be on your guard for lights with identical characters and periods, although these are usually a long way apart.

Looms A bright light beyond the horizon can be seen as a faint patch of light scattered in the air, known as the *loom* of the light. Large towns, factories and harbour installations can often be detected at some distance by their looms. The most valuable application of the loom is with navigational lights whose beams are formed by rotating lenses. The loom of such a light can be identified and a bearing taken when it is still well below the horizon.

Navigating in fog

Navigating in fog stretches the nerves and requires as much accuracy as can possibly be found, but it is not of itself hard to do.

Dead reckoning In fog, the DR becomes of paramount importance and must be kept up faithfully. If opportunity offers before the fog comes down, a good fix should be taken for a departure, and the DR plotted and assessed thereafter. This may be hard during a race, if the wind is also very light; the yacht will be going in all directions to try and make progress, leading to a plot which resembles the rambles of a drunken spider. The 95 per cent error of the DR will still be growing, and must be considered when deciding on the safety of a particular course of action.

Fixing aids All available fixing aids must be used to help reduce uncertainties in the DR. The echo sounder (if fitted) should be left on as much as possible, for insurance against running aground as much as for position lines. Electronic aids should be used to the full, especially radar which helps with collision avoidance as well as navigation. Some information can be gleaned from fog signals; too much reliance should not be placed on bearings of fog signals taken by ear, as the fog may distort the transmission of sound. On the other hand, hearing a faint fog signal (such as a bell on a buoy) is good evidence that the buoy is quite close; provided the buoy can be identified beyond doubt, this can be very helpful. If it is safe to do so, there is much to be said for homing on to such a fog signal to find and identify the buoy positively (by reading the name painted on it if necessary), to obtain a pinpoint and re-start the DR.

Navigating in heavy weather

In heavy weather everything, including navigation, is more difficult. The motion of the boat, tiredness, fright, seasickness, wet and cold are among the many handicaps the navigator has to fight.

Chart and log book Guard these carefully, as you may need them very badly later on for a second attempt at the DR when conditions improve. Keep both as dry as possible; consider whether it is essential for the chart to be kept on the chart table all the time. Wet hats should be taken off before working on the chart, and the near edge of the chart protected – wet oilskins rubbing against a wet chart will destroy it, and possibly some priceless information, in seconds.

Dead reckoning Keep this as carefully as possible in the conditions, bearing in mind that both course and speed are liable to very large errors. If lying ahull, hove to or running before under bare poles, course and distance can only

be guessed at from watching the yacht as she moves in the water.

Fixing Fixing aids can be few, especially if the heavy winds bring poor visibility with them. Visual bearings can be taken with difficulty and considerable error, as can MFDF radio bearings. Radio bearings should be repeated over and over again until some sort of consistency emerges. Radar and advanced electronic aids keep working, though radar needs proper adjustment of the clutter controls. You should not be surprised if the violent conditions cause such equipment to break down. Astronomical position lines are almost impossible to take because the horizon is obscured by huge waves nearby, but patience and practice may give you something to work on. Watch your own safety while using the sextant, and try to prevent it getting soaked.

Leeway Leeway is by far the most important and difficult factor to estimate in heavy weather. In general it is safe to say that there will be much more leeway than you expect; this arises in three ways:

1) Normal leeway caused by the pressure of the wind on the topsides and rig of the boat.
2) 'Dumping' by breaking waves. Every time the boat is picked up by a wave which breaks under her, she will be put down some distance to leeward. Each 'dump' may not move the boat very far, but over a period of time they add up.
3) Surface water movement, a sort of short-term current caused by friction between the wind and the surface of the sea. This obviously depends upon the strength of the wind and the length of time it has been blowing. It will persist for some hours after the wind that caused it moderates.

Overall, the effect of leeway is such that it no longer is sensible to treat it as a change in the course, as is done for most DR work (see page 60). Instead, the leeway can be treated as a current, the direction being downwind, and the speed at the guess of the navigator. In extreme conditions, this 'leeway current' can easily reach three knots, but will depend upon the boat and the conditions of the moment. The leeway current is naturally quite independent of any progress the boat might be making on her own account; the current must be added to the boat's course and speed.

56   Landfall

The most critical and exciting moment of any passage other than one that involves only coasting, is the landfall. However long or short a time the ship has been out of sight of land, there is a period of anxiety whilst waiting for the landfall to appear, and a great feeling of pleasure and relief when it finally shows up.

There is no other time in a passage when the principles of random error described in this book assume greater importance. A landfall can be considered as the whittling down of uncertainty. Beforehand, the 95 per cent error circle is large (sometimes very large); as land is approached and position lines based on the shore become available, the error circle is reduced until eventually it can be made so small as to be relatively unimportant and the navigator can set off on the final stages of the passage in safety and confidence.

The actual ways in which the error circle can be progressively reduced vary so much with individual circumstances that it is difficult to give specific advice. The example which follows is fairly typical of the situation which may occur at the end of a longish passage out of sight of land; it is imaginary, and designed mainly to illustrate the principles upon which the navigator should base his thinking.

The example supposes that a yacht is approaching the coast after an ocean passage. The weather has been overcast, and the last astronomical fix is now some five hundred miles behind. The navigator has been running his DR, and reckons that his 95 per cent error circle has a radius of 50 miles. By the time he gets within about 150 miles of the coast (three times his error circle radius), he begins to feel the need for better information (Fig. 1).

He first tries to take bearings of MF radio beacons on the coast; he manages to pick up two, but they are both near the limit of their range, and are situated quite close together. After correcting the bearings for half convergency (see page 114), he plots them, and decides to allow a 95 per cent error of 10° (Fig. 2). The resulting fix is poor, but better than the DR in that the error zone is much smaller. The fix is not too far from the DR, well inside the DR's error circle, so he considers the fix (as far as it goes) as being trustworthy. As the error zone is

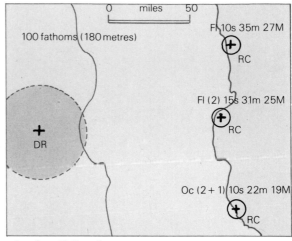

56.1 Landfall – phase 1.

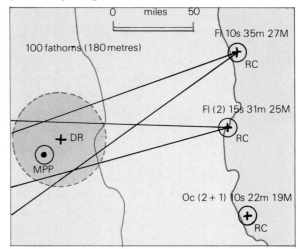

56.2 Landfall – phase 2.

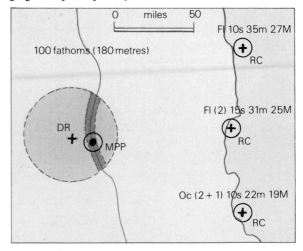

56.3 Landfall – phase 3.

56.4 Landfall – phase 4.

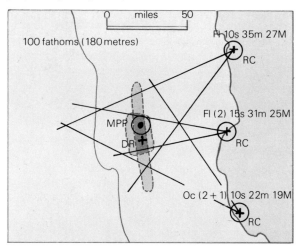

56.5 Landfall – phase 5.

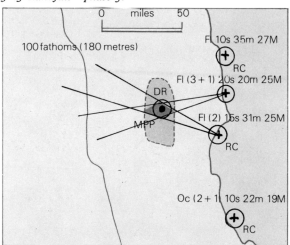

56.6 The landfall complete.

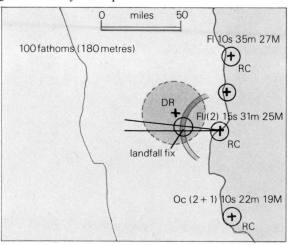

long and thin, it tells him more about his line of approach than his distance offshore.

Meanwhile, the navigator has been running his echo sounder from time to time, and some time after the radio fix he picks up the 100 fathom (180 m) line, traditionally regarded as the edge of the continental shelf. By now it is dusk, so radio bearings are for the moment unreliable, but the sounding can be used to reduce the error zone of the previous fix, which has by now grown a little through errors in the DR since the fix was taken (Fig. 3). The 100 fathom line runs more or less parallel with the coast, so he now has a much better idea how far off he is.

Later on, when the ionosphere has settled down, he tries another radio fix, and this time manages to get bearings on three beacons (Fig. 4). He notices that all three signals show signs of fading and that the nulls are not very sharp; he concludes that night effect is present, and decides to use the same 95 per cent error as before, 10°. However, the beacons are now closer and the angle of cut is better, so the fix has a smaller error circle than the one he has been using up to that time, and therefore he has improved his situation.

Some time after midnight, he sees the faint loom of two powerful landfall lights ahead. At first they are so faint and intermittent they do nothing but reassure him that land does actually exist, but as time goes by he is first able to make a positive identification, and then take useful bearings (Fig. 5). The angle of cut is not too good, but the bearings themselves are quite accurate, and the navigator uses a 95 per cent error of 4°. His error circle has now been reduced to something less than four miles across the track, and perhaps six or seven along it.

Finally, just before dawn, the landfall light for which he has been aiming is raised above the horizon. He takes a long, careful bearing (95 per cent error of 2°), and looks up the range in the table (see page 192), which has a 95 per cent error of about half a mile (Fig. 6). The landfall is complete, and the navigator can thankfully give new instructions to the watch on deck and go and get some well-earned sleep.

The problems of making a landfall are by no means confined to ocean sailing. Skipping across a wide bay, or crossing a narrow sea produce exactly the same situation, though the magnitudes of the errors may be smaller; on the other hand, in such circumstances there may be more off-lying dangers to worry about, so the situation is no easier. In poor visibility, a landfall after three miles can be more difficult than one made after 3,000 miles.

Planning the landfall

Making a landfall can be simplified to some extent by a little pre-planning. First, the actual point for the landfall should be selected with some care. It should be prominent, well marked and (if possible) free from off-lying dangers. Many of the great capes of the world have been used as landfall points.

Secondly, it should be possible to choose the time at which landfall is expected. The best time is to raise the shore lights just before dawn, as in the example above. This means that, provided visibility is all right, the light can be identified from its loom at some distance, and the process of raising it gives a valuable position line. If the destination port lies close to the landfall, it can then be entered in daylight. Unless the coast is very distinctive, it is hard to identify features at a distance in daylight, and the navigator can remain in doubt for some time after sighting land. Self-deception is very easy under these circumstances, and the navigator may persuade himself he is in a quite different position from his real one. If circumstances allow, a position line from the sun can help sort out such problems; navigators often forget about their sextants when land is in sight.

For a short passage, the time of landfall can be decided (more or less) by choosing the time of departure. On a long passage, where time is probably of less importance anyway, there is much to be gained by standing off for a while, so as to make the final approach to the coast at night.

57 Pilotage

Pilotage is the term used to describe navigation in harbours and narrow channels, where big ships would carry a pilot. Most of the normal tools of navigation are of little use, but it is during this phase of the passage that the yacht comes closest to danger. It would be a great pity to ruin an otherwise immaculate passage by putting the ship aground in the last half-mile, so pilotage deserves just as much attention as any other aspect of navigation.

The major contribution towards successful pilotage is preparation; study the chart carefully, read the *Pilot Book* and any other information, and try to form some sort of image in your mind as to what you should look for. Whilst your impression of the general scenery will almost certainly be wrong, such prominent objects as churches, beacons and breakwaters should show up as expected. Blind pilotage using radar requires very careful preparation indeed, as it can be difficult to distinguish between buoys and nearby small craft. The course and distance between each mark should be written down in advance.

The time of day can make a considerable difference to the ease of pilotage. It is much easier to feel your way up a long, winding buoyed channel at night (provided the buoys are lit) as each buoy can be identified positively by its light. During the day in a big river, this is not so easy; if in doubt, go right up to the buoy and read the name painted on it. It is not a bad idea to tick off each buoy on the chart as it is passed, as it is surprisingly easy to lose track of where you have got to.

On the other hand, it is best to enter a harbour, especially a busy one, during the day. At night it is very much harder to judge distance, and navigational marks can easily get lost in street lighting, flashing advertisement signs and traffic lights. Harbours are constantly being altered or improved, so there may well be obstructions or other changes which do not appear on your chart; it is much easier to avoid such hazards in daylight.

When entering pilotage waters, make ready by putting the *Pilot* (weighted open at the right page) and the chart (in a plastic cover if it is raining) by the helm. A hand bearing compass and binoculars will also be needed. The echo sounder will

naturally be running, and you will have worked out the state of the tide in advance, so you will be able to reduce the soundings in your head; you will also know what tidal streams to expect in different parts of the approach. A decision to be taken at this stage is whether you should take on a pilot or whether you can manage on your own. There is no disgrace involved in taking on a pilot, and it may well be the sensible and seamanlike thing to do.

The first essential on entering pilotage waters is to make sure you know exactly where you are to begin with; some form of pinpoint is best, such as passing close by the outer buoy of the approach channel. Thereafter you should keep track of the buoys as they pass on the chart, the compass course between them, the depth of water and the tidal stream. Conning by eye needs practice, as the view from sea level is at first confusing and hard to relate to the plan view given by the chart. It is necessary to watch the compass, as tidal streams or currents may otherwise lead you into trouble. In Figure 1, a yacht is steering for a buoy, but a crosstide is running. If the navigator paid no attention to the compass, he would approach the buoy along a curve which might well set him into danger.

In all pilotage, you should take your time, and not go thrusting forward into the unknown. Keep an anchor ready for letting go, so that if necessary you can stop for a good long think.

57.1 *Steering for a buoy without allowing for tide or watching the compass.*

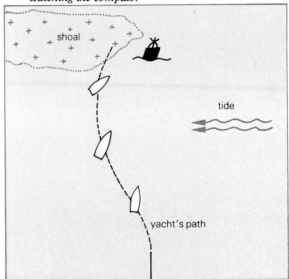

57.2 *Use transits where available.*

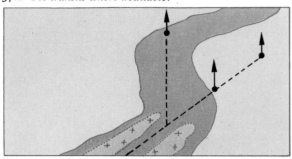

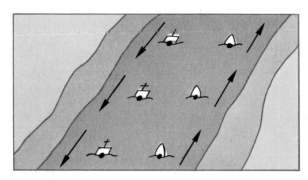

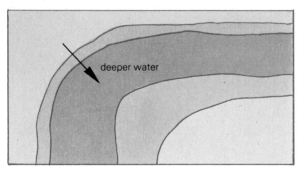

deeper water

57.3 (Centre) *Keeping clear of the main channel if depth of water permits.*

57.4 (Above) *Deeper water is generally on the outside of river bends.*

When following a long, winding channel, make use of any transits or leading lines that may be available (Fig. 2). The rule of the road at sea requires you to keep to the starboard hand of the channel, but if possible you should keep out of the deep water channel intended for big ships altogether (Fig. 3). Very often, there is plenty of water for a yacht on the 'wrong' side of the channel buoys; the correct place for a yacht in such circumstances, from everyone's point of view, is outside the channel. When following a river, the temptation to cut corners should be resisted; deeper water is normally to be found at the outside of a bend (Fig. 4).

In the final stages of the approach, you come into contact once again with the rest of the human race, in the form of harbour officials and the like who may or may not be pleased to see you. It is important to keep your temper and to listen to any instructions you may be given very carefully. Occasionally, it may be neither safe nor sensible to do what officials say, and polite obstinacy usually wins the day.

Make sure that your berth is as satisfactory as possible – that you will not dry out, perhaps, or if drying out is inevitable there are suitable conditions for this to be done safely – a firm bottom, a stout wall to lean against, ample fendering and suitable bollards. The berth should be as far protected from prevailing weather as possible and clear of passing traffic. Decisions or arguments at this stage can make you visit much more agreeable.

58 Plane sailing

Plane sailing (sometimes written: plain sailing) is a way of keeping up a dead reckoning position without actually plotting it on a chart, or of calculating the direction and distance of one point on the surface of the earth from another. Plane sailing can only be used over relatively short distances, because it assumes that the earth is flat (a plane) over the region of interest; the practical limit beyond which this assumption starts to introduce noticeable errors is about 600 miles.

What is required for plane sailing is a way of converting a particular direction and distance into a change of latitude and longitude, or conversely a way of converting changes in latitude and longitude into a direction and a distance. This problem is divided into two parts:

1) Solving the right-angled triangle on the surface of the earth, to give north-south distance in miles and east-west distance in miles from a known direction and distance, or *vice versa* (Fig. 1).

2) Because the nautical mile and the minute of latitude are equivalent, the north-south distance in miles is the same as the change in latitude and is known as the difference in latitude (D lat). However, the minute of longitude is only equivalent to the nautical mile at the equator, so in general the east-west distance in miles (known as the departure) must be converted to minutes of longitude (difference in longitude, D long), depending upon the latitude; the higher the latitude, the closer the meridians come and the shorter the minute of longitude becomes.

Plane sailing makes use of four equations, which can either be worked out on a pocket calculator (see page 185) or by means of a traverse table (see below). The equations are:

Departure = D long cos (mid latitude) (1)
Departure = distance sin (direction) (2)
D lat   = distances cos (direction) (3)

and, dividing (2) by (3):

$$\tan (\text{direction}) = \frac{\text{departure}}{\text{D lat}} \quad (4)$$

In the equations, mid-latitude is the latitude mid-way between the starting latitude and the finishing latitude.

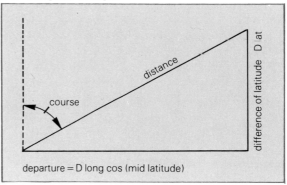

58.1 *The plane triangle.*

The plane sailing problems that a navigator may wish to solve generally take one of two forms:

1) *To find the direction and distance between two known points*: The mid latitude, D lat and D long can be worked out, and departure obtained from equation (1). Either (2) or (3) can be used to find the distance, and (4) gives the direction.

2) *To find the position after following a given direction for a given distance*: D lat and departure can be found from equations (2) and (3). From the D lat, the finishing latitude can be found, and hence the mid latitude. Equation (1) then gives the D long.

The traverse table

To help the navigator solve these equations (especially in the days before pocket calculators were invented), the traverse table was devised. A part of one page of a traverse table is shown in Table 1. A double page is provided for each degree of direction, and the various columns provide distance, D lat, departure, and D long. The traverse table only covers 45° of direction, as the values then start to repeat themselves. For the sample page shown, the four directions shown at the top of the page (025°, 155°, 205° and 335°) require that the column headings at the top of the page be used; for the directions at the bottom of the page (065°, 115°, 245° and 295°), the column headings at the bottom of the page should be used.

Thus, to find the D lat and departure for a direction of 025° and a distance of 170 miles, it is only necessary to consult the table on the page with 025° at distance 170 miles to find D lat 154.1

Table 1 *Extract from traverse tables.*

E60
TRAVERSE TABLE

25°

335°   025°

205°   155°

N

DIST	D.LAT	DEP	DIST	D.LAT	DEP	DIST	D.LAT	DEP	DIST	D.LAT	DEP	DIST	D.LAT	DEP
D.long	Dep		D.long	Dep		D.long	Dep		D.long	Dep		D.long	Dep	
1	00.9	00.4	61	55.3	25.8	121	109.7	51.1	181	164.0	76.5	241	218.4	101.9
2	01.8	00.8	62	56.2	26.2	122	110.6	51.6	182	164.9	76.9	242	219.3	102.3
3	02.7	01.3	63	57.1	26.6	123	111.5	52.0	183	165.9	77.3	243	220.2	102.7
4	03.6	01.7	64	58.0	27.0	124	112.4	52.4	184	166.8	77.8	244	221.1	103.1
5	04.5	02.1	65	58.9	27.5	125	113.3	52.8	185	167.7	78.2	245	222.0	103.5
6	05.4	02.5	66	59.8	27.9	126	114.2	53.2	186	168.6	78.6	246	223.0	104.0
7	06.3	03.0	67	60.7	28.3	127	115.1	53.7	187	169.5	79.0	247	223.9	104.4
8	07.3	03.4	68	61.6	28.7	128	116.0	54.1	188	170.4	79.5	248	224.8	104.8
9	08.2	03.8	69	62.5	29.2	129	116.9	54.5	189	171.3	79.9	249	225.7	105.2
10	09.1	04.2	70	63.4	29.6	130	117.8	54.9	190	172.2	80.3	250	226.6	105.7
11	10.0	04.6	71	64.3	30.0	131	118.7	55.4	191	173.1	80.7	251	227.5	106.1
12	10.9	05.1	72	65.3	30.4	132	119.6	55.8	192	174.0	81.1	252	228.4	106.5
13	11.8	05.5	73	66.2	30.9	133	120.5	56.2	193	174.9	81.6	253	229.3	106.9
14	12.7	05.9	74	67.1	31.3	134	121.4	56.6	194	175.8	82.0	254	230.2	107.3
15	13.6	06.3	75	68.0	31.7	135	122.4	57.1	195	176.7	82.4	255	231.1	107.8
16	14.5	06.8	76	68.9	32.1	136	123.3	57.5	196	177.6	82.8	256	232.0	108.2
17	15.4	07.2	77	69.8	32.5	137	124.2	57.9	197	178.5	83.3	257	232.9	108.6
18	16.3	07.6	78	70.7	33.0	138	125.1	58.3	198	179.4	83.7	258	233.8	109.0
19	17.2	08.0	79	71.6	33.4	139	126.0	58.7	199	180.4	84.1	259	234.7	109.5
20	18.1	08.5	80	72.5	33.8	140	126.9	59.2	200	181.3	84.5	260	235.6	109.9
21	19.0	08.9	81	73.4	34.2	141	127.8	59.6	201	182.2	84.9	261	236.5	110.3
22	19.9	09.3	82	74.3	34.7	142	128.7	60.0	202	183.1	85.4	262	237.5	110.7
23	20.8	09.7	83	75.2	35.1	143	129.6	60.4	203	184.0	85.8	263	238.4	111.1
24	21.8	10.1	84	76.1	35.5	144	130.5	60.9	204	184.9	86.2	264	239.3	111.6
25	22.7	10.6	85	77.0	35.9	145	131.4	61.3	205	185.8	86.6	265	240.2	112.0
26	23.6	11.0	86	77.9	36.3	146	132.3	61.7	206	186.7	87.1	266	241.1	112.4
27	24.5	11.4	87	78.8	36.8	147	133.2	62.1	207	187.6	87.5	267	242.0	112.8
28	25.4	11.8	88	79.8	37.2	148	134.1	62.5	208	188.5	87.9	268	242.9	113.3
29	26.3	12.3	89	80.7	37.6	149	135.0	63.0	209	189.4	88.3	269	243.8	113.7
30	27.2	12.7	90	81.6	38.0	150	135.9	63.4	210	190.3	88.7	270	244.7	114.1
31	28.1	13.1	91	82.5	38.5	151	136.9	63.8	211	191.2	89.2	271	245.6	114.5
32	29.0	13.5	92	83.4	38.9	152	137.8	64.2	212	192.1	89.6	272	246.5	115.0
33	29.9	13.9	93	84.3	39.3	153	138.7	64.7	213	193.0	90.0	273	247.4	115.4
34	30.8	14.4	94	85.2	39.7	154	139.6	65.1	214	193.9	90.4	274	248.3	115.8
35	31.7	14.8	95	86.1	40.1	155	140.5	65.5	215	194.9	90.9	275	249.2	116.2
36	32.6	15.2	96	87.0	40.6	156	141.4	65.9	216	195.8	91.3	276	250.1	116.6
37	33.5	15.6	97	87.9	41.0	157	142.3	66.4	217	196.7	91.7	277	251.0	117.1
38	34.4	16.1	98	88.8	41.4	158	143.2	66.8	218	197.6	92.1	278	252.0	117.5
39	35.3	16.5	99	89.7	41.8	159	144.1	67.2	219	198.5	92.6	279	252.9	117.9
40	36.3	16.9	100	90.6	42.3	160	145.0	67.6	220	199.4	93.0	280	253.8	118.3
41	37.2	17.3	101	91.5	42.7	161	145.9	68.0	221	200.3	93.4	281	254.7	118.8
42	38.1	17.7	102	92.4	43.1	162	146.8	68.5	222	201.2	93.8	282	255.6	119.2
43	39.0	18.2	103	93.3	43.5	163	147.7	68.9	223	202.1	94.2	283	256.5	119.6
44	39.9	18.6	104	94.3	44.0	164	148.6	69.3	224	203.0	94.7	284	257.4	120.0
45	40.8	19.0	105	95.2	44.4	165	149.5	69.7	225	203.9	95.1	285	258.3	120.4
46	41.7	19.4	106	96.1	44.8	166	150.4	70.2	226	204.8	95.5	286	259.2	120.9
47	42.6	19.9	107	97.0	45.2	167	151.4	70.6	227	205.7	95.9	287	260.1	121.3
48	43.5	20.3	108	97.9	45.6	168	152.3	71.0	228	206.6	96.4	288	261.0	121.7
49	44.4	20.7	109	98.8	46.1	169	153.2	71.4	229	207.5	96.8	289	261.9	122.1
50	45.3	21.1	110	99.7	46.5	170	154.1	71.8	230	208.5	97.2	290	262.8	122.6
51	46.2	21.6	111	100.6	46.9	171	155.0	72.3	231	209.4	97.6	291	263.7	123.0
52	47.1	22.0	112	101.5	47.3	172	155.9	72.7	232	210.3	98.0	292	264.6	123.4
53	48.0	22.4	113	102.4	47.8	173	156.8	73.1	233	211.2	98.5	293	265.5	123.8
54	48.9	22.8	114	103.3	48.2	174	157.7	73.5	234	212.1	98.9	294	266.5	124.2
55	49.8	23.2	115	104.2	48.6	175	158.6	74.0	235	213.0	99.3	295	267.4	124.7
56	50.8	23.7	116	105.1	49.0	176	159.5	74.4	236	213.9	99.7	296	268.3	125.1
57	51.7	24.1	117	106.0	49.4	177	160.4	74.8	237	214.8	100.2	297	269.2	125.5
58	52.6	24.5	118	106.9	49.9	178	161.3	75.2	238	215.7	100.6	298	270.1	125.9
59	53.5	24.9	119	107.9	50.3	179	162.2	75.6	239	216.6	101.0	299	271.0	126.4
60	54.4	25.4	120	108.8	50.7	180	163.1	76.1	240	217.5	101.4	300	271.9	126.8
D.long		Dep	D.long		Dep	D.long		Dep	D.long		Dep	D.long		Dep
DIST	DEP	D.LAT	DIST	DEP	D.LAT	DIST	DEP	D.LAT	DIST	DEP	D.LAT	DIST	DEP	D.LAT

N

295°   065°

245°   115°

65°

miles, departure 71.8 miles. This departure can be converted to D long by opening the traverse table at the page appropriate to the mid latitude and entering the columns headed *D long* and *dep*. Assume in the previous example that the mid latitude was 65° (use the bottom column headings). A departure of 71.8 miles gives a D long of 170 minutes of longitude, or 2°50'. From the D lat and the D long thus obtained, the finishing position can be established from the starting position; D lat is either north or south depending on the direction (north in this example), and similarly D long is east or west (east in the example).

The converse process of finding a direction and distance between two positions is a little more involved. First establish the mid latitude and convert D long to departure. Then scan through the tables until the values of D lat and departure are found matching each other. The distance column then shows the distance, and the page shows the direction (to be interpreted according to whether D lat is north or south, and dep is east or west).

DR by traverse table

It can sometimes be convenient to keep up the dead reckoning by traverse table rather than plotting on a chart; the most likely occasion for this is when working on a small-scale ocean chart, when accurate plotting becomes almost impossible. The following example shows the method:

Time	Course	Distance	D lat N	D lat S	Dep E	Dep W
1200–1800	240	41	–	35.5	–	20.5
1800–0100	275	50	4.4	–	–	49.8
0100–1130	220	69	–	52.9	–	44.4
Current	060	18	9.0	–	15.6	–
			13.4	88.4	15.6	114.7
				–13.4		–15.6
Total D lat and departure				75.0S		99.1W

Start lat	29°40'N	Start long	44°20'W
D lat	1°15'S	D long	1°53'.3W
End lat	28°25'N	End long	46°13'.3W

Mid lat   29°N   , so D long = 113'.3 = 1°53'.3W

For interest, the traverse table also shows that the course and distance made good over the period was:

233° — 125 n miles.

59 Mercator and great circle sailings

Mercator sailing

The ocean navigator may sometimes want to calculate the course to steer and the distance to run between two positions which are a long way apart – too far for the basic assumption that the earth is flat used in plane sailing to be valid. For distances greater than about 600 miles, mercator sailing should be used instead, which requires a special table to be found in books of nautical tables, called 'meridional parts for the terrestial spheroid'.

Without going too deeply into theory, mercator sailing is to some extent the converse of plane sailing. In plane sailing, D lat is held constant and D long is changed into departure; in mercator sailing, the D long is held constant and the D lat is changed into a quantity called DMP (difference of meridional parts) by using the table. The DMP is formed by taking out the meridional parts of the starting and the finishing latitudes and subtracting (adding if the track crosses the equator).

The two basic formulae for mercator sailing are:

$$\tan (\text{course}) = \frac{D \text{ long}}{DMP} \qquad (1)$$

$$\text{distance} = \frac{D \text{ lat}}{\cos (\text{course})} \text{ or D lat sec (course)} \quad (2)$$

(The first form is easier to use with a pocket calculator)

The results given by these formulae are exact for any distance travelled. They give the course to steer (rhumb line) and distance between the points, though it must be remembered that the resulting distance will not be the shortest possible distance between the points; this is found by great circle sailing (see below), if required.

For example: What is the rhumb line course and distance from New York (40°45′N, 74°00′W) to Bermuda (32°45′N, 65°00′W)?

New York lat 40°45′N	mer part 2666.48	long 74°00′W	
Bermuda lat 32°45′N	mer part 2069.01	long 65°00′W	
D lat 8°S	DMP 597.47	D long 9°E	
= 480′S		= 540′E	

$$\tan (\text{course}) = \frac{D \text{ long}}{DMP} = \frac{540}{597.47} = 0.90381$$

$$\text{Course} = S42°E = 138$$

$$\text{distance} = D \text{ lat sec (course)} = 480 \sec (42°) = 645.9 \text{ miles}$$

It is, of course, possible to invert the formulae if desired to solve the converse problem of finding the finishing position given the starting position and the course and distance sailed.

Great circle sailing

As has been pointed out, the shortest distance between two points on the earth's surface is on the great circle that joins them. The difference in distance between the great circle track and the rhumb line can be considerable in longer passages. For example, the great circle distance between San Francisco and Yokohama is 4517 miles, while the rhumb line distance is 4723 miles – a difference of 206 miles or the best part of two days sailing in a small craft. Of course, distance is not everything, and a sailing craft in particular will plan a route with many other factors in mind (see page 182); however, there is no point in sailing unnecessary miles if they can be avoided, so a consideration of the great circle track should be an important part of the planning.

There are two ways of determining the great circle track between two points; the graphical method described first is the more satisfactory, as it allows for the plotting of intermediate positions on a mercator chart for detailed planning. The tabular method can be used if no gnomonic chart is available, or as a quick check on the distance involved.

Graphical method The graphical method of determining a great circle track requires a gnomonic passage planning chart (see pages 16–7). On this chart, great circles are represented by straight lines. Therefore, the great circle track between two points can be found by drawing a straight line between them (Fig. 1a). The track should then be divided into convenient lengths (say every 10° of longitude), and the intermediate positions on the track recorded; these positions can then be transferred to a mercator chart, and the courses and distances of the various legs worked out, either by drawing or (preferably) by mercator sailings (Fig. 1b).

By comparing Figures 1a and 1b, it is clear that the great circle track always takes the ship closer to the pole than the rhumb line. This can take the ship into undesirably high latitudes on occasion. Thus, the great circle from the Lizard to New York

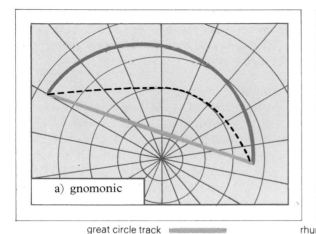

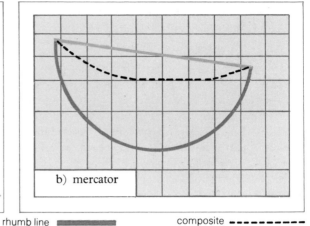

great circle track ▰▰▰▰▰   rhumb line ▰▰▰▰   composite ------

59.1 *Rhumb line, great circle and composite tracks on (a) gnomonic (b) mercator projections.*

comes within the iceberg region in winter, and a great circle from Tasmania to Cape Horn takes one within 1000 miles of the south pole! To avoid such hazards whilst still keeping the distance as short as possible, a *composite track* is used. In this case, a limiting latitude is chosen, beyond which the ship will not go. A great circle track to this latitude is followed, and the ship then sails due east or west along the limiting parallel until it is in a position to start following another great circle track to the destination.

Tabular method The problem of finding the great circle distance between two points is exactly the same as finding the calculated zenith distance between a chosen position and the geographical position of a heavenly body; therefore, the various methods of sight reduction can be applied to this problem. *The Sight Reduction Tables for Marine Navigation* (NP 401) and the haversine method can be used in all cases; the *Sight Reduction Tables for Air Navigation* (AP 3270 Vols 2 and 3) can only be used if the latitude of the destination is less than 30°N or S.

The method consists of entering the tables with the following quantities:

1) Starting latitude as latitude
2) Finishing latitude as declination (same or contrary name as appropriate)
3) Difference in longitude as LHA

With the haversine method, the answer comes out directly as zenith distance, which can be converted to distance in miles by multiplying the degrees by 60. The *Sight Reduction Tables* give the calculated altitude; this must be subtracted from 90° to give zenith distance before being converted to miles. The azimuth of the body corresponds with the initial heading for the great circle track.

A complication with this method is that it is not so easy to obtain intermediate points on the track for course changes. This can be done by plotting a suitable distance (of a day or two's sail) along the initial heading and finding the position reached, then re-computing the next great circle heading using the position reached as the starting position. Plotting a composite track by this method is very involved and best avoided if possible.

Note: The great circle track only offers significant benefits in higher latitudes and if the desired course is mainly east or west. In other circumstances, great circle sailings can be ignored.

60 Ocean passage planning

When considering an ocean passage, careful planning is an important and enjoyable aspect of the whole enterprise. A small craft is very much at the mercy of the elements, so the shortest route may not necessarily be the quickest. A sailing craft, in particular, will be able to 'afford' a substantial detour if the result is constant, moderate and favourable winds; to fall into an area of light, contrary or gale force winds can set a passage back by days or weeks.

Planning needs to begin with a study of the *Pilot Charts* (or routing charts) of the area; these give a wealth of information about the conditions that may be met, generally organized on a monthly basis throughout the year. A very large number of considerations need to be taken into account when planning an ocean passage, and the following list contains merely those most commonly regarded as important; it is for the individual to decide what is important from his own point of view.

1) *The plan* The owner or skipper (who may also be the navigator) will have a certain plan in mind – places to be visited or avoided, time available and so on. The owner's wife may offer frequent modifications.

2) *The vessel* The actual course of action decided upon may be influenced by the size and stowage capacity of the craft. Extra ports of call may be needed to replenish fuel, water or provisions.

3) *The crew* Crew considerations may also modify the plan, requiring extra ports of call for crew changes. Perhaps such ports must be chosen for the air links available for crew travel.

4) *Prevailing winds* For a sailing yacht, the route must be chosen to give the maximum chance of fair winds, preferably moderate in strength. Pages 88–9 give a general impression of global winds in the (northern) summer and (northern) winter, but much more detailed information is given on the pilot charts. Note in particular how the area of trade winds and the doldrums between moves north or south according to the season. In the Indian Ocean, monsoons are of major importance.

5) *Currents* A contrary current can have a very bad effect on passage times, and should be avoided if possible. A general view of global currents is shown on page 89, but (again) more detailed information should be gleaned from the pilot chart.

6) *Tropical revolving storms* Variously known as hurricanes, typhoons or cyclones, these intense storms should be avoided; many yachts have survived these dangerous storms, but many others have not. Tropical storms are notoriously unpredictable, and may be encountered outside their 'proper' season (see pages 92–3).

7) *Fog, ice, etc* The pilot chart also gives details of regions liable to fog, icebergs or pack ice; clearly, such areas should be avoided if possible.

8) *Gales and calms* Gales, even if favourable in direction, are far from comfortable; calms are time-consuming and frustrating, and perhaps the most likely condition to spoil the enjoyment of the whole crew. A week spent slatting in the same spot will drive the most placid soul into fits of gibbering rage. Keep away (if you can!).

Isochrones In the early part of this century, the German Hydrographic Office published some fascinating charts, which show the average duration (in days) of sailing ship journeys; the source of the data was an analysis of many hundreds of sailing ship logs. Specimens are given in Figure 1. Whilst the numbers attached to each contour represent days for large sailing ships, and hence are unlikely to relate to smaller sailing yachts, the general impression the charts give is likely to remain valid. An idea of the most favourable route can be gained by seeing where the contours 'bulge' in the general direction in which you wish to go. Thus Figure 1a, outward bound from the Lizard, suggests a course for the Cape of Good Hope, which leads close to the Portuguese coast and the Cape Verde Islands, thence across to within a few hundred miles of the South American coast, and generally south or south-west until about latitude 25° south, when course can be shaped ESE for Cape Town. Figure 1d shows that, because of the prevailing westerlies, it is always quicker to round Cape Horn rather than the Cape of Good Hope when bound from the Pacific into the Atlantic.

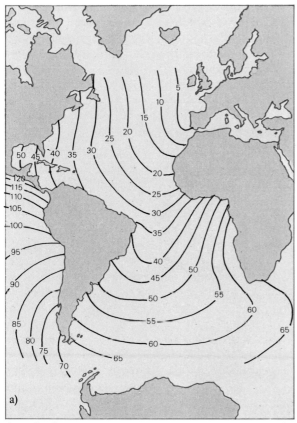

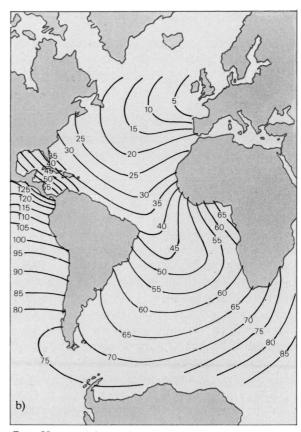

60.1 *Isochrones: (a) outward bound from the Lizard; (b) homeward bound for the Lizard; (c) from* Cape Horn and Cape of Good Hope; (d) to Cape Horn and Cape of good Hope.

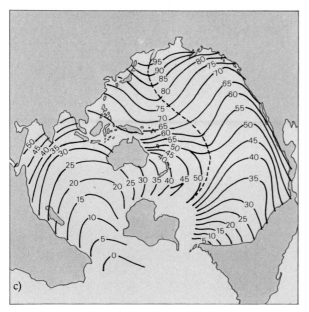

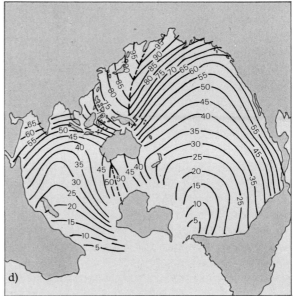

61 Pocket calculators

A pocket calculator can be a powerful aid for someone who is used to using one, provided he bears in mind that it is a vulnerable piece of equipment which is liable to fail in the adverse conditions found at sea. There must always be some form of back-up available (generally books of tables) which does not suffer from this drawback.

Calculator types

Calculators are available in a bewildering profusion, to suit all pockets and all levels of expertise. They range from specialized pre-programmed devices made specifically for use in navigation, to others which can be programmed either by inserting chips or cards, or by hand. Non-programmable calculators may be *scientific*, i.e. with trigonometrical and other functions, or purely arithmetical (+ , − , × , ÷).

A simple arithmetical calculator is not a great deal of use to a navigator, as most of the useful formulae require trig. or square root functions which means a scientific calculator. The most common source of error with a calculator is pressing the wrong button by mistake; therefore, the fewer key-strokes that need to be made, the better. This points towards a programmable calculator if possible. One drawback with calculators programmed by hand (rather than by inserting cards or memory modules) is that the programme is lost when the calculator is switched off, which can be inconvenient. Some calculators are fitted with a special type of memory which is maintained by the battery when the calculator is switched off, and so programmes and data are not lost. As with all types of equipment, the buyer must balance the needs of the job against the depth of his pocket.

Care of the calculator

The calculator faces two big risks – of being dropped or thrown about, and of getting wet. The utmost care must be taken to guard against both of these. The calculator must be held firmly when in use and immediately put away afterwards in a safe, dry place. A good way of protecting it from water is to seal it inside a transparent plastic bag; the keys can be operated and the display read through the plastic.

Many calculators, especially those with a light-emitting diode display (bright, red numbers), have a limited battery life. Spare batteries must be carried; if it is possible either to run the calculator or to recharge its battery from the ship's supply, this is an advantage.

Equations

The following useful formulae can generally be adapted to the calculator in use; the more elaborate ones become time-consuming and liable to button-pressing errors if attempted on any other than programmable machines.

Speed, time and distance

$$\text{Speed (knots)} = \frac{\text{distance (n miles)}}{\text{time (hours)}}$$

Converting metres to fathoms and feet

$$\begin{aligned}\text{Metres} &= \text{feet} \times 0.305 \\ &= \text{fathoms} \times 1.83\end{aligned}$$

Range by narrow horizontal angle (see page 70)

$$\text{Range of midpoint} = \frac{\text{distance between objects}}{2 \times \tan (\text{measured angle})}$$

Range by sound echo

$$\text{Range (n miles)} = \text{time (seconds)} \times 0.0904$$

Half convergency (see page 114)

$$\begin{aligned}\text{Half convergency} &= \tfrac{1}{2} \text{ D long (degrees)} \\ \text{(degrees)} & \quad\quad \times \sin (\text{mean lat}) \tfrac{1}{2}\end{aligned}$$

Range by vertical sextant angle (see page 71)

For short ranges (foot of the object visible)

$$\text{Distance (n miles)} = \frac{\text{height (metres)}}{1852 \times \tan (\text{angle})}$$

For all circumstances

$$R = \cos(H_s - D) \left\{ -\frac{\sin(H_s - D)}{0.0002493} \right.$$
$$\left. + \left[\left(\frac{\sin(H_s - D)}{0.0002439}\right)^2 + \frac{h_s - h_o}{0.2258} \right]^{\frac{1}{2}} \right\}$$

Where:

R = range to base of object (n miles)

H_s = sextant altitude corrected for index error (deg, min)

D = Dip of observer's horizon (min)

h_s = height of object above sea level (metres)

h_o = height of observer above sea level (metres)

The tables on pages 187–191 are based on this formula, which is after Guier W.H., *Navigation* (USA) Vol 15 No. 4 (1968) p. 368

Dipping distance of lights (see page 71)
Use the formula above with a sextant altitude of 0 — i.e., enter the value of the dip as a negative quantity.

Dip of a short sea horizon
When practising astronomical sights, it may happen that the sea horizon is obscured by intervening land. This formula gives a figure for dip which should be used instead of the normal dip found in the *Nautical Almanac*

$$\text{Dip (minutes)} = \frac{1.85 \times H}{D} + 0.423 \times D$$

Where:
H = height of eye (metres)
D = Distance to short horizon (n miles)

Plane sailing (see page 177)
Departure = D long cos (mid latitude)
Departure = distance sin (direction)
D lat $\quad$ = distance cos (direction)
$$\text{Direction} = \tan^{-1}\left(\frac{\text{departure}}{\text{D lat}}\right)$$

Note: If using a calculator with polar to rectangular co-ordinate conversion keys, note that the x direction in mathematics is conventionally east; D lat must go in the y register and departure in the x register.

Mercator sailing (see page 180)

Course
$$= \tan^{+1}\frac{\pi(\text{Lon}_1 - \text{Lon}_2)}{180\{\text{ln tan}[45 + \frac{1}{2}\text{Lat}_2] - \text{ln tan}[45 + \frac{1}{2}\text{Lat}_1]\}}$$
$$\text{Distance} = 60(\text{Lon}_2 - \text{Lon}_1)\cos(\text{Lat})$$
$$\qquad\qquad \text{if } \cos C = 0$$
$$= \frac{60(\text{lat}_2 - \text{Lat}_1)}{\cos(C)} \text{ otherwise}$$

Great circle sailing (see page 181)
$$\text{Distance} = 60 \times \cos^{-1}[\sin(\text{Lat}_1)\sin(\text{Lat}_2) + \cos(\text{Lat}_1)\cos(\text{Lat}_2)\cos(\text{D Long})]$$
Course angle
$$= \cos^{-1}\left[\frac{\sin(\text{Lat}_2) - \sin(\text{Lat}_1)\cos\left(\frac{D}{60}\right)}{\sin\left(\frac{D}{60}\right)\cos \text{Lat}_1}\right]$$

Course = course angle
$$\qquad \text{if } \sin(\text{Lon}_2 - \text{Lon}_1) < 0$$
$$= 360° - \text{course angle}$$
$$\qquad \text{if } \sin(\text{Lon}_2 - \text{Lon}_1) \geq 0$$

Note: S latitudes and E longitudes are entered as negative
Avoid passing through the poles
Do not compute a course of north or south

Interpolating Greenwich hour angle (see page 140)
First express the minutes and seconds of GMT as decimals of an hour:
Decimal = mins/60 + secs/3600.
Increment
$$= \text{Decimal of hour} \times 15° \text{ (sun, planets)}$$
$$\times 15°02'.5 \text{ (Aries)}$$
$$\times 14°19'.0 \text{ (moon)}$$
v corrections (if appropriate) are needed additionally.

Sight reduction (see page 165)
$$H_c = \sin^{-1}[\sin(D)\sin(L) + \cos(D)\cos(L)\cos(\text{LHA})]$$
$$Z = \cos^{-1}\left[\frac{\sin(D) - \sin(L)\sin(H_c)}{\cos(L)\cos(H_c)}\right]$$
$$Z_n = Z \text{ where } \sin \text{LHA} < 0$$
$$= 360° - Z \text{ where } \sin \text{LHA} \geq 0$$

Note: S latitudes and declinations are entered as negative
Where H_c = calculated altitude
$\qquad$ D = declination
$\qquad$ L = latitude
$\qquad$ LHA = local hour angle
$\qquad$ Z = azimuth angle
$\qquad$ Z_n = azimuth

Amplitude (see page 163)
$$\text{Amplitude} = \cos^{-1}\left[\frac{\sin(D)}{\cos(L)}\right]$$

Feet and metres conversion table

Feet		Metres	Feet		Metres
3.3	1	.3	167.2	51	15.6
6.6	2	.6	170.5	52	15.9
9.8	3	.9	173.8	53	16.2
13.1	4	1.2	177.0	54	16.5
16.4	5	1.5	180.3	55	16.8
19.7	6	1.8	183.6	56	17.1
23.0	7	2.1	186.9	57	17.4
26.2	8	2.4	190.2	58	17.7
29.5	9	2.7	193.4	59	18.0
32.8	10	3.1	196.7	60	18.3
36.1	11	3.4	200.0	61	18.6
39.3	12	3.7	203.3	62	18.9
42.6	13	4.0	206.6	63	19.2
45.9	14	4.3	209.8	64	19.5
49.2	15	4.6	213.1	65	19.8
52.5	16	4.9	216.4	66	20.1
55.7	17	5.2	219.7	67	20.4
59.0	18	5.5	223.0	68	20.7
62.3	19	5.8	226.2	69	21.0
65.6	20	6.1	229.5	70	21.4
68.9	21	6.4	232.8	71	21.7
72.1	22	6.7	236.1	72	22.0
75.4	23	7.0	239.3	73	22.3
78.7	24	7.3	242.6	74	22.6
82.0	25	7.6	245.9	75	22.9
85.2	26	7.9	249.2	76	23.2
88.5	27	8.2	252.5	77	23.5
91.8	28	8.5	255.7	78	23.8
95.1	29	8.8	259.0	79	24.1
98.4	30	9.2	262.3	80	24.4
101.6	31	9.5	265.6	81	24.7
104.9	32	9.8	268.9	82	25.0
108.2	33	10.1	272.1	83	25.3
111.5	34	10.4	275.4	84	25.6
114.8	35	10.7	278.7	85	25.9
118.0	36	11.0	282.0	86	26.2
121.3	37	11.3	285.2	87	26.5
124.6	38	11.6	288.5	88	26.8
127.9	39	11.9	291.8	89	27.1
131.1	40	12.2	295.1	90	27.5
134.4	41	12.5	298.4	91	27.8
137.7	42	12.8	301.6	92	28.1
141.0	43	13.1	304.9	93	28.4
144.3	44	13.4	308.2	94	28.7
147.5	45	13.7	311.5	95	29.0
150.8	46	14.0	314.8	96	29.3
154.1	47	14.3	318.0	97	29.6
157.4	48	14.6	321.3	98	29.9
160.7	49	14.9	324.6	99	30.2
163.9	50	15.3	327.9	100	30.5

Metre and fathom conversion table

Fath		Metres	Fath		Metres
.5	1	1.8	27.9	51	93.3
1.1	2	3.7	28.4	52	95.2
1.6	3	5.5	29.0	53	97.0
2.2	4	7.3	29.5	54	98.8
2.7	5	9.2	30.1	55	100.7
3.3	6	11.0	30.6	56	102.5
3.8	7	12.8	31.1	57	104.3
4.4	8	14.6	31.7	58	106.1
4.9	9	16.5	32.2	59	108.0
5.5	10	18.3	32.8	60	109.8
6.0	11	20.1	33.3	61	111.6
6.6	12	22.0	33.9	62	113.5
7.1	13	23.8	34.4	63	115.3
7.7	14	25.6	35.0	64	117.1
8.2	15	27.5	35.5	65	119.0
8.7	16	29.3	36.1	66	120.8
9.3	17	31.1	36.6	67	122.6
9.8	18	32.9	37.2	68	124.4
10.4	19	34.8	37.7	69	126.3
10.9	20	36.6	38.3	70	128.1
11.5	21	38.4	38.8	71	129.9
12.0	22	40.3	39.3	72	131.8
12.6	23	42.1	39.9	73	133.6
13.1	24	43.9	40.4	74	135.4
13.7	25	45.8	41.0	75	137.3
14.2	26	47.6	41.5	76	139.1
14.8	27	49.4	42.1	77	140.9
15.3	28	51.2	42.6	78	142.7
15.8	29	53.1	43.2	79	144.6
16.4	30	54.9	43.7	80	146.4
16.9	31	56.7	44.3	81	148.2
17.5	32	58.6	44.8	82	150.1
18.0	33	60.4	45.4	83	151.9
18.6	34	62.2	45.9	84	153.7
19.1	35	64.1	46.4	85	155.6
19.7	36	65.9	47.0	86	157.4
20.2	37	67.7	47.5	87	159.2
20.8	38	69.5	48.1	88	161.0
21.3	39	71.4	48.6	89	162.9
21.9	40	73.2	49.2	90	164.7
22.4	41	75.0	49.7	91	166.5
23.0	42	76.9	50.3	92	168.4
23.5	43	78.7	50.8	93	170.2
24.0	44	80.5	51.4	94	172.0
24.6	45	82.4	51.9	95	173.9
25.1	46	84.2	52.5	96	175.7
25.7	47	86.0	53.0	97	177.5
26.2	48	87.8	53.6	98	179.3
26.8	49	89.7	54.1	99	181.2
27.3	50	91.5	54.6	100	183.0

Range by vertical sextant angle – 5 to 15 metres

Arguments are: sextant altitude in minutes (corrected for index error and dip) and height of object minus height of eye (metres). Range is given in nautical miles.

					Height in metres						
Angle (mins)	5	6	7	8	9	10	11	12	13	14	15
−5	13.6	13.8	14.1	14.4	14.6	14.9	15.1	15.4	15.6	15.8	16.1
−4	11.5	11.8	12.1	12.4	12.7	13.0	13.2	13.5	13.7	14.0	14.2
−3	9.5	9.9	10.2	10.5	10.8	11.1	11.4	11.7	12.0	12.2	12.5
−2	7.7	8.1	8.4	8.8	9.1	9.5	9.8	10.1	10.3	10.6	10.9
−1	6.0	6.5	6.9	7.3	7.6	8.0	8.3	8.6	8.9	9.2	9.4
0	4.7	5.2	5.6	6.0	6.3	6.7	7.0	7.3	7.6	7.9	8.2
1	3.7	4.1	4.5	4.9	5.2	5.6	5.9	6.2	6.5	6.8	7.0
2	2.9	3.3	3.7	4.0	4.4	4.7	5.0	5.3	5.6	5.8	6.1
3	2.3	2.7	3.0	3.4	3.7	4.0	4.3	4.5	4.8	5.1	5.3
4	1.9	2.3	2.6	2.9	3.1	3.4	3.7	3.9	4.2	4.4	4.7
5	1.6	1.9	2.2	2.5	2.7	3.0	3.2	3.5	3.7	3.9	4.1
6	1.4	1.7	1.9	2.2	2.4	2.6	2.8	3.1	3.3	3.5	3.7
7	1.2	1.5	1.7	1.9	2.1	2.3	2.5	2.7	2.9	3.1	3.3
8	1.1	1.3	1.5	1.7	1.9	2.1	2.3	2.5	2.6	2.8	3.0
9	1.0	1.2	1.4	1.5	1.7	1.9	2.1	2.2	2.4	2.6	2.7
10	.9	1.1	1.2	1.4	1.6	1.7	1.9	2.1	2.2	2.4	2.5
12	.8	.9	1.0	1.2	1.3	1.5	1.6	1.7	1.9	2.0	2.2
14	.7	.8	.9	1.0	1.2	1.3	1.4	1.5	1.6	1.8	1.9
16	.6	.7	.8	.9	1.0	1.1	1.2	1.3	1.5	1.6	1.7
18	.5	.6	.7	.8	.9	1.0	1.1	1.2	1.3	1.4	1.5
20	.5	.6	.6	.7	.8	.9	1.0	1.1	1.2	1.3	1.4
22	.4	.5	.6	.7	.7	.8	.9	1.0	1.1	1.2	1.2
24	.4	.5	.5	.6	.7	.8	.8	.9	1.0	1.1	1.1
26	.4	.4	.5	.6	.6	.7	.8	.8	.9	1.0	1.1
28	.3	.4	.5	.5	.6	.7	.7	.8	.9	.9	1.0
30	.3	.4	.4	.5	.6	.6	.7	.7	.8	.9	.9
32	.3	.3	.4	.5	.5	.6	.6	.7	.7	.8	.9
34	.3	.3	.4	.4	.5	.5	.6	.7	.7	.8	.8
36	.3	.3	.4	.4	.5	.5	.6	.6	.7	.7	.8
38	.2	.3	.3	.4	.4	.5	.5	.6	.6	.7	.7
40	.2	.3	.3	.4	.4	.5	.5	.6	.6	.6	.7
42	.2	.3	.3	.4	.4	.4	.5	.5	.6	.6	.7
44	.2	.3	.3	.3	.4	.4	.5	.5	.5	.6	.6
46	.2	.2	.3	.3	.4	.4	.4	.5	.5	.6	.6
48	.2	.2	.3	.3	.3	.4	.4	.5	.5	.5	.6
50	.2	.2	.3	.3	.3	.4	.4	.4	.5	.5	.6
52	.2	.2	.2	.3	.3	.4	.4	.4	.5	.5	.5
54	.2	.2	.2	.3	.3	.3	.4	.4	.4	.5	.5
56	.2	.2	.2	.3	.3	.3	.4	.4	.4	.5	.5
58	.2	.2	.2	.3	.3	.3	.4	.4	.4	.4	.5
60	.2	.2	.2	.2	.3	.3	.3	.4	.4	.4	.5

Range by vertical sextant angle – 18 to 48 metres

Arguments are: sextant altitude in minutes (corrected for index error and dip) and height of object minus height of eye (metres). Range is given in nautical miles.

Angle (mins)	18	21	24	27	30	33	36	39	42	45	48
					Height in metres						
0	8.9	9.6	10.3	10.9	11.5	12.1	12.6	13.1	13.6	14.1	14.6
1	7.8	8.5	9.2	9.8	10.4	11.0	11.5	12.0	12.5	13.0	13.4
2	6.9	7.5	8.2	8.8	9.4	9.9	10.5	11.0	11.5	11.9	12.4
3	6.0	6.7	7.3	7.9	8.5	9.0	9.5	10.0	10.5	11.0	11.4
4	5.4	6.0	6.6	7.2	7.7	8.2	8.7	9.2	9.7	10.1	10.6
5	4.8	5.4	5.9	6.5	7.0	7.5	8.0	8.5	8.9	9.4	9.8
6	4.3	4.9	5.4	5.9	6.4	6.9	7.4	7.8	8.2	8.7	9.1
7	3.9	4.4	4.9	5.4	5.9	6.3	6.8	7.2	7.6	8.1	8.5
8	3.5	4.0	4.5	5.0	5.4	5.9	6.3	6.7	7.1	7.5	7.9
9	3.2	3.7	4.1	4.6	5.0	5.4	5.8	6.2	6.6	7.0	7.4
10	3.0	3.4	3.8	4.3	4.7	5.1	5.4	5.8	6.2	6.6	6.9
11	2.7	3.2	3.6	4.0	4.3	4.7	5.1	5.5	5.8	6.2	6.5
12	2.6	2.9	3.3	3.7	4.1	4.4	4.8	5.1	5.5	5.8	6.1
13	2.4	2.8	3.1	3.5	3.8	4.2	4.5	4.8	5.1	5.5	5.8
14	2.2	2.6	2.9	3.3	3.6	3.9	4.2	4.6	4.9	5.2	5.5
15	2.1	2.4	2.8	3.1	3.4	3.7	4.0	4.3	4.6	4.9	5.2
20	1.6	1.9	2.1	2.4	2.6	2.9	3.1	3.4	3.6	3.9	4.1
25	1.3	1.5	1.7	1.9	2.2	2.4	2.6	2.8	3.0	3.2	3.4
30	1.1	1.3	1.5	1.6	1.8	2.0	2.2	2.3	2.5	2.7	2.9
35	.9	1.1	1.3	1.4	1.6	1.7	1.9	2.0	2.2	2.3	2.5
40	.8	1.0	1.1	1.2	1.4	1.5	1.6	1.8	1.9	2.0	2.2
45	.7	.9	1.0	1.1	1.2	1.3	1.5	1.6	1.7	1.8	1.9
50	.7	.8	.9	1.0	1.1	1.2	1.3	1.4	1.5	1.6	1.8
55	.6	.7	.8	.9	1.0	1.1	1.2	1.3	1.4	1.5	1.6
60	.6	.6	.7	.8	.9	1.0	1.1	1.2	1.3	1.4	1.5
65	.5	.6	.7	.8	.9	.9	1.0	1.1	1.2	1.3	1.4
70	.5	.6	.6	.7	.8	.9	.9	1.0	1.1	1.2	1.3
75	.4	.5	.6	.7	.7	.8	.9	1.0	1.0	1.1	1.2
80	.4	.5	.6	.6	.7	.8	.8	.9	1.0	1.0	1.1
85	.4	.5	.5	.6	.7	.7	.8	.8	.9	1.0	1.0
90	.4	.4	.5	.6	.6	.7	.7	.8	.9	.9	1.0
95	.4	.4	.5	.5	.6	.6	.7	.8	.8	.9	.9
100	.3	.4	.4	.5	.6	.6	.7	.7	.8	.8	.9
105	.3	.4	.4	.5	.5	.6	.6	.7	.7	.8	.8
110	.3	.4	.4	.5	.5	.6	.6	.7	.7	.8	.8
115	.3	.3	.4	.4	.5	.5	.6	.6	.7	.7	.8
120	.3	.3	.4	.4	.5	.5	.6	.6	.6	.7	.7

Range by vertical sextant angle – 50 to 100 metres

Arguments are: sextant altitude in minutes (corrected for index error and dip) and height of object minus height of eye (metres). Range is given in nautical miles.

Angle (mins)	Height in metres										
	50	55	60	65	70	75	80	85	90	95	100
0	14.9	15.6	16.3	17.0	17.6	18.2	18.8	19.4	20.0	20.5	21.0
1	13.7	14.5	15.2	15.8	16.5	17.1	17.7	18.2	18.8	19.4	19.9
2	12.7	13.4	14.1	14.7	15.4	16.0	16.6	17.2	17.7	18.3	18.8
3	11.7	12.4	13.1	13.8	14.4	15.0	15.6	16.2	16.7	17.2	17.8
4	10.9	11.5	12.2	12.9	13.5	14.1	14.6	15.2	15.8	16.3	16.8
5	10.1	10.7	11.4	12.0	12.6	13.2	13.8	14.3	14.9	15.4	15.9
6	9.4	10.0	10.6	11.3	11.8	12.4	13.0	13.5	14.1	14.6	15.1
7	8.7	9.4	10.0	10.6	11.1	11.7	12.2	12.8	13.3	13.8	14.3
8	8.1	8.8	9.3	9.9	10.5	11.0	11.6	12.1	12.6	13.1	13.6
9	7.6	8.2	8.8	9.3	9.9	10.4	10.9	11.4	11.9	12.4	12.9
10	7.1	7.7	8.3	8.8	9.3	9.9	10.4	10.8	11.3	11.8	12.3
11	6.7	7.3	7.8	8.3	8.8	9.3	9.8	10.3	10.8	11.2	11.7
12	6.3	6.9	7.4	7.9	8.4	8.9	9.3	9.8	10.3	10.7	11.1
13	6.0	6.5	7.0	7.5	8.0	8.4	8.9	9.3	9.8	10.2	10.6
14	5.7	6.2	6.6	7.1	7.6	8.0	8.5	8.9	9.3	9.8	10.2
15	5.4	5.9	6.3	6.8	7.2	7.6	8.1	8.5	8.9	9.3	9.7
20	4.3	4.7	5.0	5.4	5.8	6.2	6.5	6.9	7.3	7.6	8.0
25	3.5	3.8	4.2	4.5	4.8	5.1	5.4	5.8	6.1	6.4	6.7
30	3.0	3.3	3.5	3.8	4.1	4.4	4.6	4.9	5.2	5.5	5.7
35	2.6	2.8	3.1	3.3	3.6	3.8	4.0	4.3	4.5	4.8	5.0
40	2.3	2.5	2.7	2.9	3.1	3.4	3.6	3.8	4.0	4.2	4.4
45	2.0	2.2	2.4	2.6	2.8	3.0	3.2	3.4	3.6	3.8	4.0
50	1.8	2.0	2.2	2.4	2.5	2.7	2.9	3.1	3.3	3.4	3.6
55	1.7	1.8	2.0	2.2	2.3	2.5	2.6	2.8	3.0	3.1	3.3
60	1.5	1.7	1.8	2.0	2.1	2.3	2.4	2.6	2.7	2.9	3.0
65	1.4	1.6	1.7	1.8	2.0	2.1	2.3	2.4	2.5	2.7	2.8
70	1.3	1.4	1.6	1.7	1.8	2.0	2.1	2.2	2.4	2.5	2.6
75	1.2	1.4	1.5	1.6	1.7	1.8	2.0	2.1	2.2	2.3	2.4
80	1.2	1.3	1.4	1.5	1.6	1.7	1.8	2.0	2.1	2.2	2.3
85	1.1	1.2	1.3	1.4	1.5	1.6	1.7	1.8	1.9	2.1	2.2
90	1.0	1.1	1.2	1.3	1.4	1.5	1.6	1.7	1.8	1.9	2.0
95	1.0	1.1	1.2	1.3	1.4	1.5	1.6	1.6	1.7	1.8	1.9
100	.9	1.0	1.1	1.2	1.3	1.4	1.5	1.6	1.7	1.8	1.8
105	.9	1.0	1.1	1.1	1.2	1.3	1.4	1.5	1.6	1.7	1.8
110	.8	.9	1.0	1.1	1.2	1.3	1.3	1.4	1.5	1.6	1.7
115	.8	.9	1.0	1.0	1.1	1.2	1.3	1.4	1.4	1.5	1.6
120	.8	.8	.9	1.0	1.1	1.2	1.2	1.3	1.4	1.5	1.5
125	.7	.8	.9	1.0	1.0	1.1	1.2	1.3	1.3	1.4	1.5
130	.7	.8	.9	.9	1.0	1.1	1.1	1.2	1.3	1.4	1.4
135	.7	.8	.8	.9	1.0	1.0	1.1	1.2	1.2	1.3	1.4
140	.7	.7	.8	.9	.9	1.0	1.1	1.1	1.2	1.3	1.3
145	.6	.7	.8	.8	.9	1.0	1.0	1.1	1.1	1.2	1.3
150	.6	.7	.7	.8	.9	.9	1.0	1.0	1.1	1.2	1.2
155	.6	.7	.7	.8	.8	.9	1.0	1.0	1.1	1.1	1.2
160	.6	.6	.7	.8	.8	.9	.9	1.0	1.0	1.1	1.2

Range by vertical sextant angle – 150 to 650 metres

Arguments are: sextant altitude in minutes (corrected for index error and dip) and height of object minus height of eye (metres). Range is given in nautical miles.

Angle (mins)	Height in metres										
	150	200	250	300	350	400	450	500	550	600	650
0	25.8	29.8	33.3	36.5	39.4	42.1	44.6	47.1	49.4	51.5	53.7
1	24.6	28.6	32.1	35.3	38.2	40.9	43.5	45.9	48.2	50.4	52.5
2	23.5	27.5	31.0	34.1	37.1	39.8	42.3	44.7	47.0	49.2	51.3
3	22.4	26.4	29.9	33.0	36.0	38.7	41.2	43.6	45.9	48.1	50.2
4	21.4	25.4	28.8	32.0	34.9	37.6	40.1	42.5	44.8	47.0	49.1
5	20.5	24.4	27.8	31.0	33.9	36.5	39.1	41.5	43.7	45.9	48.0
6	19.6	23.5	26.9	30.0	32.9	35.5	38.1	40.4	42.7	44.9	47.0
7	18.7	22.6	26.0	29.0	31.9	34.6	37.1	39.4	41.7	43.9	46.0
8	17.9	21.7	25.1	28.1	31.0	33.6	36.1	38.5	40.7	42.9	45.0
9	17.2	20.9	24.2	27.3	30.1	32.7	35.2	37.5	39.8	41.9	44.0
10	16.5	20.1	23.4	26.4	29.2	31.8	34.3	36.6	38.8	41.0	43.0
11	15.8	19.4	22.6	25.6	28.4	31.0	33.4	35.7	37.9	40.1	42.1
12	15.2	18.7	21.9	24.8	27.6	30.1	32.6	34.9	37.1	39.2	41.2
13	14.6	18.1	21.2	24.1	26.8	29.3	31.8	34.0	36.2	38.3	40.3
14	14.0	17.4	20.5	23.4	26.1	28.6	31.0	33.2	35.4	37.5	39.5
15	13.5	16.8	19.9	22.7	25.4	27.8	30.2	32.5	34.6	36.7	38.7
20	11.3	14.3	17.1	19.7	22.2	24.5	26.8	28.9	31.0	32.9	34.9
25	9.6	12.3	14.9	17.3	19.6	21.8	23.9	25.9	27.8	29.7	31.6
30	8.3	10.8	13.1	15.3	17.4	19.5	21.4	23.3	25.2	27.0	28.7
35	7.3	9.5	11.6	13.7	15.6	17.5	19.4	21.2	22.9	24.6	26.2
40	6.5	8.5	10.5	12.3	14.1	15.9	17.6	19.3	20.9	22.5	24.1
45	5.9	7.7	9.5	11.2	12.9	14.5	16.1	17.7	19.2	20.7	22.2
50	5.3	7.0	8.7	10.3	11.8	13.4	14.9	16.3	17.8	19.2	20.6
55	4.9	6.4	8.0	9.4	10.9	12.3	13.7	15.1	16.5	17.8	19.1
60	4.5	5.9	7.4	8.7	10.1	11.5	12.8	14.1	15.4	16.6	17.9
65	4.2	5.5	6.8	8.1	9.4	10.7	11.9	13.2	14.4	15.6	16.8
70	3.9	5.1	6.4	7.6	8.8	10.0	11.2	12.3	13.5	14.6	15.8
75	3.6	4.8	6.0	7.1	8.3	9.4	10.5	11.6	12.7	13.8	14.9
80	3.4	4.5	5.6	6.7	7.8	8.9	9.9	11.0	12.0	13.0	14.0
85	3.2	4.3	5.3	6.4	7.4	8.4	9.4	10.4	11.4	12.4	13.3
90	3.1	4.0	5.0	6.0	7.0	8.0	8.9	9.9	10.8	11.7	12.7
95	2.9	3.8	4.8	5.7	6.6	7.6	8.5	9.4	10.3	11.2	12.1
100	2.8	3.7	4.6	5.4	6.3	7.2	8.1	8.9	9.8	10.7	11.5
105	2.6	3.5	4.3	5.2	6.0	6.9	7.7	8.5	9.4	10.2	11.0
110	2.5	3.3	4.2	5.0	5.8	6.6	7.4	8.2	9.0	9.8	10.5
115	2.4	3.2	4.0	4.8	5.5	6.3	7.1	7.8	8.6	9.4	10.1
120	2.3	3.1	3.8	4.6	5.3	6.1	6.8	7.5	8.3	9.0	9.7
125	2.2	2.9	3.7	4.4	5.1	5.8	6.5	7.2	8.0	8.7	9.4
130	2.1	2.8	3.5	4.2	4.9	5.6	6.3	7.0	7.7	8.3	9.0
135	2.0	2.7	3.4	4.1	4.7	5.4	6.1	6.7	7.4	8.0	8.7
140	2.0	2.6	3.3	3.9	4.6	5.2	5.9	6.5	7.1	7.8	8.4
145	1.9	2.5	3.2	3.8	4.4	5.0	5.7	6.3	6.9	7.5	8.1
150	1.8	2.5	3.1	3.7	4.3	4.9	5.5	6.1	6.7	7.3	7.9
155	1.8	2.4	3.0	3.6	4.1	4.7	5.3	5.9	6.5	7.0	7.6
160	1.7	2.3	2.9	3.4	4.0	4.6	5.1	5.7	6.3	6.8	7.4

Dip of a short horizon
To be used when the sea horizon is obscured by land

Arguments are observer's height of eye in metres and distance to the land in nautical miles. Dip is in minutes of arc, always subtracted. This table replaces the dip table in the *Nautical Almanac*.

| Distance (miles) | Height of eye (metres) | | | | | | | | |
	2	3	4	5	6	7	8	9	10
.5	7.6	11.3	15.0	18.7	22.4	26.1	29.8	33.5	37.2
.6	6.4	9.5	12.6	15.7	18.8	21.8	24.9	28.0	31.1
.7	5.6	8.2	10.9	13.5	16.2	18.8	21.4	24.1	26.7
.8	5.0	7.3	9.6	11.9	14.2	16.5	18.8	21.2	23.5
.9	4.5	6.6	8.6	10.7	12.7	14.8	16.8	18.9	20.9
1.0	4.1	6.0	7.8	9.7	11.5	13.4	15.2	17.1	18.9
1.1	3.8	5.5	7.2	8.9	10.6	12.2	13.9	15.6	17.3
1.2	3.6	5.1	6.7	8.2	9.8	11.3	12.9	14.4	15.9
1.3	3.4	4.8	6.3	7.7	9.1	10.5	11.9	13.4	14.8
1.4	3.2	4.6	5.9	7.2	8.5	9.9	11.2	12.5	13.8
1.5	3.1	4.3	5.6	6.8	8.0	9.3	10.5	11.7	13.0
1.6	3.0	4.2	5.3	6.5	7.6	8.8	9.9	11.1	12.3
1.7	2.9	4.0	5.1	6.2	7.3	8.4	9.4	10.5	11.6
1.8	2.8	3.9	4.9	5.9	6.9	8.0	9.0	10.0	11.1
1.9	2.8	3.7	4.7	5.7	6.7	7.6	8.6	9.6	10.6
2.0	2.7	3.6	4.6	5.5	6.4	7.3	8.3	9.2	10.1
2.1	2.7	3.6	4.4	5.3	6.2	7.1	8.0	8.8	9.7
2.2	2.6	3.5	4.3	5.2	6.0	6.8	7.7	8.5	9.4
2.3	2.6	3.4	4.2	5.0	5.8	6.6	7.4	8.2	9.0
2.4	2.6	3.3	4.1	4.9	5.7	6.4	7.2	8.0	8.7
2.5	2.6	3.3	4.0	4.8	5.5	6.3	7.0	7.7	8.5
2.6	2.5	3.3	4.0	4.7	5.4	6.1	6.8	7.5	8.2
2.7	2.5	3.2	3.9	4.6	5.3	6.0	6.6	7.3	8.0
2.8	2.5	3.2	3.9	4.5	5.2	5.8	6.5	7.2	7.8
2.9	2.5	3.2	3.8	4.4	5.1	5.7	6.4	7.0	7.6
3.0	2.5	3.1	3.8	4.4	5.0	5.6	6.2	6.8	7.5
3.1	2.5	3.1	3.7	4.3	4.9	5.5	6.1	6.7	7.3
3.2	2.5	3.1	3.7	4.3	4.9	5.4	6.0	6.6	7.2
3.3	2.5	3.1	3.7	4.2	4.8	5.3	5.9	6.5	7.0
3.4	–	3.1	3.6	4.2	4.7	5.3	5.8	6.4	6.9
3.5	–	3.1	3.6	4.2	4.7	5.2	5.7	6.3	6.8
3.6	–	3.1	3.6	4.1	4.6	5.2	5.7	6.2	6.7
3.7	–	3.1	3.6	4.1	4.6	5.1	5.6	6.1	6.6
3.8	–	3.1	3.6	4.1	4.6	5.0	5.5	6.0	6.5
3.9	–	3.1	3.6	4.1	4.5	5.0	5.5	6.0	6.4
4.0	–	3.1	3.6	4.0	4.5	5.0	5.4	5.9	6.4
4.1	–	3.1	3.6	4.0	4.5	4.9	5.4	5.8	6.3
4.2	–	3.1	3.6	4.0	4.5	4.9	5.3	5.8	6.2
4.3	–	3.1	3.6	4.0	4.4	4.9	5.3	5.7	6.2
4.4	–	–	3.6	4.0	4.4	4.8	5.3	5.7	6.1
4.5	–	–	3.6	4.0	4.4	4.8	5.2	5.6	6.1
4.6	–	–	3.6	4.0	4.4	4.8	5.2	5.6	6.0
4.7	–	–	3.6	4.0	4.4	4.8	5.2	5.6	6.0
4.8	–	–	3.6	4.0	4.4	4.8	5.2	5.5	5.9
4.9	–	–	3.6	4.0	4.4	4.8	5.1	5.5	5.9
5.0	–	–	3.6	4.0	4.4	4.8	5.1	5.5	5.9

Table of amplitudes in degrees

Arguments are: declination (top) and latitude (side); apply eastward on rising and westward on setting, from north or south according to name of declination. Below latitude 10, use 90°-declination.

Latitude	Declination																							
	0	1	2	3	4	5	6	7	8	9	10	11	12	13	14	15	16	17	18	19	20	21	22	23
10	90	89	88	87	86	85	84	83	82	81	80	79	78	77	76	75	74	73	72	71	70	69	68	67
11	90	89	88	87	86	85	84	83	82	81	80	79	78	77	76	75	74	73	72	71	70	69	68	67
12	90	89	88	87	86	85	84	83	82	81	80	79	78	77	76	75	74	73	72	71	70	69	67	66
13	90	89	88	87	86	85	84	83	82	81	80	79	78	77	76	75	74	73	72	70	69	68	67	66
14	90	89	88	87	86	85	84	83	82	81	80	79	78	77	76	75	73	72	71	70	69	68	67	66
15	90	89	88	87	86	85	84	83	82	81	80	79	78	77	75	74	73	72	71	70	69	68	67	66
16	90	89	88	87	86	85	84	83	82	81	80	79	78	76	75	74	73	72	71	70	69	68	67	66
17	90	89	88	87	86	85	84	83	82	81	80	78	77	76	75	74	73	72	71	70	69	68	67	66
18	90	89	88	87	86	85	84	83	82	81	79	78	77	76	75	74	73	72	71	70	69	68	67	66
19	90	89	88	87	86	85	84	83	82	80	79	78	77	76	75	74	73	72	71	70	69	68	67	66
20	90	89	88	87	86	85	84	83	81	80	79	78	77	76	75	74	73	72	71	70	69	68	67	65
21	90	89	88	87	86	85	84	82	81	80	79	78	77	76	75	74	73	72	71	70	69	67	66	65
22	90	89	88	87	86	85	84	82	81	80	79	78	77	76	75	74	73	72	71	69	68	67	66	65
23	90	89	88	87	86	85	83	82	81	80	79	78	77	76	75	74	73	71	70	69	68	67	66	65
24	90	89	88	87	86	85	83	82	81	80	79	78	77	76	75	74	72	71	70	69	68	67	66	65
25	90	89	88	87	86	84	83	82	81	80	79	78	77	76	75	73	72	71	70	69	68	67	66	64
26	90	89	88	87	86	84	83	82	81	80	79	78	77	76	74	73	72	71	70	69	68	67	65	64
27	90	89	88	87	86	84	83	82	81	80	79	78	77	75	74	73	72	71	70	69	67	66	65	64
28	90	89	88	87	85	84	83	82	81	80	79	78	76	75	74	73	72	71	70	68	67	66	65	64
29	90	89	88	87	85	84	83	82	81	80	79	77	76	75	74	73	72	70	69	68	67	66	65	63
30	90	89	88	87	85	84	83	82	81	80	78	77	76	75	74	73	71	70	69	68	67	66	64	63
31	90	89	88	86	85	84	83	82	81	79	78	77	76	75	74	72	71	70	69	68	66	65	64	63
32	90	89	88	86	85	84	83	82	81	79	78	77	76	75	73	72	71	70	69	67	66	65	64	63
33	90	89	88	86	85	84	83	82	80	79	78	77	76	74	73	72	71	70	68	67	66	65	63	62
34	90	89	88	86	85	84	83	82	80	79	78	77	75	74	73	72	71	69	68	67	66	64	63	62
35	90	89	88	86	85	84	83	81	80	79	78	77	75	74	73	72	70	69	68	67	65	64	63	62
36	90	89	88	86	85	84	83	81	80	79	78	76	75	74	73	71	70	69	68	66	65	64	62	61
37	90	89	87	86	85	84	82	81	80	79	77	76	75	74	72	71	70	69	67	66	65	63	62	61
38	90	89	87	86	85	84	82	81	80	79	77	76	75	73	72	71	70	68	67	66	64	63	62	60
39	90	89	87	86	85	84	82	81	80	78	77	76	74	73	72	71	69	68	67	65	64	63	61	60
40	90	89	87	86	85	83	82	81	80	78	77	76	74	73	72	70	69	68	66	65	63	62	61	59
41	90	89	87	86	85	83	82	81	79	78	77	75	74	73	71	70	69	67	66	64	63	62	60	59
42	90	89	87	86	85	83	82	81	79	78	76	75	74	72	71	70	68	67	65	64	63	61	60	58
43	90	89	87	86	85	83	82	80	79	78	76	75	73	72	71	69	68	66	65	64	62	61	59	58
44	90	89	87	86	84	83	82	80	79	77	76	75	73	72	70	69	67	66	65	63	62	60	59	57
45	90	89	87	86	84	83	81	80	79	77	76	74	73	71	70	69	67	66	64	63	61	60	58	56
46	90	89	87	86	84	83	81	80	78	77	76	74	73	71	70	68	67	65	64	62	61	59	57	56
47	90	89	87	86	84	83	81	80	78	77	75	74	72	71	69	68	66	65	63	61	60	58	57	55
48	90	89	87	86	84	83	81	80	78	76	75	73	72	70	69	67	66	64	62	61	59	58	56	54
49	90	88	87	85	84	82	81	79	78	76	75	73	72	70	68	67	65	64	62	60	59	57	55	53
50	90	88	87	85	84	82	81	79	77	76	74	73	71	70	68	66	65	63	61	60	58	56	54	53
51	90	88	87	85	84	82	80	79	77	76	74	72	71	69	67	66	64	62	61	59	57	55	53	52
52	90	88	87	85	83	82	80	79	77	75	74	72	70	69	67	65	63	62	60	58	56	54	53	51
53	90	88	87	85	83	82	80	78	77	75	73	72	70	68	66	65	63	61	59	57	55	53	52	50
54	90	88	87	85	83	81	80	78	76	75	73	71	69	67	66	64	62	60	58	56	54	52	50	48
55	90	88	87	85	83	81	79	78	76	74	72	71	69	67	65	63	61	59	57	55	53	51	49	47
56	90	88	86	85	83	81	79	77	76	74	72	70	68	66	64	62	60	58	56	54	52	50	48	46
57	90	88	86	84	83	81	79	77	75	73	71	69	68	66	64	62	60	58	55	53	51	49	47	44
58	90	88	86	84	82	81	79	77	75	73	71	69	67	65	63	61	59	57	54	52	50	47	45	42
59	90	88	86	84	82	80	78	76	74	72	70	68	66	64	62	60	58	55	53	51	48	46	43	41
60	90	88	86	84	82	80	78	76	74	72	70	68	65	63	61	59	57	54	52	49	47	44	41	39
61	90	88	86	84	82	80	78	75	73	71	69	67	65	62	60	58	55	53	50	48	45	42	39	36
62	90	88	86	84	81	79	77	75	73	71	68	66	64	61	59	57	54	51	49	46	43	40	37	34
63	90	88	86	83	81	79	77	74	72	70	68	65	63	60	58	55	53	50	47	44	41	38	34	31
64	90	88	85	83	81	79	76	74	71	69	67	64	62	59	57	54	51	48	45	42	39	35	31	27
65	90	88	85	83	80	78	76	73	71	68	66	63	61	58	55	52	49	46	43	40	36	32	28	22
66	90	88	85	83	80	78	75	73	70	67	65	62	59	56	54	50	47	44	41	37	33	28	23	16

Navigational Terms in Five Languages

English	French	German	Dutch	Spanish
Across	en travers	hinuber	dwarsover	al costado
Abeam	par le travers	querab	dwarsscheeps	por el traves
Aground	echoué	auf Grund	gestrand	encallado
Ahead	en avant	voraus	vooruit	avante
Almanac	Ephemerides	Jahrbuch	Almanak	Almanaque
Alongside	à couple	längsseit	langszij	al lado
Anchor	Ancre	Anker	Anker	Ancia
Anchorage	Mouillage	Ankerplatz	Ankerplaats	Fondeadero
Anchoring prohibited	Défense de mouiller	Ankern verboten	Verboden ankerplaats	Fondeadero prohibido
Anemometer	Anémomètre	Windmesser	Windmeter	Anemómetro
Around	autour	herum	rond	alrededor
Astern	en arrière	achtern	achteruit	atras
Bands (horizontal)	bandé	waagrechtgestreift	horizontaal gestreept	fajas horizontales
Bar	Barre	Sandbank	Drempel	Barra
Bay	Baie	Bucht	Bocht	Bahia
Beach	Plage	Strand	Strand	Playa
Beacon	Balise	Bake	Baken	Baliza
Bearing	Relèvement	Peilung	Peiling	Marcacion
Before	devant	vor	voor	antes
Bell	Cloche	Glocke	Mistklok	Campana
Between	entre	zwischen	tussen	entre
Black	noir	schwarz	zwart	negro
Blue	bleu	blau	blauw	azul
Breadth	largeur	Breite	breedte	ancho
Breakers	Brisants	Brecher	Brekers	Rompientes
Breakwater	Brise-lames	Wellenbrecher	Dam	Escollera
Bridge	Pont	Brucke	Brug	Puente
Buoy	Bouée	Boje	Boei	Boya
Calm	calme	glatt	kalm	en calma
Canal	Canal	Kanal	Kanaal	Canal
Cape	Cap	Kap	Kaap	Cabo
Channel marker	Bouée de chenal	Fahrwasser-tonne	Markering van de vaargeul	Boya de canal
Chart	Carte	Seekarte	Zeekaart	Carta nautica
Chart table	Table à cartes	Kartentisch	Kaartentafel	Mesa de cartas
Chequered	à damier	gewürfelt	geblokt	damero
Chimney	Cheminée	Schornstein	Schoorsteen	Chimenea
Church	Eglise	Kirche	Kerk	Iglesia
Cliff	Falaise	Klippe	Klip	Acantilado
Coast	Côte	Küste	Kust	Costa
Compass	Compas	Kompass	Kompas	Compas
Compass adjuster	Compensateur de compas	Kompensierer	Kompassteller	Compensador de compases
Conical	conique	kegelförmig	kegelvormig	conico
Creek	Etier	Bach	Kreek	Arroyo
Current	Courant	Strömung	Stroom	Corriente
Danger	Danger	Gefahr	gevaar	peligro
Dark	foncée	dunkel	donker	obscuro
Degrees	Degrés	Grad	Graden	Grados
Depth	Profondeur	Tiefe	Diepte	profunidad
Diamond (shape)	losange	Raute	ruitvormig	rombo
Diaphone	Diaphone	Kolbensirene	Diafoon	Diafono
Dividers	Pointes sèches	Stechzirkel	Passer	Compas de puntas

English	French	German	Dutch	Spanish
D/F Radio	Radio-gonio	Funkpeiler	Radio-richtingzoeker	Radio-goniómetro
Dock	Bassin	Dock	Dok	Dique
Dolphin	Bouée de corps-mort	Dalben	Dukdalf	Boya de amarre
Downstream	en aval	flussabwärts	stroomafwaarts	rio abajo
Draught	Tirant d'eau	Tiefgang	Diepgang	Calado
Dries	assèchant	trockenfallend	droogvallend	en seco
Dunes	Dunes	Dünen	Duinen	Dunas
East	Est	Ost	Oost	Este
Ebb (tide)	Marée descendante	Ebbe	Eb	Vaciante
Echo sounder	Sondeur	Echolot	Echolood	Eco sonda
Entrance	Entrée	Einfahrt	Toegang	Entrada
Estuary	Estuaire	Mündung	Zeegat	Estuario
Fairway	Chenal	Fahrwasser	Vaargeul	Canal
Ferry	Ferry	Fähre	Veerboot	Ferry
Fixed light	Feu fixe	Festfeuer	Vast licht	Luz fija
Flag	Pavillon	Flagge	Vlag	Bandera
Flares	Fusées éclairantes	Leuchtsignale	Hand-stakellichten	Bengalas
Flashing light	Feu à éclats	Blinkfeuer	Schitterlicht	Luz de destellos
Flood (tide)	Marée montante	Flut	Vloed	Entrante
Fog	Brume	Nebel	Mist	Niebla
Gale	Coup de vent	Sturm	Stormachtig	Temporal
Green	vert	grün	groen	verde
Hand bearing compass	Compas de relèvement	Handpeilkompass	Handpeilkompas	Compas de marcar
Harbour	Port	Hafen	Haven	Puerto
High water	Pleine mer	Hochwasser	Hoogwater	Pleamar
Hill	Colline	Hügel	Heuvel	Colina
Horn	Nautophone	Nautofon	Natofoon	Nautofono
Index error	Erreur de collimation	Indexfehler	Indexfout	Error de indice
Inner	interieur	inner	binnen	interior
Island	Ile	Insel	Eiland	Isla
Jetty	Jetée	Steg	Steiger	Malecon
Latitude	Latitude	Breite	Breedte	Latitud
Leading light	Feu d'alignment	Leitfeuer	Geleidelicht	Luz de efilación
Leeward	sous le vent	Lee	aan lij	sotavento
Left (side)	gauche	links	links	izquierdo
(Sea) Level	Niveau	Wasserstand	Waterstand, Peil	Nivel
Lifeboat	Canot de sauvetage	Rettungsboot	Reddingboot	Bote salvavidas
Light	Feu	Feuer	Licht	Luz
Lighthouse	Phare	Leuchtturm	Vuurtoren	Faro
Light vessel	Bateau-feu	Feuerschiff	Lichtschip	Buque faro
Lock	Ecluse	Schleuse	Sluis	Esclusa
(Patent) Log	Loch enregistreur	Patentlog	Sleeplog	Corredera mecanica
Logbook	Journal de bord	Logbuch	Logboek	Cuaderno de bitacora
Longitude	Longitude	Lange	Lengte	Longitud
Low water	Basse mer	Niedrigwasser	Laagwater	Bajamar

English	French	German	Dutch	Spanish
Marina	Marina	Marina	Jachthaven	Puerto deportivo
Mast	Mât	Mast	Mast	Palo
Mean (average)	moyen	mittlere	gemiddeld	media
Minutes	Minutes	Minuten	Minuten	Minutos
Moon	Lune	Mond	Maan	Luna
Mooring prohibited	Accostage interdit	Anlegen verboten	Verboden aan te leggen	Amarradero prohibido
Mountain	Montagne	Berg	Berg	Montana
Mud	Boue	Schlick	Modder	Lodo
Neap tide	Morte eau	Nipptide	Doodtij	Aguas muertas
North	Nord	Nord	Noord	Norte
Obstruction	Obstruction	Hindernis	Hindernis	Obstrución
Occasional	occasionnel	gelegentlich	facultatief	ocasional
Occulting light	Feu a occultation	Mischfeuer	Onderbroken licht	Luz de ocultacion
Orange	orange	orange	oranje	naranja
Outer	avant	äusser	buiten	exterior
Overfalls	Remous	Stromkabbelung	Stroomrafeling	Escarceos
Parallel ruler	Règle parallele	Parallel-lineal	Parallel-lineaal	Regla paralelas
Peninsula	Peninsule	Halbinsel	Schiereiland	Peninsula
Pilot	Pilote	Lotse	Loods	Piloto
Pilot book	Instructions nautiques	Seehandbuch	Zeemansgids	Derrotero
Pilot cutter	Bateau-pilote	Lotsenboot	Loodsbooot	Barco del practico
Planets	Planètes	Planeten	Planeten	Planetas
Pole Star	Etoile polaire	Polarstern	Poolster	Estrella polar
Port (side)	Babord	backbord	bakboord	babor
Port tack	babord amure	auf steuerbord-bug*	over bakboord	con amuras a babor
Protractor	Rapporteur	Winkelmesser	Gradenboog	Transportador
Pencil	Crayon	Bleistift	Potlood	Lapiz
Pontoon	Ponton	Ponton	Ponton	Ponton
Quay	Quai	Kai	Kade	Muelle
Radiobeacon	Radiophare	Funkfeuer	Radiobaken	Radiofaro
Radio receiver	Poste récepteur	Empfangsgerät	Radio-ontvangtoestel	Receptor de radio
Range (of light)	Distance	Reichweite	Bereik	Alcance
Range (of tide)	Amplitude	Tidenhub	Verval	Repunte
Red	rouge	rot	rood	rojo
Reef	Récif	Riff	Rif	Arrecife
Right (side)	droit	rechts	rechts	derecha
River	Rivière	Fluss	Rivier	Rió
Rocks	Rochers	Felsen	Rotsen	Rocas
Rough (sea)	dure, agité	rauh	ruw	agitado
Round	circulaire	rund	rond	redondo
Rubber (Eraser)	Gomme	Gummi	Vlakgom	Goma
Sand	Sable	Sand	Zand	Arena
Seaward	vers le large	seewärts	zeewaarts	hacia la mar
Seconds	Secondes	Sekunden	Seconden	Segundos
Sextant	Sextant	Sextant	Sextant	Sextante
Shoal	Haut-fond	Untiefe	Ondiepte	Bajio
Shore	Côte	Land	Kust	Costa

English	French	German	Dutch	Spanish
Shoreward	vers la terre	landwärts	kustwaarts	hacia tierra
Sight reduction tables	Tables de navigation	Höhentafeln	Zeevaartkundige tafels	Tablas rapidas
Siren	Sirène	Sirene	Mistsirene	Sirena
Slipway	Slip	Slip	Helling	Varadero
Spring tide	Vive eau	Springtide	Springtij	Marea viva
Squall	Grain	Bö	Bui	Chubasco
Square	carré	viereckig	vierkant	cuadrangular
Stand (of tide)	Etale	Wasserstand	Stilwater	Margen
Star	Etoile	Stern	Ster	Estrella
Starboard	Tribord	Steuerbord	Stuurbord	Estribor
Starboard tack	Tribord amure	auf backbord-bug*	over stuurboord	con amuras a estribor
Steep	raide	steil	steile	empinado
Stones	Pierres	Steine	Steenen	Piedras
Strait (narrows)	Détroit	Meerenge	Straat	Estrecho
Stripes (vertical)	raiée	senkrecht gestreift	vertikaal gestreept	fajas verticales
South	Sud	Süd	Zuid	Sur
Sun	Soleil	Sonne	Zon	Sol
Surf	Surf	Brandung	Branding	Resaca
Swell	Houle	Dünung	Deining	Mar de fondo
Temporary	temporaire	zeitweilig	tijdelijk	provisional
Tide tables	Table des marées	Tidenkalender	Getijtafels	Tabla de mareas
Topmark	Voyant	Toppzeichen	Topteken	Marea de tope
(a) Tow	Remorque	Schlepper	Sleep	Remolque
Tower	Tour	Turm	Toren	Torre
Town	Ville	Stadt	Stad	Ciudad
Triangle	Triangle	Dreieck	Driehonk	Triangulo
Tug	Remorqueur	Schlepper	Sleepboot	Remolcador
Upstream	en amont	flussaufwärts	stroomopwaarts	rio arriba
Water	Eau	Wasser	Water	Agua
Wave	Vague	Welle	Golf	Ola
Weather forecast	Prévisions météo	Wetterbericht	Weers-voorspelling	Pronostico
West	Ouest	West	West	Oeste
Whistle	Sifflet	Heuler	Fluit	Silbato
White	blanc	weiss	wit	blanco
Wind	Vent	Wind	Wind	Viento
Windward	au vent	luv	aan loef	barlovento
Wreck	Epave	Wrack	Wrak	Naufragio
Yacht club	Yacht-club	Yachtclub	Watersport-vereniging	Club nautico
Yellow	jaune	gelb	geel	amarillo

*N.B. Note different terminology in German

INDEX

Page numbers in *italic* refer to illustrations.

Tart Love

To warm hearts and
delicious tarts!
Bon appetit—

Holly Herick

"The Queen of Hearts, she made some tarts

All on a summer day

The Knave of Hearts, he stole those tarts,

And took them quite away

The King of Hearts

Called for Those Tarts

And beat the Knave fell sore

The Knave of Hearts

Brought back those Tarts

And vow'd he'd steal no more"

—excerpted from "The King and Queen of Tarts," by Charles Lamb (1775–1834)

Tart Love

SASSY, SAVORY, AND SWEET

HOLLY HERRICK

PHOTOGRAPHS BY HÉLÈNE DUJARDIN

First Edition
15 14 13 12 11   5 4 3 2 1

Text © 2011 Holly Herrick
Photographs © 2011 Hélène Dujardin

Published by
Gibbs Smith
P.O. Box 667
Layton, Utah 84041

1.800.835.4993 orders
www.gibbs-smith.com

Cover and book design by Michelle Farinella Design

Gibbs Smith books are printed on paper produced from sustainable PEFC-
certified forest/controlled wood source. Learn more at www.pefc.org.
Printed and bound in Hong Kong

Library of Congress Cataloging-in-Publication Data

Herrick, Holly.
  Tart love : sassy, savory, and sweet / Holly Herrick ; photographs by Hélène
Dujardin. — 1st ed.
     p. cm.
  ISBN 978-1-4236-1894-2
1. Pies. 2. Cooking, American—Southern style. I. Title.
  TX773.H447 2011
  641.8'652—dc22
                  2011006580

For Dori and Simone

Thank you for kindly introducing me to the brave,

versatile, and delicious world of tarts and pastry

—forever banishing my former tart terrors.

You will always be my reigning Queens of Tarts,

nestled deeply in my heart and

ever present in my kitchen.

Contents

Preface

My relationship with tarts has not always been sweet. In fact, it could more accurately be defined as a mild dislike that eventually developed into a true love—a little like that pesky boy you knew in third grade who by the time high school rolled around had morphed into the man of your dreams.

My first exposure to the term *tart* had nothing to do with food. It came via my older brother Tom when he was in tenth grade and just beginning to expand his vocabulary for upcoming college exams. He learned in English class that a tart was a kind of wanton woman. He couldn't resist throwing the term relentlessly at my twin sister Heather and me, declaring almost daily for what seemed like a very long time, "You silly tarts," with aggravating adolescent swagger punctuated by an obnoxious giggle. Of course, at least at that young age, we were nothing of the kind, but it sent my mind wondering about the true meaning of tarts, and especially their edible casing, pastry. That wouldn't come until a decade later when I got married and simultaneously met and adopted Doris Herrick as my mother-in-law.

Dori, as she was affectionately called, amazed me. She cooked three delicious meals a day, always neatly coiffed and made up, wearing heels and a pretty dress. She never looked flustered in the kitchen, certainly never perspired, and practically always whistled while she worked. An Iowa farm girl at heart, she ate pig virtually three meals a day and never gained an ounce. But the thing that impressed me more than anything else was that Dori could make pie pastry that could make a grown man cry, or at least come begging for more. I came to believe it was this skill that in no small part contributed to her very happy 50-plus year marriage to the love of her life, Walt.

I marveled at Dori's deftness with pastry and told her so. Slowly but surely, she began to teach me in her gentle, motherly way. For Dori, pastry was always made by hand, using a pastry blender and a bowl, and it always included equal parts lard (she swore by leaf lard, the rendered lard from the fat surrounding the pig's kidney) and sweet butter to two parts flour. After that, it was simply a matter of adding just enough water to hold it together. The rest was elementary, or so she said. She never fussed with tart pans and was ardently committed to the world of deep-dish pies, usually fruit or pecan.

At home, in my own kitchen, I tried to replicate Dori's pastry for several years, but I always felt that mine fell short. It just didn't have the right flake factor or buttery deliciousness. I didn't hold that against Dori. She became

one of my best friends, and though she's now passed, remains the same in my heart. She was the person who set me on the path of learning the joys of cooking. I can never make pastry without thinking of her.

Dori was my inspiration for pursuing culinary training at Le Cordon Bleu, Paris, France, where I learned the mechanics of pastry (we'll get there in "Perfecting Pastry," page 16), was introduced to tarts, and finally got comfortable in my own tart skin. But it was a petite woman with a huge heart who I met in the soulfully beautiful Pays Cathare in the Languedoc-Roussillon region of France that fully opened the doors of my mind to the limitless possibilities of tarts.

After graduating from cooking school in Paris and falling in love with France, my by now tart-happy husband and I decided to buy a small house in that rugged part of the country. Simone lived in a tiny village about 12 kilometers from mine called St.-Jean-de-Paracol. We met through mutual friends in her beautiful, bougainvillea-walled garden over glasses of Blanquette de Limoux and a savory platter of—what else?—tarts.

Besides her celebrated couscous and *choucroute garni* (sausage and sauerkraut dish), Simone was best known for her tarts, especially the savory kind. A frugal widow of limited financial means and mother of two young girls, she was most often found in her rocky garden with a Mediterranean view, cultivating the foods that fed her family and, often, friends. Winter squash, fennel, figs, tomatoes, zucchini, mushrooms, apples, cherries, onions, arugula, spinach, endives and assorted cheeses and meats from the local *marches*—any and all—were delicious tart-topping fare. Encased in simple pastry, and often puff pastry, these became low-cost, high-nutrient meals-in-one and were frequent features at her always delicious table.

Before Simone, I thought of tarts as sweet, a kind of dessert. After Simone, the universe of tarts became literally limitless.

In *Tart Love*, it is my desire to share some of Dori's, Simone's and my pastry and tart wisdom so that you, too, can revel in the joy and delicious diversity of tarts. As you read the following pages and practice the techniques, hopefully you, like I did, will shed any trepidation you may have about pastry and experience firsthand the pleasure of flour-dusted hands, the heady aroma of baking butter, and the unparalleled beauty of the tart. Perhaps with patience and renewed confidence, you'll even fall in love.

Introduction

So what exactly is a tart? Literally, a tart is an open-faced, skinny kind of pie. Usually only one inch deep and straight-sided, tarts are pies' sleeker, sexier culinary cousins. A tart never has a double crust with a pastry lid (like an apple pie might) and can be filled with anything from custard to Camembert. The pastry can be baked ahead (see Blind Baking, page 19) and filled, or filled and then baked. Tarts come in all shapes and sizes (see Tart Equipment Cupboard, page 13), the smallest of which is the diminutive, single-serving tartlet. The pastry can be a savory or sweet short pastry, a puff pastry, or even a crumble pastry ("Perfecting Pastry," page 16).

But the figurative definition of tarts is so much more fun! I think of them as delectable, delicate and beautiful food vessels. With tarts, the filling and presentation possibilities are endless. I had more fun coming up with recipe ideas for this book than any other I have ever written. Saturday mornings at the Charleston Farmers Market, from early spring through late fall, became inspirational forays into the infinite realm of possibilities for tarts. Rhubarb one hot summer day was the imaginational fodder for Rosy Rhubarb and Apricot Tartlets (page 134), while small green baskets brimming with fat, purple, early fall figs would eventually become Panna Cotta Tart with Roasted Fresh Figs in Balsamic Honey Sauce (page 34). I eventually started calling myself "queen of tarts" because tarts were all I thought about for months on end. There were days when I was so distracted by the tart head phenomenon I questioned whether it was safe to drive. Once you get started thinking about the vast universe of sassy tart flavor and texture possibilities, I think and hope you'll become similarly and happily tart-obsessed, except for the dangerous driving potential part, of course.

I am a southern woman. Although there are variations on southern themes such as cheese, buttermilk, or sweet potato custards, this book is not southern in the sense that it is chock full of classic southern tart and pie fillings. Rather, it's southern in the sense that it follows the South's long growing season for fresh inspiration and includes whimsical, delicious recipes that are essentially fresh tart versions of old southern favorites like Feisty Fried Shrimp and Grits Pockets (page 85), Lowcountry Boil Puff Tart (page 43), and Lavender Buttermilk Tart (page 103). Recipes are organized in each chapter by season. With limited exceptions, such as scuppernongs

(large grapes of the muscadine family, native to the Southeast), most of the ingredients are available anywhere, though they may grow at a different time of year depending on the region.

Like Simone, always keep Mother Nature and her seasonal produce bounty close to your heart in your tart kitchen. The results will be fresher, more delicious, more nutritious and kinder to planet Earth.

Because everyone loves them and because they showcase the versatility of pastry, I've also included a few tart variations in pot pie recipes, such as Pot Roast Pot Pies (page 63) and fried pie pocket recipes, such as Deep Purple Fresh Cherry Pie Pockets (page 123).

As you delve into the world of tarts and in all cooking adventures, always remember the most important ingredient is love. If you sprinkle it into all you do, in both your kitchen and your life, everything will taste, look and feel better.

The Complete Tart Kitchen

Making tarts does not require a fully stocked professional kitchen, but it makes things easier if you have a few basic ingredients and equipment on hand. Below are some of the items I find to be useful in my kitchen. Start small and build your tart-preparing supplies as you go. In general, I find it's better to lean more heavily on quality than quantity in both ingredients and equipment, as both will take you the distance much more efficiently and deliciously than cheap substitutes.

Tart Ingredients Pantry

White Lily Flour—Milled from 100 percent soft winter wheat, which is naturally lower in protein, White Lily Flour yields exceptionally tender pastry every time. Aptly nicknamed "the light baking flour," it is pre-sifted and all-purpose. Find it locally or visit *www.whitelily.com*. Before measuring, simply fluff the flour bag with a fork. I use White Lily for all my pastries and find it makes a remarkable difference in the texture over other brands of flour I've tested. It stores well in the refrigerator unopened. Once opened, store in a sealed, wide-mouth dry-goods container for easy measuring access.

AA Grade Unsalted Butter—Butter makes up nearly half of the content of the Master Pastry recipes in this book, so buy the best you can afford. Unsalted butter is best because you get to decide how much salt you want to add to a recipe. More perishable than salted butter, it's best stored in the freezer until ready to use. I use Land O' Lakes Sweet Cream Unsalted butter because it's readily available and I find it to be very dependable in quality. If you're lucky enough to know an artisanal dairy/cheese/butter vendor at your local farmers market, go for it—you're in for a treat.

Sea salt or kosher salt—Both sea salt and kosher salt are additive-free and therefore devoid of the strong chemical flavor present in processed salt. Use these whenever possible. Measured salt (and pepper) quantities are suggested when necessary throughout the book, but generally speaking, I suggest that you season to taste. Tasting as you cook and to your liking will make your food taste better and make you happier.

Pure Vanilla Extract—The FDA requires 13.35 ounces of vanilla beans per gallon during the flavor extraction process, ensuring a beautifully aromatic wave of pure vanilla flavor. Buy the best quality you can afford and try to avoid imitation vanilla at all costs.

Honey—Buy local honey produced near where you live for multi-dimensional, additive-free antibody-building goodness. It is well worth the extra cost for the rich flavor and color dividends it delivers.

Tart Equipment Cupboard

Tart Pans—Tart pans are like people: they come in all shapes and sizes, but for different reasons. In the case of tarts, the selected form is dependent on the function and especially the filling. Think of it like pairing shoes with a dress. stiletto heels work with a black evening gown but would look ridiculous with a flowing muumuu. Similarly, a tender, fragile filling, such as in the Butterscotch and Caramel Apple Tarts (page 104), demand a long, lean, rectangular shape that makes cutting through less pastry than you would in a wedge cut from a large round tart pan, for example, a snap. A quiche pan is slightly deeper and thus better suited to ensuring that the custard and pastry cook at the right speed for a sinfully silky custard. Round, rectangular, square, big or small, tart pan variety is a large part of what makes tart-making fun. I prefer the stainless steel variety with removable bottoms. The removable bottom makes removing the pastry from the tart pan truly fuss-free. For each recipe, I make suggestions for pan sizes to match with different filling and presentations, but feel free to explore the myriad possibilities as your tart pan collection grows.

To clean tart pans, wash thoroughly in hot soapy water after using, and dry completely in a warm oven before storing. Some suggested sources for tart pan shopping include *surlatable.com*, *williams-sonoma.com*, and *amazon.com*.

Round Pastry Cutters—Ideal for forming tartlets, pot pie lids, and pockets, I rely heavily on my 4-inch-wide round pastry cutter, but it comes nestled with several smaller sizes for added variety. If you don't have one, a small, roughly 4-inch-wide, round plate will work just as well, as a guide

for your paring knife to cut around. As with tart pans, clean and dry pastry cutters thoroughly before storing.

Rolling Pin—Rolling pin preferences are as personal as perfume. I love my simple, unadorned, 18-inch-long, 1½-inch-wide wooden dowel and have been using it for about as long as I've been wearing Cabotine de Gres perfume. It's the right length for rolling or shaping almost any tart size and is free of the clunky, rolling extra handles so prevalent on fatter rolling pins. Do a little investigating to see what works best for you. Rolling pins need simply to be brushed down with a damp towel after using. Avoid submerging in soapy water.

Pie Weights—These are used when blind baking (see page 19) is necessary to hold the pastry in place as it cooks. Lead pie weights are priccy alternatives to humble legumes, which I re-use over and over again in my kitchen. Dried pinto, navy or kidney beans (or a combination of these) work just fine. Store them, cooled, in a sealed container between uses.

Work/Rolling Surface—While many pastry cooks swear by marble or granite boards or surfaces, my large wooden cutting board works beautifully. No matter what surface you use, it should be flat, clean, and cool, or at least room temperature.

Dry/Wet Measuring Cups and Measuring Spoons—Have a complete set of each on hand for accurate measuring.

Whisk—Crucial for blending custards, blending sauces, and mounting cream, I find that a stainless steel, mid-size whisk works perfectly for all of these uses. I couldn't survive without my whisk!

Pastry Brush—A standard-size pastry brush is necessary for brushing egg washes, glazes and such onto tarts. Synthetic and natural brushes work equally well. Clean thoroughly in soapy water and dry before storing.

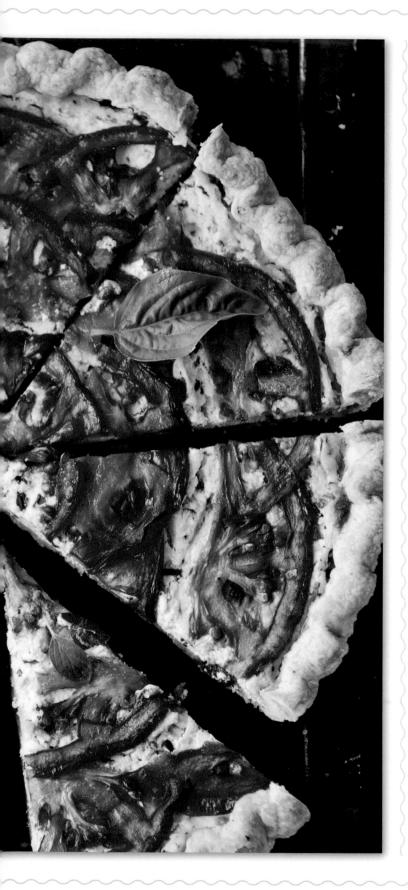

Hand-Held Mixer—Helpful but not crucial in doing all the same things a whisk can do. If you have one, use it!

Pastry Blender—With this and a large bowl you can cut the fat into the flour that becomes the backbone of a delicious, flaky pastry.

Food Processor—Because I have one, I use my large Cuisinart food processor fitted with a plastic blade to make multiple batches of pastry. It's great to have on hand, but if you don't have one, a pastry blender (see above) will do the same thing.

Baking Pans—You'll need at least one good-quality stainless steel rimmed baking sheet. All tarts, especially those with fragile custard fillings (such as quiche), should be baked on a sheet. This helps evenly conduct heat and acts as a safeguard against spilled fillings. It also makes removing tarts/tartlets from the oven both easier and safer.

Stacked Mixing Bowls—I received a set of four stacked glass mixing bowls as a wedding gift over twenty years ago, and they're still as good as new. Stainless steel and ceramic work great too. Try to have at least one small, one medium and one large bowl in your tart equipment cupboard.

Parchment Paper/Aluminum Foil—Useful for lining raw pastry for blind baking (see page 19) and for lining pastry pans for puff pastry tarts/tartlets and free-form tarts/tartlets.

Also suggested—Spatulas, cherry pitter, ice cream machine, wooden spoons, sauté pans, saucepans, good-quality knives (at least one paring and one chef's knife), potato masher or ricer, and lemon zester. These will all work wonders in both your savory and sweet tart-making endeavors!

Perfecting Pastry

Over the years, I've read and used literally hundreds of recipes for pastry. Ingredients can include eggs, sour cream, milk, lard and more. As with so many things in the kitchen, and in life, I tend to adhere to the "simple is best" theory. The Master Sweet Pastry and Master Savory Pastry recipes I use are personalized versions of the pâte brisée and pâte sucrée recipes I learned at Le Cordon Bleu. Essentially a "short" pastry, or a pastry with a high ratio of fat to flour, it is crumbly, flaky, flexible and delicious. In its sweet form, it's reminiscent of a sugar cookie, while in its savory form it recalls a buttery cracker—think Ritz on fancy steroids.

Unlike Dori, my mother-in-law, I don't fancy lard in my pastry. For one, it can be difficult to find the real thing, unless you render your own. For another, nothing surpasses the aroma of baking butter or its deep-seated nutty, milky flavor. Feel free to formulate what you like best. And unlike Simone, my friend in St.-Jean-de-Paracol, I'm opposed to using processed, frozen pastry. Ever-practical Simone lives in France, where processed pastry was, and still is, of a much higher quality than anything I've been able to find Stateside. More importantly, making your own pastry is so much more rewarding. When mastered, it's a cathartic, joyful process that takes just minutes. The only exception I make to that rule is using processed puff pastry.

Making puff pastry is an extremely involved, long process (Julia Child gives an excellent explanation in *The Way to Cook*) that could frustrate even the most experienced cook, and we don't want that! I've found Pepperidge Farms brand puff pastry to be consistently delicious and easy to work with, and that's what I recommend. (If you insist on buying processed tart pastry, I understand, but buy the best brand out there—Mrs. Smith's is a good bet—and roll it out as you would homemade pastry. See On a Roll, page 18).

The only other pastry used in these recipes is a cookie crumb pastry for the delicious Peanut Butter Fluff and Chocolate Tart (page 116).

Master Savory Pastry

Makes two 9-inch tart crusts

2 1/2 cups White Lily all-purpose flour
2 teaspoons sea salt or kosher salt
2 sticks (1 cup) AA grade unsalted butter,
    cold and cut into 1/4-inch cubes
3 tablespoons ice-cold water, or just
    enough to hold the pastry together

Master Sweet Pastry

Makes two 9-inch tart crusts

2 1/4 cups White Lily all-purpose flour
1/4 cup sugar
Generous pinch sea salt or kosher salt
2 sticks (1 cup) AA grade unsalted butter,
    cold and cut into 1/4-inch cubes
About 3 tablespoons ice-cold water, or just
    enough to hold the pastry together

Let's Make Pastry!

Besides great ingredients, the biggest key to flaky, perfect pastry is minimal manipulation of the dough. Flour contains gluten. The last thing you want to do is get it all worked up, or you will have tough, miserable pastry. Begin by having all your ingredients measured and nearby in a preferably cool kitchen. Butter should be very cold but not frozen solid, or it will rattle a food processor or a pastry blender. I take mine out of the freezer for 10 minutes before I cut it and then use it immediately. Refrigerator-cold is not quite cold enough. Freeze refrigerated butter for at least 30 minutes before using it. Water should be literally ice-cold. I fill up my liquid measuring cup with ice and top it off with cold tap water and place it in the freezer for 15 minutes before using it.

Once you've got your pastry workspace set up, it's time to make pastry. This can be done either with a food processor or by hand, blending the ingredients in a large bowl using a pastry blender.

First, combine the dry ingredients by pulsing 10–12 times in the processor or blending with your pastry blender. The next and very important step is incorporating the butter. Do this with love and use your eyes. Think of this step as "wrapping" the butter with tiny packages of flour that will help the pastry rise as it bakes. The butter needs to be quickly blended in until it resembles the size of very coarse sand or sea salt. In the processor, this should take between 40 and 50 quick, successive pulses. With a pastry blender, it takes about the same number of times cutting the butter into the flour. Don't be afraid to look, but don't touch, at least not excessively: hot hands are pastry's worst enemy.

Similarly, you don't want to over-water the pastry, which is the next step, and the one that took me so long to master. Too much water wreaks havoc with the gluten and requires over-manipulation and additional flour—both of which make for tough pastry. The amount of water the pastry will take largely depends on the humidity level of the flour. For me, it's usually between 2 and 3 tablespoons. Whether in a processor or in a bowl with a blender, trickle the water very slowly into the pastry while pulsing/cutting. At the second the pastry begins to form a big, messy ball, you're there. STOP! (Note: If it's gummy and sticky and messy, if 2 tablespoons of flour can't fix it, throw it out and try again. You'll get it right the next time!)

Turn out the pastry onto a lightly floured surface, and very quickly shape it into a 2-inch-thick round disk with your hands, scooping up any stray bits and working them into the disk. It should feel and look a little like Play-Doh, or, as I once thought to myself, a very firm little baby's bottom. Look for bits of butter peeking through the pastry—this is a good thing.

Now wrap the pastry and refrigerate it for at least 30 minutes, or better yet, overnight. Pastry can also be made in double batches on slow days, prepared as above, double-wrapped in plastic wrap and foil, and frozen for 1 to 2 months. Thaw in the refrigerator overnight before using.

The master recipes each make enough to line two normal-size (9 inch) tarts. If preparing only one tart, just cut the pastry in half and store it in the refrigerator or freezer until ready to use.

Flavor: It's in the Crust

One of the loveliest things about a tart or tartlet is that every bite contains pastry. For that reason, many recipes in this book get additional flavors—from grated cheese to chives to crackers—worked or rolled into the crust. Follow recipe directions for the best way and time to incorporate the extra ingredient into the pastry.

On a Roll

After the pastry has chilled out in the refrigerator for at least 30 minutes, you're ready to roll. Have the intended tart pan(s) out and ready to fill. Unwrap the dough and place it on a lightly floured (as in 1–2 tablespoons of flour), dry work surface. Give the pastry a few little love taps to break it in and prepare it for rolling. I do this by pressing the top of the pastry three times with a horizontal impression of the rolling pin. Then turn it over and start rolling. Keep the top and bottom of the pastry lightly coated with flour at all times, and turn the pastry intermittently in quarter turns as you work. Roll gently but quickly, pushing out evenly as you go along. Work toward forming the dough into the shape of the tart pan you intend to fill. For instance, form a rectangle for a rectangular tart pan, form a circle for a round tart pan, etc. You're done when the pastry is even and about 1/4 inch thick.

Remember that your rolling pin is your friend; use it to guide the pastry into the pan(s). It's easiest to roll the pastry around the pin and then slowly drape it into the pan(s), starting from the outside in. This way it literally falls into place without being touched. Nudge the pastry further into place by gently pressing it into the sides and bottoms of the tart pan. How you finish it depends on what's going into the tart. Here are your options:

Flush Tart Border

Probably the most common tart pastry edge finish, the flush tart border is best used for tartlets or tarts with a particularly delicate filling. This is also the easiest border to form. Once the pastry is draped into the pan, simply roll the pin over the edges of the tart pan. Any excess pastry will drop off and you have an instant border.

Elevated Tart Border

This is pretty and appropriate when you want a visual lift to the edge of the tart. It has one more step than the flush tart border. After the pastry is draped into the pan, lift about 1/2 inch of the hanging pastry back into the interior edges of the pan, continuing all around the circumference. Now roll the pin over the entire pan, and cut off the excess pastry (like with the flush tart border). To finish, press the pastry edge between your thumb and forefinger to raise, or elevate, it. It can be crimped lightly if you like.

Forming Tartlets

Roll out the pastry as usual and find a pastry cutter that equals the size of the tartlet pan. For example, for my 3 5/8-inch round tartlet pans, cutting the pastry with a 4-inch round pastry cutter works perfectly. Cut the rounds and place the pastry into the tartlet pans, pressing gently to fit it into the pans.

No matter the shape or the size of the tart, all pastry needs to chill again once it has been formed and arranged in

the pan. Give each and all of these another 20 minutes in the fridge before filling and/or baking. Save any scraps for filling holes in the pastry or for another use. Just ball it up, wrap it, and refrigerate or freeze for later.

Egg Wash

An egg wash serves two purposes: 1) it helps to seal the pastry and hold it together, and 2) it helps the pastry develop a sheen and color as it cooks. Depending on the seasoning and small amount of liquid you add to an egg yolk or to a whole egg, the effect will be altogether different:

- A whole egg plus salt yields a shiny surface
- A whole egg plus milk yields a slightly shiny surface
- A whole egg plus water yields a golden color and matte surface
- An egg yolk plus water yields a shiny, golden surface
- An egg yolk plus cream yields a shiny, dark golden to brown color
- An egg white makes for a crunchy, light-colored surface

I like a light shine on my tarts, so in this book, the egg wash is consistently a yolk, salt and water. Experiment as you wish; it only makes you a better cook. The egg wash is applied after the pastry has been rolled, formed and chilled, and just before it goes into the oven, except in the case of blind baking (below).

Blind Baking

Blind baking is essentially pre-cooking the tart shell before filling it. The pastry can be entirely baked for a tart that is to be filled with something fully cooked, as in the Roasted Pumpkin Ice Cream and Candied Pecan Tartlets (page 110), or partially baked for something that's going to continue cooking along with the pastry after it is set,

as in any of the quiches in the "Savory Quiches" chapter, pages 70–81. The whole point of blind baking is to keep the pastry in its place in the fragile first few minutes of cooking, so that it literally doesn't fall on its face. This is accomplished by weighting the pastry. I use dried legumes/beans, but pie weights are another, pricier option. Simply shape parchment paper to fit your pan (it should be slightly higher than the pan to hold the weights), crumple it up to soften it, and line the tart pans with the paper and fill almost completely with the weights. Press gently to make sure that the beans are evenly distributed. Then bake as directed. Cooking times vary depending on the recipe, but generally, it will need to cook for at least 20 minutes before the paper and weights are removed. The pastry then gets brushed with an egg wash and continues on its merry way, baking another 10 minutes to brown before being filled. This may seem like an annoying extra step, but it's worth it. Every time I've tried to skip it, especially for custard pies and quiches, I've regretted it. Once, I lost an entire quiche filling just for being blind-baking lazy.

Now that you know the whys and hows of making pastry and getting your workspace ready, choose a tart recipe and get on your way to mastering the art of tart making!

Savory Tarts and Tartlets

Of the entire tantalizing universe of tarts and tartlets, the savory planet is my most preferred. Savory tarts are such a sexy and flexible way to utilize an entire garden full of produce—figs, tomatoes, squash, peaches, corn, apples, fennel, mushrooms, you name it—with myriad savory flavorings in assorted shapes and sizes. They remind me of feminine, dressed-up pizzas, with limitless ingredient opportunities. The Sage Green Apple and Aged Cheddar Tart (page 46) makes a snappy, smart alternative to wine and cheese with cocktails, for example, while the gorgeous Panna Cotta Tart with Roasted Fresh Figs in Balsamic Honey Sauce (page 34) is so glossy, smooth, beautiful, and delicious, it would be very much at home as a main course with a salad at a fancy dinner party or even a wedding reception. Other favorites in this chapter included the Roasted Tomato and Garlic Tart with Fresh Marjoram and Fontina (page 25) and the Lowcountry Boil Puff Tart (page 43).

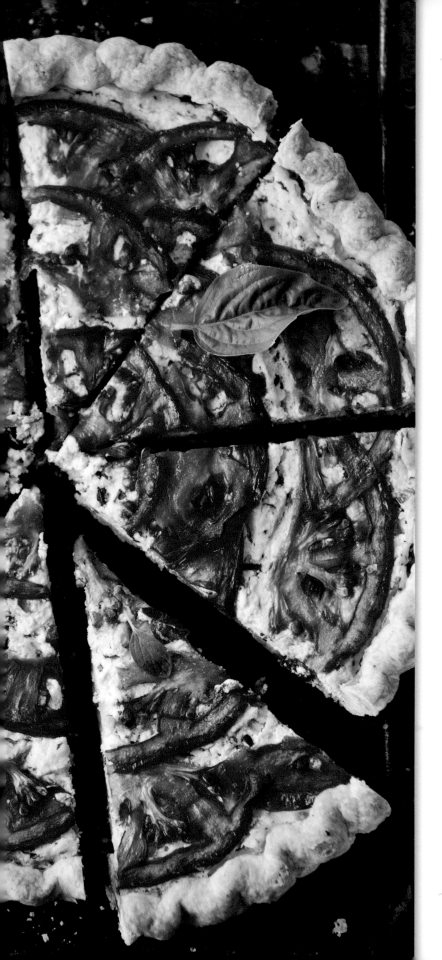

Tomato Tart a la Margherita

Serves 8

Summer This is a lighter, thinner riff on a traditional southern deep-dish tomato pie held together with cheese and lots of mayonnaise. A bed of seasoned sweet ricotta puffs up in this tart, absorbing the juice and the flavor of the tomatoes. Don't overdo it on the tomatoes or the tart will get soggy. A single fanned layer on top does just the trick, and slicing with a sharp serrated knife does a much neater job than a standard chef's knife.

EQUIPMENT NEEDED **One 12 x 1-inch round tart pan with a removable bottom**

1 recipe Master Savory Pastry (page 17)
2 tablespoons chopped fresh oregano
2 tablespoons chopped fresh basil
1½ cups whole-milk ricotta
1 teaspoon half-and-half
Zest from 1 small lemon
1 egg yolk
Salt and freshly ground pepper, to taste
2 scallions, green and white, finely chopped
2 large vine-ripened tomatoes, thinly sliced
Drizzle of extra virgin olive oil

Prepare and rest one recipe of Master Savory Pastry as described in "Perfecting Pastry" (pages 17–18). Chill at least 30 minutes or overnight. Roll it out, forming a ¼-inch-high border (see Elevated Tart Border, page 18). Chill in the refrigerator for at least 20 minutes while preparing the filling.

Preheat oven to 375 degrees F.

To prepare the filling, place the oregano, basil, ricotta, half-and-half, zest, egg yolk, salt, and pepper in a medium-size bowl. Whisk thoroughly to combine. Fold in the scallions. Taste and adjust seasoning as needed.

To assemble the tart, remove the pastry from the refrigerator. Line the bottom with the filling, smoothing it out flat with a spatula. Stack the sliced tomatoes and cut them in half to form half-circle shapes. Moving from the outside of the tart inward, arrange the slices in a single-layer fan, overlapping just slightly on the edges to close any gaps. You should have just enough to go all around the tart and to cover its interior. At the center, make a small fan of three tomato slices to finish. Sprinkle with salt and pepper and drizzle with olive oil.

Bake for 50 minutes, or until the pastry is golden brown and the tomatoes are slightly shrunken, lightly colored and slightly juicy. Increase heat to 400 degrees F and continue baking another 10 minutes, or until any excess juice has cooked off. Cool at room temperature for 20 to 30 minutes.

Remove from the pan, slice and serve. This tart is magnificent warm from the oven but also at room temperature.

Roasted Tomato and Garlic Tart with Fresh Marjoram and Fontina

Serves 4

Summer *This beautiful square tart dances with flavor. Two-toned tomatoes (I used yellow and red heirloom tomatoes from the farmers market) are roasted prior to going into the tart to concentrate their flavor and reduce their juices. This, combined with a protective and flavorful coating of roasted garlic paste that forms the first layer of the tart, prevents the pastry from getting soggy.*

EQUIPMENT NEEDED **Parchment paper, pastry brush, roasting pan**

One 6 x 6-inch square prepared puff pastry
3 medium-size heirloom tomatoes, trimmed, halved and sliced ⅛ inch thick
1 whole head garlic
Extra virgin olive oil for drizzling
Aged balsamic vinegar for drizzling
Salt and freshly ground pepper, to taste
1 egg wash (yolk, splash water, pinch salt blended together)
1 small onion, peeled and sliced very finely
8 thick, 2-inch-long slices fontina cheese
1 tablespoon finely chopped fresh marjoram

Fontina is a nutty, flavorful cow's milk cheese that originated from Italy. It's a super-great "melter" and is excellent for grilled cheese sandwiches. It's readily available in most groceries. Feel free to substitute fresh mozzarella if fontina is unavailable where you are.

Preheat the oven to 400 degrees F.

Remove the puff pastry from the freezer and thaw according to manufacturer's directions. Keeping the colors separate, arrange tomato slices on a baking sheet in a single layer. Season with salt and pepper. Trim the top off of the whole head of garlic and drizzle lightly with olive oil. Wrap tightly with aluminum foil and place on the corner of the baking sheet. Place the tray in the center rack of the oven; roast the tomatoes until they've just shriveled, about 15 minutes. Remove from oven and let cool completely. Keep the garlic in the oven another 15 minutes, or until it's softened. Then remove foil and let garlic cool.

Drizzle tomatoes lightly with olive oil and balsamic vinegar. When the garlic is cool enough to handle, remove the pulp by squeezing the garlic gently to extrude the "flesh" of the individual cloves; discard garlic casings and spread the roasted flesh into a paste with the back of your chef's knife; let cool completely.

Unfold the thawed pastry and arrange on a baking sheet lined with parchment paper. Press gently to form into its (already) square shape. Brush the entire square lightly with egg wash using a pastry brush, then use the same brush to coat the pastry with the garlic paste, leaving a 1-inch border all around the square. Arrange a single layer of onions within the border, and season with salt and pepper. Arrange the tomatoes on top, forming two parallel vertical lines of two different-colored tomatoes. Wedge 4 slices of cheese evenly between the tomatoes on each of the two vertical rows of tomatoes. Bake about 20 minutes, until crisp, brown and bubbly.

While the tart is still warm, sprinkle with the fresh marjoram, salt, and pepper and drizzle with a tiny bit of oil. To serve, cut into four large squares.

Plenty of "Thyme" Parmesan and Black Pepper–Encrusted Summer Squash Tart

Serves 8 to 10

Summer Ribbons of lemony yellow summer squash and lime-green zucchini thread throughout this tart. The pastry is prepared with grated aged Parmesan cheese. A barely there custard holds it all together with the nuances of grated sweet onion. If you have a mandolin, use it to get whisper-thin squash slices; otherwise use a sharp knife and slice as thinly as possible. Ideally, you'll be able to see through the ribbons.

EQUIPMENT NEEDED **One 12 x 1-inch round tart pan with removable bottom**

1 recipe Master Savory Pastry (substitute ¼ cup of the flour with finely grated Parmigiano-Reggiano and add 1 teaspoon coarsely ground black pepper to the dry ingredients
2 tablespoons butter
1 medium-size zucchini, trimmed, halved horizontally, and cut into very thin ribbons
2 medium-size yellow summer squash, trimmed, halved horizontally, and cut into very thin ribbons
Salt and freshly ground pepper, to taste
1 medium onion
3 tablespoons heavy cream

1 large egg yolk
Zest of 1 lemon
1 tablespoon chopped fresh thyme
1 egg wash (yolk, splash water, pinch salt blended together)

Preheat the oven to 375 degrees F.

Prepare and chill the Master Savory Pastry recipe, with substitution and addition according to "Perfecting Pastry" (pages 17–18). Chill at least 30 minutes or overnight. Roll out according to Elevated Tart Border directions (page 18). Chill for at least 20 minutes.

Meanwhile, prepare the filling. Heat the butter in a large skillet over medium heat. When melted, add sliced squash, season liberally with salt and pepper, and cook over medium heat for about 10 minutes, tossing occasionally, until the squash has softened and given up some of its juices. Place in a bowl and refrigerate to cool. Grate the onion, reserving juice; set aside on a plate. Whisk cream, egg yolk, zest, thyme, salt, and pepper together in a small bowl.

To assemble the tart, brush the bottom, sides and tops of chilled pastry with egg wash using a pastry brush. Drain any excess onion juice and whisk it into the prepared egg/cream mixture. Line bottom of the tart evenly with the onion. Squeeze any excess liquid out of the squash between your palms in small batches, and line the squash evenly into the tart pan. Drizzle egg/cream mixture over top of the squash. Bake about 1 hour, until golden and bubbly. Remove from the oven and cool. It is best served warm, but is also delicious cold or at room temperature.

Dainty Ratatouille Tartlets with Pine Nut Pastry and Fresh Pesto Sauce

Makes 10 tartlets

Summer Ratatouille is one of the long-reigning flavor princes of the Provence region of France. A fragrant, chunky stew of eggplant, zucchini, peppers, tomatoes and garlic, it can take on a very rustic appearance. Sized down into tiny cubes, however, ratatouille becomes glamorous and is thus perfectly suited to the individual serving size of tartlets.

Though it may seem like an unnecessary step to sauté the eggplant and zucchini separately before adding them to the tomato and pepper sauce, it makes a big difference in achieving the all-important effect of subtle, layered flavors. Salting the eggplant for a few minutes prior removes excess water, adding further to the delicious flavor concentration in these pretty little tarts. I love the crunch of toasted pine nuts worked into the pastry and the bright green, garlicky brush of fresh pesto as a light sauce.

These tarts may look delicate, but they are powerfully flavorful and delicious warm, cold or at room temperature. They hold up nicely for a day or two in the fridge after being prepared and make perfect picnic fare. If you have any filling left over, work it into an omelet for a stunning breakfast, lunch or dinner.

EQUIPMENT NEEDED Ten 3 x ⅝-inch round tartlet pans with removable bottoms, one 4-inch round pastry cutter

¼ cup pine nuts

1 recipe Master Savory Pastry (substitute ¼ cup of the flour with ¼ cup roasted pine nuts) plus flour for rolling

Filling

2 small Japanese eggplant, cut into ⅛-inch dice (about 3 cups)

2 tablespoons kosher salt or sea salt

6–7 tablespoons olive oil, divided

Salt and freshly ground pepper, to taste

2 small zucchini, trimmed and cut into ⅛-inch dice (about 2½ cups)

1 small onion, finely diced

2 cloves garlic, smashed and diced

1 small green bell pepper, seeded and cut into ⅛-inch dice

1 medium tomato, finely chopped (about 1 cup)

2 tablespoons dry white wine

Light drizzle honey

Pinch red pepper flakes

Pesto

6 cloves garlic, peeled

1½ cups loosely packed fresh basil leaves, stems removed

⅓ cup pine nuts

⅓ cup grated Parmigiano-Reggiano

Salt and freshly ground pepper, to taste

⅔ cup extra virgin olive oil

1 egg wash (yolk, splash water, pinch salt blended together)

Preheat oven to 375 degrees F.

Saute the pine nuts in a small sauté pan over high heat, tossing for about 3 minutes, just until golden. Set aside to cool.

Prepare Master Savory Pastry (see page 17), substituting $^1/_4$ cup of the flour with $^1/_4$ cup cooled pine nuts and following directions for "Perfecting Pastry" (pages 17–18). Pulse with the flour and salt to combine and proceed as usual. Chill 30 minutes or overnight. Roll out as directed in Flush Tart Border (see page 18). Chill at least 20 minutes.

To prepare the filling, chop the eggplant and toss with salt. Place in a colander and drain for at least 10 minutes. Rinse thoroughly and drain, squeezing any excess liquid out of the eggplant by pressing between your palms. Heat 2–3 tablespoons olive oil over medium-high heat, then add eggplant and season with salt and pepper. Cook, tossing, for about 10 minutes, or until eggplant has just softened. Set aside to cool.

Meanwhile, heat 2 tablespoons olive oil in a separate skillet over medium heat. Add zucchini, salt and pepper. Cook about 10 minutes, until just softened. Set aside to cool.

In a large sauté pan, heat 2 tablespoons olive oil over medium heat. Add onion, garlic, and bell pepper. Cook, tossing, about 3 minutes, until just softened. Season generously with salt and pepper. Add the tomato and cook about 5 minutes to soften and break down the fruit. Season generously with salt and pepper. Increase heat to high and add wine, honey and red pepper flakes. Cook until the liquid has reduced to almost nothing. Taste and adjust seasoning as needed. Set aside to cool.

To prepare the pesto, combine garlic, basil, pine nuts, and cheese in the bowl of a food processor fitted with a steel blade. Pulse 5 or 6 times to combine. Season with salt and pepper. While running the processor, gradually stream in the olive oil until it's all incorporated. Taste and adjust seasoning.

In a large bowl, combine the cooled eggplant, zucchini, and tomato/pepper sauce with $^1/_2$ cup of the prepared pesto.

To assemble, arrange the pastry-lined tartlets pans on a baking sheet. Brush each lightly with egg wash. Fill each with about $^1/_2$ cup of the filling mixture, tapping lightly to flatten the tops. Bake about 40 minutes, until bubbly and golden. Remove from oven and let cool slightly.

Remove tartlets from their pans and serve warm, at room temperature, or cold with a small pool of the pesto for sauce. (*Note:* The pesto and the tartlets can be made a day in advance. Store both in separate airtight containers in the refrigerator, pouring a thin top "film" of olive oil over the pesto to prevent oxidation.)

Salad Niçoise Tart

Serves 8 to 10

Summer This recipe takes its nod from Nice, in the heart of Provence country in France. The pastry is pulsed together with salty, black Niçoise olives and gets a gentle flavor brush from fresh thyme. Like the salad that inspired it, the Salade Niçoise, the tart is composed of and beautifully layered with classic Niçoise players like haricot verts, boiled potatoes, roasted red pepper, capers, and pan-seared fresh tuna.

A plucky aioli, rife with garlic and anchovies, is the classic accompaniment, drizzled over the tart or pooled off to its side. Aioli is basically a flavored mayonnaise. It's a breeze to whip up in a food processor, or it can be done by hand using a whisk or a mortar and pestle. As with any emulsion sauce, the trick is to trickle the oil in slowly so that it blends nicely with the other ingredients. Assemble the tart in just minutes before serving, and pair with some fresh bread for a completely French and delicious feast made for fêtes that you will not soon forget.

EQUIPMENT NEEDED Two 13 x 4 x 1-inch rectangular tart pans with removable bottoms

1 recipe Master Savory Pastry plus 2 tablespoons freshly chopped thyme leaves and ½ cup coarsely chopped pitted Niçoise olives (or substitute Greek olives)

1 egg wash (yolk, splash water, pinch salt blended together)

Aioli

4 cloves garlic

2 tablespoons Dijon mustard

2 egg yolks

½ (2-ounce) can anchovies packed in olive oil, oil reserved

Reserved oil from anchovies plus ½ cup extra virgin olive oil

Salt and freshly ground pepper, to taste

Filling

10 baby potatoes, scrubbed, skin-on

1 red bell pepper

40 haricots verts (or standard fresh green beans), trimmed and rinsed

½ pound fresh tuna steak

Salt and pepper, to taste

2 tablespoons olive oil

2 cups arugula

Juice of ½ lemon

½ (2-ounce) can anchovies

1 tablespoon capers

Prepare the Master Savory Pastry the day before. The addition of the olives slows down the "setting up" process. Prepare according to "Perfecting Pastry" (pages 17–18), adding olives and thyme to the pastry after the butter has been pulsed in and before the water is added. Chill overnight. Roll out into a large square (see On a Roll, page 18) and fill the tart pans according to Flush Tart Border (page 18). Chill for at least 20 minutes or overnight.

Preheat oven to 375 degrees F and blind bake (page 19) pastry, brushing down pastry with egg wash after the weights are removed (20 to 30 minutes into the cooking). Finish baking until golden and crisp, a total of about 45 minutes. Remove from oven and cool. (*Note:* This can be done a day ahead. Keep the tart shells in an airtight container once cooled.)

To prepare the aioli, pulse the garlic, mustard, egg yolks, and the anchovies together in the bowl of a food processor fitted with a metal blade until chunky/smooth. Very slowly drizzle the olive oil into the mouth of the food processor while it's running. The aioli will start to set up almost immediately, resembling the texture of a thick mayonnaise. Continue until all the oil is gone, adding the reserved oil from the anchovy tin. Season to taste with salt and pepper. Scrape into a bowl and refrigerate (up to 24 hours) until ready to use. Bring to room temperature before serving.

To prepare the tart filling, pierce potatoes with a knife and boil in generously salted water until firm/tender, about 20 minutes depending on size. Drain and set aside.

Meanwhile, either roast the pepper directly over the open flame of a gas stove or place it under a hot broiler, turning occasionally, until nearly all of the surface is charred. Set aside to cool. When able to handle, remove the blackened flesh (under running water), seeds, ribs, and stem. Cut into thin strips and cut in half again, lengthwise. Set aside.

Boil beans in salted water about 4 minutes, until crisp/ tender. Remove from heat and drain, then plunge into icy water to stop the cooking. Cut into 1/4-inch lengths and set aside.

Rinse and pat the tuna steaks dry. Season generously on both sides with salt and pepper. Heat a medium-size sauté pan over medium-high heat and add the oil. When hot, add steaks and cook for 2 1/2 to 3 minutes, depending on thickness and desired temperature (I prefer medium-rare, pink on the inside); turn over and repeat. Remove from heat and set aside to rest, then cut into thin slices.

To assemble the tart, toss arugula with 2 tablespoons aioli and season lightly with salt and pepper. Arrange a bed of greens evenly on the bottom of each tart shell. Drizzle pepper, beans and tuna with lemon juice, then top the arugula with a generous helping of the roasted pepper and beans. Top with prettily arranged slices of the tuna. Quarter the still-warm potatoes lengthwise and toss lightly with a few tablespoons of aioli. Arrange along the top of the tart vertically. Scatter anchovies and capers on top.

To serve, cut the tarts into 4-inch wedges (you'll get about 4 from each tart) and serve on a plate with a pool of aioli, a sprig of thyme and a few olives if desired. Pure deliciousness!

Peach and Pancetta Tartlets with Crystallized Ginger–Spiked Fresh Chèvre

Makes 12 tartlets

Summer *The sweetness and mild acidity of a beautiful summer peach just begs for a savory companion. What better than a match with salty bacon or its Italian cured cousin, pancetta? For creaminess and tang, fresh goat cheese is blended with peach-friendly crystallized ginger. A kiss of local honey while the warm tartlets are fresh out of the oven gives the final, love-struck flavor blow. Because the peach halves are roughly the same size as the tartlets, this is an ideal individual tartlet candidate. Another big plus is that these tarts can be prepped, assembled and refrigerated several hours or a full day before baking and serving.*

EQUIPMENT NEEDED **Twelve 3 x ⅝-inch round tartlet pans with removable bottoms, one 4-inch round pastry cutter, two baking sheets**

1 recipe Master Savory Pastry (page 17)
1 tablespoon olive oil
2 cups pancetta* cut in ¼-inch cubes, divided
Salt and freshly ground pepper
1 cup fresh chèvre goat cheese
2 teaspoons coarsely chopped
    crystallized ginger**
1 egg wash (yolk, splash water, pinch
    salt blended together)
6 fresh ripe peaches, peeled, halved, and pitted
About ¼ cup local honey, to glaze

Preheat oven to 375 degrees F.

Prepare and chill the Master Savory Pastry as instructed in "Perfecting Pastry" (pages 17–18). Chill at least 30 minutes or overnight. Roll out and form the tartlets as instructed in Flush Tart Border (page 18). Arrange the prepped tartlets on two baking sheets, 6 on each, and refrigerate for 20 minutes.

Meanwhile, heat the oil in a large skillet over medium-high heat. When hot, add pancetta and season lightly with salt and pepper. Brown on all sides, tossing occasionally, for about 10 minutes, or until golden. Using a slotted spoon, transfer pancetta to a plate lined with a paper towel and refrigerate until cool. Combine cheese with ginger, blending thoroughly in a medium bowl. Season lightly with salt and pepper, if desired.

To assemble the tarts, brush the bottoms, sides and edges of the cool tart lightly with egg wash, using a pastry brush. Spread about 1 tablespoon of the cheese mixture gently along the bottom of each tartlet. Use your fingers; a spoon or spatula is clumsy and might tear the pastry. Top this with about 1 tablespoon of the cooled pancetta. Finish the tarts with a peeled peach half placed cut side down in the center of each tart. Place tart-laden baking sheets on two central oven racks and bake about 1 hour, until golden and bubbly. Remove and set to cool slightly. Brush the peaches and edges of the tart with a light honey glaze using a pastry brush. Serve warm.

*Ask for the pancetta in its whole, rolled form and then slice and cut it into little cubes at home. Great-quality bacon can be substituted.

**You can substitute about ¼ teaspoon dried ginger.

Panna Cotta Tart with Roasted Fresh Figs in Balsamic Honey Sauce

Serves 8

Summer/Fall Of all things "fruit," figs are indisputably my favorite. Sensual, satisfying, nutritious, and highly versatile, figs are as delicious fresh off the tree as they are in a sauce, or in this case, a tart. The sweetness of the figs roasted in a balsamic vinegar and honey glaze plays beautiful texture and flavor contrasts with a savory, thyme-infused, Roquefort panna cotta (a "cooked cream" thickened lightly with gelatin). "Lining" the bottom of the prepped, rolled pastry with a layer of pretty pink prosciutto (Italian cured ham) gives a necessary salty kick to another thin layer of fig preserves, while simultaneously sealing the pastry from the soft filling to ensure crispness. This recipe works equally well prepared as a single tart or as individual tartlets, depending on your mood. I prefer it as a single tart because the sliced wedges show off the beautiful layers of the tart. Both the roasted figs/sauce and tart can be made a day ahead and refrigerated, but don't dress the tart slices (or tartlets) with the figs/sauce until service, or the glaze will bleed into the lovely, white panna cotta.

EQUIPMENT NEEDED One 9 x 1-inch round tart pan with removable bottom.

1 recipe Master Savory Pastry (page 17)
1 egg wash (yolk, splash water, pinch
   salt blended together)

Fig Sauce
2½ cups fresh whole figs, any
   tough, long stems removed
3 tablespoons aged Modena balsamic vinegar
2 tablespoons honey (preferably local)
Salt and freshly ground pepper

Panna Cotta
1 packet powdered gelatin
   (about 4½ teaspoons)
3 tablespoons cold water
2 cups half-and-half
½ cup Roquefort or other mild
   blue cheese, crumbled
1 tablespoon chopped fresh thyme leaves
Salt and freshly ground pepper, to taste

Additional Fillings
3 very thin slices prosciutto
4 tablespoons fig preserves

Preheat oven to 375 degrees F.

Prepare Master Savory Pastry following directions for "Perfecting Pastry" (pages 17–18). Chill 30 minutes or overnight. Roll out with an Elevated Tart Border (see page 18). Chill for at least 20 minutes before using. Brush with egg wash and blind bake (see page 19) about 30 minutes, until golden brown. Remove from oven and cool at room temperature.

While the tart shell is baking, roast the figs in the same 375 degree F oven. Combine the fresh figs with the balsamic vinegar, honey, salt and pepper in a medium bowl, tossing gently with your hands to coat. Arrange in a single layer in a roasting pan and bake about 20 minutes, until somewhat softened and the juices have reduced to form a thick, dark glaze. Remove from the oven and set aside to cool. When cool enough to handle, slice each fig in half vertically, then return to the sauce. (Note: This can be made a day or two before serving the tarts and refrigerated in an airtight container. Bring to room temperature before serving).

For the panna cotta, combine the gelatin and water in a medium bowl, stirring to dissolve. Set aside for 10 minutes. In a medium pot, combine the half-and-half, cheese, thyme, salt, and pepper. Bring to a simmer over medium-high heat for about 5 minutes, whisking constantly to combine and melt the cheese and to prevent scalding. Taste and adjust seasoning as needed. Let cool slightly. Now whisk the warm milk mixture slowly into the prepped gelatin mixture, whisking constantly to combine. Set aside. (Note: The mixture should be just warm to the touch before pouring it into the prepped tart shell, so prepare it as the shell is nearly finished baking or has already come out of the oven. The shell needs to be fully cooled before filling).

To assemble, brush the bottom of the cooled shell with the fig preserves, using a pastry brush to form an even, smooth layer. Arrange the three slices of prosciutto so their edges just overlap and they fully "line" the bottom of the tart. Pour in the just warm panna cotta, being careful not to spill or overfill. Refrigerate until the panna cotta has set fully, about 4 hours. (Note: This can be done the day before serving. Be sure to wrap the tart securely with plastic wrap.)

To serve, slice the tart into eight wedges using a sharp bread knife to get clean edges. Dress each tart wedge with several roasted fig halves and a generous drizzle (about 1 tablespoon) of the glaze. Garnish with fresh thyme.

Great Party Idea!

I intentionally create more panna cotta than the tart can hold for this recipe, because any extra double as a fabulously simple and delicious alternative to a cheese plate. Simply pour the extra panna cotta into a small bowl lightly oiled with a flavorless oil like vegetable or canola. Fill with the warm mixture, cover and refrigerate overnight. Un-mold the panna cotta onto a pretty platter. Put a ramekin full of fig preserves and some crisp crackers alongside. Top the panna cotta with any remaining roasted figs and some sliced prosciutto, and garnish with fresh thyme.

Eggplant and Cream Cheese Tapenade Tartlets

Makes 12 Tartlets

Summer/Fall Mellow eggplant sits atop a bed of cream cheese blended with sweet basil and salty olives for these sophisticated tartlets. Pair with a chilled Rose for an indulgent late-summer aperitif for easy entertaining.

EQUIPMENT NEEDED **One 3½-inch round pastry cutter, parchment paper**

2 sheets Pepperidge Farms puff pastry

1 small eggplant, trimmed, peeled, and
    cut into ¼-inch-thick slices

¼ cup extra virgin olive oil

Sea salt or kosher salt and
    freshly ground pepper

Cream Cheese Filling

½ cup cream cheese

1 tablespoon finely chopped fresh basil

Zest of 1 lemon

1 large clove garlic, peeled, smashed
    and finely chopped

¼ cup finely chopped pitted green olives

Sea salt or kosher salt and freshly
    ground pepper, to taste

1 egg wash (yolk, pinch salt, splash
    water blended together)

Fresh basil sprigs, for garnish

Thaw puff pastry according to package directions, about 40 minutes at room temperature.

Preheat oven to 400 degrees F.

Arrange eggplant on a baking sheet in a single layer. Drizzle lightly with olive oil. Season liberally with salt and pepper. Bake about 15 minutes, until softened and slightly shrunken. Remove from the oven and set aside to cool, but leave the oven on. When the eggplant is cool, chop it with a chef's knife into pieces about the size of peas.

Meanwhile, prepare the cream cheese filling by combining all the ingredients, except garnishing basil, in a small bowl, stirring well with a wooden spoon to combine. Taste and adjust seasonings as needed.

To assemble the tarts, arrange the thawed pastry sheets on a lightly floured work surface. Gently press out any rough seams with your fingertips to smooth. Cut the pastry with the round cutter to form rounds; avoid wasting pastry. You should get 12 rounds from the pastry. Arrange each on a baking sheet lined with parchment paper, spacing them about ½ inch apart to allow space for them to "puff." Gently coat the top (not the sides) of the pastry with egg wash. Fill each tartlet with one tablespoon of the cream cheese mixture, spreading with a spoon. Leave ¼ inch border of naked pastry, which will become the sides of the tart as the pastry rises. Top cream cheese with 1 heaping tablespoon of eggplant. Bake for 25 minutes, or until puffy and golden. Remove and let cool slightly. Serve warm on a platter or on individual cocktail plates sprinkled with fresh basil.

Crunchy Crab Cup Canapés

Makes 18 individual canapés

Summer/Fall Seasonal fresh crab availability varies depending on where you live. The fattest season for blue crab in Charleston, South Carolina, is summer, but it sweetly wades its way into early fall. If you can find fresh lump crabmeat (which comes from the body of any crab), feel free to gently sauté it in a bit of butter over medium-high heat, seasoning lightly. Be careful not to break up the big chunks of crab as you go. Alternatively, pasteurized lump crab is available in the refrigerated section of the fish department of most groceries throughout the year and does not require cooking. I love it here in these bite-size cups of crab love. They're the perfect canapé for an easy, sophisticated cocktail party and are a snap to put together.

EQUIPMENT NEEDED **2-inch round pastry cutter, two 12-cup mini-muffin pans**

1 recipe Master Savory Pastry (page 17)
1 egg wash (yolk, pinch salt, splash
    water blended together)

Crabmeat Filling

1½ cups pasteurized lump crabmeat
2 tablespoons capers
½ cup finely chopped red onion
1 tablespoon finely chopped fresh chives
Zest of 1 lime
1 teaspoon Old Bay Seasoning

3 tablespoons mayonnaise
1 tablespoon Dijon or sweet/hot mustard
2 teaspoons fresh lime juice
Generous dash hot sauce
Salt and freshly ground pepper, to taste

Preheat oven to 375 degrees F.

Prepare Master Savory Pastry following directions for "Perfecting Pastry" (pages 17–18). Chill 30 minutes or overnight. Roll out to ⅛-inch thickness, following directions for On a Roll (page 18). Using the pastry cutter, cut out the rounds, working tightly to avoid pastry waste. Gently ease the rounds into the mini-muffin molds. The border should be flush with the top of the mold. Chill for at least 20 minutes. Blind bake (see page 19) until lightly browned. Remove pie weights and brush each lightly with the egg wash. Bake an additional 15 minutes, or until completely cooked and deep, golden brown. Set aside to cool. (Note: The pastry cups can be made a day ahead, cooled fully, and stored in an airtight container for up to 24 hours.)

To prepare the filling on the day of service, very gently place the crab, capers, onion, chives, and zest in a medium bowl. In a small bowl, whisk together the remaining ingredients. Whisk vigorously to combine. Top the crab mixture with the blended mixture and fold gently with a wooden spoon to combine, being careful not to break up the crab. Taste and adjust seasoning as needed.

Fill the canapé cups within an hour of serving. Keep cold prior to service. Garnish with a few short spears of fresh chives, if desired.

Pimento Cheeseburger Tartlets

Makes 10 individual tartlets

Summer/Fall **Plucky, prepared**
pimento cheese (see Purely Pimento, page 81)
bubbles along the top of miniature burgers
nestled within golden tartlet shells to create
these five- or six-bite wonders. I like to think
of them as dressed-up, open-faced sliders. The
perfect mess-free *party food, they work equally*
as well for football watching get-togethers as
they do for elegant cocktail parties.

EQUIPMENT NEEDED **Ten 3⅝ x 1-inch round
tartlet pans with removable bottoms, one 4-inch
round pastry cutter**

1 recipe Master Savory Pastry (page 17)
1 egg wash (yolk, pinch salt, splash
    water blended together)

Filling

1 pound 85% lean ground chuck beef or sirloin
2 tablespoons finely chopped fresh parsley
½ teaspoon kosher salt or sea salt
½ teaspoon freshly ground black pepper
2 teaspoons Worcestershire sauce
2 cloves garlic, mashed and finely chopped
1 teaspoon Dijon mustard

Topping

¼ red onion, peeled and very thinly sliced
½ pound preferred brand prepared
    pimento cheese
10 small fresh parsley leaves, for garnish
Ketchup

Preheat oven to 375 degrees F.

Prepare Master Savory Pastry following directions for
"Perfecting Pastry" (pages 17–18). Chill 30 minutes
or overnight. Roll out to ⅛-inch thickness, following
directions for On a Roll (page 18). Using the pastry cutter,
cut out the rounds, working tightly to avoid pastry waste.
Gently ease the rounds into tartlet pans, pressing to guide
the pastry into the sides of the pans. The border should
be flush with the top of the mold. Using a pastry brush,
lightly brush the bottoms, sides and top of the pastry with
the egg wash. Arrange on a baking sheet and chill in the
refrigerator for at least 20 minutes.

Meanwhile, in a medium bowl, combine the beef,
parsley, salt, pepper, Worcestershire sauce, garlic, and
mustard. Using clean hands, blend until uniform and well
combined. Verify taste by forming a tiny patty and cooking
it either in the microwave or in a small sauté pan. Taste
and adjust seasoning as needed. Form 10 small patties
using 3 tablespoons of the filling for each. Press the patties
into the prepared tart shells, gently guiding the meat to
all sides of the pastry. The top of the patties should be flat
and the thickness should be even once they're inside the
pastry shells. Bake for 15 minutes.

Remove the tartlets from the oven and top each
with 4 or 5 slivers of the onion and 1 tablespoon of
the pimento cheese in the center of each. Bake for
15 additional minutes, or until bubbly and golden.
Remove from the oven and cool at room temperature for
10 minutes. Garnish each with a parsley leaf and a tiny
drop of ketchup at the base of the parsley. Serve warm.
(Note: The pastry and the filling can be prepared and
refrigerated, covered, overnight; assemble and bake just
before serving).

Lowcountry Boil Puff Tart

Makes 8 entrée or 32 appetizer portions

Summer/Fall *This delectable tart brings together the fabled Lowcountry boil ingredients of corn, shrimp, kielbasa, potatoes and a kiss of Old Bay. But instead of being poured out onto newspaper for greedy, messy consumption, as is usually done, the ingredients are encased in a crunchy, buttery puff pastry shell. The shrimp cooks through perfectly while the pastry bakes, and the pre-cooked kielbasa warms to a gleaming golden brown without drying out.*

EQUIPMENT NEEDED **Baking sheet, parchment paper**

2 sheets Pepperidge Farm Puff Pastry Sheets

1 egg wash (yolk, pinch salt, splash water blended together)

1 large Yukon Gold potato, peeled and cut into 1-inch cubes (making 2 cups)

$1/2$ teaspoon kosher salt or sea salt

Cold water to cover

2 tablespoons butter

$1/2$ cup heavy cream

Kosher salt or sea salt and freshly ground black pepper, to taste, divided

1 teaspoon Old Bay Seasoning

$3/4$ cup raw corn, fresh and seasonal, or substitute frozen

$3/4$ pounds raw shrimp, peeled, deveined and cut into $1/2$-inch lengths (making 2 cups)

1 tablespoon olive oil

$1/2$ teaspoon dried thyme (or $1 1/2$ teaspoons fresh thyme leaves)

$1 1/2$ cups pre-cooked kielbasa, cut into $1/2$-inch cubes

Fresh thyme or parsley sprigs for garnish

Forty minutes before compiling and baking, thaw the pastry according to pastry directions. Prepare the egg wash and set aside.

For the filling, place potatoes and salt in a medium sauce pan with enough cold water to just cover. Bring to a boil over high heat, then reduce to medium. Cook about 15 minutes, until the potatoes are fork-tender. Drain the potatoes thoroughly and return to the same pan they were cooked in. Add butter, cream, salt, pepper, and Old Bay Seasoning. Mash with a potato masher until all the liquid and seasonings are incorporated and the potatoes have a chunky/smooth texture. Taste and adjust seasonings. Add more liquid if needed. Potatoes should be stiff enough to stand up in a spoon. Fold in the corn with a wooden spoon. Turn out into a shallow bowl and refrigerate until room temperature or cool. (Note: The potatoes can be prepared the day before and refrigerated covered).

Meanwhile, combine the shrimp, oil, salt and pepper to taste, thyme and kielbasa in a medium bowl and toss to coat. Unfold the thawed pastry and arrange squares evenly spaced on a parchment paper–lined baking sheet. Brush each square with egg wash, being careful to brush the entire top but not letting the wash drip down the sides.

Preheat oven to 400 degrees F.

To assemble, plop half of the cooled potato mixture into the middle of each tart. Using a spatula, evenly spread the potatoes around the pastry, forming a potato square and leaving $1/2$ inch of naked pastry that will rise to form the puff pastry borders. Evenly arrange the shrimp/kielbasa mixture on top of the potatoes. Bake 20 to 25 minutes, until bubbly and golden. Serve warm as an appetizer portion or main course. Garnish with fresh parsley or thyme sprigs.

Beefy Pear, Roquefort and Walnut Free-Form Tarts

Makes two tarts, serves 8 to 12

Fall *This free-form savory/sweet tart (a.k.a. galette) is drenched in the pungent flavors of the Mediterranean. Local honey and fresh lemon juice provide the sauce that gently envelops soft Bartlett pears and toothsome walnuts. Bresaola—air-dried salted beef that hails from Italy—gives it beefy depth and chew. It all gets topped off with mild Roquefort cheese and a generous dusting of freshly ground black pepper. This tart is a wonderful celebration of the fall season and is fabulous for entertaining both for its simplicity and its rustic elegance.*

EQUIPMENT NEEDED **Baking sheet, parchment paper**

1 recipe Master Savory Pastry plus
    2 teaspoons dried thyme leaves

Filling

3 ripe but still firm Bartlett pears,
    cored and thinly sliced
Juice of 1 lemon
3/4 cup coarsely chopped dried apricots
6 slices bresaola (available at most grocery
    deli counters), coarsely chopped
3/4 cup coarsely chopped walnuts
3/4 cup local honey
1 teaspoon coarsely ground black pepper
Pinch salt
Generous dash cinnamon
2 tablespoons flour
1 egg wash (yolk, pinch salt, splash
    water blended together)

Topping

1/2 cup Roquefort or another mild
    blue cheese, crumbled
Freshly ground pepper

Preheat oven to 375 degrees F.

Prepare Master Savory Pastry (see page 17). Add 2 teaspoons thyme to the master recipe after the butter has been pulsed in pastry and before adding the water. Follow directions for "Perfecting Pastry" (pages 17–18). Chill 30 minutes or overnight.

In a large bowl, gently toss together all of the filling ingredients, being careful to coat all the fruit and filling completely. Chill for 20 minutes.

Roll out the pastry on a lightly floured surface in two 10–12-inch rounds, following directions from On a Roll (page 18). Using your rolling pin, ease each pastry onto a baking sheet lined with parchment paper. Plop the filling into the center of the pastry circle and spread evenly into a circle, until the filling is about 1 inch thick. Trim borders of the pastry circle with kitchen scissors so you have about 2 inches of free pastry space all around the filling. (Note: It does not have to be perfectly symmetrical. You are shooting for a rustic, country look). Use your palm to cup the pastry around the filling, folding in creases about every two inches as you move around the filling. Press gently with the palm of your hand to make sure everything is sealed. Brush the pastry top and sides lightly with egg wash. Sprinkle the open part of the filling with cheese and pepper. Bake 45 to 50 minutes, until golden and bubbly.

Serve warm or at room temperature as an appetizer, main course or dessert.

Sage Green Apple and Aged Cheddar Tart

Makes 9 appetizer portions or 4 entrée portions

Fall *Apples sit firmly atop my preferred autumnal food heap. Winesap, Honeycrisp, McIntosh and oodles of heirloom varieties tempt me with their tart, sweet, crispness. Eaten raw out of the palm or nestled into a tart, they offer infinite variety and goodness.*

In this tart, the play is on the perennial pairing of apples and cheese. The edgy tartness of Granny Smith apples is idyllic with a best-quality aged, extra sharp cheddar cheese. Sage seals the deal with its effortlessly earthy touch.

This tart comes together in minutes. Assemble it just before your cocktail guests arrive and bake while they wait. The house is filled with wonderful aromas and the tart bakes in just 20 to 25 minutes. Serve it very warm, while the cheese is still gooey and gently oozing from the edges of the tart wedges. This tart makes the perfect appetizer companion to a sturdy red wine, or pair it with a salad to make a complete meal.

EQUIPMENT NEEDED **Parchment paper, baking sheet**

1 sheet Pepperidge Farm puff pastry, thawed per box directions
1 egg wash (yolk, pinch salt, splash water blended together)
2 Granny Smith apples, halved and cored
2 tablespoons butter
1 teaspoon ground black pepper
Pinch kosher salt or sea salt
1 tablespoon dried sage leaves, plus extra for garnish
3 cups grated extra sharp yellow cheddar cheese

Thaw pastry at room temperature according to package directions (about 40 minutes). Preheat oven to 400 degrees F.

Arrange thawed puff pastry on a baking sheet lined with parchment paper. Refrigerate while preparing the filling. Prepare the egg wash and set aside.

Cut the apples, skin-on, so thin that you can practically see through them. Heat the butter in a large skillet over medium-high heat. Add apples, pepper, salt, and sage. Toss to coat, then cook, tossing occasionally, for 5 minutes, or until the apples have begun to soften and lightly brown. Remove from heat, transfer to a bowl, and refrigerate to let cool.

Meanwhile, grate cheese at a medium-size grate. When the apples are cool, toss half of the cheese with the apples. Arrange this mixture in the center of the puff pastry sheet, spreading gently and evenly to the edges, leaving 1/2 inch border of naked pastry. Top apples evenly with the remaining cheese, taking care not to drizzle over the border. Brush the naked border lightly with egg wash. Bake for 20 to 25 minutes, or until the pastry is fully puffed and a rich golden brown and the cheese is melted and bubbly. Let cool for 10 minutes then serve immediately. For appetizer portions, cut through the tart in 3 bars vertically and horizontally. For entrée portions, cut the tart into 4 even squares. Garnish with a final pass of ground black pepper and a light drizzle of dried sage if desired.

Elegant Oyster Mushroom Pearl Puffs

Makes 18 individual servings

Fall *Though mushrooms are available most of the year, I think of mushroom dishes when summer heat cedes to the shorter, cooler days of fall. The creamy, pale gray color of the mild, silky oyster mushroom does indeed resemble a beautiful fresh oyster. Its gentle texture and fluttery edges are embraced here with delicate puff pastry. The mushrooms are topped with a blend of cream cheese, grated Parmigiano-Reggiano, and fresh herbs. Use these highly perishable mushrooms the day you buy them, or as soon as possible. Don't season with salt until after they've given off their high water content during the saute phase.*

EQUIPMENT NEEDED parchment paper, baking sheet, 2¾-inch round pastry cutter

1 box (2 sheets) Pepperidge Farm Puff Pastry

Mushroom Filling

2 tablespoons olive oil

1 medium onion, finely chopped

2 cloves garlic, mashed and finely chopped

1 pound oyster mushrooms, tough
   stems discarded, chopped in ¼-
   inch dice (yields about 5 cups)

2 tablespoons sherry vinegar

2 tablespoons dry sherry

2 teaspoons honey

Salt and freshly ground pepper, to taste

Cream Cheese Topping

½ cup cream cheese

½ cup grated Parmigiano-Reggiano

7 tablespoons chopped chives, divided

1 tablespoon finely chopped parsley

Salt and freshly ground pepper, to taste

1 egg wash (yolk, pinch salt, splash
   water blended together)

Thaw pastry at room temperature according to package directions (about 40 minutes). Preheat oven to 400 degrees F.

Meanwhile, prepare the mushroom filling. Heat oil in a large, deep saute pan over medium heat. Saute onion and garlic about 5 minutes, until both have softened and are translucent. Add mushrooms and cook, stirring, another 5 minutes. Increase heat to high and add the vinegar, tossing to coat. Cook for 1 minute to reduce, then add the sherry. Cook for 1 minute to reduce. Stir in the honey, and season to taste with salt and pepper. Remove from heat and turn out onto a large plate. Refrigerate to cool.

Prepare the cheese topping. In a small bowl, combine cheeses, chives, parsley, salt, and pepper, blending gently with a fork or spoon to combine. Refrigerate. (Note: Both fillings can be prepared a day ahead and refrigerated in airtight containers.)

To assemble tarts, gently unfold the thawed puff pastry sheets and arrange on a lightly floured work surface. Gently press out any kinks in the pastry folds with your fingertips. Working quickly, cut rounds out of the pastry with your pastry round. Arrange them on a baking sheet lined with parchment paper. Top each round with a tablespoon of the cooled mushroom mixture, then a heaping teaspoon of the cheese mixture, leaving ¼ inch rim of naked pastry around the edges. Brush the naked pastry lightly with egg wash, using a pastry brush or your fingertips. Refrigerate for 10 minutes to chill. Bake on the center rack of the hot oven about 20 to 25 minutes, until golden and puffed. Serve warm with a little pool of the warm mushroom mixture (you will have some left over), and sprinkle bits of freshly chopped chives over the top.

Tasso Tussled Sweet Potato and Arugula Tartlets

Makes 10 to 12 Tartlets

Fall/Spring Sweet potatoes and arugula (also called "rocket") grow best in the cooler seasons of fall and spring. Though sweet potatoes are often served loaded with sugar and fat at calorie-drunk Thanksgiving tables, they have a rich, nutty, savory flavor and deep color in their virgin state. Arugula provides a deep green lining at the bottom of the tartlets that gives a peppery taste surprise in every bite. Crumbled candied pecans scattered over the top add just the right sweetness to counter the Cajun kick of tasso ham, which is prepared from cured and smoked pork butt. I'm lucky enough to find it a my local farmers market at Meathouse's stand, featuring the tasty works of the charming husband and wife team of Jason and Katie Houser. If you can't find it, substitute bacon or pancetta, and feel free to spice up either with a little cayenne and fresh garlic as it cooks.

EQUIPMENT NEEDED Ten to twelve $3\frac{5}{8}$ x 1-inch round tartlet pans with removable bottoms, one 4-inch round pastry cutter

1 recipe Master Savory Pastry
1 egg wash (yolk, pinch salt, splash water blended together)

Fillings

2 large sweet potatoes, skin on and pierced with a fork
1 tablespoon olive oil
1 cup ¼-inch cubes tasso ham
4 cups coarsely chopped fresh arugula, stems removed
Salt and freshly ground pepper, to taste

Candied Nuts

1 tablespoon butter
1 cup fresh pecan halves, coarsely chopped
Salt and freshly ground pepper, to taste
½ teaspoon ground chipotle chili pepper
2 teaspoons granulated sugar

Finish the Fillings

½ teaspoon salt and freshly ground pepper
2 tablespoons (local) honey
½ teaspoon ground cinnamon
½ cup half-and-half
1 egg

Prepare Master Savory Pastry as described in "Perfecting Pastry" (pages 17–18). Chill at least 30 minutes or overnight. Roll out on a lightly floured surface to about ¼-inch thickness. Working tightly to avoid waste, cut

rounds with the pastry cutter. Line the tartlet pans with the pastry, pressing it delicately into the edges and forming a small, ¼-inch-high border (see Elevated Tart Border, page 18). Chill in the refrigerator for at least 20 minutes. Preheat oven to 375 degrees F. Bake the tartlets according to Blind Baking (pages 19) for 20 minutes, or until the tartlets have begun to set. Remove the pie weights and their liners and, using a pastry brush, coat with a light layer of egg wash. Continue baking for 20 additional minutes.

While the pastry is pre-baking, place the two sweet potatoes in the hot oven to bake, skin-on. Bake until softened, 40 to 50 minutes. Remove to cool at room temperature.

Meanwhile, heat olive oil in a large saute pan over medium-high heat. When sizzling, add the ham and brown on all sides (about 5 minutes), tossing from time to time. Add the arugula all at once, and stir to coat. It will wilt and break down almost immediately. Cook only about 3 minutes so it retains its bright green color and chewy texture. Season liberally with salt and pepper to taste. Set aside to cool, draining off any excess liquid.

To prepare the candied nuts, heat butter in a medium saute pan. When sizzling, add pecans, salt, peppers, and sugar. Toss to coat, stirring occasionally. Cook about 5 minutes, until just evenly browned; watch carefully so the nuts do not burn. Drain on paper towels and set aside.

Once the potatoes are cool enough to handle, peel, and place the cooked flesh in a large bowl with salt and pepper, honey, cinnamon, half-and-half, and egg. Beat with a hand-held mixer on medium-high until frothy and light, about 2 minutes. Taste and adjust seasonings as needed.

To assemble the tartlets, line each with about 1 tablespoon of the cooled arugula mixture. Top with 3 tablespoons of the potato mixture. Arrange the tartlets on a baking sheet and bake at 375 degrees F for 40 to 45 minutes. Remove from the oven and let cool for 10 to 15 minutes. Finely chop the cooled nuts and sprinkle about 1 tablespoon over each tartlet. Serve tartlets warm, drizzling lightly with a bit of honey if desired.

Confit of Onion and Fennel on an Orange-Basil Ricotta Bed

Makes two 6 x 6-inch tarts and serves 16 appetizer portions or 8 full portions

Spring *Because onion and fennel are readily available throughout late summer, fall and spring, this is technically a tart for all seasons. The pale green color, light licorice taste of fennel and citrus edge of fresh orange juice somehow seem to say spring, however, especially with the fluffy ricotta bed and light, flaky pastry. This tart strikes me as particularly feminine and, as such, just the perfect item to serve at a bridal luncheon or bridge party. Pernod, an anise-flavored liqueur, enhances the subtle nuance of the fennel flavor, while salty, black kalamata olives make flavorful topping focal points. Because the flavors are so delicate in this tart, you'll want to use best-quality extra virgin olive oil. This tart is super easy to make and comes together in just minutes.*

EQUIPMENT NEEDED 1 sheet pan, parchment paper

2 square sheets Pepperidge Farms puff pastry

Filling
2 tablespoons extra virgin olive oil
3 small fennel bulbs, green fronds and
　　stems removed (but reserved),
　　halved, cored, and thinly sliced
1 large white onion, peeled, halved, thinly sliced
Salt and freshly ground pepper
Juice of 1/2 orange (about 3 tablespoons)
1/2 cup Pernod
2 tablespoons chopped green fronds

Ricotta Bed
1/2 cup whole or part-skim ricotta
Zest of 1 orange
6 leaves fresh basil, cut into chiffonade
　　(see sidebar, page 55)
1 egg yolk
Salt and freshly ground pepper
About 30 pitted kalamata olives
1 egg wash (yolk, pinch salt, splash
　　water blended together)

About 40 minutes before baking, remove the prepared puff pastry from the freezer and thaw at room temperature. Preheat oven to 400 degrees F.

Prepare the filling by heating the olive oil over medium heat in a large skillet. When hot, add fennel and onion. Season with salt and pepper. Toss to coat and continue cooking for about 20 minutes, until it's very soft and tender but not browned. Add orange juice, increase heat to high, and cook until the juice is reduced to a glaze. Add Pernod. Taste and adjust seasoning as needed. Remove from heat and stir in the reserved feathery fennel fronds. Turn out the mixture onto a large plate and refrigerate to cool completely.

Meanwhile, combine the ricotta, zest, basil, egg yolk, salt, and pepper in a small bowl, stirring well to combine. Set aside.

Gently unfold the puff pastry sheets and arrange each on a parchment-lined baking sheet. If there are any creases, use your fingertips to even them out and "repair" the pastry. Place equal parts of ricotta in the center of each sheet.

Spread out evenly to form a thin layer, leaving $1/2$ inch naked space around the edge of pastry. (This will rise to form the border.) Top this with equal parts of the cooled fennel and onion confit. Scatter olives across the tops of both tarts, avoiding pastry edges. Brush the naked edges of the puff pastry using a pastry brush. Bake the tarts about 15 to 20 minutes, until golden and puffed. Serve fresh from the oven or at room temperature.

Chiffonade is a French word that simply means "cut into thin strips." It works particularly well with basil, which is a tender herb that can bruise and discolor if roughly handled. To chiffonade, simply stack and gently roll the leaves into a cigar-like bundle. Then quickly and neatly cut through it to form $1/8$-inch-thick strips, and you have beautifully green basil confetti.

Vidalia Onion Tart with Bacon, Honey and Fresh Thyme

Serves 10 to 12

Spring/Summer **This tart, featured in my Southern Farmers Market Cookbook, is so delicious that I decided to include it in this book as well. It features those sweet belles from Vidalia, Georgia, known as Vidalia onions.** *They are available through spring and summer and are quickly snatched up from market bins. Vidalia's signature sweetness is gorgeous with the saltiness of bacon and the mild, lemony bite of fresh thyme in this savory tart. I like this best served in a big, dramatic round tart pan for lean, long slivers and a special presentation, so I use the biggest one I own. Regardless of size, this tart hits a home run with tart fans every single fail-proof time.*

EQUIPMENT NEEDED **One 12 x 1-inch round tart pan with removable bottom**

1 recipe Master Savory Pastry
Egg wash (yolk, pinch salt, splash
　　water blended together)

Filling

4 slices bacon
5 large Vidalia onions peeled,
　　halved and thinly sliced
Kosher salt or sea salt and freshly
　　ground pepper, to taste
2 tablespoons coarsely chopped
　　fresh thyme leaves
1/2 cup dry white wine

3 tablespoons honey
1 egg, beaten
2 tablespoons whole cream

Prepare and rest Master Savory Pastry as described in "Perfecting Pastry" (pages 17–18). Chill at least 30 minutes or overnight. Preheat oven to 375 degrees F. Roll out the pastry according to On a Roll (page 18) and form an elevated border according to Elevated Tart Border (page 18). Refrigerate for at least 20 minutes. Blind bake (see Blind Baking, page 19), brushing down with egg wash once the pie weights are removed, about 20 minutes into the cooking. Cook another 10 minutes, until just golden. Remove from the oven and set aside until ready to fill.

To prepare the filling, heat a large sauté pan over medium-high heat. Add the bacon in a single layer and cook, turning as needed, until it is crispy and the fat has been rendered. Transfer bacon to drain and cool on paper towels; chop coarsely once cool enough to handle. Reserve 2 tablespoons bacon fat in the pan and reduce heat to medium. Add onions, salt, pepper, and thyme. Cook over medium heat until onions have softened, stirring about every 5 minutes. Do not let the onions brown! After about 20 minutes, add wine and increase heat to medium-high. Cook the wine down to a glaze, about 3 minutes. Reduce heat to medium-low and add the honey and reserved chopped bacon. Stir and cook 5 minutes more. Remove onion mixture from the heat and spoon into a shallow pan; refrigerate to cool. When cool, drain off any excess pan juices and stir in the egg and cream. Adjust seasonings as needed.

Reduce oven temperature to 350 degrees F. Fill the pastry crust with the onion mixture and bake about 35 minutes, until golden brown and the filling is set. Serve warm or at room temperature.

Savory Pies and Pot Pies

Comforting little individual servings of pot pie bring out the kid in everyone and are the consummate comfort food. Breaking through a rustic, golden brown crust to find out what treasure lurks just below the surface and nabbing a bite of pastry along the way is just part of their charm. What I love about all the pies in this chapter is that the pastry and fillings can (and really should) be prepared a day or two in advance. They can be assembled the day you want to use them and baked just before service. This provides the cook the pleasures of calm, quiet assembly the day of cooking and inhaling their buttery goodness as they bake.

Shapely Shepherd's Pie

Serves 8

Spring Fluffy mashed potatoes topped with fragrant grass-fed beef and a layer of spring peas wrapped with a casing of buttery pastry make this dish a winner any time of year. In the spring, grass-fed beef (which has a distinctly sweet, herbaceous flavor, is lower in fat and higher in Omega-3's) and peas are at their freshness and flavor peak. So it's perhaps best to try this recipe on cooler, early spring evenings. Grass-fed beef can be exchanged for ground lamb, or traditional beef and frozen peas work just fine as a substitute for fresh spring peas. Look for grass-fed beef at your local farmers market. You'll be glad you did. The soulful heartiness of this pie, which typically comes without a pastry wrapper, demands a deep-dish pie pan and a big appetite for deliciousness.

EQUIPMENT NEEDED One 9-inch deep-dish (2–3 inches) pie pan

1 recipe Master Savory Pastry

Mashed Potatoes
2 russet potatoes, peeled and cut into 2-inch cubes (about 4 cups)
2 teaspoons kosher salt, divided
Water to cover
1/4–1/2 cup whole cream (depending on desired texture)
2–3 tablespoons sweet butter
1/2 teaspoon prepared horseradish
Salt and freshly ground pepper to taste

Peas
2 cups shelled fresh peas, blanched and refreshed, or 2 cups frozen peas
1 tablespoon plus 2 teaspoons salt

Meat Filling
1 tablespoon olive oil
1 pound ground grass-fed beef
Salt and freshly ground pepper to taste
1 small onion, peeled and finely chopped
2 cloves garlic, smashed
1 1/2 cups minced fresh carrots
2 tablespoons finely chopped fresh parsley
2 scallions, trimmed and coarsely chopped
1 tablespoon Worcestershire sauce
1 tablespoon Dijon mustard

Finishing
1 egg wash (yolk mixed with a sprinkle of water, dash of salt)
1 cup sour cream
1 tablespoon Dijon mustard
1 tablespoon prepared horseradish
Freshly ground black pepper

Prepare the Master Savory Pastry according to "Perfecting Pastry" (pages 17–18). Chill 30 minutes or overnight. Roll out to form an elevated pie border (see Elevated Tart Border, page 18). Chill completely for at least 20 minutes.

For the mashed potatoes, place the peeled, chopped potatoes in a medium pan with salt and enough water to cover. Bring to a boil then reduce to a gentle simmer and cook until potatoes are tender, about 15 to 20 minutes. Drain potatoes in a colander; return to the same pan and let them steam over low heat for 1 to 2 minutes to remove any excess water. Add the cream, butter, horseradish, and seasoning. Mash with a potato masher, stirring to incorporate all of the ingredients. Taste and adjust seasoning as needed. Let cool, then refrigerate to chill completely.

For the peas, bring a medium pot of generously salted water to a boil. Add peas and blanch for about 1 minute. Drain in a colander and "shock" by running very cold water over the peas. (If using frozen peas, skip this step.)

To make the meat filling, heat olive oil in a large skillet over medium-high heat. Add beef, season generously with salt and pepper, and brown for 4 to 5 minutes, stirring to break up and cook evenly. Drain off any excess fat, leaving 1–2 tablespoons in the pan. Reduce heat to medium. Add onion, garlic, and carrots; stir to coat. Let vegetables cook into the meat and just wilt, about 3 minutes. Remove from heat and stir in parsley, scallions, Worcestershire, and mustard. Taste and adjust seasonings as necessary. Refrigerate to chill the meat mixture completely.

Putting it together: Preheat the oven to 375 degrees F. Gently brush the bottom, sides and edges of the chilled pastry shell with the egg wash using a pastry brush. Spoon about 1 cup of the potatoes into the bottom of the prepared pie pastry, smoothing to distribute gently along the bottom and about 2 inches of the sides. Add all of the cooled beef mixture, and spread evenly. Top this with the cooled blanched peas or 2 cups of frozen. Top with the remaining mashed potatoes, smoothing gently with a spatula and leaving at least ½ inch (including the elevated crust) free of filling, since the potatoes "puff" while they cook. Cook for 45 to 60 minutes, or until the crust is golden brown.

Meanwhile, whisk together the sour cream, mustard, horseradish, and pepper. Bring to room temperature before serving. Place a generous dollop on or near each slice of pie.

Pot Roast Pot Pies

Makes 6 to 8 individual pot pies

Spring Pot roast, that soul-warming classic, gets all dressed up with a flaky pastry lid in this dish. Braising the meat with the vegetable aromatics of garlic, celery, tomatoes, and onion until the meat is tender and the vegetables are dissolved into the sauce ensures layers of flavor. Fresh baby spring carrots, baby spring potatoes, and collards are added near the end so they retain their individual flavors and bright colors. A jolt of red pepper flakes provides a little flavor surprise.

EQUIPMENT NEEDED **Six to eight 8–10-ounce ovenproof ramekins or bistro bowls, one 6-inch round pastry cutter**

1 recipe Master Savory Pastry
2 tablespoons butter
2 tablespoons olive oil
3 pounds pot roast
Salt and freshly ground pepper, divided
1 onion, peeled, quartered and sliced
3 cloves garlic, peeled and smashed
2 ribs celery, trimmed and sliced ¼ inch thick
1 teaspoon herbes de Provence
½ cup red wine
2½ cups coarsely chopped tomatoes
2 cups beef or vegetable stock (or enough to cover the roast halfway)
1 teaspoon red chili flakes
¼ cup chopped fresh parsley
2 cups baby carrots

3 cups collards, washed, tough stems removed, and cut into 1-inch squares (can substitute kale, spinach, or arugula)
3 cups fresh baby potatoes, scrubbed and pierced with a fork
1–2 tablespoons ketchup
Salt and freshly ground pepper to taste
1 egg wash (yolk mixed with a sprinkle of water, dash of salt)

The day before serving, prepare the Master Savory Pastry according to "Perfecting Pastry" (pages 17–18). Chill overnight.

Prepare the braised stew filling. Heat a large, heavy-bottomed pot or Dutch oven over medium-high heat. Add butter and oil. Season the roast generously on all sides with salt and freshly ground pepper. When the fat is sizzling (but not burning!), add the roast to the pan. Let brown, undisturbed, for about 5 minutes, or until golden brown. Turn the roast and repeat on the other side. Remove the browned roast from the pan and set aside. Add onion, garlic, celery, salt and pepper, and herbes de Provence to the pan. Stir to coat and pick up any brown bits. Cook until softened, about 5 minutes. Deglaze with red wine, stirring to pick up brown bits, and reduce wine by half.

Return the roast to the pan. Add the tomatoes and stock. Reduce heat to a simmer and cover, leaving the lid slightly ajar. After about 4 hours, add the red chili flakes and parsley, stirring in. Remove meat from the pan and allow to rest and cool. Meanwhile, using a shallow ladle, skim any excess fat off the surface. When the meat is cool enough to handle, chop it coarsely, removing and

discarding any excess fat or sinew. Return meat to the pot and add the carrots, collards, potatoes, and ketchup. Taste and adjust seasonings as needed. If too much liquid has evaporated, add enough water to thin to a stew consistency. Simmer, covered, another 40 minutes, or until vegetables are just tender. Remove from heat, cool, and refrigerate overnight.

The day of service, roll out the prepped pastry into a large circle (about ¼ inch thick) on a lightly floured surface (see On a Roll, page 18). Cut into 6-inch rounds, using your pastry cutter. Return rounds to the refrigerator to chill for about 20 minutes. Meanwhile, remove the stew from the refrigerator and remove any remaining fat (which will have coagulated overnight). Arrange the ramekins or bistro bowls on a baking sheet. Fill each with 1¼ cups of the stew. Top each with a prepped round of pastry, sealing the excess pastry down around the rim of the bowl (it should be about ½ inch deep). Cut three slits in the top of each pastry, and brush the top and sides of each lightly with egg wash. (Note: The pies can be assembled and refrigerated for several hours before baking or go directly into the oven at this point).

Preheat the oven to 375 degrees F and bake for 35 to 40 minutes, until bubbly and golden. Let cool for 15 minutes before serving.

Braised Pork Shank, Fresh Fig, and Sweet Potato Pot Pies

Makes 6 to 8 individual pot pies

Late Summer/Fall As summer bids an almost imperceptible farewell to long, hot, lazy days, autumn comes knocking on our doors, inviting the nostalgia of long-simmering stews and warming weekend afternoons in front of the fire. Where I live, fresh figs make a return to farmers markets in October, so I snap them up. They are absolutely lovely in this dish of long-braised pork shank, enveloping the sauce with a chunky sweetness and texture that is beautiful in contrast to the bright orange of the sweet potatoes and virginal whiteness of the fresh onions. Cinnamon and cloves give the stew Moroccan moxie and provide hours of aromatic pleasure as the shanks break down.

EQUIPMENT NEEDED **Six to eight 8–10-ounce ovenproof ramekins or bistro bowls, one 6-inch round pastry cutter**

1 recipe Master Savory Pastry

1 tablespoon butter

2 tablespoons olive oil

2½ pounds pork shank (or substitute pork shoulder, lamb or beef shank, or beef short ribs)

Salt and freshly ground pepper, divided

½ teaspoon ground cloves

1 teaspoon ground cinnamon

4 slices bacon, coarsely chopped

1 onion, peeled, quartered, and thinly sliced

3 cloves garlic, peeled and smashed

2 stalks celery, thinly sliced

1 cup red wine

2 cups fresh figs, halved (or substitute 1 cup dried figs)

2 cups vegetable or beef stock, or enough to cover by half

2 bay leaves

1 teaspoon dried orange peel or 2 tablespoons fresh orange zest

1 tablespoon local honey

20 small fresh sweet onions, with green tops trimmed to ½ inch (reserve green tops for garnish)

2 sweet potatoes, peeled and cut in ¼-inch dice

1 cup reserved green onion tops, finely sliced, for garnish

1 egg wash (yolk mixed with a sprinkle of water, dash of salt)

The day before serving, prepare the Master Savory Pastry according to "Perfecting Pastry" (pages 17–18). Chill overnight.

Prepare the braised stew filling. Heat a large, heavy-bottomed pot or Dutch oven over medium-high heat. Add the butter and olive oil. Meanwhile, generously season the shank on all sides with salt, pepper, cloves and cinnamon. Brown the shank well on all sides until it has turned a handsome golden brown, about 5 minutes per side. Remove shank from the pan and set aside. Add the bacon, onion, garlic, and celery. Season with salt and pepper. Stir to brown and coat with the fat and cook until just softened, about 5 minutes. Deglaze the pan with wine, stirring to pick up any brown bits. Reduce wine to ½ cup. Return shank to the pan and add the figs, stock, bay leaves, orange peel or zest, and honey. Season again with salt

and pepper. Bring to a simmer then cover and reduce to low heat. Cook about 4 to 5 hours, until the meat is very tender and falling off the bone.

Remove shank from the pot and set aside to cool. When cool enough to handle, pull the meat off the bone and shred or chop, discarding the bone and any fat or sinew. Skim any excess fat off the top of the stew and discard. Return meat to the stew, add the onions and sweet potatoes, and simmer, covered, over medium-high for about 40 minutes, or until the vegetables are tender. Taste and adjust seasonings and skim fat again. Stir in the reserved green onions; set aside to cool. Remove the bay leaves and discard. Refrigerate, covered, overnight.

The day of service, roll out the prepped pastry into a large circle (about ¼ inch thick) on a lightly floured surface (see On a Roll, page 18). Cut into 6-inch rounds using your pastry cutter. Return rounds to the refrigerator to chill for about 20 minutes. Meanwhile, remove the stew from the refrigerator and discard any fat that has congealed overnight.

Arrange the ramekins or bistro bowls on a baking sheet. Fill each with 1¼ cups of the stew. Top each with a prepped round of pastry, sealing the excess pastry down around the rim of the bowl (it should be about ½ inch deep). Cut three slits in the top of each pastry, and brush the top and sides of each lightly with egg wash. (Note: The pies can be assembled and refrigerated for several hours before baking or go directly into the oven at this point.)

Preheat the oven to 375 degrees F and bake for 35 to 40 minutes, until bubbly and golden. Set aside to cool for 15 minutes before serving. Dig in! It doesn't get any better than this.

A Word or Two on Braising

Braising is another way of saying "low 'n' slow" in a pot with liquid, and it applies to both meats and vegetables. The cuts that are best suited to braising are the tough, working muscles of any beast, such as the shoulder, pot roast, round, shank, brisket, or top shank.

The extra good news is that these cuts are usually the least expensive, but with a little patience, time and love, they become taste treasures when braised.

Use only enough water to half-cover the meat and add whatever vegetables you like. It is key to first beautifully brown the meat on all sides, as this (when de-glazed) will create the first layer of luscious flavor in the sauce.

If you don't own a Dutch oven, consider getting one. The enamel coating over cast iron is ideal for slow and steady heat distribution and for the browning process. However, a sturdy, heavy-bottomed pot of any kind will work. Cooking can be done on the stovetop or in the oven on low heat. The main thing to remember is that braising can't be rushed. Once you try braising, you'll want to use this method more often. Your house will smell fantastic, and the olfactory orgy will linger for days. The little pots of tender, braised love will not.

Hearty Chicken, Fennel, and Fresh Corn Pot Pies

Makes 6 to 8 individual pot pies

Fall Maybe it's because of the fronds that flutter in the late summer winds like deep green lace from the stalks of the perennial fragrant herb we call fennel, that it strikes me as a particularly delicate thing to be used with extreme care. The entire herb is used in these light, beautifully fragrant pot pies.

A whole chicken is gently poached with the stalks to lend to the stock its signature anise kiss. Thin slices or fennel bulb are in the soup, and freshly chopped fronds are added at the very end just before these pot pies get their pastry lids.

These precious pies would be perfect on a late summer to early fall evening, just when your mind is starting to think about Halloween or you're lighting the very first fire of the season. Serve with a salad prepared with mild greens such as bibb or iceberg lettuce topped with pungent, creamy buttermilk and black pepper dressing.

EQUIPMENT NEEDED Six to eight 8–10-ounce ovenproof ramekins or bistro bowls, one 6-inch round pastry cutters

1 recipe Master Savory Pastry

Chicken and Stock

One 3½–4 pound whole chicken
1 onion, peeled and quartered
4 cloves garlic, skin on
1 rib celery, rinsed and cut in half
Stalks from 1 fennel bulb cut ½ inch above
    bulb (handful of feathery fronds reserved)
5 black peppercorns
1 tablespoon sea salt or kosher salt
1 bay leaf
3–4 sprigs fresh parsley
Water to cover

Soup

2 tablespoons butter
1 tablespoon olive oil
1 medium onion, peeled and finely chopped
2 bulbs fennel, stalks and fronds removed,
    vertically halved and thinly sliced*
Corn from 1 cob (about ½ cup),
    husk and silk removed
Salt and freshly ground pepper
2 tablespoons Pernod
3 tablespoons all-purpose flour
5 cups reserved stock (from stock recipe above)
3 tablespoons whole cream
2 tablespoons finely chopped fennel fronds
2 tablespoons finely chopped fresh chives
Reserved chicken meat
½ teaspoon local honey
Salt and freshly ground pepper, to taste
1 egg wash (yolk mixed with a sprinkle
    of water, dash of salt)

*Note: If there is a tough, sinewy white
    core near the base of the bulb, cut
    it out before slicing and discard.

The day before serving, prepare the Master Savory Pastry according to "Perfecting Pastry" (pages 17–18). Chill overnight.

The day before serving, prepare the chicken stock. Rinse the chicken and place the whole bird in a stock pot or large Dutch oven along with the onion, garlic, celery, fennel fronds, peppercorns, salt, bay leaf and parsley. Bring to a boil then reduce to a simmer. Cover and cook about 1½ hours, until chicken is thoroughly cooked and almost falling off the bone. Set aside until cool enough to handle, about ½ hour. Using two sturdy forks on either end, lift chicken out of the pot. Remove all skin. Gently pull the meat off the bones, pulling into long strands. Discard bones and any sinew or veins. Place the chicken in an airtight container and refrigerate overnight.

Using a sieve, strain solids from the stock. Discard solids and refrigerate the stock overnight in a large airtight container. (Note: You can continue with the recipe at this point if you want to do it all in one day. I think it's preferable to break it down, however, as it makes service day more enjoyable. Just make sure that greedy, chicken-loving hands don't nab all the chicken overnight!)

The day of service, finish the soup. In a large Dutch oven or soup pot, heat the butter and olive oil over medium heat. Add the onion, fennel, and corn and stir. Cook for 5 minutes, or until the ingredients have begun to soften. Add the salt and pepper; stir to coat. Increase heat to medium-high. Add the Pernod and reduce to a glaze. Drizzle flour evenly over the top of the mixture and stir to combine. Reduce heat to medium and continue cooking the flour into the mixture for 1 minute. Add 5 cups reserved chicken stock, increase heat to high, and bring to a boil. Cook for 10 minutes, or until the broth has started to thicken. Reduce heat to medium and add the cream, fennel fronds, chives, all of the reserved, pulled chicken

meat, honey, and salt pepper to taste. Set aside to cool. Ladle the still-warm soup into the ramekins, filling just shy of ½ inch of the top. Line these up on a baking sheet and refrigerate to further cool the soup.

Roll out the prepped pastry into a large circle (about ¼ inch thick) on a lightly floured surface (see On a Roll, page 18). Cut into 6-inch rounds, using your pastry cutter. Return the rounds to the refrigerator to chill for about 20 minutes. Top each of the cooled, prepped soup pots with a round of pastry, sealing the excess pastry down around the rim of the bowl (it should be about ½ inch deep). Cut three slits in the top of the pastries, and brush the top and sides of each lightly with egg wash. (Note: The pies can be assembled and refrigerated for several hours before baking or go directly into the oven at this point).

About 1 hour before desired service time, preheat the oven to 375 degrees F and bake for 35 to 40 minutes, until bubbling and golden. Let cool for 15 minutes before serving.

Savory Quiches

Long associated with French cuisine, quiche was actually born in Germany in the Middle Ages. Essentially an open pie of an egg-and-cream custard, quiche is a delectable springboard for myriad flavor pairings and can be the central star of any meal. Despite its once wimpy reputation, quiche has resumed its rightful place at the top of the culinary dynasty charts in recent years, probably due to its versatility, practicality, relative simplicity, and flat-out deliciousness.

When you're working with quiche, the goal is to keep the custard in the shell, so never pierce a quiche dough with a fork (to prevent bubbling, as with other non-liquid pies), and always keep any dough scraps on hand to patch little gaps or openings that may appear in the pastry once it's in the pan. It's for this reason, that I recommend an entire recipe of pastry for the quiches in this chapter. You will have plenty left over to fill any holes in the crust, and having more rolled-out pastry makes it easier to guide the pastry into the deeper quiche pans.

To get the most lift and lightness, the custard is aerated in either a blender or with a hand-held mixture. This makes all the difference! All other fillings (with rare exception, see Creamy Blue Crab and Salmon Quiche, page 73), whether it's onion or bacon or veggies, need to be cooked in advance to cook off excess water that will muddle the custard, and they should be added to the quiche between alternating layers of custard to keep everything from floating to the bottom of the pie.

Finally, to get a nice clean slice, allow your quiche to cool for a good 30 minutes before cutting. Better yet, bake it the day before, cool completely, and refrigerate overnight before cutting. Reheat the slices gently in a moderate 350 degree F oven after bringing them to room temperature.

Follow these tips, and you'll never say no to quiche! As outstanding for lunch as it is for supper, there is no limit to the wonders of quiche.

Creamy Blue Crab and Salmon Quiche

Serves 6 to 8

Spring/Summer During the warmer months in the south, crab pots are as prolific as the fat, sweet blue crabs that troll the fish-rich coastal waters. If you can get your hands on fresh blue crabs for this delicate seafood quiche, ask your fish monger to gently pull the lump meat that comes from the body of the crab. It's pesky business but well worth the effort. If not, find whatever fresh lump crab is available at your local grocer. Pasteurized, imported lump crab (usually from Asia) will work, but the flavor is slightly medicinal and soapy, in my opinion. Neither fresh nor pasteurized crab (like the salmon in this dish) needs to be cooked in advance, as it cooks in the custard without giving off unwanted water. Cream cheese whipped into the custard gives this quiche an extra-smooth and airy touch. Fresh chives gently worked into the pastry add a breath of fresh spring flavor.

EQUIPMENT NEEDED **One 8 x 1¾-inch fluted quiche pan with removable bottom**

1 recipe Master Savory Pastry (page 17) plus
    2 tablespoons finely chopped fresh chives
1 egg wash (yolk, splash water, pinch
    salt blended together)

½ pound (or 1¾ cup) fresh blue lump crabmeat
    or pasteurized blue lump crabmeat
½ pound fresh salmon fillets (sockeye
    is recommended for its color)
4 scallions, finely chopped

Custard

4 eggs, room temperature
¼ cup cream cheese, room temperature
1½ cups heavy cream, room temperature
½ teaspoon salt
Generous dash ground white pepper

Prepare Master Savory Pastry (see "Perfecting Pastry," pages 17–18), adding the chives after pulsing in the butter and before adding the water. Chill 30 minutes or overnight. Roll out according to instructions on Elevated Tart Border (page 18). Chill 20 to 30 minutes.

Preheat the oven to 375 degrees F. Place the prepared shell on a baking pan and blind bake the pastry (see Blind Baking, page 19) about 25 minutes, or until set and becoming golden. Remove the pie weights, brush down the pastry with egg wash, and return to the oven to finish baking until golden brown, another 20 to 25 minutes. Remove the pre-baked shell from the oven and reduce the oven temperature to 350 degrees F. Let shell cool slightly at room temperature.

Meanwhile, prepare the filling. Slice the salmon into ¼-inch dice. Arrange salmon, crab, and scallions in separate piles on your workspace.

For the custard, blend together the eggs, cream cheese, cream and seasonings in a blender for 30 seconds, or until light, frothy, and doubled in volume.

Arrange the crab and salmon on the bottom of the pan. Top with the custard, filling to about ¼ inch below the top of the shell. Sprinkle with scallions.

Bake on a baking sheet at 350 degrees F about 45 minutes, until the quiche is just set in the center but slightly wobbly to the touch. Cool for at least 30 minutes before slicing, or cool completely and refrigerate overnight. Slice and reheat in a 350 degree F oven before serving.

Summer Squash, Cheddar, Fresh Mozzarella and Bacon Quiche

Serves 6 to 8

Summer *The sweetness of fresh-off-the-vine yellow summer squash is magical paired with the mellow creamy custard and the gutsy flavor notes of bacon, mozzarella, and cheddar cheeses. The pastry is rolled out in crumbled Cheez-Its for added crunch and golden color, and the squash is grated before being cooked so it threads sweetly through every bite.*

EQUIPMENT NEEDED One 8 x 1¾-inch fluted quiche pan with removable bottom

1 recipe Master Savory Pastry (page 17)

1 cup Cheez-Its (or other cheese cracker), crushed and blended with 2–3 tablespoons flour

1 egg wash (yolk, splash water, pinch salt blended together)

3 slices bacon

2 tablespoons extra virgin olive oil

2 small yellow summer squash, coarsely grated (about 2 cups)

¼ teaspoon sea salt or kosher salt, divided

⅛ teaspoon ground white pepper, divided

2 scallions, finely chopped

Custard

5 eggs, room temperature

1 pint (2 cups) heavy cream

Salt and pepper, to taste

Pinch ground nutmeg

1½ cups loosely packed grated extra sharp yellow cheddar cheese, divided

¾ cup perlini (tiny) fresh mozzarella balls

Prepare Master Savory Pastry (see "Perfecting Pastry," pages 17–18). Chill 30 minutes or overnight. Roll out according to instructions on Elevated Tart Border (page 18). However, instead of rolling out exclusively in flour, roll out the dough in the crushed Cheez-Its blended with flour, adding more flour as needed to prevent the pastry from sticking. Chill 20 to 30 minutes.

Preheat the oven to 375 degrees F. Place the prepared shell on a baking pan and blind bake the pastry (see Blind Baking, page 19) about 25 minutes, until set and becoming golden. Remove the pie weights, brush the pastry with egg wash, and finish baking until golden brown, another 20 to 25 minutes. Remove the pre-baked shell from the oven and reduce oven temperature to 350 degrees F. Let the shell cool slightly at room temperature.

Meanwhile, sear bacon in a medium-size sauté pan over medium-high heat. Drain on paper towels. When cool, chop coarsely and set aside. Heat the olive oil in a medium sauté pan and add the squash, salt and pepper. Cook over medium heat about 5 minutes, until squash has wilted. Stir in the chopped scallions and set aside.

For the custard, combine eggs, cream, salt, pepper and nutmeg in a blender or a large bowl using a hand-held mixer. Blend for 1 minute, or until the custard is very frothy and foamy on top. Pour a third of the custard into the prepared pie shell. Add a third of both cheeses and half each of the squash and bacon. Add the remaining custard and top off with remaining squash, bacon and cheeses. Bake on a baking sheet at 350 degrees F about 45 minutes, or until the quiche is just set in the center but slightly wobbly to the touch. Cool for at least 30 minutes before slicing and serving, or cool completely and refrigerate overnight; slice and reheat in a 350 degree F oven before serving.

Mellow Yellow Sweet Corn Quiche with Fresh Shrimp, Bacon, Provolone and Chives

Serves 6 to 8

Summer Sweet, summer-fresh corn literally pops in this fabulous, sophisticated quiche. The mellow flavor of fresh shrimp (local if possible), bright lift of fresh chives, rich bacon, and melted goodness of provolone cheese work in perfect taste and texture combination. Because this is a "dressy" quiche, I like to prepare it in a fancier, fluted deep-dish quiche pan. If you like, you can work the chives into the pastry (after pulsing in the butter), but I especially like the way the green looks peeking out from the top of the quiche.

EQUIPMENT NEEDED **One 8 x 1¾-inch fluted quiche pan with removable bottom**

1 recipe Master Savory Pastry
1 egg wash (yolk, splash water, pinch
    salt blended together)

Filling

4 strips bacon
1 tablespoon butter
1 cup fresh corn, cut off the cob
Salt and freshly ground pepper
1 cup fresh shrimp, peeled and de-veined
¼ cup cut chives (½-inch lengths)
1 cup fresh provolone cheese
    chopped into a ¼-inch dice

Custard

5 eggs, room temperature
1 pint heavy cream
½ teaspoon sea salt or kosher salt
⅛ teaspoon ground pepper

Prepare the Master Savory Pastry (see "Perfecting Pastry," pages 17–18). Refrigerate at least 30 minutes or overnight. Roll out (see On a Roll, page 18) on a lightly floured surface and shape into the quiche pan, forming a flush border (see Flush Tart Border, page 18). Chill the formed crust for at least 20 minutes. Blind bake (see Blind Baking, page 19) the pastry for 20 minutes, remove the pie weights, and brush the pastry down quickly with egg wash. Continue baking for 20 to 30 minutes, or until the pastry is golden brown and set.

Meanwhile, prepare the filling. Sauté the bacon in a single layer over medium-high heat, flipping once or twice, until brown and crispy, about 5 minutes. Remove and drain on paper towels. Remove all but 1 tablespoon of the bacon fat. Add butter and corn. Season lightly with salt and pepper. Reduce heat to medium and cook for about 3 minutes, stirring the corn to coat. Add shrimp and cook about 3 minutes, until just opaque. Season gently with salt and pepper; set aside.

Just before the pastry shell is through blind baking, blend together the custard ingredients in a blender for about 1 minute, until frothy and light. Season to taste with salt and pepper.

To assemble the quiche, remove the baked pastry from the oven and reduce heat to 350 degrees F. Gently, evenly place half of the corn/bacon/shrimp mixture, half of the chives, and half of the provolone cheese on the bottom of the pastry-lined pan. Top with half of the custard mixture. Repeat, topping off with the remaining custard. Bake on the center rack on a baking sheet for 45 to 50 minutes, until golden and bubbly. Serve warm.

Roasted Grape Tomato and Pimento Cheese Quiche

Serves 8

Summer/Early Fall Grape tomatoes *are roasted at a high heat to concentrate their flavor and maximize their "pop" factor before going into this sunset-hued quiche. Pimento cheese, a southern staple of (usually) yellow or white cheddar studded with roasted pimento peppers (deeply sweet and aromatic peppers) gives it a rustic, relaxing twist that begs for a deep-dish pie pan for shaping and baking. The basil, cut into a kind of confetti in the blender with the custard, weaves its way all the way through the flavor of the delicate custard. Feel free to garnish the quiche with fresh basil when serving.*

EQUIPMENT NEEDED **One 8 x 1³⁄₄-inch fluted quiche pan**

1 recipe Master Savory Pastry
1 egg wash (yolk, splash water, pinch
    salt blended together)

Filling
2 cups grape tomatoes, rinsed
2 tablespoons olive oil
Sea salt or kosher salt and freshly ground pepper
6 scallions, white and green parts, finely chopped
1 cup pimento cheese (see sidebar, page 81)

Custard
5 eggs
1 pint heavy cream
¹⁄₄ teaspoon kosher salt or sea salt
¹⁄₈ teaspoon freshly ground pepper
10 fresh basil leaves

Prepare Master Savory Pastry (see "Perfecting Pastry," pages 17–18). Chill 30 minutes or overnight. Roll out on a lightly floured surface according to instructions on Elevated Tart Border (page 18). Chill 20 to 30 minutes.

Just before baking, preheat the oven to 375 degrees F. Place the prepared shell on a baking pan and blind bake (see Blind Baking, page 19) about 25 minutes, until pastry is set and becoming golden. Remove the pie weights, brush down the pastry with egg wash, and return to the oven to finish baking until golden brown, another 20 to 25 minutes. Remove the pre-baked shell from the oven and reduce the oven temperature to 350 degrees F. Let the shell cool slightly at room temperature.

Meanwhile, roast the tomatoes in the oven. Toss tomatoes in oil, salt and pepper, and arrange in a single layer on a rimmed baking sheet; place it on a rack below the pastry. Roast for about 25 minutes, until tomatoes have just popped and shrunken in size. Remove and set aside to cool.

To prepare the custard, combine eggs, cream, salt and pepper in a blender for 1 minute on high, until frothy and light. Add the basil and blend for 3 seconds, until just shredded. Set aside.

To assemble the quiche, line the bottom of the pre-baked pie shell with half of the scallions, half of the tomatoes and half of the custard. Repeat. Top the quiche with large dollops of the pimento cheese scattered over the top. Bake at 350 degrees F for about 45 to 50 minutes, until golden and bubbly. Serve warm.

Cheesy, Meaty, Hungry-Man Quiche

Serves 6 to 8

Winter My certified therapy dog and best friend, a handsome chocolate cocker named Tann Mann, and I visit our local VA Hospital every Friday morning. We regularly join the guys on the fourth-floor nursing home. One morning, as I was writing this book, I had the occasion to visit with an especially endearing young vet, Karl, and his mother, Sher. She told me about the post-Lent Italian tradition of meat pies (pizzagiani, or "pizzachino"), which are beefy, cheesy delights intended to be savored on Easter Day as a celebratory break from the lean days of Lent. They are traditionally quiche-like, though most use less custard than the other recipes in this chapter. Even though Easter falls in spring, I think of this recipe as more of a winter tart.

EQUIPMENT NEEDED **One 8 x 1¾-inch fluted quiche pan**

1 recipe Master Savory Pastry
1 egg wash (yolk, splash water, pinch
    salt blended together)

Filling

1 tablespoon olive oil
1 onion, finely chopped
4 cloves garlic, peeled and mashed to pulp
Salt and freshly ground pepper, to taste
1 pound ground beef (85% lean)
1 pound ground pork sausage
Salt and freshly ground pepper, to taste
1 tablespoon fennel seeds
1 tablespoon chopped fresh rosemary
1½ teaspoons red chili flakes
2 tablespoons balsamic vinegar
Generous dash Worcestershire sauce
3 very thin slices prosciutto
¼ cup fresh ricotta cheese
1 cup Manchego cheese cut into ¼-inch cubes
½ cup fresh mozzarella cheese,
    cut into ¼-inch cubes

Custard

2 eggs, room temperature
½ cup half-and-half
Salt and freshly ground pepper to taste
½ cup Parmigiano-Reggiano, for the topping

Prepare Master Savory Pastry (see "Perfecting Pastry," pages 17–18) and chill 30 minutes or overnight. Roll out on a lightly floured surface according to instructions on Elevated Tart Border (page 18). Chill 20 to 30 minutes.

Just before baking, preheat the oven to 375 degrees F. Place the prepared shell on a baking pan and blind bake the pastry (see Blind Baking, page 19) about 25 minutes, until set and becoming golden. Remove the pie weights, brush down the pastry with egg wash, and then finish baking until golden brown, another 20 to 25 minutes. Remove the pre-baked shell from the oven and reduce the oven temperature to 350 degrees F. Let the shell cool slightly at room temperature.

Meanwhile, prepare the filling. Heat oil in a large, deep sauté pan over medium heat. Add onion, garlic, and a dash of salt and pepper. Cook about 5 minutes, stirring, until softened. Avoid browning. Increase heat to medium-high. Break up the beef and sausage with

your hands and drop into the pan. Season with salt and pepper, fennel seeds, rosemary, and chili flakes. Cook for about 10 minutes, stirring and draining off excess fat as you go, until lightly browned. Deglaze the pan with vinegar and reduce to a glaze, about 2 minutes. Add the Worcestershire. Set aside to cool. Season to taste. Turn out into a large bowl and refrigerate to bring down to room temperature.

Meanwhile, line the bottom of the pre-cooked shell with prosciutto slices to form a cohesive pastry "lining," Top with an even layer of ricotta.

Once cooled to room temperature, toss the meat mixture with the cheeses.

Separately, place the eggs, half-and-half, salt, and pepper in a blender, and blend until the custard is frothy and doubled in volume. Taste and adjust seasonings as necessary.

To assemble, place the meat and cheese mixture into the procsciutto-lined pastry. Pour custard over the top. Sprinkle the Parmigiano-Reggiano evenly. Bake at 350 degrees F for 45 minutes, or until brown and bubbly. Serve warm.

Purely Pimento

I like all different types of pimento cheese except those that look and taste fake—all orange and ugly like a very bad hair dye job. A reliably delicious and easy-to-find brand, and the one I used for this recipe, is Palmetto Cheese (brand) pimento cheese. Their motto is true to its word: "Real Cheese, Real Southern , Really Good"! You can find it at www.palmettocheese.com and assorted retailers, including Costco. Another preferred brand is Callie's (see page 89).

To make your own, coarsely grate some good-quality aged cheddar and mix with just enough mayonnaise to hold it together, about 3 tablespoons. Fold in some chopped, roasted pimento peppers (they're in season during summer and fall and are also available canned at most supermarkets), a dash of Worcestershire, a dash of hot sauce, and salt and pepper to taste. One of my favorite chefs in the world, Robert Stehling of Charleston's Hominy Grill, adds a few tablespoons of bourbon to his, and it's ever so good! It will hold for a week or more refrigerated in an airtight container.

Savory Meat and Veggie Pockets

Fried fruit pockets are a favorite southern tradition. In this short and extra tasty chapter, they're rendered savory using some preferred southern seasonal staples from shrimp to grits, bacon and more. These little guys take patience and care but are so much more rewarding than those processed, frozen pockets from the grocery store. A little advance planning and prep work will yield show-stopping party fare or a light lunch for a big group, paired with a simple salad. For a lighter, less caloric pocket, each of these recipes can alternatively be baked at 375 degrees F on a parchment-lined baking sheet for about 25 minutes, until golden. Be sure to give the pockets a gentle egg wash glaze before popping them into the oven.

Feisty Fried Shrimp and Grits Pockets

Makes 24 pockets

Summer/Fall *Shrimp and grits is one of the most distinctive dishes of the Lowcountry, a magically scenic and fertile area that envelops lovely Charleston. Seek out stone-ground, preservative-free grits, which are essentially the larger fragments left behind after the cornmeal is sifted from the ground, dried corn. They can be white or yellow, cooked with cream or water, but should never be rushed. The toothsome texture of these grits will reward you again and again. (Note: I use Charleston's Own in this recipe. They're easily ordered at www.charlestonspecialtyfoods.com. Another good source is Boykin Grits at www. boykinmillfarms.com).*

These surprise hot pockets, with their perfect crunch and ooze factor, make idyllic party food or can be a central player for a Sunday brunch buffet. As with so many recipes in this book, the best plan is to prep the fillings and the pastry the day before, fill them on cooking day, keep cold for several hours, and fry or bake just before serving.

EQUIPMENT NEEDED **4-inch round pastry cutter, large pot for deep-frying**

2 recipes Master Savory Pastry

Grits Filling

¾ cup Charleston's Own yellow stone ground
    grits (see web site above to order)
1½ cups half-and-half
1 cup water
½ teaspoon kosher salt or sea salt
Freshly ground black pepper to taste
¾ cup grated Gouda cheese

Shrimp Filling

3 strips bacon
1 tablespoon butter
2 cloves garlic, smashed
1 stalk celery, trimmed and finely chopped
¼ cup dry wine
1½ cups boxed seafood stock
Generous dash hot sauce
2 teaspoons Worcestershire sauce
3 Roma tomatoes, finely chopped
4 scallions, finely chopped
1 tablespoon ketchup
1 tablespoon cream
1 tablespoon herbes de Provence or dried thyme
3 thin slices prosciutto, cut into thin strips
1 teaspoon honey
1 pound fresh white or brown shrimp,
    peeled, deveined, coarsely chopped
Salt and freshly ground pepper to taste
4 cups vegetable, canola or peanut oil
Sliced scallions, for garnish, optional
Chopped parsley, for garnish, optional

Prepare Master Savory Pastry (see "Perfecting Pastry," pages 17–18). Chill 30 minutes or overnight. (I recommend the latter.)

The day before service, bring the grits, half-and-half, water, salt and pepper to a boil in a medium pot over medium-high heat, whisking constantly. Reduce to a low simmer and continue whisking regularly. Add more water as needed and adjust seasonings carefully along the way. Count on about 30 minutes for the grits to cook. The grits are done when they're tooth-tender but still have a tiny

"bite." Remove from the heat, whisk in the cheese until melted, and set aside to cool. Refrigerate overnight in an airtight container.

To prepare the shrimp filling, cook bacon in a large, deep skillet over medium-high heat until crisp and golden, turning once or twice. Remove from pan and drain on paper towels. Discard all but two tablespoons of the bacon fat and continue. Heat over medium-low heat and add the butter, garlic and celery. Cook about 5 minutes, until just softened. Add wine and seafood stock and cook over medium heat until reduced by two-thirds. Add hot sauce, Worcestershire, tomatoes, scallions, ketchup, cream, herbes de Provence or thyme, prosciutto, and honey. Cook through for a few minutes. At the last minute, season to taste with salt and pepper. Crumble the reserved bacon and stir in along with the raw shrimp. Stir through just to coat. (Note: You don't really want the shrimp to cook at this point, as they will cook when frying. Be careful to barely heat the shrimp through, or they will be tough. Remove shrimp from the heat and refrigerate overnight in an airtight container.

On the day of service, several hours before serving, roll out the pastry according to On a Roll (page 18), one batch at a time. Cut pastry into 4-inch rounds, lightly dusted with flour, and arrange neatly on a baking pan. Chill for 20 minutes. To fill the pockets, place 1 tablespoon of the cold grits on the right side of the circle, flattening gently with the back of a spoon. Top with a heaping tablespoon of cooled shrimp mixture, leaving 1/4 inch naked pastry border. Pull the top gently over the filling, guiding the top pastry to meet the naked pastry border. Seal gently with your fingertips, then press the border gently with the tines of a fork to seal. The pockets should look like fat, crimped pastry crescent moons. Continue until all the pastry and filling has been used. Chill pockets for 30 minutes and up to several hours.

About 40 minutes before serving, preheat oven to 325 degrees F. Heat oil of choice in a large pot over medium-high heat, until to 360–375 degrees F, or until the oil begins to squirm and zigzag around the bottom of the pan and sizzles aggressively when the pastry enters the pan. Fry in batches of 2 or 3 pockets, gently placing each into the hot oil (do not plop or you might get burned!). Cook for 7 minutes, or until the pockets float on the top and are deep, golden brown. Remove with a slotted spoon and drain on paper towels. Keep warm in the preheated oven while frying the remainder. Serve immediately, garnished with fresh scallions or parsley if desired. If you have a little filling left over, cook that through in a sauce pan and serve a little pool on a plate alongside the pie pocket.

Hot Frying Tips

These pockets, like anything being fried (including the Deep Purple Cherry Pie Pockets, page 123), demand oil with a high smoking point, meaning oil that can handle high heat without smoking. Olive oil cannot be substituted or you'll have a huge, stinky mess on your hands. However, vegetable, peanut, and canola will all work perfectly well. When frying, be alert. The oil gets hot and stays that way long after it's off the heat. Turn any pan handles in and away from the edge of the stove, and make sure young children and pets cannot get to the hot oil. Once it's thoroughly cool, pour the oil into a plastic bag and discard it in the outside trashcan. Do not re-use the oil after frying the pockets.

Cheesy Cauliflower and Bacon Pockets

Makes 14 to 16 pockets

Fall/Spring Cauliflower is a wonderful cool-weather vegetable that often gets reduced to a watery, bland, overcooked mess in an extended steam bath. Not here! Tiny florets are roasted in the oven, enhancing cauliflower's natural nuttiness, and tossed with bacon. They're held together with a thick béchamel (a white sauce formed with flour, fat and milk) and finished with chunks of pungent Edam cheese and scallions. The mixture gets a pastry wrap and is then formed into pockets. The pudding-like filling practically quivers with deliciousness. The cheese melts while cooking and oozes out of the hot pockets with every bite. This makes for great party food.

EQUIPMENT NEEDED One 4-inch round pastry cutter, small roasting pan, large deep skillet

2 recipes Master Savory Pastry plus ½ cup white or yellow cornmeal for rolling and flour for dusting the rolling surface
½ cauliflower, rinsed, cored and cut into small florets (yield should be about 2½ cups)
¼ cup extra virgin olive oil
Sea salt or kosher salt and freshly ground pepper to taste
4 slices bacon, diced into ¼-inch cubes

Béchamel
2 tablespoons reserved bacon fat
2 tablespoons all-purpose flour
1 cup whole milk
Sea salt or kosher salt and ground pepper to taste

Filling
3 scallions, white and green parts thinly sliced
½ cup Edam cheese, cut into ¼-inch cubes (or substitute yellow cheddar)
4 cups vegetable, peanut or canola oil for frying

Prepare Master Savory Pastry (see "Perfecting Pastry," pages 17–18). Chill 30 minutes or overnight. (I recommend the latter unless you're in a hurry to get these done.)

Prepare filling a day ahead. When ready to go, preheat the oven to 400 degrees F.

Cut the cauliflower in half, reserving the other half for another use. Cut the half in half and cut out the tough center core. Break the florets into small, mini-florets, about the size of the tip of your pinky, cutting out any additional tough cores or stems. Rinse the florets in a

colander and drain. Toss cauliflower with olive oil, salt and pepper and arrange in a small roasting pan. Roast for 20 to 25 minutes, tossing once or twice, until just softened and beginning to turn golden.

Meanwhile, heat a large, deep skillet or sauté pan over medium-high heat. Sear the bacon for about 4 minutes, stirring occasionally until it's browned and cooked through. Remove bacon with a slotted spoon and drain on paper towels. Reserve 2 tablespoons of the rendered bacon fat in the cooking pan, discarding the rest.

Prepare the béchamel. Heat reserved bacon fat in the same skillet over medium heat. Add the flour, and blend thoroughly with a whisk, cooking for 1 minute. Add the milk gradually, whisking the entire time. Cook on medium heat for 2 minutes, whisking constantly. Remove from heat and season to taste with salt and pepper. When the cauliflower is cooked, fold it into the béchamel along with the reserved bacon. Pour the mixture into a small bowl and refrigerate overnight.

The day of service, several hours in advance, roll out the pastry according to On a Roll (page 18), one pastry batch at a time. However, instead of dusting your work surface with flour alone, add the cornmeal, dusting the top and bottom of the pastry as you roll. Cut the pastry into 4-inch rounds and arrange neatly on a baking pan. Chill for 20 minutes. Meanwhile, fold the scallions and cheese into the chilled cauliflower filling.

To fill the pockets, place 1 tablespoon of filling on the right side of the circle, flattening gently with the back of a spoon. Leave ¼ inch naked border. Pull the top gently over the filling, guiding the top pastry to meet the naked pastry border. Seal gently with your fingertips, then press the border gently with the tines of a fork to seal. Continue until all the pastry and filling have been used. Chill pockets for 30 minutes and up to several hours.

About 40 minutes before serving, preheat oven to 325 degrees F. Heat the oil of choice in a large pot over medium-high heat to 360–375 degrees F, until the oil begins to squirm and zigzag around the bottom of the pan and sizzles aggressively when the pastry enters the pan. Fry in batches of 2 or 3 pockets, gently placing each into the hot oil. Cook for 5 minutes, or until the pockets float on top and are deep, golden brown. Remove with a slotted spoon and drain on paper towels. Keep warm in the preheated oven while frying the remainder. Serve immediately, garnished with a sprinkling of freshly chopped scallions or parsley.

Callie's Pimento, Bacon, and Fresh Basil Pockets

Serves 8 (makes 16 pockets)

All Seasons *Callie's is a top-quality, chunky, spicy-sweet pimento cheese that is hand produced in Charleston, South Carolina. It's the best pimento cheese you can find and better than any I can make. Because it's a snap to purchase online at www. calliesbiscuits.com, I recommend using this brand whenever pimento cheese is needed (see Purely Pimento, page 81). Fresh basil and pepper bacon are folded into these impossible-to-resist pie pockets. My neighbor's unusually polite little girls, Margaret and Elizabeth, uncharacteristically snatched these off their mother's plate when I delivered them for tasting, declaring, "Miss Holly, you are the best cooker ever!" Bet your friends will say the same about you when you serve these baked pie pockets.*

EQUIPMENT NEEDED **One 4-inch round pastry cutter, parchment paper, baking sheet**

1 recipe Master Savory Pastry plus flour for rolling

4 slices pepper bacon

1 1/2 cups Callie's Old Southern Style Pimento
    Cheese or best quality available

2 tablespoons fresh basil, cut into thin strips

1/4 teaspoon freshly ground black pepper

1 tablespoon all-purpose flour

1 egg wash (yolk, pinch salt, splash
    water, blended together)

16 tiny basil leaves, for garnish

16 Parmigiano-Reggiano shavings, for garnish

Prepare Master Savory Pastry according to "Perfecting Pastry" (pages 17–18). Wrap in plastic or parchment paper and refrigerate at least 1 hour (or overnight).

To prepare the filling, brown the bacon and drain on paper towels. Coarsely chop. Combine bacon, cheese, basil, pepper, and flour in a medium-size bowl, folding gently. Cover and chill for at least 1 hour (or overnight).

At least 1 hour before you plan to serve the pockets, roll out the pastry according to On a Roll (page 18). Cut the pastry into 4-inch rounds, dusting lightly with flour. Arrange the rounds neatly on a baking sheet and chill for at least 20 minutes.

To fill the pockets, place 1 heaping tablespoon of filling on the right side of the circle, flattening gently with the back of a spoon and leaving 1/4 inch naked border on the right side of the circle. Pull the top gently over the filling, guiding the top pastry to meet the naked pastry border. Seal gently with your fingertips, then press the border gently with the tines of a fork to seal. Line a baking sheet with parchment paper and place the filled pockets in neat, well-spaced rows on the sheet. Chill for at least 20 minutes. (Note: These can be rolled and filled then chilled overnight, tightly wrapped with plastic wrap, in the fridge before baking.)

To bake, preheat the oven to 375 F. Just before baking, brush the top of each pocket with egg wash. Cut three short slits in the top of each pocket with a paring knife. Top each pocket with a basil leaf; brush these with a dot of egg wash, then sprinkle each with a few broken shavings of Parmigiano-Reggiano shavings. Bake in the center of the oven for 30 minutes, or until golden brown and puffy. Serve warm.

Sweet Custard and Cream Tarts and Tartlets

Cool, silky custards and pastry creams are a natural base for crisp, fruit tart toppings, and have been so through the ages. But, lovely as they are, this tart chapter is not limited to straightforward custards.

In the friendly, delicious Strawberry 'n' Cream Dream Tart (page 92), the base is a simple blend of mascarpone and ricotta with a fresh strawberry coulis. It forms a pale pink, creamy base to showcase the strawberries that top it. Buttermilk gets infused with the delicate flavor of lavender to form the luscious Lavender Buttermilk Tart (page 103), while a rich, nutty butterscotch pudding forms the base for the show-stopping Butterscotch and Caramel Apple Tart (page 104). The Vanilla-Dipped Pear and Chocolate Tartlets (page 107) are a heady mix of vanilla bean and syrup-poached pears atop a fluffy truffle ganache and are so easy to make, you'll be pleased with your first effort.

Strawberry 'n' Cream Dream Tart

Serves 12

Spring/Summer Strawberries and cream take center stage in this simple, refreshing tart prepared with mascarpone cheese flavored with a fresh strawberry coulis and topped with fresh berry slices. In a rectangular tart pan shell, the slices can be cut easily horizontally, without breaking up excessive amounts of pastry or mussing up the pretty strawberry pattern on top.

EQUIPMENT NEEDED **Two 13 x 4 x 1-inch rectangular tart pans with removable bottoms**

1 recipe Master Sweet Pastry (page 17) plus 2 tablespoons yellow cornmeal and flour for rolling
1 egg wash (yolk, splash water, pinch salt blended together)

Coulis
1 1/2 cups fresh strawberries, tops trimmed, rinsed and dried
1/3 cup confectioners' sugar
1/4 teaspoon fresh lemon juice

Filling
Prepared coulis (above)
Zest of 1 lemon
1 teaspoon pure vanilla extract
8 ounces (1 cup) mascarpone cheese*
1/2 cup confectioners' sugar
2 tablespoons heavy cream
1/4 cup whole milk ricotta cheese
1 cup fresh strawberries, rinsed, dried, trimmed, and thinly sliced, for topping

1/4 cup strawberry jelly plus 1 tablespoon water for glazing

Preheat oven to 350 degrees F. Prepare Master Sweet Pastry according to "Perfecting Pastry" (pages 17–18). Chill for 30 minutes or overnight. Roll out the dough according to Flush Tart Border directions (page 18), adding cornmeal to the flour used for rolling. (Note: For this shape pan, roll out the dough into a large rectangle and cut in half, vertically, to create two separate pieces of pastry to line the pans). Chill the pastry for 20 minutes. Blind bake (see page 19) in a 375 degree F oven for about 25 minutes, until golden. Remove the pie weights and brush the sides and top with egg wash. Bake 15 to 20 minutes more, or until the crust is completely baked and golden. Remove from the oven and set aside to cool. (Note: This can be done a day in advance, as long as the pastry is stored in an airtight container at room temperature.)

To prepare the coulis, puree the strawberries, sugar and lemon juice in the bowl of a food processor fitted with a metal blade or in a blender. Puree until smooth. To complete the filling, combine the coulis, zest, vanilla, mascarpone, sugar, cream, and ricotta. Whisk to combine.

To assemble, fill the tarts with the filling, gently scraping the top flush with the border using the back of a knife. Arrange the strawberries in neat vertical or horizontal lines on top of the filling, overlapping the edges slightly to seal any gaps. Heat the jelly and water in a small cup in the microwave until just melted (about 30 seconds on High). Stir to combine. Using a pastry brush, gently brush the top of the tarts with a fine layer of the jelly glaze. Chill thoroughly before serving. Serve within 3 to 4 hours.

*Mascarpone is an Italian triple cream version of crème fraîche that has been denatured to remove the whey. Its texture is ultra smooth and its flavor faintly sweet and nutty. It's available at most groceries and specialty stores.

Sweet Green Tea Cream and Fresh Peach Tart with "Grawnola" Crunch

Makes about 12 servings

Summer In the Deep South, where I live, sweet tea is consumed in thirsty gallons during the sweltering months of July and August, which also happens to be peak peach season. Voila! Inspiration for these refreshing and light tarts.

The creamy filling, which forms the flavor backbone of the pastry cream (see Pastry Cream Panache, page 96), is infused with both green and peach tea. Underneath the pastry cream sits the curious crunch of a fabulous "raw" variation on granola that can be purchased online at www.grawnola.com. Or substitute another lightly sweetened granola of choice. In addition to the pleasing crunch, putting the granola underneath the pastry cream protects the pastry from getting soggy. Enjoy these pretty-as-a-peach fresh treats!

(Note: Do NOT substitute the cream with a lower fat product like milk or half-and-half or the cream will curdle once the lemon juice is added.)

EQUIPMENT NEEDED Two 13 x 4 x 1-inch rectangular tart pans with removable bottoms

1 recipe Master Sweet Pastry (page 17)
Egg wash (yolk, splash water, pinch
    salt blended together)

Pastry Cream

2 ¼ cups cream or light cream
1 bag each green tea and peach tea
6 large egg yolks
⅔ cup sugar
⅓ cup cornstarch
1 teaspoon pure vanilla extract
Zest of 2 lemons
Juice of ½ lemon

Tart Filling

1 cup grawnola or brand of your choice,
    crumbled into small pieces
8 peaches, peeled, pitted and sliced ¼ inch thick
¼ cup peach or apricot jelly
Confectioners' sugar, for garnish, optional

Preheat oven to 375 degrees F. Prepare Master Sweet Pastry according to "Perfecting Pastry" (pages 17–18). Chill 30 minutes or overnight. Roll out to form an Elevated Tart Border (page 18). Chill for 20 minutes. Blind bake (see page 19) in a 375 degree F oven for about 25 minutes, until golden. Remove the pie weights and brush the sides and top with egg wash. Bake 15 to 20 minutes more, or until the crust is completely baked and golden. Remove from the oven and set aside to cool. (Note: The tart can be baked, cooled and sealed in an airtight container up to a full day in advance of filling it.)

Prepare the pastry cream. Bring the cream up to a simmer in a medium-size pot over medium-high heat. Drop both tea bags into the cream and set aside to steep (i.e., infuse) for 15 minutes. Meanwhile, in a large bowl, whisk eggs vigorously until they are light and lemon-colored. All at once, add the sugar, cornstarch, vanilla, zest, and juice. Continue whisking until thoroughly combined and light. Set aside.

Remove tea bags from the milk and squeeze gently to release any additional tea flavor. Discard bags. Bring the milk back up to a simmer. Secure the bowl containing the egg mixture by wrapping a damp kitchen towel, rat-tail style, around the bottom of the bowl so it will not move while you're working. Slowly stream the warm milk into the egg mixture, whisking constantly. Once all of the milk has been poured into the bowl, return the entire mixture to the pan and continue cooking over medium heat at a very gently simmer, whisking constantly. The cream will thicken quickly, in about 3 minutes. Remove from heat and turn out into a clean bowl to cool. Cover the top tightly with plastic wrap, pressing onto the top of the cream to prevent air pockets. Refrigerate to cool and set completely, about 4 hours. (Note: This can be done a day in advance).

To assemble the tarts, crumble grawnola evenly into the bottom of each shell. Top with equal quantities of the cooled cream, spreading evenly with a spatula. Arrange sliced peaches in two attractive vertical rows. Keep the slices tight to one another, avoiding gaps. Heat the jam with a few drops of water in a small cup in the microwave on high for 3 seconds, or until soft and melted. Stir to blend, then brush the tops of the peaches, cream and edges of the tart with the glaze. Garnish the edges with a flurry of sifted confectioners' sugar, if desired. Refrigerate until serving, no more than 3 or 4 hours for maximum freshness.

Pastry Cream Panache

Pastry cream is essentially a crème anglaise (which is used to make everything from ice cream to sauces) that gets additional thickening from cornstarch. It (along with whipped cream, or a combination of the two) is frequently the "bed" for fresh fruit tarts, and it is a delicious one! It's not hard to make, but like a crème anglaise, it needs your constant attention. Watch and "feel" the custard as it sets, whisking constantly or you will end up with a fine mess of scrambled eggs. Invest in a fine sieve (the best are the cone-shaped chinois, available at most fine cooking stores), and if you happen to get a scramble, gently press the warm cream quickly through the sieve with a wooden spoon to strain out any solids. This usually does the trick.

Chocolate-Covered Cherry "Sundae" Tartlets

Makes 12 tartlets

Summer *Fuss-free and virtually cooking-free (except for baking the pastry), these pretty little tartlets look just like little chocolate sundaes in tartlet shells. A bright red maraschino cherry on top continues the theme that kids especially love. A cherry pitter (available at most specialty cooking shops) "pops" the pesky pit right out of the cherries— a job kids love doing. These are perfect for birthday parties! In fact, make it a tart-making birthday party for extra fun! The tartlet shells can be made a day ahead and the filling and toppings come together in minutes.*

EQUIPMENT NEEDED **Twelve 3 x ⅝-inch tartlet pans with removable bottoms, one 4-inch round pastry cutter, one cherry pitter**

1 recipe Master Sweet Pastry (page 17)
1 egg wash (yolk, splash water, pinch
　　salt blended together)

Cream Topping
1 cup whole cream
1 large bar (3.17 ounces) dark (86%
　　cacao) chocolate, coarsely chopped
Pinch sea salt or kosher salt
36 whole Bing cherries (about 1½
　　cups), stems removed and pitted
2 vanilla beans
1 cup whole milk ricotta cheese
¼ cup sugar
1 tablespoon half-and-half
12 maraschino cherries, for garnish

Prepare Master Sweet Pastry according to "Perfecting Pastry" directions (pages 17–18). Chill for 20 minutes or overnight. Roll out according to Flush Tart Border (page 18) and cut into 4-inch circles with a pastry cutter. Chill for at least 20 minutes. Blind bake (see page 19) in a 375 degree F oven for about 25 minutes, until golden. Remove the pie weights and brush the sides and top with egg wash. Bake 15 to 20 minutes more, or until the crust is completely baked and golden. Remove from the oven and set aside to cool. (Note: The tartlets can be baked, cooled and sealed in an airtight container up to a full day in advance of filling them).

To prepare the topping, bring the cream to a simmer over medium-high heat. Place the chopped chocolate and salt in a medium bowl. Pour hot cream over the chocolate and blend with a whisk to melt. Stir in the prepped cherries and coat. Meanwhile, cut the vanilla beans in half, vertically, and scrape the seeds from the interior with a small, sharp paring knife. Combine the seeds with the ricotta, sugar, and half-and-half. Using a spatula, fill each cooled tartlet with about 3 tablespoons of the ricotta mixture, leveling the filling flush with the edges of the tart. Top each tartlet with three chocolate-covered cherries, drizzling a little extra chocolate over each. Top the center of each tartlet with a maraschino cherry. Chill for 20 minutes to set the chocolate. Serve within 4 to 6 hours.

Raspberry Crème Brûlée Tartlets

Makes 8 single-serving tartlets

Summer *In this recipe, we take crème brûlée and literally turn it upside down. It's normally baked in little "pots," chilled, dusted with sugar and then broiled or "burned." Here, we start the same way but then turn out the well-chilled crème to top the fresh raspberry bed in each tartlet. Afterwards, the top is dusted with sugar and browned with a kitchen torch. The crème clings to this mid-summer fruit like a cloud, and the brûlée finish delivers a fine crunch factor. A layer of raspberry jam on the bottom of the tarts helps glue the berries in place. The crème and pastry can, and should, be prepped the day before. Keep the tartlets cold before serving, and serve within a few hours of assembly.*

EQUIPMENT NEEDED **Eight 3⅝ x 1-inch tartlet pans, one 4-inch round pastry cutter, kitchen torch, three 8-ounce ramekins**

1 recipe Master Sweet Pastry (page 17)
1 egg wash (yolk, splash water, pinch
 salt blended together)

Crème

1 pint heavy cream
1 vanilla bean, split and seeds
 scraped and reserved
¼ cup sugar
3 large egg yolks
½ cup best-quality raspberry jam (with seeds)
1 pint fresh raspberries
¼ cup granulated sugar, for the brûlée

Prepare Master Sweet Pastry according to "Perfecting Pastry" directions (pages 17–18). Chill for 20 minutes or overnight. Roll out according to Flush Tart Border (page 18) and cut into 4-inch circles with a pastry cutter. Chill for at least 20 minutes. Blind bake (see page 19) in a 375 degree F oven for about 25 minutes, until golden. Remove the pie weights and brush the sides and top with egg wash. Bake 15 to 20 minutes more, or until the crust is completely baked and golden. Remove from the oven and set aside to cool.

The day before serving, prepare the cream. Preheat oven to 325 degrees F. Simmer the heavy cream and vanilla bean and reserved seeds together over low heat for 20 minutes to infuse the flavor of the bean. Set aside and let steep another 30 minutes. Remove the vanilla bean.

Meanwhile, combine sugar and egg yolks in a medium bowl. Whisk thoroughly until the mixture is light, airy and lemon-colored. Bring the cream back to a low boil then gradually drizzle it into the egg/sugar mixture, whisking constantly. Once all of the cream has been incorporated, set aside. Arrange the ramekins in a roasting pan and fill each with the cream, leaving ½ inch free border at the top. Fill the roasting pan to half the height of the ramekins with very hot or boiling water. Bake on the center rack of the oven about 1 hour, until the cream is just set but still has a bit of a jiggle. Remove from the oven and set aside to cool. Refrigerate overnight (and up to 3 days) covered with plastic wrap.

To assemble the tarts, fill the bottom of each pre-baked tartlet with a generous tablespoon of jam, spreading it to the edges. Fill the bottom of each tart with raspberries arranged concentrically, bottom-side down. Place a heaping tablespoon of the well-chilled cream on top of the raspberry base of each tartlet. Sprinkle the top of each tartlet evenly with 1 teaspoon sugar. Brown the tops using a kitchen torch or brown under a hot broiler, so they get an even caramelized glow. Place a fresh raspberry in the center of each tart. Chill at least one hour (and up to 3) before serving.

'Nana and Nilla Pudding Tart with a Chocolate Kiss

Serves 8 to 10

Summer Even though bananas do not have a "season" in the South, there is a peak season for barbecue, and that's summer. For barbecue and all its sordidly indulgent fixings, from corn pudding to coleslaw, banana and Nilla Wafer pudding is the dessert of choice. Cold, slithery, silky pudding (actually pastry cream) softens the edge of the crunchy Nilla Wafers as it sits awaiting eager consumption.

In this tart, I add a cushioning layer of ganache to line a Nilla Wafer crust and give it chocolatey pluck. Additional wafers are partially dipped in the stuff to set off the top of the border. Fresh bananas are mashed into the warm pudding to infuse it with the fruit's signature sweet flavor, and whipped cream tops it all off. This is an excellent tart to pre-bake the pastry and pre-make the fillings the day before and put it all together an hour or so before serving.

EQUIPMENT NEEDED One 8 x 1¾-inch fluted quiche/tart pan with removable bottom

1 recipe Master Sweet Pastry
1 egg wash (yolk, splash water, pinch salt blended together)

Pastry Cream

2¼ cups light cream or whipping cream
1 vanilla bean, split and seeds scraped and reserved
6 egg yolks
⅔ cups granulated sugar
⅓ cup cornstarch
Pinch sea salt or kosher salt
2 large bananas, peeled

Ganache

2 ounces 60% cacao dark chocolate (I like Ghirardelli Intense Dark)
2 tablespoons whole cream
24 Nilla Wafers, divided
1 banana, peeled and cut into thin diagonal slices

Whipped Cream

1 cup whole cream
¼ cup granulated sugar
1 teaspoon pure vanilla extract

Prepare Master Sweet Pastry according to "Perfecting Pastry" directions (pages 17–18). Chill for 30 minutes or overnight. Roll out according to Flush Tart Border (page 18). Chill for at least 20 minutes. Blind bake (see page 19) in a 375 degree F oven for about 25 minutes, until golden.

Remove the pie weights and brush the sides and top of the tart with egg wash. Bake 15 to 20 minutes more, or until the crust is completely baked and golden. Remove tart from the oven and set aside to cool. (Note: The tart can be baked, cooled and sealed in an airtight container up to a full day in advance of filling it.)

Prepare the pastry cream/pudding. In a medium-size pan, heat the cream over medium-high heat with the vanilla bean seeds until simmering at a low boil. Meanwhile, combine the egg yolks, sugar, cornstarch, and salt in a large bowl, whisking thoroughly for 1 to 2 minutes, until light and lemon-colored. Gradually pour the hot cream into the egg yolk mixture, whisking constantly. Return the mixture to the same cooking pan, over medium heat, whisking constantly for about 3 minutes, until thickened and set. Remove from heat and mash bananas into the warm mixture. Turn out into a fresh bowl and refrigerate overnight to set, wrapping with plastic wrap pressed down to the top of the pudding to prevent the formation of a skin.

To assemble the tart, prepare the ganache. Melt the chocolate and cream together in a small, nonreactive bowl in the microwave for 1 minute on High. Whisk to combine. Using a pastry brush, coat the bottom and sides of the prepared tart shell with the hot chocolate ganache. Refrigerate for 10 minutes to set the chocolate. Meanwhile, dip 12 of the Nilla Wafers in the remaining chocolate, coating one half of each. Line up on a sheet of parchment paper to set. Whip the cold cream, sugar and vanilla together (see Getting the Best Whip Out of Your Cream, page 111) in a cold bowl. Reserve in the refrigerator.

Arrange 12 un-coated Nilla wafers in the bottom of the chocolate-lined tart. Top with several thin slices of banana. Top this with a layer of cold pastry cream, smoothing with a spatula to flatten the top. Insert the non-chocolate end of the prepped chocolate-dipped Nilla wafers into the edges of the tart in a concentric pattern. Fill in the middle with whipped cream, forming a rounded mound with your pastry spatula. Refrigerate for 1 to 2 hours before serving.

Lavender Buttermilk Tart

Serves 6 to 8

Fall *Any time of year is just right for buttermilk pie. I love the fluttery femininity of the delicate custard, kissed here with the hardly detectable nuance of lavender leaves. It leaves an inviting flavor trail that leads to pastoral dreams. In slender tart form, the buttermilk custard is even more delicate and quivers ever so slightly as it reaches the plate. It's the perfect dessert to be enjoyed after dinner, in front of a blazing fire on a cool fall evening with a loved one or two.*

EQUIPMENT NEEDED **One 8 x 1¾-inch fluted quiche/tart pan with removable bottom**

1 recipe Master Sweet Pastry (page 17)
1 egg wash (yolk, splash water, pinch
    salt blended together)

Lavender-Infused Buttermilk

1½ cups buttermilk
½ cup whole cream
1 tablespoon dried lavender flowers or leaves

Custard

¼ cup all-purpose flour
¾ cup sugar
¼ teaspoon kosher salt or sea salt
3 large eggs
6 tablespoons sweet butter, melted
1 teaspoon pure vanilla extract
Whipped cream, optional
Lavender for garnish, optional

Prepare Master Sweet Pastry (see "Perfecting Pastry," pages 17–18). Chill 30 minutes or overnight. Roll out according to instructions on creating Elevated Tart Border (page 18). Chill 20 to 30 minutes.

Preheat the oven to 375 degrees F. Place the prepared shell on a baking pan and blind bake the pastry (see Blind Baking, page 19) about 20 minutes, until set and becoming golden. Remove the pie weights, brush down the pastry with egg wash, and return to the oven to finish baking another 10 minutes, until golden brown. Remove the pre-baked shell from the oven and reduce the oven temperature to 350 degrees F. Let the shell cool slightly at room temperature.

Meanwhile, infuse the buttermilk with the lavender. Combine the buttermilk, cream and lavender flowers in a saucepan, whisking to combine. Turn the heat on high and bring to a low boil; reduce heat to medium-low and simmer for 10 minutes. Remove from heat and set aside to steep 5 minutes. Using a fine sieve, strain buttermilk into a medium bowl and refrigerate to cool.

In a large bowl, whisk together the flour, sugar, and salt. In a medium bowl, whisk eggs for 1 minute, until lemon-colored and fluffy. Whisk in butter and vanilla. When the buttermilk has cooled to body temperature or cooler, add it to the egg mixture, slowly streaming in and whisking to combine. To finish the custard, stream the milk/egg mixture into the flour mixture, whisking constantly. Pour the custard into the prepared tart shell. Bake 35 minutes, or until the custard has browned to a light tan and the custard still quivers to the touch. Remove from oven and cool for at least 1 hour before slicing. It's best refrigerated, covered, for several hours or overnight and served cold with a dollop of whipped cream (see Getting the Best Whip Out of Your Cream, page 111). Garnish with a few lavender leaves or flowers scattered on the plate.

Butterscotch and Caramel Apple Tarts

Makes 2 tarts, approximately 10 servings

Fall Super-silky and delicate butterscotch pudding (a beloved southern dish) forms the first layer of this delightful tart. It's topped with see-through-thin slices of skin-on, tart Granny Smith apples, which provide a protective layer for the hot caramel that tops it all off.

A decadent ode to autumn, this tart is surprisingly simple to make and divine to eat. Take extra care with the caramel. It's not difficult to make, but it gets dangerously hot once the sugar turns to caramel and can do serious damage to exposed skin. Use a deep, broad-sided pan and add the cream very gradually, as the sauce will bubble up vigorously as the cream is added. The pudding, caramel, and pastry shells can be made a full day ahead and the tarts can be assembled up to 3 or 4 hours before serving. Make sure it's nice and cool when you serve it. Drizzle the plates with the leftover caramel sauce. I add just a touch of molasses to the pudding for deeper color and a flavor surprise.

EQUIPMENT NEEDED Two 13 x 4 x 1-inch rectangular tart pans

1 recipe Master Sweet Pastry (page 17)
1 egg wash (yolk, splash water, pinch salt blended together)

Butterscotch Pudding

2¾ cup whole milk, divided
¾ cup firmly packed dark brown sugar
¼ teaspoon kosher salt or sea salt
4 egg yolks
¼ cup plus 1 tablespoon cornstarch
2 tablespoons cold butter, cut into small cubes
2 teaspoons pure vanilla extract
1 teaspoon molasses

Caramel

1½ cups sugar
9 tablespoons cold butter (1 stick plus 1 tablespoon), cut into small cubes
¾ cup whipping cream
1–2 large Granny Smith apples, halved, cored, and sliced very thinly, for garnish

Prepare the Master Sweet Pastry according to "Perfecting Pastry" (pages 17–18). Wrap with plastic wrap and refrigerate 30 minutes or overnight. Roll out into a large square (see On a Roll, page 18) and fill the tart pans according to Flush Tart Border (page 18). Chill for at least 20 minutes. Blind bake (see page 19) in a 375 degree F oven for about 25 minutes, until golden. Remove the pie weights and brush the sides and top of the tart with egg wash. Bake about 15 to 20 minutes more, or until the crust is completely baked and golden. Remove from oven and set aside to cool. (Note: This can be done a day ahead. Keep the tart shells in an airtight container once cooled.)

Prepare the pudding. In a large bowl, whisk together ½ cup milk, brown sugar, salt, egg yolks, and cornstarch. Whisk until frothy and well blended. Meanwhile, bring the remaining milk up to a boil in a heavy-bottomed, deep saucepan over medium-high heat, watching closely to avoid scalding or spills. As soon as it just bubbles to a boil, gradually stream the warm milk into the mixture in the bowl. Whisk in until well incorporated. Return the mixture to the same pan and place over medium heat. Whisk vigorously for about 2 minutes, until the pudding starts to set. It should be smooth and firm with a pliable consistency. Remove the pan from the heat and whisk in the butter, vanilla, and molasses. Taste and adjust seasoning (especially salt) if desired. Transfer the pudding into a clean medium bowl and refrigerate until fully cold or overnight. Cover with plastic wrap pressed to the surface of the pudding to prevent a skin from forming.

Meanwhile, prepare the caramel. Place the sugar in a medium-size heavy-bottomed pan with high sides. Heat over medium-high heat, gently stirring the sugar to help it melt and start to caramelize. Once the sugar has completely melted, stop stirring. It will caramelize very quickly, bubbling up a bit in the pan (be careful!). Once it has turned a luscious caramel color, remove from the heat and whisk in the butter until it is melted. Very gradually whisk in the cream. Set aside to cool. When cool enough to handle, either use it to assemble the tart or refrigerate it in a covered container for up to 2 weeks.

To assemble the tarts, place equal quantities of the cooled pudding in the bottom of the two cooled pastry shells. Using a spatula, even out the pudding so it fully fills the tart shells and is flat and smooth. Slice the apples, then quickly arrange them along the top of the tarts in two rows, forming a kind of layered apple "spine" down the center of each tart. Top with a generous amount of caramel (about ¾ cup for each tart), brushing it with a pastry brush to evenly disperse and to cover the pudding and apples. Chill the tarts for 2 to 3 hours before serving. Slice and serve on a plate drizzled with extra caramel sauce.

Vanilla-Dipped Pear and Chocolate Tartlets

Makes 10 individual tartlets

Fall/Winter My petite, talented, French firecracker of a photographer/food stylist and I met at the farmers market one beautiful Saturday morning last fall. She started telling me about some recipe development she was doing for her blog using diminutive Forelle pears. "They would be perfect in a tartlet," she exclaimed in sheer joy. Voila! The next day, I found some at my local grocery store. They are beautiful, tiny little things that are just packed with juicy flavor. Even though they are grown in the Pacific Northwest, they taste just as delicious in the fall here, and their little size is perfectly suited to an individual-size tartlet.

In these delicious, vanilla-drenched tartlets (there is even vanilla in the pastry!), the vanilla-cinnamon-poached pear halves nestle into virtually flourless chocolate cake pillows of deliciousness. They are best served warm with a drizzle of the poaching syrup and a fat scoop of vanilla ice cream.

pans with removable bottoms, one 4-inch round pastry cutter, baking sheet

1 recipe Master Sweet Pastry (page 17), plus
the seeds scraped from 1 fresh vanilla bean

Poached Pears

1 cup sugar
2½ cups water
¼ cup Poire William or other pear liqueur
1 fresh vanilla bean, split and seeds
scraped and reserved
3 star anise (see sidebar, page 109)
1 cinnamon stick
Generous pinch kosher salt or sea salt
5 ripe but firm Forelle pears, peeled, halved
and gently cored (stem on, if possible)

Chocolate Filling

1 bar (4.25 ounces) mildly sweet dark chocolate
1 cup heavy cream, warm
Generous pinch salt
½ teaspoon pure vanilla extract
2 egg yolks
½ cup all-purpose flour

Preheat the oven to 375 degrees F. Prepare the Master Sweet Pastry and roll out as described in "Perfecting Pastry" (pages 17–18). Chill 30 minutes or overnight. Roll out, cut the pastry into 4-inch circles using a pastry cutter, and line the tartlet pans according to Flush Tart Border (page 18). Arrange the lined tartlets on a baking sheet and chill for at least 20 minutes.

pears (including the vanilla bean and reserved seeds) in a medium saucepan. Heat over high until it reaches a low boil, whisking to help melt the sugar. Reduce heat to medium-low and arrange pears cut side down in a single layer in the poaching liquid. Poach for 10 minutes, or until a knife can gently penetrate the pears without breaking them up (this will depend on their ripeness). Using a slotted spoon, gently remove the pears from the pan and arrange on paper towels to drain. Remove the vanilla bean, cinnamon stick and star anise and discard.

To prepare the chocolate filling, break the chocolate bar into small chunks and place in a medium bowl. Heat the cream in a nonreactive container until very warm. Pour cream over the chocolate and whisk to blend. Whisk in the salt and vanilla extract. Set aside or refrigerate for a few minutes, until the chocolate cools to body temperature. Whisk in the egg yolks and then the flour until fully incorporated.

To assemble the tarts, ladle just under ½ cup of chocolate mixture into each prepped tartlet shell. Place a pear half, round side down, in the center of each tartlet. It will partially submerge, and this is fine. Bake at 375 degrees F for 25 minutes, or until the chocolate filling has puffed up and surrounded the pretty little pear. Remove from oven, cool slightly. Remove tartlets from the pans and serve individually with a pool of the warm poaching liquid and whipped cream.

Star anise is so named because it is shaped like a star that contains a tiny seed of flavor in each of its eight star sections. A member of the magnolia family, its taste resembles anise. It's usually available at Asian markets and increasingly at mainstream grocery stores. If you cannot find it, just add another cinnamon stick to the poaching liquid in this recipe.

Roasted Pumpkin Ice Cream and Candied Pecan Tartlets

Serves 8

Fall/Winter *Oven-roasting gives fall's beacon cool-weather squash and pumpkin a special sweetness that swirls deliciously with a simple ice cream custard and pumpkin pie spice. A lightly sweetened tart crust envelops the ice cream with crunchy, buttery panache, while nutty southern pecans take a quick caramelized sugar bath to provide the finishing touch.*

These are too cute not to be made into individual tartlets, but if you must, a standard tart form will work, as well. You will have ice cream left over for midnight indulging.

EQUIPMENT NEEDED **Eight 3 x ⅝-inch round tartlet pans, one 4-inch round pastry cutter**

1 recipe Master Sweet Pastry (page 17)
1 egg wash (yolk, splash water, pinch
    salt blended together)

Ice Cream

1 pie pumpkin
1¼ cups whole milk
2 cups whipping cream
¾ cup granulated sugar
6 egg yolks
1 teaspoon vanilla extract
1 teaspoon pumpkin pie spice
1 teaspoon cinnamon
Pinch cloves

Candied Pecans

2 tablespoons butter
½ cup pecan halves
½ teaspoon sugar

Whipped cream (see Classic Whipped
    Cream in Getting the Best Whip Out
    of Your Cream, facing page)

Preheat the oven to 375 degrees F. Prepare the Master Sweet Pastry as described in "Perfecting Pastry" (pages 17–18). Chill 30 minutes or overnight. Roll out, cut into circles with a 4-inch pastry cutter, and line the tartlet pans according to Flush Tart Border (page 18). Arrange the lined tartlets on a baking sheet and chill for at least 20 minutes. Blind bake (see page 19) in a 375 degree F oven for about 25 minutes, until golden. Remove the pie weights and brush the sides and top with egg wash. Bake 15 to 20 minutes more, or until the crust is completely baked and golden. Remove from the oven and set aside on a wire rack to cool. (Note: The tart can be baked, cooled and sealed in an airtight container up to a full day in advance of filling it.)

Meanwhile, preheat the oven to 425 degrees F. Cut the pumpkin in half, horizontally, scoop out and discard the seeds, and place pumpkin halves cut side down on a baking sheet. Roast for 1 hour, or until the flesh is soft. Cool, then peel off the skin and discard. Puree the flesh in a food processor until smooth. Reserve ¾ cup for the ice cream. (Note: Any remaining pumpkin can be refrigerated for several days or frozen for several months.) Refrigerate the puree until completely cold.

Bring the milk and cream to an aggressive simmer in a saucepan over medium-high heat. In a large bowl, whisk

colored. Whisk in the remaining ingredients, including the reserved pumpkin puree, until smooth. Once the milk and cream come to a simmer, slowly whisk them into the egg mixture, stirring constantly. Return mixture to the saucepan and cook over medium heat, stirring constantly with a wooden spoon. The custard is done once it starts to coat the back of the spoon and the bubbles on top have disappeared. Remove it from the heat and strain through a fine strainer into a bowl set into a bed of ice; let cool completely, stirring occasionally. Freeze in an ice cream maker according to manufacturer's directions.

(Note: Both the ice cream custard and tartlet shells can be made a day ahead and filled just before serving. Keep tart shells in an airtight container.)

Meanwhile, prepare the whipping cream. Refrigerate until ready to use. To prepare the pecans, melt the butter in a small sauté pan over medium-high heat. Add the pecan halves and sugar and toss to coat. Continue cooking (tossing occasionally) about 3 minutes, until the pecans have caramelized on all sides. Set aside on a paper towel to drain and cool.

To put together the tartlets, scoop a heaping ¼ cup of the prepared ice cream into the tart shells and level with your spatula so the ice cream is flush with the tartlet borders. Place the tartlets on a baking sheet and place in the freezer about 20 minutes so the ice cream sets even more firmly. To finish, top each with a generous dollop of whipped cream and 3 or 4 candied pecan halves.

Getting the Best Whip Out of Your Cream

Cream needs to be "heavy" or "whipping" cream, to mount well. These are two names for essentially the same thing: a cream that contains 36 percent or more milk fat, which enables the air to work its way into the cream and stay there. Try whipping skim milk to save calories and you'll be there all day! To get the best results, the cream needs to be very cold, and it needs to be whipped in a cold bowl.

An electric blender works just fine, but for small quantities like this, I like to whisk it with a large wire whisk. Chill a glass, stainless steel or copper bowl, as well as the cream, in your freezer for several minutes before starting. When ready, combine the cream, sugar and vanilla in the bowl, wrap a rolled-up kitchen towel around the base of the bowl to keep it in place, and whisk away. Bring the whisk under and over the cream in a rapid motion, slowly turning the bowl as you go. If done in this manner, the cream should be fluffy and mounted within less than two minutes. Stop when you have firm, fluffy peaks or your sweet cream will quickly become sweet butter. Store for up to an hour ahead in the refrigerator, if desired, and whisk lightly just before serving.

Classic Whipped Cream

Yields 8 to 10 service toppings

1 cup cold whipping cream
¼ cup granulated sugar
1 teaspoon pure vanilla extract
Tiny pinch kosher salt or sea salt

Drunken Pumpkin-Bourbon Tart

Serves 8 to 10

Fall/Winter **This tart utilizes the distinctly delicious flavor and color of roasted fresh pie pumpkin. (Substitute canned pumpkin only if nothing else is available.) The custard gets pumped up with bourbon and plenty of spice so that it takes on a beautiful, burnt caramel color and layers of festive flavor. It is best served cold or at room temperature with a generous dollop of freshly whipped cream (see Getting the Best Whip Out of Your Cream, page 111).**

EQUIPMENT NEEDED **One 9 x 1-inch round tart pan with removable bottom**

1 recipe Master Sweet Pastry (page 17)
1 egg wash (yolk, splash water, pinch
    salt blended together)
1 pie pumpkin

Filling

2 cups roasted pumpkin flesh
3 large eggs
½ cup light brown sugar
1 cup heavy cream
2 tablespoons bourbon
1 teaspoon pure vanilla extract
1 teaspoon kosher salt or sea salt
2 tablespoons molasses
2 teaspoons ground cinnamon
½ teaspoon ground ginger
¼ teaspoon ground cloves
¼ teaspoon ground nutmeg

Preheat the oven to 375 degrees F. Prepare the Master Sweet Pastry and roll out as described in "Perfecting Pastry" (pages 17–18). Chill 30 minutes or overnight. Line the tart pan according to Elevated Tart Border (page 18). Chill for at least 20 minutes. Blind bake (see Blind Baking, page 19) for 20 minutes. Remove the parchment paper and pie weights, and brush down the bottom, sides and edges of the tart with egg wash. Return tart pan to the oven and bake another 10 minutes, or until golden and nearly fully set. Remove from the oven and set aside.

Meanwhile, cut the pumpkin in half and remove the pulp and seeds. Turn pumpkin halves cut side down on a roasting sheet and bake in the preheated oven about 45 minutes, until the flesh is soft to the touch and beginning to implode. (Note: If you bake the pumpkin and tart shell simultaneously, place pumpkin below the tart shell so it does not impede even coloring). When the pumpkin is done, remove from oven and let cool.

Reduce oven temperature to 350 degrees F.

To prepare the filling, scoop 2 cups roasted pumpkin flesh out of the pumpkin halves and place in a large bowl. Using a hand-held mixer, blend the pumpkin for 2 minutes on medium speed to a smooth consistency. Add eggs and brown sugar, and blend together on medium for 1 minute, or until fully incorporated. Add the remaining ingredients and blend on medium until fluffy, aerated and fully incorporated. Gently pour the custard into the prepared tart shell, leaving a ¼-inch-deep tart border. Place on a baking sheet and bake on the center oven rack. After 15 minutes, reduce heat to 325 degrees F, and continue baking about 30 minutes, until custard has just set and quivers slightly to the touch. Cool completely before slicing, or refrigerate for several hours or overnight before serving. (Note: If you have a bit of custard left over, pour it into a small oven-proof bowl or ramekin and bake it along with the tart until it's set. It makes a wonderful midnight custard snack!)

Peanut Butter Fluff and Chocolate Tart

Serves 8

Fall/Winter What kids, regardless of their "real" age, don't love peanut butter, marshmallow cream, and chocolate all wrapped up in one? On a recipe development grocery run, I spied the fluffy stuff staring at me brazenly from a shelf, right next to the peanut butter. My neighbor Lucie had recently turned me on to the wonders of chocolate graham crackers, so that became the crust that cradles this decadent tart filled with a mousse-like blend of cream cheese, marshmallow cream, and peanut butter. It can be fully assembled ahead of time and chilled overnight. However, save whipping the cream until just a few hours before service. This is heartbreakingly good and beautiful to look at! Its richness and pumpkin-colored hue are perfect for fall and winter indulgences.

EQUIPMENT NEEDED One 9 x 1-inch round tart pan with a removable bottom

Chocolate Crust

1 stick soft butter

3 cups crumbled chocolate graham cracker crust (about 1½ wrapped plastic packets)

Filling

1 cup creamy peanut butter

4 ounces (½ cup) cream cheese

¾ cup marshmallow cream (suggest Kraft's Jet-Puffed brand)

¼ cup light brown sugar

Topping

½ cup whipping cream

3 tablespoons sugar

1 teaspoon vanilla

½ cup semi-sweet chocolate chunks or chips

Preheat the oven to 375 degrees F.

To prepare the crust, crush the graham crackers with a rolling pin and continue until they are about the size of tiny peas. Combine the cracker crumbs and butter in a small bowl, using your hands, until thoroughly mixed. Press the crust evenly into the bottom of the tart pan, pressing the crumbs into the edges. It's okay if it looks a little rough and rustic. Fill with parchment paper and beans or pie weights, and blind bake (see page 19) for 25 minutes. (Note: No egg wash required.) Remove parchment and pie weights and continue baking another 20 minutes, or until the crust starts to dry out and crisp. Remove from oven and set aside to cool. Chill to refrigerate. (Note: You can make the crust a day ahead and refrigerate, tightly wrapped.)

Meanwhile, prepare the filling. Combine the peanut butter, cream cheese, marshmallow cream and brown sugar in a medium-size bowl. Whisk to combine, or blend with a hand-held mixer until very fluffy and smooth.

To assemble, add the filling to the completely cooled crust. Smooth with a spatula to the edges of the tart. Refrigerate for several hours, or overnight if desired. If serving within the next few hours, proceed to whip the cream, sugar and vanilla together (see Getting the Best Whip Out of Your Cream, page 111) in a cold medium-size bowl until firm peaks have formed. All at once, place the whipped cream on top of the tart. Spread with a spatula to level it out, leaving ½ inch visible border of the peanut butter filling. Sprinkle chocolate chunks or chips over the whipped cream. Chill for at least 1 hour and up to 3 hours before serving.

Toasty and Nutty Chocolate Hazelnut Tart

...and works wonderfully in this tart that is chock full of hazelnuts, Nutella, and a dark, rich custard that holds it all together. Warm from the oven, this rich tart begs to be eaten in front of a blazing fire on a cold fall or winter evening. Serve with warm mugs of cocoa or coffee and top off the tart with freshly whipped cream. I like this tart best in a round tart pan, but it would also work wonderfully in a rectangular or square tart pan or as individual tartlets.

EQUIPMENT NEEDED **One 9 x 1-inch round tart pan with removable bottom**

1 recipe Master Sweet Pastry (page 17)
1 egg wash (yolk, splash water, pinch
　　salt blended together)
1 cup Nutella
4 tablespoons butter, cut into small cubes
1/2 cup half-and-half
1/2 cup dark corn syrup
1 teaspoon vanilla
1/4 teaspoon kosher salt or sea salt
3 eggs, beaten
1 cup finely chopped hazelnuts
Whipped cream

neat to gently warm and melt the butter. Off the heat, stir in the half-and-half. Let stand to cool slightly.

Separately, combine the corn syrup, vanilla, salt, and eggs in a large bowl. Whisk thoroughly to combine. When fluffy and light, whisk in the Nutella mixture until smooth. Fold in the hazelnuts using a spatula or wooden spoon. Pour into the prepared pastry shell and bake at 375 degrees F about 40 minutes, until golden and puffy. Let cool at least 45 minutes before cutting and serving, or chill overnight. It's delicious warm or cold from the refrigerator. Either way, serve with whipped cream!

Coco-nutty Sweet Potato Tart

Serves 10 to 12

Fall/Winter/Spring **In this simple tart, the pure flavor of sweet potatoes really comes through. Hardly a custard with just two eggs to bind one large potato, it's more like a fluffy puree that's lightly sweetened and seasoned. A final layer of sweet coconut flakes on top forms a pleasing crunch and an attractive toasty hue. I baked this in my fat rectangular tart pan and cut it into bars, which makes a really nice presentation. It would also work well in a round tart pan. Serve this just as it is, either warm or cold. It's delicious either way.**

EQUIPMENT NEEDED **One 8 x 11 x 1-inch rectangular tart pan with removable bottom**

1 large sweet potato, scrubbed, trimmed
   of bad spots, and pierced with a fork
1 recipe Master Sweet Pastry (page 17)
1 egg wash (yolk, splash water, pinch
   salt blended together)

Filling

2 cups (yield) flesh from the pre-baked,
   peeled sweet potato
2 large eggs
1/2 teaspoon kosher salt or sea salt
1 cup whole cream
1/4 cup light brown sugar
1 teaspoon ground ginger
1 teaspoon ground cinnamon
1/4 teaspoon ground cloves
1/4 cup dark corn syrup
1 cup sweet coconut flakes

Preheat the oven to 400 degrees F. Bake the sweet potato on the middle rack until soft and tender, about 1 hour. Remove and set aside to cool.

Meanwhile, prepare the Master Sweet Pastry and roll out as described in "Perfecting Pastry" (pages 17–18). Chill 30 minutes or overnight. Roll out and line the tart pan according to Elevated Tart Border (page 18). Chill for at least 20 minutes. Brush bottoms, sides and edges lightly with egg wash using a pastry brush.

Reduce oven heat to 350 degrees F.

Prepare the filling. Remove the skin from the cooled sweet potato and combine in a large bowl with the eggs, salt, cream, brown sugar, ginger, cinnamon, cloves and corn syrup. Using a hand-held blender, blend on medium about 2 minutes, until smooth, fluffy and incorporated, using a spatula to scrape down the sides and bottom of the bowl.

Fill the prepared pastry shell with the sweet potato mixture, smoothing it evenly with a spatula. Sprinkle the coconut evenly over the top of the tart, leaving 1/2 inch border of the filling uncovered. Bake at 350 degrees F for 45 minutes, until golden and just barely firm to the touch. Serve warm or cool, or refrigerate overnight and serve cold.

Sweet Fruit Tarts
and Pockets

The buttery, nutty flavor of perfect pastry has no better filling match than fruit, whether it's a hand-held pie pocket, an open tart, or an assembled tartlet. Tart, acidic fruits with just the right amount of sugar make this a most decadent flavor marriage that is absolutely impossible to resist. Paired with ice cream or whipped cream, the juicy, dripping deliciousness Deep Purple Fresh Cherry Pie Pockets (page 123) is one of my top five favorite recipes in this entire book. The fast assembly of the Super Sexy Scuppernong and Pomegranate Tartlets (page 135) is deceiving, as these beauties look like colorful clouds of cream and ruby and taste like heaven. The tart-sweet crunch of the Winesap Apple and Walnut "Wow" Tart (page 138) just begs for a big, fat scoop of fresh vanilla ice cream.

Strawberry, Rhubarb and Rosemary Pocket Pies

Serves 8 to 16 (makes 16 pockets)

Spring/Summer **The sweet/tart combination of fresh strawberries and lip-smacking rhubarb is a warm-weather classic. In these pie pockets, the flavors are super-concentrated and fabulous. A handful of raisins give a little sweet bite and girth, while fresh rosemary folded into the pastry gives a gentle flavor surprise with every bite. All these baked pockets need for a finish is a dusting of powdered sugar while they're still warm from the oven. Serve leftover compote warm on the side.**

EQUIPMENT NEEDED **4-inch round pastry cutter, parchment paper, baking sheet**

1 recipe Master Sweet Pastry (page 17) plus
    2 tablespoons freshly chopped rosemary

Filling

2½ cups fresh strawberries, stemmed,
    rinsed and quartered
4 medium stalks fresh rhubarb, trimmed,
    rinsed and cut into ¼-inch dice, divided
¼ cup water
⅓ cup granulated sugar plus
    2 tablespoons, divided
Generous pinch sea salt or kosher salt
1 tablespoon freshly squeezed orange juice
1 tablespoon cornstarch blended into
    a paste with a few drops water
½ cup raisins or currants
Powdered sugar, for garnish
1 egg wash (yolk, pinch salt, splash
    water blended together)
Fresh rosemary sprigs, for garnish, optional

Prepare Master Sweet Pastry according to "Perfecting Pastry" (pages 17–18). Add the rosemary after the butter has been incorporated and before adding the water. Wrap tightly with plastic wrap or parchment paper and chill at least 1 hour (or overnight).

To prepare the filling combine the strawberries, 2 cups rhubarb, water, ⅓ cup sugar, salt, and orange juice in a large saucepan. Bring to a boil over high heat then reduce to a lively simmer. Cook, uncovered, about 20 minutes, until the compote has thickened and reduced by half, stirring from time to time. Remove from heat and stir in remaining rhubarb, cornstarch paste, and raisins. Return to heat and simmer another 5 minutes. Remove from heat and turn out the compote into a shallow bowl. Freeze, covered, for at least 3 hours (or overnight), until very cold and semi-frozen.

At least 30 minutes before filling the pockets, remove the compote from the freezer and set out at room temperature to soften slightly. Preheat the oven to 425 F.

Roll out the pastry according to On a Roll (page 18). Cut the pastry into 4-inch rounds, and arrange on a lightly dusted baking sheet. Chill for at least 20 minutes. To fill the pockets, place a heaping tablespoon of the compote on the right side of each chilled pastry circle, leaving ¼ inch naked border on the right. Pull the top over the filling, guiding the top pastry to meet the naked pastry border. Seal gently with your fingertips, then press the border gently with the tines of a fork to seal. Arrange pockets on a parchment-lined baking sheet and chill another 20 minutes. Before baking, gently brush the tops of the pockets with egg wash, dust evenly with the 2 tablespoons granulated sugar, and cut three short slices in the top of each. Bake for 15 minutes. Reduce heat to 375 F and bake another 15 minutes, or until golden brown and bubbling.

Serve warm, dusted with powdered sugar and placing fresh rosemary sprigs for garnish, if desired.

Deep Purple Fresh Cherry Pie Pockets

Makes 14 individual pies

Summer *A great bargain on beautiful Bing cherries and a lingering curiosity about, and deep love of, fried fruit pies (a hot southern tradition) inspired me to take the plunge into the wonderful world of deep-fried pies. Like so many things, once you try it, you realize it is not as difficult as you may have thought.*

I recently purchased a cherry pitter, which makes easy and fun work of removing the pits. I highly recommend the small investment (mine costs less than $10) in this highly useful kitchen gadget.

Frequently, these empanada-like pie pockets call for lard as a substitute for butter. But I like the way butter tastes and the special flakiness that it offers. The trick is this: the pies go in cold and dry; the oil temperature is right (between 360 and 375 degrees F); they're not overcrowded; they're treated with care when turning.

The fresh cherries are cooked down with cassis (or you could substitute a nice merlot) and finished with dried cranberries, some citrus and exotic spices from cinnamon to allspice. The filling is gently chewy and has a gorgeous deep purple hue. It all merges exquisitely with each flaky warm bite, fresh from the fryer. Amazingly, they're almost as delicious cold the next day, if there are any left over. I recommend you prep the filling and the pastry the day before, assemble the little pies the next morning, chill for several hours, and fry just before serving.

EQUIPMENT NEEDED 1 cherry pitter, 1 deep-fryer thermometer (optional, see directions below), one 4-inch round pastry cutter

1 recipe Master Sweet Pastry (page 17)

Filling

3 ½ cups fresh, pitted whole Bing cherries, or another seasonal variety

½ cup dried cherries

½ cup dried cranberries

½ cup freshly squeezed orange juice (do not substitute concentrate)

½ cup Cassis (or good-quality merlot)

1 vanilla bean, halved lengthwise

⅓ cup sugar

2 teaspoons ground cinnamon

Pinch sea salt or kosher salt

Pinch allspice

Juice of ½ lemon

For Frying

2 cups canola oil (or peanut or vegetable oil)

½ cup powdered sugar, for garnish

Ideally, begin the day before you plan to serve the pies by preparing the Master Sweet Pastry. Allow the dough to rest for several hours or overnight. Roll out the pastry on a lightly floured surface to a large round shape, about ¼ inch thick (see On a Roll, page 18).

Working quickly and tightly, to avoid waste, cut the dough into rounds with your pastry cutter. Ball up any pastry scraps and roll out, repeating, so that you use all, or nearly all, of the pastry. Set the rounds on a plate or platter and refrigerate, covered with plastic wrap.

Meanwhile, prepare the filling. If you don't have a cherry pitter, cut the cherries in half with a paring knife and do the best you can to extricate the pit without losing too

much of the fruit or its juices. Place the pitted cherries into a medium-size saucepan along with the remaining filling ingredients. Bring to a simmer over medium-high heat, and cook until the juices/wine have cooked down to about ½ cup and the fruit has softened and thickened to a compote-like consistency. Set aside to cool. Remove the vanilla bean and scrape out the seeds. Return the seeds to the compote, stirring, and discard the bean. Refrigerate, covered, overnight.

Fill the pies 1 to 2 hours before frying. Arrange the prepared pastry disks on a lightly floured surface. Working quickly, form each tart individually. Take about 1½–2 tablespoons of filling and place it on the right side of the pastry round, leaving about ¼ inch space for the border. Guide the free side of the pastry over the top to make a crescent turnover shape. Seal the edges gently with your fingers and then finish by pressing along the edge with the tines of a fork. Repeat until complete. Place the pies on a large plate or platter and refrigerate as you work.

To fry the pies, use a pan with deep sides that is large enough to ensure you have at least 2 inches of free room at the top. Add the oil and heat over medium-high heat to about 365 degrees F. If you don't have a thermometer, look for movement of the oil at the bottom of the pan, smell for the scent of warm oil, and listen for the occasional pop. To be sure, place a cube of bread in the pan. If the oil is appropriately hot, the bread will brown to a golden color in about 1 minute and will sizzle gently in the oil.

When the oil is hot, gently guide 2 to 3 pies at a time into the oil to fry for 2 minutes on the first side, until golden. Flip gently with a spatula to turn, and cook another 2 minutes on the second side, or until golden and puffy. Drain on paper towels. Repeat with the remaining pies. Discard the used oil after it has cooled.

Serve the pies warm from the fryer. I like them served on individual plates, with a spoonful or two of the remaining compote, and sprinkled with a light coating of powdered sugar. If desired, serve with vanilla ice cream. You're going to be so proud of yourself!

Berry Peachy Free-Form Tarts

Serves 6 to 8

Summer *Free-form, open tarts (also called galettes) have always seemed a little bit daunting to me. They seem to defy gravity, baking all alone without anything to wrap around them to help them hold their shape. As long as the pastry stays cold and the individual tarts are not overfilled, they're basically fuss-free. Substitute any fruit (with the exception of 100 percent citrus) in this recipe and you're golden.*

Ultra-fresh blackberries, blueberries and peaches do a beautiful taste dance in these oven-warm little pies that practically scream for fresh vanilla ice cream.

EQUIPMENT NEEDED **One 4-inch round pastry cutter, parchment paper, baking sheet**

1 recipe Master Sweet Pastry (page 17)
    plus 2 tablespoons yellow
    cornmeal and flour for rolling

Filling

1½ cups fresh blueberries, rinsed and dried
1½ cups fresh blackberries
1 cup fresh, ripe peaches, peeled,
    pitted and coarsely chopped
½ cup granulated sugar
1 teaspoon fresh orange juice
1 teaspoon fresh lemon juice
1 tablespoon cornstarch
1 teaspoon ground cinnamon
1 egg wash (yolk, splash water, pinch
    salt blended together)
Vanilla ice cream, optional

Preheat oven to 375 degrees F. Prepare the Master Sweet Pastry according to "Perfecting Pastry" (pages 17–18). Roll out the dough to about ¼ inch thickness on a work surface lightly dusted with the cornmeal and flour (see On a Roll, page 18). Cut the pastry into 4-inch circles using the pastry cutter. Repeat, working quickly and tightly, to avoid waste, until you have six to eight rounds or have used up all of the pastry. Place the baking sheet in the fridge and chill for at least 20 minutes.

Meanwhile, gently toss the blueberries, blackberries, peaches, sugar, orange and lemon juices, cornstarch and cinnamon together in a medium-size bowl. Prepare the egg wash and set aside.

Working quickly, arrange the pastry rounds on the lined baking sheet with at least 2 inches separating them. Scoop about ½ cup of the filling into the center of one pastry round. Using both of your palms to "cup" the pastry edges, work around the edge to bring the pastry up and around the fruit, pressing gently but firmly to hold the seams together. Press gently with your fingertips to urge them to stay together. Repeat with the remaining pastry rounds. Brush the top and sides of the pastry lightly with egg wash using a pastry brush. Be careful not to over-brush the tarts and let the wash drip down over and under the pastry. Return the pies to the refrigerator and chill 10 to 15 minutes.

Place the sheet in the center rack of the preheated oven and bake about 40 minutes, until set and golden. Serve warm with ice cream. (Note: Though not ideal, the pies can be made a day ahead, fully cooled, fully sealed and re-heated for 10 minutes in a 350 degree F oven before serving.)

Pecan-Peach Tartlets

Makes 8 tartlets

Summer *The contrast of a sweet/tart, juicy peach and a nutty, soft pecan is divine, as you'll taste in these lovely tartlets. The chopped pecans are scattered at the bottom of the tarts before baking, creating a "shield" to prevent the juicy peaches from dampening the pastry. Of course, they also deliver an inviting crunch that plays deliciously with the peaches.*

EQUIPMENT NEEDED **Eight 3⅝ x 1-inch round tartlet pans with removable bottoms, one 4-inch round pastry cutter, baking sheet**

1 recipe Master Sweet Pastry (page 17)
1 egg wash (yolk, splash water, pinch
      salt blended together)

Filling
½ cup finely chopped pecans
6–7 ripe, medium-size peaches (about 2
      cups, peeled, pitted and thinly sliced)
2 tablespoons local honey
1 teaspoon fresh lemon juice
¼ teaspoon cinnamon
Pinch ground cloves
Pinch salt
1 teaspoon cornstarch

Preheat the oven to 375 degrees F. Prepare the Master Sweet Pastry according to "Perfecting Pastry" (pages 17–18). Chill, roll out, cut into 4-inch circles using a pastry cutter, and shape according to Flush Tart Border (page 18). Arrange the pastry-lined tartlet pans on a baking sheet and refrigerate for at least 20 minutes. Brush the bottoms, edges and tops lightly with egg wash, using a pastry brush.

To assemble the tarts, sprinkle the pecans evenly on the pastry bottoms, pressing lightly with your fingers to "set" the pecans. In a medium bowl, toss the remaining ingredients together gently, using clean hands. Arrange the peaches in a circular fan around each tartlet and drizzle with the juices. Bake about 40 minutes, until the pastry is golden brown and the fruit is bubbling.

Almond Crumble Nectarine Tart

Serves 8 to 10

Summer *This delicious, crumbly nectarine recipe delight came to me via an editor friend, Pat Wilens. Her sister, Leslie Wilens Curley, won the blue ribbon and $10 at the 2008 Arlington, Virginia Country Fair for this juicy, beautiful, deep tart, which begs for a generous scoop of vanilla ice cream while it's still warm from the oven. Use the freshest, sweetest nectarines you can find and pile them high!*

EQUIPMENT NEEDED **One 8 x 1¾-inch fluted tart/quiche pan with removable bottom**

1 recipe Master Sweet Pastry (page 17)
1 egg wash (yolk, splash water, pinch
    salt blended together)

Filling
½ cup light brown sugar, divided
2½ tablespoons cornstarch
6 cups pitted, sliced ripe nectarines, unpeeled
1½ tablespoons fresh lemon juice
Zest of 1 lemon
1 teaspoon almond extract

Crumble Topping
¾ cup slivered almonds
½ cup light brown sugar
½ cup all-purpose flour
¼ teaspoon kosher salt or sea salt
6 tablespoons cold, unsalted butter,
    cut into ¼-inch pieces

Prepare the Master Sweet Pastry according to "Perfecting Pastry" (pages 17–18). Chill 30 minutes or overnight. Roll out following directions for Flush Tart Border (see page 18). Chill for at least 15 minutes. (Leslie likes to put her pastry in the freezer to chill out).

Preheat the oven to 400 degrees F.

To prepare the filling, mix 2 tablespoons of the sugar with the cornstarch in a small bowl and set aside. Combine the remaining sugar, nectarines, lemon juice, and zest in a large bowl. Let stand for 10 minutes. Mix the cornstarch mixture into the fruit, tossing gently with your hands to coat thoroughly. Blend in the almond extract. Brush the bottom, sides, and top edges of the chilled tart pastry with egg wash using a pastry brush. Place the filling in the chilled tart shell and bake at 400 degrees F for 30 minutes.

To prepare the crumble topping, combine the almonds and sugar in the bowl of a food processor fitted with a metal blade. Pulse until the almonds are finely chopped. Add the flour and salt; pulse to mix. Add the butter and pulse until the mixture resembles the texture of fine crumbs. Refrigerate until ready to use.

Once the pie has baked for 30 minutes, remove it from the oven and reduce the temperature to 375 degrees F. Spread the topping carefully over the pie and press down lightly. Return tart to the oven and bake for 35 to 40 minutes, until the filling is bubbly and the crumble topping is golden brown. Cool 2 hours on a wire rack before serving.

Plum Perfect Almond Ginger Tart

Serves 8

Summer/Fall **A huge basket brimming with shimmering purple plums kicked my mind into plum tart gear. This is a classically satisfying combination. A simple almond cream of pureed nuts, butter and flavorings makes a gentle bed for this soulful, early fall fruit. The pastry crust is generously seasoned with a peppery kick of ground ginger. Super easy to make and delicious at any temperature, this beautiful tart could easily find its way onto your go-to list for fret-free entertaining.**

EQUIPMENT NEEDED **One 9 x 1-inch round tart pan with a removable bottom**

1 recipe Master Sweet Pastry (Page 17)
    plus 1½ tablespoons ground ginger

Almond Cream
1 cup slivered almonds
¼ cup light brown sugar
3 tablespoons soft butter
2 large eggs
¼ teaspoon pure vanilla extract
¼ teaspoon almond extract
2 tablespoons all-purpose flour
Pinch kosher salt or sea salt

Finishing
6 ripe plums
1 egg wash (yolk, splash water, pinch
    salt blended together)
2 tablespoons warm honey, for glaze
Vanilla ice cream, optional

Prepare the Master Sweet Pastry according to "Perfecting Pastry" (pages 17–18), adding the ginger with the flour, salt and sugar. Chill at least 30 minutes or overnight. Roll out into a round shape approximately ¼ inch thick on a lightly floured surface, following directions in On a Roll (page 18). Delicately place into the tart pan and form the edges according to Elevated Tart Border (page 18). Chill for 20 minutes.

Preheat the oven to 375 degrees F.

To prepare the almond cream, pulse the almonds in the bowl of a food processor fitted with a metal blade until very fine. Add the sugar, butter, eggs, extracts, flour and salt, and pulse to combine thoroughly. The mixture should have the consistency of soft pudding. Remove and refrigerate in a medium bowl for 30 minutes.

Meanwhile, prep the plums by pitting and slicing each into 6 even slices.

To assemble the tart, brush the border and bottom of the prepped tart pastry with egg wash. Place the pastry cream into the tart shell, spreading with a spatula or knife to make it smooth. Top with sliced plums. Arrange them tightly, working concentrically starting at the outside of the shell. The thin edge should be tucked under the thicker, skin-on edge as you go. When you get to the middle, arrange a few slices (3 to 5) in a circular pattern to finish. Bake for 45 minutes, or until golden and bubbly. Remove from the oven. While still warm, brush the top and pastry borders with warm honey. Best served warm with a heaping scoop of vanilla ice cream.

Rosy Rhubarb and Apricot Tartlets

Makes 8 individual tartlets

Summer/Fall As I was thinking about what ingredient would counter the extra-tart flavor of rhubarb (a pink and green vegetable stalk that resembles celery and is a member of the buckwheat family), the morning sun mysteriously shone through the Mason jar on my kitchen counter that houses pale orange dried apricots, as if telling me what to use. Indeed, the chew and color of the apricots offset the rhubarb beautifully here.

This is a light, refreshing after-dinner dessert for a summer evening. Using prepared puff pastry makes the tarts extra easy and quick to put together. They are unbeatable fresh out of the oven and served with a scoop of premium vanilla ice cream. But they also make an excellent breakfast when served cold, and they store well overnight in the fridge. (Note: This filling also works out very well in a free-form pie using the Master Sweet Pastry recipe as in the Berry Peach Free-Form Pie, page 126).

EQUIPMENT NEEDED **One 4-inch round pastry cutter, baking sheet, parchment paper**

1 package (2 sheets) Pepperidge Farm Puff Pastry

Filling

5 cups sliced rhubarb (about 5 large stalks, trimmed)

1 cup water

1 cup coarsely chopped dried apricots

1 cup granulated sugar

1 tablespoon ground cinnamon

½ teaspoon dried Valencia orange peel

Pinch salt

1 egg wash (yolk, splash water, pinch salt blended together)

Vanilla ice cream, optional

Preheat oven to 400 degrees F. Remove the puff pastry from the freezer and thaw to room temperature for 40 minutes, according to package directions. Line the baking sheet with the parchment paper.

Combine all of the filling ingredients in a medium-size pot and bring to a boil. Reduce to a simmer and cook until the mixture becomes a stew-like consistency and the rhubarb has broken down into tender shreds. Set aside to cool. Turn out into a bowl and refrigerate until cold. (Note: This can be prepared a day ahead and refrigerated, covered, until ready to use).

To assemble the tarts, arrange the two sheets of thawed puff pastry on a lightly floured work surface. Using the round pastry cutter, cut 4 rounds out of each sheet, for a total of 8 pastry rounds. Arrange them about ¼ inch apart on the parchment paper–lined baking sheet. Working quickly, place two heaping tablespoons of the cold rhubarb mixture in the center of each, leaving about ½ inch of naked pastry. This will eventually rise to form the border of the tarts. Using a pastry brush, lightly coat the naked pastry with egg wash. Bake for 15 to 20 minutes, or until the pastry has puffed and is golden brown. Allow to cool at least 15 minutes before serving. If desired, sprinkle with powdered sugar. Serve with ice cream, if desired

Super-Sexy Scuppernong and Pomegranate Tartlets

Makes 12 individual servings

Fall Petite, ruby-red pomegranate seeds and clunky-looking scuppernongs may seem like strange tart-fellows. Though the former is a berry and the latter is a variety of the muscadine grape, they have much in common. Both are harvested during cool weather, both are tart-sweet, and both have a very long history. The scuppernong is the state fruit of North Carolina, where it has been harvested (as well as throughout the Southeast) for centuries. It is named after a river that runs through that lush state. The pomegranate dates back to ancient times in the Middle East, where it was grown in Asia and India, though now it is grown throughout the world.

The flavor of a scuppernong is intensely grape-like. The outer skin is bitter, while the interior is sweet and gelatinous, which is the foundation for the thickness of the coulis in this recipe. Pomegranate juice adds brilliant, deep red color and a sweet, acidic edge. The pairing of this duo produces a smashing result!

The crunchy, pop-in-your mouth pomegranate seeds form the first layer of the filling, which is topped with a lemony, cotton-white mousse. Prepared puff pastry shells form the tart casings, while the coulis swirls around the plate in unrestrained regal splendor. All can be prepped ahead and plated at the last second, making these perfect for any festive occasion where elegance is on the menu. If scuppernongs are not available where you are, substitute Concord grapes or another full-flavored grape.

EQUIPMENT NEEDED Parchment paper, baking sheet

2 packages Pepperidge Farm Puff Pastry Shells (or 2 Pepperidge Farm Puff Pastry sheets cut into rounds with 2-inch round pastry cutters)
1 egg-wash (yolk, splash water, pinch salt blended together)

Coulis

3 cups whole fresh scuppernongs, rinsed
1 cup pomegranate juice
½ cup water
1 cinnamon stick
2 tablespoons sugar

Mousse

1 packet Knox unflavored gelatin
1 tablespoon warm water
1 cup 2% plain Greek yogurt
Zest from one lemon
½ cup local honey
1 cup cold whipping cream
1 teaspoon pure vanilla extract
Seeds from one pomegranate, for garnish

Preheat oven to 400 degrees F. Line the baking sheet with parchment paper and arrange the pastry shells on it, about 1 inch apart. Brush the tops (not sides!) of each lightly with egg wash. Bake about 25 minutes, until fluffy and golden. Set aside to cool when done.

To prepare the coulis, combine the scuppernongs, pomegranate juice, water, cinnamon stick and sugar in a medium saucepan. Bring to a boil and reduce to a simmer. Cook, stirring occasionally, about 20 minutes, until the scuppernongs have popped and the liquid has reduced by half. Set aside to cool.

To prepare the mousse, combine the gelatin and water in a small glass or cup. Stir to dissolve. Once fully dissolved, whisk the gelatin in a medium bowl with the yogurt, zest and honey. In a separate cold bowl, using a hand mixer or a whisk (see Getting the Best Whip Out of Your Cream, page 111), mount the whipping cream with the vanilla. Whip until fluffy and firm. To finish the mousse, whisk one-third of the cream into the yogurt mixture. Fold the remaining cream, in two batches, into the yogurt mixture. Chill, covered, in the refrigerator. (Note: This can be made several hours in advance).

To finish the coulis, remove and discard the cinnamon stick and smash the cooled mixture with a masher or a fork to release as much flesh as possible from the scuppernongs. Drain the mixture through a fine sieve into a small bowl, pressing with the back of a ladle to release the juices. Discard the grape skin/seed solids. The remaining liquid is your wonderful coulis! Chill.

Now separate the seeds from the pomegranate. To do this, cut the pomegranate into quarters. Peel the seeds away from their pulp (also called aril). Do this with patience, it takes a little time. Your goal is to separate the bitter pulp from the seeds and discard the pulp.

To assemble the tartlets, gently peel the "tops" off the baked pastry shells, along with some of the inside pastry, to form a "home" for the tart filling. Place one tablespoon of pomegranate seeds in the bottom of each. Top with 2 heaping tablespoons of mousse. Serve on individual plates with a generous swirl of the coulis and a sprinkling of pomegranate seeds. Keep cold for up to 1 hour until serving. Better yet, serve immediately.

Winesap Apple and Walnut "Wow" Tart

Serves 10 to 12

Fall/Winter/Spring The Winesap
*apple is equally as delicious raw as it is baked.
Other kinds of apples, particularly a tart
variety such as McIntosh or Granny Smith,
will work just fine. This tart is well suited to
a pan that will yield long, slender slivers of
sliced, soft, cooked apples on a bed of crispy,
lightly candied walnuts.*

EQUIPMENT NEEDED **One 12 x 1-inch round tart
pan with removable bottom**

1 recipe Master Sweet Pastry (page 17)
1 egg wash (yolk, splash water, pinch
    salt blended together)

Candied Walnut Filling

3 tablespoons unsalted butter
2½ cups finely chopped walnuts
¼ cup light brown sugar
1 teaspoon ground cinnamon
Generous pinch kosher salt or sea salt

Apple Filling

6 large Winesap apples
Juice of 1 lemon
3 tablespoons butter, melted
1 tablespoon ground cinnamon
1 tablespoon ground ginger
Generous pinch salt
¼ cup light brown sugar
1 teaspoon pure vanilla extract

Glaze

3 tablespoons apricot jelly mixed
    with 1 tablespoon water

The day, or at least 20 minutes, before rolling out the
pastry, prepare the Master Sweet Pastry according to
"Perfecting Pastry" (pages 17–18). Let it rest in the
refrigerator, sealed in plastic wrap for 30 minutes or
overnight. On a lightly floured surface roll out a ¼-inch-
thick disc following On a Roll directions (page 18). Line
the tart pan with the pastry, creating a Flush Tart Border
(page 18). Refrigerate for 20 minutes.

When ready to bake, preheat the oven to 375 degrees F.
Brush the prepared pastry shell with egg wash, gently
covering the bottom, sides and pastry top. Refrigerate briefly.

Prepare the candied walnut filling by heating the butter
over medium-high heat until melted and bubbly. Add the
nuts, brown sugar, cinnamon and salt all at once. Toss to
coat and continue cooking, stirring every minute or so,
until lightly browned. Remove from the heat and turn out
onto a large plate. Refrigerate to completely chill.

Meanwhile, prepare the apple filling. Slice and peel the
apples one by one; toss apple slices in lemon juice in a
large bowl as you go along to prevent discoloration. After
all the apples are tossed with the juice, add the remaining
apple filling ingredients and toss thoroughly with your
hands to coat.

To assemble the tart, crumble the completely cooled
candied walnuts evenly along the bottom of the pastry
shell. Top with an attractively arranged fan of apples
to neatly cover the nuts in a single layer. Bake at 375
degrees F for about 35 minutes, until bubbly and golden
and the apples are soft and pliable to the touch. Remove
from the oven and set aside to cool for about 10 minutes.
Heat the apricot jelly with water in a small bowl in the
microwave on high for a few seconds, until it's melted. Stir
to combine. Gently brush the top of the tart and the tart
borders with the glaze for a pretty finishing touch. Best
served warm for the ultimate wow factor.

Acknowledgments

The book wouldn't be a reality without Gibbs Smith publisher and Christopher Robbins. Thank you, Christopher, and the entire Gibbs team for believing in me a second time. Madge Baird, my razor-sharp and enthusiastic editor, thank you for jumping into this project with a keen eye, boundless energy, and great advice. Thank you, also, to book designer Michelle Farinella and production editor Renee Bond for their exquisite work. Hélène Dujardin, my super-talented food stylist and photographer, made the photography leg of this journey a pure delight while making some of the most delicious-looking pictures I've ever seen. *Un grand merci,* Tartelette! Huge thanks to fellow food writer and friend Devany Vickery-Davidson for a great book title idea in "Tart Love."

I think this year I became even closer with the wonderful cast of characters and dear friends that share life's moments on our usually quiet little street in Charleston, South Carolina. Despite a year of construction clamor directly across from my office/writing window, tight parking, and swirling dust clouds, we survived new-house construction with our sanity and friendships intact. Many afternoons, I combed the crowded street bearing warm tarts in search of at-home neighbors for tastings and opinions. Thank you to my neighborly tart tasters: Lucie, Bobbie, Derek, Kim, Jennie, Selby, Elizabeth, Peter, Apple, Veronica, Leiza, Lydia, David, Claudia and assorted members of the construction crew across the street.

For Kyle Klawetter, Keshaun Jones, Farmer King Paul Nelson, and everyone who has talked me through tumultuous and joyful tart times, thank you for being my special angels. My sweet chocolate cocker spaniel and best friend Tann Mann, thanks for patiently hanging out with me in the kitchen and for enduring all of those hours of butter-wafting tart temptation. You and chubby Chutney Cat make life sweet indeed.

Finally, here's to you, Dori and Simone!

Index

Metric Conversion Chart

VOLUME MEASUREMENTS		WEIGHT MEASUREMENTS		TEMPERATURE CONVERSION	
U.S.	Metric	U.S.	Metric	Fahrenheit	Celsius
1 teaspoon	5 ml	½ ounce	15 g	250	120
1 tablespoon	15 ml	1 ounce	30 g	300	150
¼ cup	60 ml	3 ounces	90 g	325	160
⅓ cup	75 ml	4 ounces	115 g	350	180
½ cup	125 ml	8 ounces	225 g	375	190
⅔ cup	150 ml	12 ounces	350 g	400	200
¾ cup	175 ml	1 pound	450 g	425	220
1 cup	250 ml	2¼ pounds	1 kg	450	230

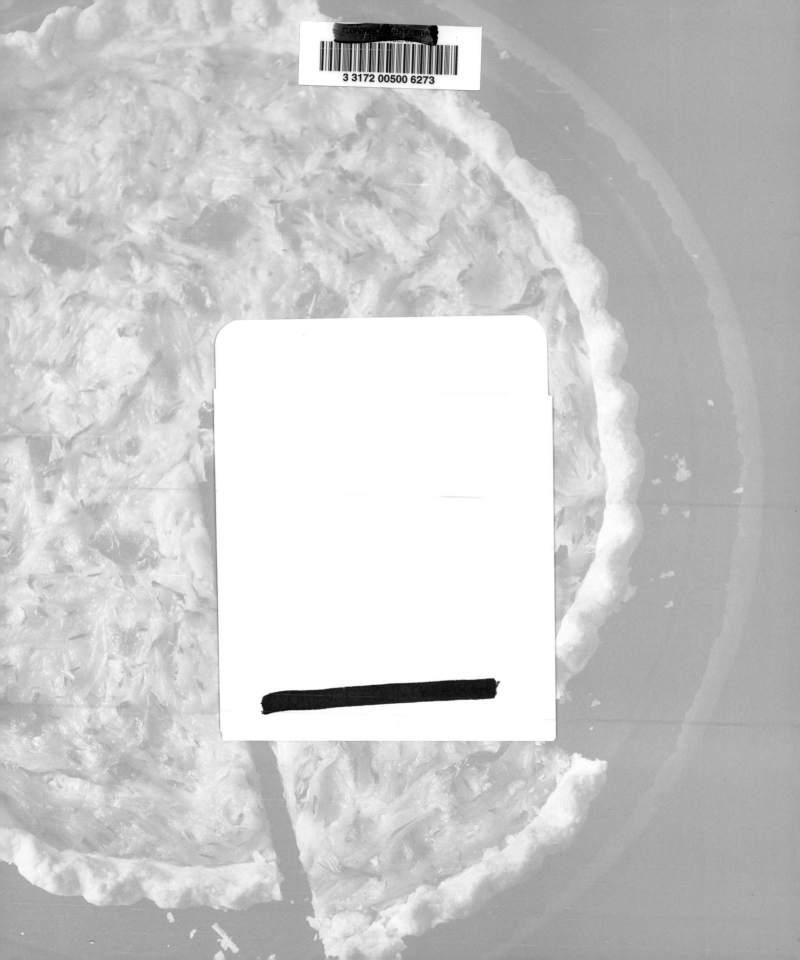